Instructor's Resource Manual with  W9-AOD-578

to accompany

Hess, Hess Orthmann and Cho's

CRIMINAL INVESTIGATION

TENTH EDITION

DELMAR
CENGAGE Learning·

Australia·Brazil·Japan·Korea·Mexico·Singapore·Spain·United Kingdom·United States

DELMAR
CENGAGE Learning·

Instructor's Resource Manual with Test Bank to Accompany Hess, Hess Orthmann and Cho's Criminal Investigation
Tenth Edition

Vice President, Careers & Computing:
Dave Garza

Director of Learning Solutions: Sandy Clark

Senior Acquisitions Editor: Shelley Esposito

Managing Editor: Larry Main

Senior Product Manager: Anne Orgren

Editorial Assistant: Diane Chrysler

Vice President, Marketing: Jennifer Baker

Marketing Director: Deborah Yarnell

Senior Marketing Manager: Mark Linton

Marketing Coordinator: Erin DeAngelo

Production Director: Wendy Troeger

Production Manager: Mark Bernard

Senior Content Project Manager: Betty Dickson

Art Director: Riezebos Holzbaur Group

Media Editor: Debbie Bordeaux

For product information and technology assistance, contact us at
Cengage Learning Customer & Sales Support, 1-800-354-9706
For permission to use material from this text or product,
submit all requests online at **www.cengage.com/permissions.**
Further permissions questions can be e-mailed to
permissionrequest@cengage.com

Library of Congress Control Number: 2011945716

ISBN-13: 978-1-1330-1893-3

ISBN-10: 1-133-01893-9

Delmar
5 Maxwell Drive
Clifton Park, NY 12065-2919
USA

Cengage Learning is a leading provider of customized learning solutions with office locations around the globe, including Singapore, the United Kingdom, Australia, Mexico, Brazil, and Japan. Locate your local office at:
international.cengage.com/region

Cengage Learning products are represented in Canada by Nelson Education, Ltd.

To learn more about Delmar, visit **www.cengage.com/delmar**

Purchase any of our products at your local college store or at our preferred online store **www.cengagebrain.com**

Notice to the Reader
Publisher does not warrant or guarantee any of the products described herein or perform any independent analysis in connection with any of the product information contained herein. Publisher does not assume, and expressly disclaims, any obligation to obtain and include information other than that provided to it by the manufacturer. The reader is expressly warned to consider and adopt all safety precautions that might be indicated by the activities described herein and to avoid all potential hazards. By following the instructions contained herein, the reader willingly assumes all risks in connection with such instructions. The publisher makes no representation or warranties of any kind, including but not limited to, the warranties of fitness for particular purpose or merchantability, nor are any such representations implied with respect to the material set forth herein, and the publisher takes no responsibility with respect to such material. The publisher shall not be liable for any special, consequential, or exemplary damages resulting, in whole or part, from the readers' use of, or reliance upon, this material.

Printed in the United States of America
1 2 3 4 5 6 7 16 15 14 13 12

CONTENTS

CRIMINAL INVESTIGATION: AN OVERVIEW

OUTLINE

- A Brief History of Criminal Investigation
- Criminal Investigation Definitions
- Other Terms Defined
- Goals of Criminal Investigations
- Basic Functions of Investigators
- Characteristics of an Effective Investigator
- An Overview of the Investigative Process
- The Preliminary Investigation: Basic Considerations
- Crime Scene Investigators
- The Follow-Up Investigation
- Computer-Aided Investigation
- Problem-Oriented Policing
- Investigative Productivity
- The Investigative Function: The Responsibility of All Police Personnel
- Interrelationships with Others—Community Policing
- Major-Case Task Forces
- Law Enforcement Resources
- Avoiding Civil Liability

Chapter 1
Criminal Investigation: An Overview

Key Terms

• civil liability	• exculpatory evidence
• community policing	• felony
• crime	• forensic science
• crime mapping	• hot spots
• criminal intent	• inductive reasoning
• criminal investigation	• intuition
• criminal statute	• investigate
• criminalist	• leads
• criminalistics	• Locard's principle of exchange
• culturally adroit	• misdemeanor
• data mining	• modus operandi (MO)
• deductive reasoning	• ordinance
• elements of the crime	• *res gestae* statements

Learning Objectives
After reading this chapter, students should be able to

• Describe what criminal investigation is.	• Explain how the crime scene and evidence are protected and for how long.
• Define the major goals of criminal investigation.	• Report on the responsibilities that are included in the preliminary investigation.
• Explain the basic functions investigators perform.	• Define the meaning and importance of *res gestae* statements.
• Describe what effective investigators do.	• Describe how to determine whether a crime has been committed.
• Describe which characteristics are important in investigators.	• Discuss who is responsible for solving crimes.
• Explain who usually arrives at a crime scene first.	• Explain with whom investigators must relate.
• Discuss what should be done initially at a crime scene.	• Discuss how to avoid civil lawsuits.
• Describe what to do if a suspect is still at a crime scene or has recently fled the scene.	

Internet Assignments

These are ideas for student assignments, classroom discussion, and student interaction.

1. Complete a search of the Internet and list five federal agencies or even military agencies that handle criminal investigations.
2. Have students search out the following Web sites:

    *   Integrated Automated Fingerprint Identification System (IAFIS)
    *   Combined DNA Index System (CODIS)
    *   National Integrated Ballistic Information Network

    Ask students to read the information on each site and then describe how each system works.
3. Have students split into three groups. Assign one of the following to each group:

    *   The Police Foundation, "CompStat in Practice: An In-Depth Analysis of Three Cities"
    *   National Institute of Justice, "Automated Information Sharing: Does It Help Law Enforcement Officers Work Better?" *NIJ Journal*, no. 253, January 2006.
    *   A local police or sheriff's department's experience with CompStat, including success stories that can be attributed to the use of the CompStat system. For example, information on the Philadelphia Police Department's CompStat program can be found online on the Philadelphia Police Department's Web site.

    Have the three groups search the Internet for the article or site, read it and then convene and share information on what they found.

Class Assignments

1. Use a "think-pair-share" assignment: Split the students into pairs or even triads, and let them come up with their various responses. You may wish to have them list their responses so then you can compare and contrast them to the other groups' responses. Ideas for group discussion could include:

    *   How are criminalistics used in investigations today? What are some of the latest developments?
    *   What is the importance in investigating exculpatory evidence and what is its effect on the case?
    *   How is the latest technology used in investigations? What do you think will be available to investigators in the next 5, 10 or 20 years and how will these new technologies change investigations?
    *   How can police use their community policing efforts to enhance investigations? What are some of the barriers and how can the police overcome them?

2.   Split the class into three sections:

- fingerprints
- DNA
- firearms

Have each section prepare a short presentation to share with the class on the purpose of using each of these tools to investigate crime and how computerized databases are used for each tool to fight crime.

Chapter Outline

I.   A Brief History of Criminal Investigation

II.   Criminal Investigation Definitions

III. Other Terms Defined

IV.   Goals of Criminal Investigations

    A.   Determine whether a crime has been committed
    B.   Legally obtain information and evidence to identify the responsible person
    C.   Arrest the suspect
    D.   Recover the stolen property
    E.   Present the best possible case to the prosecutor

V.   Basic Functions of Investigators

    A.   Provide emergency assistance
    B.   Secure the crime scene
    C.   Photograph, videotape and sketch
    D.   Take notes and write reports
    E.   Search for, obtain and process physical evidence
    F.   Obtain information from witnesses and suspects
    G.   Identify suspects
    H.   Conduct raids, surveillances, stakeouts and undercover assignments
    I.   Testify in court

VI.   Characteristics of an Effective Investigator

    A.   Intellectual characteristics

        1.   Able to obtain and retain information
        2.   Able to apply technical knowledge
        3.   Remain open-minded, objective and logical
        4.   Must be culturally adroit

    B.   Psychological characteristics

        1.   Emotionally well balanced
        2.   Detached

          3.   Inquisitive
          4.   Suspecting
          5.   Discerning
          6.   Self-disciplined
          7.   Persevering

    C.   Physical characteristics

          1.   Physically fit
          2.   Good vision and hearing

VII.   An Overview of the Investigative Process

    A.   Initial report
    B.   Initial investigation/police contact
    C.   Incident review
    D.   Follow-up investigations
    E.   Case preparation and approval
    F.   Prosecution and charging of crime
    G.   Conclusion

VIII.   The Preliminary Investigation: Basic Considerations

    A.   Initial response

          1.   First response is usually a patrol officer
          2.   Preplanning routes to high crime areas is critical to rapid response

    B.   The point of arrival

          1.   Officers need to take charge immediately
          2.   Officers must be flexible and understanding

    C.   Setting priorities

          1.   Handle emergencies first
          2.   Secure the scene
          3.   Investigate

    D.   Handling emergency situations

          1.   A suspect at or near the scene
          2.   If the suspect has fled
          3.   If a person is seriously injured
          4.   If a dead body is at the scene

    E.   Protecting the crime scene
    F.   Conducting the preliminary investigation

          1.   Questioning victims, witnesses and suspects
          2.   Conducting a neighborhood canvass

3. Measuring, photographing, videotaping and sketching the scene
4. Searching for evidence
5. Identifying, collecting, examining and processing physical evidence
6. Recording all statements and observations in notes
7. Determining whether a crime has been committed and when
8. Field tests
9. Establishing a command center
10. Dealing with the news media

G. A final consideration about initiating investigations

1. Patrol officers should handle a case from beginning to end whenever possible
2. Whether patrol officers or detectives investigate a case, crime scene investigators become involved in many instances

IX. Crime Scene Investigators

A. A crime scene investigator is a specialist in the organized scientific collection and processing of evidence
B. Crime scene investigators collect, handle and process all physical evidence

X. The Follow-Up Investigation

A. The follow-up phase builds on what was learned during the preliminary investigation
B. Coordination between patrol officers and investigators is critical

XI. Computer-Aided Investigation

A. Computers help analyze information, and information is a critical tool of investigators
B. Crime analysis, mapping and geographic information systems (GIS)
C. Data mining

XII. Problem-Oriented Policing

A. Problem-oriented policing (POP) is a departmental-wide strategy aimed at solving persistent community problems
B. Data collected during criminal investigations can be extremely valuable to problem-oriented policing
C. Problem-oriented strategies can be used in criminal investigations in many ways

XIII. Investigative Productivity

A. It is possible to screen cases for how easily they can be solved and assign only cases that have a higher probability of being solved

B.   This approach can lead to a better understanding of investigative workload

XIV.   The Investigative Function: The Responsibility of All Police Personnel

XV.   Interrelationships with Others—Community Policing

A.   Community policing
B.   Uniformed patrol
C.   Dispatchers
D.   Prosecutor's staff
E.   Defense counsel
F.   Community corrections personnel
G.   Social services
H.   Physicians, coroners and medical examiners
I.   Forensic crime laboratories
J.   Citizens
K.   Witnesses
L.   Victims

XVI.   Major-Case Task Forces

XVII.   Law Enforcement Resources

A.   Federal law enforcement resources
B.   INTERPOL

XVIII.   Avoiding Civil Liability

A.   Civil liability refers to a person's degree of risk of being sued
B.   Section 1983
C.   Leaving out exculpatory evidence

XIX.   Summary

DOCUMENTING THE CRIME SCENE: NOTE TAKING, PHOTOGRAPHING AND SKETCHING

OUTLINE

- Field Notes: The Basics
- Characteristics of Effective Notes
- Filing Notes
- Admissibility of Notes in Court
- Investigative Photography: An Overview
- Basic Photographic Equipment
- Training in and Using Investigative Photography
- Types of Investigative Photography
- Identifying, Filing and Maintaining Security of Evidence
- Admissibility of Photographs in Court
- Crime Scene Sketches: An Overview
- The Rough Sketch
- Steps in Sketching the Crime Scene
- File the Sketch
- The Finished Scale Drawing
- Computer-Assisted Drawing
- Admissibility of Sketches and Drawings in Court

Chapter 2
Documenting the Crime Scene:
Note Taking, Photographing and Sketching

Key Terms

• backing	• mug shots
• baseline method	• overlapping
• compass-point method	• Pictometry®
• competent photograph	• pixel
• cross-projection sketch	• PPI
• finished scale drawing	• rectangular-coordinate method
• forensic photogrammetry	• relevant photograph
• immersive imaging	• resolution
• laser-beam photography	• rogues' gallery
• legend	• rough sketch
• macrophotography	• scale
• marker	• sketch
• material photograph	• trap photography
• megapixel	• triangulation
• microphotography	• ultraviolet-light photography

Learning Objectives
After reading this chapter, students should be able to

• Explain why notes are important in an investigation.	• Describe technical errors to avoid.
• Demonstrate when to take notes.	• Compare and contrast the types of photography used in criminal investigations.
• Discuss what to record.	
• Describe characteristics of effective notes.	• Illustrate the basic rules to which evidence photographs must adhere.
• Decide which notes to retain and where to file them.	• Explain the various purposes of crime scene sketches.
• Discuss purposes of crime scene photography.	• Identify what evidence to sketch.
• Compare and contrast advantages and disadvantages of crime scene photography and videography.	• Determine what materials are needed to make rough sketches.
• Decide on proper photographic equipment needed.	• Write the steps to take in making a rough sketch.
• Determine what to photograph at a crime scene and in what sequence.	• Differentiate between the different plotting methods used in sketches.
	• Clarify when a sketch or a scale drawing is admissible in court.

Internet Assignments

1. Have students search the following Web sites for information on crime scene sketches and photographs:

    *   FBI
    *   Crime-scene-investigator.net
    *   National Criminal justice Reference Service

    Then, hold the following discussion:

    *   Discuss at least five similarities between the sites.
    *   Discuss how photographs and sketches can aid in criminal profiling.
    *   Describe the role the FBI and the NJRS provide as a resource for law enforcement.

2. Have students go to the FBI's Integrated Automated Fingerprint Identification System (IAFIS) Web site and review this national fingerprint and criminal history system maintained by the FBI, Criminal Justice Information Services (CJIS) Division. Ask students to describe the function of the IAFIS. (The IAFIS provides automated fingerprint search capabilities, latent searching capability, electronic image storage and electronic exchange of fingerprints and responses.) Then have students search local police and sheriff's department's Web sites to see how they integrate with the FBI and IAFIS.

3. Have students search the Web for information on crime scene sketching. Ask them to report their findings.

Class Assignments

1. Split the class into three large groups and then assign each group one of the following topics:

    *   Describe the importance of note taking, particularly in establishing the integrity of the crime scene.
    *   Compare and contrast the advantages of digital versus film photography.
    *   Compare and contrast the advantages of hand-drawn sketches and finished reports versus computer-aided crime scene imaging.

2. Have the class split into eight groups, with each group using one of the following methods to sketch the classroom. Set up a small mock crime scene using everyday items in a corner of the room for the "scene." Afterward, discuss pros and cons of the different styles.

    *   Rectangular-coordinate method
    *   Baseline method
    *   Center-baseline method
    *   Diagonal-baseline method
    *   Outdoor-baseline method
    *   Triangulation method

- Compass-point method
- Cross-projection method

Chapter Outline

I. Field Notes: The Basics

A. When to take notes
B. What to record: As you take notes, ask yourself specific questions such as these:

1. When: did the incident happen? was it discovered? was it reported? did the police arrive on the scene? were suspects arrested?
2. Where: did the incident happen? was evidence found? stored? do victims, witnesses and suspects live? do suspects frequent most often? were suspects arrested?
3. Who: are suspects? accomplices? Complete descriptions would include gender, race, coloring, age, height, weight, hair (color, style, condition), eyes (color, size, glasses), nose (size, shape), ears (close to head or protruding), distinctive features (birthmarks, tattoos, scars, beard), clothing, voice (high or low, accent) and other distinctive characteristics such as walk
4. Who: were the victims? associates? was talked to? were witnesses? saw or heard something of importance? discovered the crime? reported the incident? made the complaint? investigated the incident? worked on the case? marked and received evidence? was notified? had a motive?
5. What: type of crime was committed? are the elements of the crime? was the amount of damage or value of the property involved? happened? (narrative of the actions of suspects, victims and witnesses; combines information included under "How") evidence was found? preventive measures (safes, locks, alarms, etc.) had been taken? knowledge, skill or strength was needed to commit the crime? was said? did the police officers do? further information is needed? further action is needed?
6. How: was the crime discovered? does this crime relate to other crimes? did the crime occur? was evidence found? was information obtained?
7. Why: was the crime committed? (was there intent? consent? motive?) was certain property stolen? was a particular time selected?
8. Information establishing a suspect's innocence is as important as establishing a suspect's guilt
9. Include all evidence, both inculpatory and exculpatory
10. Record everything you observe in the overall scene: all services rendered, including first aid, description of the injured, location of wounds, who transported the victim and how

11. Record complete and accurate information regarding all photographs taken at the scene
12. As the search is conducted, record the location and description of evidence and its preservation
13. Record information to identify the type of crime and what was said and by whom. Include the name, address and phone number of every person present at the scene and all witnesses
14. Take notes on everything you do in an official investigative capacity. Record all facts, regardless of where they may lead. Information establishing a suspect's innocence is as important as that establishing guilt
15. When evidentiary conflicts exist, the general rule is that *all* of the evidence, both inculpatory and exculpatory should be reported to the prosecutor for evaluation

C. Where to record notes

1. Opinions vary about whether it is better to use a loose-leaf notebook or separate spiral-bound notebooks for each case
2. If you use a loose-leaf notebook, you can easily add paper for each case you are working on as the need arises, and you can keep it well organized
3. Most investigators favor the loose-leaf notebook because of its flexibility in arranging notes for reports and for testifying in court
4. However, use of a loose-leaf notebook opens the opportunity of challenge from the defense attorney that the officer has fabricated the notes, adding or deleting relevant pages
5. This can be countered by numbering each page, followed by the date and case number, or by using a separate spiral notebook for each case
6. Disadvantages of the latter approach are that the spiral notebook is often only partially used and therefore expensive and may be bulky for storage
7. If other notes are kept in the same notebook, they also will be subject to the scrutiny of the defense
8. A final disadvantage is that if you need a blank sheet of paper for some reason, you should not take it from a spiral notebook because most of these notebooks indicate on the cover how many pages they contain

D. How to take notes

1. Note taking is an acquired skill. Time does not permit a verbatim transcript
2. Learn to select key facts and record them in abbreviated form
3. Do not include words such as *a, and* and *the* in your notes. Omit all other unnecessary words

4. If you make an error, cross it out, make the correction and initial it. Do *not* erase. Whether intentional or accidental, erasures raise credibility questions

5. Whenever possible, use standard abbreviations such as *mph, DWI, Ave*

6. Do *not,* however, devise your own shorthand

7. Using a digital recorder

   a. Advantage of recording exactly what was stated with no danger of misinterpreting, slanting or misquoting

   b. Disadvantages of digital recording:

      (1) The most serious is that they can malfunction and fail to record valuable information

      (2) Weak batteries or background noise can also distort the information recorded

      (3) In addition, transcribing recordings is time consuming, expensive and subject to error

      (4) The recordings themselves, not the transcription, are the original evidence and thus must be retained and filed

II. Characteristics of Effective Notes

   A. Effective notes describe the scene and the events well enough to enable a prosecutor, judge or jury to visualize them

   B. Effective notes are complete, accurate, specific, factual, clear, arranged in chronological order and well organized

   C. The basic purpose of notes is to record the *facts* of a case, accurately and objectively

III. Filing Notes

   A. If department policy is to keep the notes, place them in a location and under a filing system that makes them available months or even years later

   B. As long as the system is logical, the notes will be retrievable

   C. If they are retrievable, in any way, they are "discoverable"

IV. Admissibility of notes in court

   1. The use of notes in court is probably their most important legal application

   2. They can help discredit a suspect's or a defense witness's testimony; support evidence already given by a prosecution witness, strengthening that testimony; and defend against false allegations by the suspect or defense witnesses

   3. They must be legally retrievable and "discoverable" by both the prosecution and the defense

V.   Investigative Photography: An Overview

    A.   Advantages of photographs

        1.   The basic purpose of crime scene photography is to record the scene permanently

        2.   They can be taken immediately, accurately represent the crime scene and evidence, create interest and increase attention to testimony

        3.   They accurately represent the crime scene in court

        4.   The effect of pictures on a jury cannot be overestimated

        5.   Photographs are highly effective visual aids that corroborate the facts presented

        6.   Digital photographs are quickly adaptable as e-mail attachments; additional technical information is recorded in a text file associated with the image; image degradation is avoided; physical storage space is reduced

    B.   Disadvantages of photographs

        1.   They are not selective

        2.   They do not show actual distances

        3.   They may be distorted and damaged by mechanical errors in shooting or processing

    C.   Advantages and disadvantages of video

        1.   A video or DVD, played before a jury, can bring a crime scene to life and offers some distinct advantages over photographs, such as showing distance and including audio capability

        2.   A slow pan of a crime scene is more likely than a series of photographs to capture all evidence, including that in the periphery of view, which might seem rather inconsequential at the time

        3.   Many agencies fail to provide adequate training to those tasked with videotaping a crime scene

        4.   The negative consequences of poor video is that it can damage a case

        5.   Untrained crime scene videographers may shoot without planning ahead, not shooting enough, shooting too much (resulting in a boring presentation), poor focusing, overusing the zoom feature, making jerky camera movements, including unintentional audio and failing to use a tripod or proper lighting

VI.   Basic Photographic Equipment

    A.   Departments are advised to purchase a variety of photographic equipment for different applications

    B.   At a minimum, have available and be skilled in operating a Polaroid-type instant-print camera, a point-and-shoot camera, a digital single-lens reflex (DSLR) camera, a fingerprint camera and video equipment

C.   Instant-print cameras

    1.   These cameras provide pictures at low cost per image
    2.   They are simple to operate
    3.   The photographer can tell immediately whether the photo is good

D.   Point-and-shoot cameras

    1.   These have a fixed lens, have become relatively inexpensive and are easy to use
    2.   Some models are ruggedized to resist water, shock and extreme temperatures
    3.   They provide instant feedback regarding a photo's quality

E.   Digital single-lens reflex (DSLR) cameras

    1.   These have interchangeable lenses
    2.   They offer significantly higher image quality and resolution, but are more difficult to use properly and are often more expensive
    3.   With accessories, they can be adapted to take better photos in more challenging situations

F.   Fingerprint cameras

    1.   These are specially constructed to take pictures of fingerprints without distortion
    2.   They provide their own light through four bulbs
    3.   A tripod and cable release should be used when photographing latent prints
    4.   This camera can also photograph trace evidence

G.   Video cameras

    1.   These are used to record alleged bribery, payoffs and narcotics buys (surveillance)
    2.   Permanently installed units frequently photograph crimes being committed
    3.   They have the advantage of immediacy and eliminate a middle processing step in the chain of evidence
    4.   They can be used for in-station recording of bookings, for testing of suspects in driving-while-intoxicated stops, for crime scene investigations, and can be mounted on the dashboard of a patrol vehicle

H.   Accessories

    1.   These can include an exposure meter, flash attachments, flood lamps and high-intensity spotlights
    2.   Special lenses and filters can be used for different purposes, such as photographing evidence, distant subjects or an entire room in one frame

I.   Computer software

    1.   A major advance is the ability of computer software to stitch together digital photos of 180 degrees or more to create one 360-degree photo—a panoramic view of a crime scene that is interactive, allowing viewers, including jury members, to walk through it as though they were there

    2.   This type of 360-degree photographic view is called immersive imaging

    3.   Crime Scene Virtual Tour (CSVT) software lets jurors virtually step into a crime scene

    4.   The software allows the scene to be viewed from any angle with zoom, pan, tilt and rotate features

VII.   Training in and Using Investigative Photography

    A.   Training in the use of photographic equipment

        1.   Training is needed for all types of photography

        2.   It is important to understand the basic terms of digital technology and resolution

    B.   What to photograph or videotape

        1.   Photograph the crime scene as soon as possible and photograph the most fragile areas of the crime scene first

        2.   Plan a sequence of shots showing the entire scene using the technique called overlapping

        3.   First photograph the general area, then specific areas and finally specific objects of evidence

        4.   Take exterior shots first because they are the most subject to alteration by weather and security violations

        5.   This progression of shots or video will reconstruct the commission of a crime:

            a.   Take *long-range* shots of the locality, points of ingress and egress, normal entry to the property and buildings, exterior of the buildings and grounds, and street signs or other identifiable structures that will establish location

            b.   Take *medium-range* shots of the immediate crime scene and the location of objects of evidence within the area or room

            c.   Take *close-range* shots of specific evidence such as hairs, fibers, footprints and bloodstains. The entire surface of some objects may be photographed to show all the evidence; for example, a table surface may contain bloodstains, fingerprints, hairs and fibers

            d.   Zoom lenses allow close shots without disturbing the crime scene, and close-ups are possible with macro lenses

            e.   Such close-range shots usually should include a marker, or scale

        f.   Forensic photogrammetry, the technique of extrapolating three-dimensional (3-D) measurements from two-dimensional photographs, can be used at most crime scenes

C.   Errors to avoid

1.   To obtain effective photographs and videos, be familiar with your equipment and check it before you use it
2.   Take photographs and/or videos before anything is disturbed
3.   If something has been moved, do *not* put it back; it is legally impossible to return an object to its original position
4.   To minimize distortion or misrepresentation, maintain proper perspective, and attempt to show the objects in a crime scene in their relative size and position
5.   Take pictures from eye level, the height from which people normally observe objects

D.   Checklists

1.   Checklists are a critical aspect of the law enforcement function, especially when it comes to crime scene photography
2.   Checklists can include the following:

    a.   Are the batteries in the camera?
    b.   Is the memory media loaded?
    c.   Is the camera on?
    d.   Is the lens cap removed?
    e.   Are spare batteries and memory media readily available?

VIII.   Types of Investigative Photography

A.   Surveillance photography

1.   With a well-thought-out plan, surveillance tapes can increase the efficacy of a law enforcement agency
2.   Surveillance photography is also called trap photography
3.   Many agencies are switching to digital formats rather than videotapes
4.   Video analysis is the "new DNA of law enforcement"
5.   Soon forensic video evidence will have the Regional Forensic Video Analysis Labs—a national database of criminals caught on tape
6.   Enhanced surveillance capability can be provided by using robots
7.   Small video cameras have also been attached to radio-controlled model airplanes

B.   Aerial photography

1.   Geographical Information Systems (GIS)
2.   Pictometry: computer technology that integrates various aerial shots of a land-based artifact taken straight down (orthogonal) and

from numerous angles (oblique). The software also features extreme zooming capabilities, allowing investigators to rotate and zoom in on a particular structure

C. Night photography
D. Laboratory photography

    1. Microphotography takes pictures through a microscope and can help identify minute particles of evidence such as hairs or fibers
    2. In contrast, macrophotography enlarges a subject. For example, a fingerprint or a tool mark can be greatly enlarged to show the details of ridges or striations
    3. Laser-beam photography

        a. Reveals evidence indiscernible to the naked eye
        b. For example, it can reveal the outline of a footprint in a carpet, even though the fibers have returned to normal position

    4. Ultraviolet-light photography

        a. Uses the low end of the color spectrum, which is invisible to human sight, to make visible impressions of bruises and injuries long after their actual occurrence
        b. Bite marks, injuries caused by beatings, cigarette burns, neck strangulation marks and other impressions left from intentional injuries can be reproduced and used as evidence in criminal cases by scanning the presumed area of injury with a fluorescent or blue light

E. Mug shots

    1. The pictures of people in police custody are kept in department files for identification and are known as *mug shots*
    2. Gathered in files and displayed in groups, they are called a *rogues' gallery*

F. Lineup photographs

    1. Officers can select 6 to 12 other "hits" to be used for presentation with the suspect's photo
    2. Videotapes or photographs of people included in lineups may be taken to establish the fairness of the lineup
    3. Laptop Lineup I software quickly assembles appropriate lineups from a photo database

IX. Identifying, Filing and Maintaining Security of Evidence

A. Identifying
    1. In the field notes, the photographs taken should be dated and numbered sequentially

      2.   Include the case number, type of offense and subject of the picture

      3.   Record the photographer's name, location and direction of the camera, lens type, approximate distance in feet to the subject, film and shutter speed, lighting, weather conditions and a brief description of the scene in the picture

      4.   Backing: On the back of the photo, write your initials, the date the photo was taken, what the photo depicts and the direction of north

B. Filing

      1.   File the picture and negatives for easy reference

      2.   Pictures in the case file are available to others

      3.   Use a filing system just for photographs

      4.   Always cross-reference by case number

      5.   File digital images appropriately as evidence or within the department's internal secured hard drive

C. Maintaining security

      1.   Record the chain of custody of the film and photographs in the field notes or in a special file

      2.   Mark and identify the film as it is removed from the camera

      3.   Each time the film changes possession, record the name of the person accepting it

X. Admissibility of Photographs in Court

A. Photographs must be

      1.   Material

      2.   Relevant

      3.   Competent

XI. Crime Scene Sketches: An Overview

A. Crime scene sketches should

      1.   Accurately portray the physical facts

      2.   Relate to the sequence of events at the scene

      3.   Establish the precise location and relationship of objects and evidence at the scene

      4.   Help create a mental picture of the scene for those not present

      5.   Be a permanent record of the scene

      6.   Be usually admissible in court

B. A crime scene sketch assists in

      1.   Interviewing and interrogating people

      2.   Preparing the investigative report

      3.   Presenting the case in court

XII.   The Rough Sketch

    A.   This is the first pencil-drawn outline of a scene and the location of objects and evidence within this outline

        1.   It is not usually drawn to scale, although distances are measured and entered in the appropriate locations

        2.   Sketch all serious crime and crash scenes after photographs are taken and before anything is moved. Sketch the entire scene, the objects and the evidence

    B.   Sketching materials

        1.   Materials for the rough sketch include clipboard, paper, pencil, long steel measuring tape, carpenter-type ruler, straightedge, eraser, compass, protractor and thumbtacks

        2.   Plain white or graph paper is best

        3.   Today's contemporary crime scene specialist is likely to be equipped with a GPS (Global Positioning System) instrument for extreme accuracy

XIII.   Steps in Sketching the Crime Scene

    A.   Step One: Once photographs have been taken and other priority steps in the preliminary investigation performed, you can begin sketching the crime scene

        1.   Observe and plan

        2.   Decide where to start

    B.   Step Two: Measure and outline the area

        1.   Always measure from fixed objects

        2.   Always position north at the top of the paper

        3.   Determine the scale: Use the largest, simplest scale possible

    C.   Step Three: Plot objects and evidence

        1.   Plotting methods

        2.   Rectangular-coordinate method

            a.   Uses two adjacent walls as fixed points from which distances are measured at right angles

            b.   Locates objects by measuring from one wall at right angles and then from the adjacent wall at right angles

            c.   This method is restricted to square or rectangular areas

        3.   Baseline method

            a.   Establishes a straight line from one fixed point to another, from which measurements are taken at right angles

            b.   Take measurements along either side of the baseline to a point at right angles to the object to be located

    4.   Triangulation method

        a.   Uses straight-line measures from two fixed objects to the evidence to create a triangle with the evidence in the angle formed by the two straight lines

        b.   Commonly used outdoors but can be used indoors also

    5.   Compass-point method

        a.   Uses a protractor to measure the angle formed by two lines

    6.   Cross-projection method

        a.   The room is flattened out much like a box cut down at the four corners and opened flat

        b.   Presents the floor and walls as though they were one surface

  D.   Step Four: Take notes and record details

  E.   Step Five: Identify the scene

    1.   Prepare the legend

    2.   Legend should contain the case number, type of crime, name of victim or complainant, location, date, time, investigator, anyone assisting, scale of the sketch, direction of north and name of the person making the sketch

  F.   Step Six: Reassess the sketch

XIV.   File the Sketch

XV.   The Finished Scale Drawing

XVI.   Computer-Assisted Drawing

  A.   Forensic software programs, such as Crime Zone, are easy to use and can create diagrams with great precision and attention to detail, giving the drawing greater credibility in court

  B.   Software graphics have been used to diagram the trajectory of bullets, to document the scene of a carjacking and to help a jury visualize the locations of witnesses, victims and suspects at the scene of a shooting

  C.   Speed and portability are two other features investigators look for when selecting a CAD program

XVII.   Admissibility of Sketches and Drawings in Court

  A.   An admissible sketch is drawn or personally witnessed by an investigator and accurately portrays a crime scene

  B.   A scale drawing also is admissible if the investigating officer drew it or approved it after it was drawn and if it accurately represents the rough sketch

  C.   The rough sketch must remain available as evidence

  D.   Well-prepared sketches and drawings help judges, juries, witnesses and other people to visualize crime scenes

XVIII. Summary

WRITING EFFECTIVE REPORTS

OUTLINE

Chapter 3
Writing Effective Reports

Key Terms

• active voice	• first person
• chronological order	• form
• concise	• mechanics
• conclusionary language	• narrative
• connotative	• objective
• content	• past tense
• denotative	• slanting
• disposition	

Learning Objectives
After reading this chapter, students should be able to

• Explain why reports are important to an investigation.	• Describe characteristics of effective investigative reports.
• Describe how reports are used.	• Compare how to differentiate among facts, inferences and opinions.
• Discuss who reads the reports.	
• Summarize the common problems which occur in many police reports.	• Explain why reports should be well written.
• Explain whether form or content is more important.	

Internet Assignments

1. For report-writing tips, have students search police report writing tips and review Web sites such as "Becoming A Police Officer," "REAL POLICE: Law Enforcement Resource" and "Police One"

2. Have the class use the Internet to search for a recent major crime in the community. Have students write a report based on the newspaper account of the incident, using the outline process mentioned in the chapter.

Class Assignment

Have the class watch a TV show or movie of virtually any police drama, and have them create a one-page narrative of what actually occurred during the "crime." Afterward, discuss how different it is to watch or hear about a crime and then have to write about it, keeping the elements of the crime in mind.

Chapter Outline

I.   The Importance of Reports

    A.   An estimated 20 percent of an officer's time is spent writing reports
    B.   Reports are used, not just filed
    C.   Your reputation as an officer or investigator often rests on your report-writing skills
    D.   Poor police reporting can jeopardize effective criminal prosecution

II.   Uses of Reports

    A.   Reports are permanent records of all important facts in a case
    B.   Reports are initially used to continue the investigation of the offense. They also may be used for other purposes, such as to

        1.   Examine the past
        2.   Provide a documented record of incidents
        3.   Keep other officers informed
        4.   Continue investigations
        5.   Prepare court cases
        6.   Provide the courts with relevant facts
        7.   Coordinate law enforcement activities
        8.   Plan for future law enforcement services
        9.   Evaluate individual officer and department performance
        10.   Refresh a witness's memory about what he or she said occurred
        11.   Refresh the investigating officer's memory during the trial
        12.   Compile statistics on crime in a given jurisdiction
        13.   Provide information to insurance investigators
        14.   Aid in assessing police performance and investigating possible abusive police practices, such as racial profiling

III.   The Audience

    A.   Other officers
    B.   Supervisors
    C.   Attorneys and judges
    D.   Jurors
    E.   City officials
    F.   Insurance adjusters and investigators
    G.   Civil rights groups
    H.   Citizens
    I.   Media

IV.   Common Problems with Many Police Reports

    A.   Confusing or unclear sentences
    B.   Conclusions, assumptions and opinions presented as facts
    C.   Extreme wordiness and overuse of police jargon and abbreviations
    D.   Missing or incomplete information
    E.   Misspelled words and grammatical/mechanical errors

F. Referring readers to "the information above," rather than restating the information for them

V. The Well-Written Report: From Start to Finish

    A. Organizing information

        1. Chronological order
        2. Structuring the narrative

            a. The opening paragraph of a police report states the time, date and type of incident, and how you became involved
            b. The next paragraph contains what you were told by the victim or witness. For each person you talked to, use a separate paragraph
            c. Next, record what you did based on the information you received
            d. The final paragraph states the disposition of the case
            e. A brief look at law enforcement report forms

                (1) Law enforcement report forms vary greatly in format
                (2) Some report forms contain boxes or separate category sections (e.g., property loss section) for placement of descriptive information, addresses and phone numbers of those involved. It is unnecessary to repeat this information in the narrative *unless it is needed for clarity* because it tends to interrupt the flow of words and clutter the narrative
                (3) In contrast, narrative reports that do *not* use the box-style format include descriptive information, addresses and phone numbers within the body of the narrative

    B. Characteristics of effective reports: content and form

        1. Content—what is said

            a. The elements of the crime
            b. Descriptions of suspects, victims, etc.
            c. Evidence collected
            d. Actions of victim, witnesses and suspects
            e. Observations: weather, road conditions, smells, sounds, oddities, etc.

        2. Form—how it is said

            a. Word choice
            b. Sentence and paragraph length
            c. Spelling
            d. Punctuation
            e. Grammar
            f. Mechanics

C.   "The ability of investigators to explain both verbally and in writing how inferences (e.g., clues, evidence, etc.) lead them to draw logical and reasonable conclusions (e.g., probable cause, facts, etc.) remains a critical skill in investigative work." (Jetmore, 2007, p.22)

D.   Factual

E.   Fact, inference or opinion

    1.   Fact: A statement that can be proven. *Example:*

        a.   "The man has a bulge in his black leather jacket pocket."
        b.   "The suspect had long red hair."

    2.   Inference: A conclusion based on reasoning; also referred to as "conclusionary language." *Examples:*

        a.   "The man is *probably* carrying a gun."
        b.   "They *denied* any involvement in the crime."
        c.   "She *confessed* to seven more arsons."
        d.   "He *admitted* breaking into the warehouse."
        e.   "He *consented* to a search of the trunk."
        f.   "She *waived* her rights per Miranda."

    3.   Opinion: A personal belief. *Example:*

        a.   "Black leather jackets are cool."
        b.   "The suspect's hair is beautiful."

F.   Accurate

    1.   To be accurate, you must be specific and correct
    2.   Verify all spellings, phone numbers, addresses, e-mails, etc.
    3.   Ensure accuracy of measurements, location of evidence, skid marks, bullet holes, etc.
    4.   You don't need to say "PC for the stop," because only reasonable suspicion is needed, not probable cause

G.   Objective

    1.   Keep reports objective and factual
    2.   Word choice is important in report writing

        a.   Denotative, objective words have little emotional effect, for example, *cried* versus *wept*
        b.   Connotative words evoke empathy or sympathy
        c.   Avoid derogatory or biased terms
        d.   Avoid "slanting" your reports—remain objective
        e.   Include both inculpatory as well as exculpatory statements

H.   Complete

    1.   What officers write in their reports stays with them forever
    2.   If it isn't written, it didn't happen
    3.   Answer six basic questions: Who? What? When? Where? How? Why?

I.   Concise

    1.   Avoid wordiness; length alone does not ensure quality
    2.   You can reduce wordiness in two basic ways:

        a.   Leave out unnecessary information
        b.   Use as few words as possible to record the necessary facts

J.   Clear

    1.   Use specific, concrete facts and details
    2.   Keep descriptive words and phrases as close as possible to the words they describe
    3.   Use diagrams and sketches when a description is complex
    4.   Do not use uncommon abbreviations
    5.   Use short sentences, well organized into short paragraphs

K.   Grammatically and mechanically correct

    1.   Check the mechanics—spelling, capitalization and punctuation
    2.   Spelling is perhaps the most important part of writing
    3.   A good rule is, "If you can't spell it, don't use it"

L.   Written in Standard English

    1.   Note differences between spoken English and the written word
    2.   Follow rules for what words are used when

M.   Paragraphs

    1.   Discuss only one subject in each paragraph
    2.   Start a new paragraph when changing speakers, time or ideas, or when moving from observations or descriptions to statements

N.   Past tense

    1.   Write in the past tense
    2.   Use verbs that show that events have already occurred

O.   First person
P.   Active voice
Q.   Audience focused

    1.   Remember who your audience is
    2.   Write for the people who will read the report and need to use the reports
    3.   Avoid "Cop Speak," or police jargon
    4.   Articulate any use of force in everyday language

        a.   Note objective reasonableness test under *Graham v. Connor*
        b.   Were the officer's actions reasonable under the circumstances as viewed by the "objectiveness" of a jury?

R. Write reports that are legible and turn them in on time

    1. A key factor in legibility is speed
    2. Most officers need to slow down their writing speed

VI. Recording and Dictating Reports

    A. In effect, recording or dictating reports shifts the bulk of writing/ transcribing time to the records division
    B. Even with recording or dictating, however, officers must still take final responsibility for what is contained in the report

VII. Computerized Report Writing

    A. Computer hardware/software is now in many police vehicles for immediate reporting
    B. Software selection may be tailored for specific departmental needs and linked to state and national databases for inquiries
    C. Digital FTO and Presynct streamline data handling and workflow management

VIII. Evaluating Your Report

    A. Proofread before submitting
    B. Ask a colleague to proofread because it is difficult to proofread your own writing
    C. Evaluating your report: A checklist (see Table 3.4 in core text)

IX. Citizen Online Report Writing

    A. Some departments are allowing citizens to write and submit reports using online systems
    B. These are often used for discovery crimes: minor thefts, lost property, vandalism and graffiti and will vary by agency
    C. This prevents busy or understaffed departments from having to create "no-response" policies for low-priority calls
    D. Staff resources also can be better allocated as online reports gradually replace telephone reports and the workload for desk officers becomes manageable compared with a never-ending stream of citizens visiting police station lobbies to report crimes
    E. The monetary savings are quite substantial when considering the volume of reports that are taken online rather than having officers take reports and write them
    F. Depending on the vendor an agency chooses, online reporting systems also can facilitate crime tips, special form submissions and volunteer applications and can even serve as a 3-1-1 system, so that citizens can conveniently report abandoned vehicles, barking dogs or even streetlight outage

X. The Final Report

    A. The culmination of the preceding steps is the final, or prosecution, report, containing all essential information for bringing a case to trial

XI. A Final Note on the Importance of Well-Written Reports

    A. A report written well the first time means less time spent rewriting it. A well-written report also keeps everyone involved in the case current and clear about the facts, which can lead to higher prosecution rates, more plea bargains, fewer trials and an easing of caseloads on the court system

    B. A well-written report also can save an investigator from spending an inordinate amount of time on the witness stand, attempting to explain any omissions, errors or points of confusion found in poorly written reports

    C. All these benefits ultimately save the department time and expense

    D. Every police report must jump over the substantial hurdle of the *exclusionary rule*—which states that illegally obtained evidence cannot be used against a defendant in a criminal trial—by explaining in detail how and under what conditions a person's preexisting individual rights were provided during the investigative process

    E. The investigative report may be the one pivotal piece of documentation that makes a difference in the prosecution of a murderer or a serial-rapist

    F. Well-written reports can reduce legal liability for both the officer and the department by clearly documenting the actions taken throughout the investigation

XII. Summary

SEARCHES

OUTLINE

Chapter 4
Searches

Key Terms

• anticipatory warrant	• inevitable-discovery doctrine
• *Buie* sweep	• lane-search pattern
• *Carroll* decision	• nightcapped warrant
• *Chimel* decision	• no-knock warrant
• circle search	• particularity requirement
• curtilage	• patdown
• "elephant-in-a-matchbox" doctrine	• plain feel/touch evidence
• exclusionary rule	• plain-view evidence
• exigent circumstances	• probable cause
• frisk	• protective sweep
• "fruit-of-the-poisonous-tree" doctrine	• strip-search pattern
• good-faith doctrine	• *Terry* stop
• immediate control	• totality-of-the-circumstances test
	• true scene
	• uncontaminated scene
	• zone

Learning Objectives
After reading this chapter, students should be able to

• Identify which constitutional amendment restricts investigative searches.	• Discuss what a successful crime scene search accomplishes.
• Outline what is required for an effective search.	• Outline what is included in organizing a crime scene search.
• Define what basic restriction is placed on all searches.	• Explain what physical evidence is.
• Describe what the exclusionary rule is and how it affects investigators.	• Define and compare interior and exterior search patterns.
• Clarify what the preconditions and limitations of a legal search are.	• Describe whether evidence left in plain view may be lawfully seized and whether it is admissible in court.
• Discuss when a warrantless search is justified.	• Describe how to search a vehicle, a suspect and a dead body.
• Describe what precedents are established by the *Weeks, Mapp, Terry, Chimel, Carroll* and *Chambers* decisions.	• Outline how to use dogs in searches.

Internet Assignments

1. Have students read Deputy Robert Phillips's Legal Update site, particularly his update on "The Fourth Amendment and Search & Seizure." After reviewing the Web site, students break into small groups. Each group will discuss one topic:

    - Searches of houses
    - Searches of vehicles
    - Third-party searches
    - Curtilage issues
    - Exigent circumstances

2. Have students visit the Web site of Terry Fleck, an expert in canine legalities. Ask students to outline the case law pertaining to the use of canines in searches.

3. Ask students to choose a case cited in the text to research using the Internet. Students should then report to the class or to their small group the details of the case and how the case relates to searches or exclusionary rules.

Class Assignments

1. Set up a mock crime scene that allows the students to search for evidence of a crime. If time permits, use an indoor and an outdoor crime scene. The students are to identify the nature of the search pattern they used and why. Tell the students that the crime involves an assault with a knife. If time for a mock crime scene does not exist, then have a class discussion of what the students would do to process the crime scene.
2. Have students research *Mapp v. Ohio* (1961), and then have them discuss what the police officers did or did not do that warranted the case decision. Split the class into two sides for the discussion, and have one side advocate for the prosecution, and the other for the defense or dissenting view.

Chapter Outline

I. Legal Searches and the Fourth Amendment

    A. Investigators need an understanding of the Fourth Amendment to the U.S. Constitution
    B. The Fourth Amendment forbids unreasonable searches and seizures
    C. The Fourth Amendment strikes a balance between individual liberties and the rights of society
    D. The courts are bound by rules and can admit evidence only if it is obtained constitutionally. Thus, the legality of a search must always be kept in mind during an investigation
    E. To conduct an effective search, know the legal requirements for searching, the items being searched for and the elements of the crime being investigated; be organized, systematic and thorough

II. Basic Limitations on Searches

    A. The most important limitation on any search is that the scope must be narrow

    B. General searches are unconstitutional

    C. It is critical, however, that officers responsible for criminal investigations know these laws and operate within them

    D. No evidence obtained during an illegal search will be allowed at a trial, as established by the exclusionary rule

III. The Exclusionary Rule

    A. The *exclusionary rule* established that courts may not accept evidence obtained by unreasonable search and seizure, regardless of its relevance to a case

    B. *Weeks v. United States* (1914) made the rule applicable at the federal level

    C. *Mapp v. Ohio* (1961) made it applicable to *all* courts

    D. The *"fruit-of-the-poisonous-tree" doctrine* established that evidence obtained as a result of an earlier illegality must be excluded from trial

    E. The *inevitable-discovery doctrine*

        1. Derived from *Nix v. Williams* (1984)

        2. This doctrine states that if illegally obtained evidence would in all likelihood eventually have been discovered legally, it may be used

    F. The *good-faith doctrine*

        1. Derived from *United States v. Leon* (1984)

        2. This doctrine established that illegally obtained evidence may be admissible if the police were truly not aware they were violating a suspect's Fourth Amendment rights

IV. Justification for Reasonable Searches

    A. A search can be justified and therefore considered legal if any one of the following conditions are met:

        1. A search warrant has been issued

        2. Consent is given

        3. The officer stops a suspicious person and believes the person may be armed

        4. The search is incidental to a lawful arrest

        5. An emergency exists

B.   Search with a warrant

   1.   To obtain a valid search warrant, officers must appear before a judge, establish that there is *probable cause* to believe that the location contains evidence of a crime and specifically describe the evidence

   2.   Probable cause is more than reasonable suspicion. Here are explanations of probable cause:

      a.   "Probable cause is a commonsense, non-technical conception that deals with the factual and practical considerations of everyday life on which reasonable and prudent men, not legal technicians, act" (Scarry, 2007b, p.59)

      b.   Jetmore (2007b, p.28) explains probable cause as "less than proof, but more than suspicion that a crime is being, has been or will be committed. Thus, probable cause requires a higher standard than reasonable suspicion, but less than the proof beyond a reasonable doubt required for a conviction in court."

      c.   A list of guilt-laden or other facts to build probable cause includes: flight, furtive movements, hiding, an attempt to destroy evidence, resistance to officers, evasive answers, unreasonable explanations, contraband or weapons in plain view, a criminal record, police training and experience, unusual or suspicious behavior and information from citizens

   3.   Using informants

      a.   The Supreme Court has established requirements for using informants in establishing probable cause

      b.   Two separate tests were established in *Aguilar v. Texas* (1964):

         (1)   Is the informant reliable/credible?
         (2)   Is the information believable?

      c.   This two-pronged approach was upheld in *Spinelli v. United States* (1969)

      d.   However, the Supreme Court most recently changed the two-pronged test to a *totality-of-the-circumstances test, Illinois v. Gates* (1983), which most states have adopted

      e.   Note that federal courts are still guided by the two-pronged *Aguilar-Spinelli* test, and several states also adhere to this more stringent requirement for establishing probable cause

   4.   Other requirements

      a.   In addition to establishing probable cause for a search, the warrant must contain:

         (1)   The reasons for requesting it (probable cause)

        (2)   The names of the people presenting affidavits (officers)

        (3)   What specifically is being sought (evidence, weapons, drugs)

        (4)   The signature of the judge issuing it

    b. The warrant must be based on facts and sworn to by the officer requesting the warrant (affidavit)

    c. An address and description of the location must be given—for example, "100 S. Main Street, the ABC Liquor Store," or "1234 Forest Drive, a private home"

    d. Warrants can be issued to search for and seize the following:

        (1)   Stolen or embezzled property

        (2)   Property designed or intended for use in committing a crime

        (3)   Property that indicates a crime has been committed or that a particular person has committed a crime

    e. In *Groh v. Ramirez* (2004), the Supreme Court sent a message to law enforcement on the importance of paying attention to detail. The Supreme Court ruled that "It is incumbent upon the officer executing a search warrant to ensure the search is lawfully authorized and lawfully conducted"

    f. Once a warrant is obtained, it should be executed promptly

        (1)   In some states the warrant is good for a set number of days and is to be executed during daytime hours

        (2)   A *nightcapped warrant* authorizes a search or arrest at any time, day or night

        (3)   Nightcapped warrants can be served when a suspect is in any public area regardless of time

        (4)   If officers attempting to serve a search warrant are not admitted by occupants following a knock-notice announcement, forcible entry may be made, but unnecessary damage to the structure may make the entry unreasonable

5.   The knock-and-announce rule: Officers are required to knock, announce themselves and wait "a reasonable length of time" before attempting entry

    a. In *Wilson v. Arkansas* (1995), the Court made this centuries-old rule a constitutional mandate

    b. Officers may obtain a *no-knock warrant* if the evidence may be easily destroyed, explosives are present or other dangers exist

    c. Unnecessary damage to the structure may make the entry unreasonable

d. This rule is intended to

    (1)   protect citizens' right to privacy

    (2)   reduce the risk of possible violence to police and residence occupants

    (3)   prevent needless destruction of private property

e. Case law:

    (1)   In a unanimous ruling in *United States v. Banks* (2003), the Supreme Court upheld the forced entry into a suspected drug dealer's apartment 15 to 20 seconds after police knocked and announced themselves

    (2)   In 2006, the Supreme Court ruled in *Hudson v. Michigan* that the Constitution does not require the government to forfeit evidence gathered through illegal "no-knock" searches while executing a search warrant. In the *Hudson* case, the police only waited approximately 3 to 5 seconds before making their entry. In effect, the court upheld the evidence (gun and drugs) despite the officers' "error" in not waiting longer

    (3)   Officers must still balance the knock, announce and wait requirements against both officer safety and evidence destruction issues, and the entry must still be reasonable

f. Video recording of knock-notice announcement and entry provides evidence of compliance with the rule as well as the amount of time officers waited before entry

g. The *particularity requirement*

    (1)   *Stanford v. Texas* (1965) states that a search conducted with a warrant must be limited to the specific area and specific items named in the warrant

    (2)   During a search conducted with a warrant, items not specified in the warrant may be seized if they are similar to the items described, if they are related to the particular crime described or if they are contraband

6. Anticipatory search warrants

a. The Court approved use of an *anticipatory search warrant* (*United States v. Grubbs*, 2006)

b. This is defined as one "based upon an affidavit showing probable cause that at some future time (but not presently) certain evidence of crime will be located at a specified place"

C. Search with consent

1. Searching without a warrant is allowed if consent is given by a person with the authority to do so (*United States v. Matlock,* 1974)

2. Examples of relationships where third-party consent may be valid include:

    a. Parent/child
    b. Employer/employee
    c. Host/guest
    d. Spouses

3. Examples of instances when individuals cannot give valid consent to search include:

    a. Landlord/tenant
    b. Hotel employee/hotel guest

4. If the police believe the person giving consent has authority, they may act on this belief, even though it later turns out the person did not have authority (*Illinois v. Rodriguez*, 1990)
5. The consent must be voluntary and the search limited to the area for which consent is granted
6. The consent must not be in response to an officer's claim of lawful authority and may not be in response to an officer's command or threat
7. Silence is *not* consent. A genuine affirmative reply must also be given
8. When possible, it is a good practice to ask for consent
9. Under the *consent once removed* exception to the search warrant requirement, officers can make a warrantless entry to arrest a suspect if consent to enter was given earlier to an undercover officer or informant
10. Denial of consent by one resident

    a. In *Georgia v. Randolph* (2006), the Supreme Court changed the rules governing some consent searches of private premises
    b. Result: "If any party who is present and has authority to object to the search does object to the search, the police may not conduct the search on the authority of that party who gave consent"

D. Patdown or frisk during a "stop"

1. Two situations require police officers to stop and question individuals:

    a. to investigate suspicious circumstances
    b. to identify someone who looks like a suspect named in an arrest warrant or whose description has been broadcast in an all-points bulletin (APB)

2. The prime requisite for stopping, questioning and possibly frisking someone is *reasonable suspicion*

3. A stop and a frisk are two separate actions, and each must be separately justified

4. The *Terry* decision established that a *patdown* or *frisk* is a "protective search for weapons" and as such must be "confined to a scope reasonably designed to discover guns, knives, clubs and other hidden instruments for the assault of a police officer or others." This is called a "*Terry* stop"

   a. The Court warned that a patdown or frisk is "a serious intrusion upon the sanctity of the person which may inflict great indignity and arouse strong resentment, and it is not to be undertaken lightly"

   b. The "search" in a frisk is sometimes referred to as a *safety search*

   c. Officers may ask the stopped individual for his or her name. In *Hiibel v. Sixth Judicial District Court of Nevada, Humboldt County* (2004), the Court ruled that state statutes requiring individuals to identify themselves as part of an investigative stop are constitutional and do not violate the Fourth or Fifth Amendments

   d. Officers do not need to advise individuals *of their right not to cooperate with police* on a bus that has been stopped (*United States v. Drayton*, 2002)

   e. The Court has also ruled (*Illinois v. McArthur*, 2001) that officers may detain residents outside their homes until a search warrant can be obtained if necessary

E. Search incident to arrest

   1. Every lawful arrest is accompanied by a search of the arrested person to protect the arresting officers and others and to prevent destruction of evidence

   2. The *Chimel* decision established that a search incidental to a lawful arrest must be made simultaneously with the arrest and must be confined to the area within the suspect's immediate control (*Chimel v. California*, 1969)

   3. The police can search within a person's *immediate control*, which encompasses the area within the person's reach

   4. *Maryland v. Buie* (1990) expanded the area of a premises search following a lawful arrest to ensure officers' safety

   5. The Supreme Court added authority for the police to search areas immediately adjoining the place of arrest

      a. Called a "protective sweep" or "*Buie* sweep," this is justified when reasonable suspicion exists that another person might be present who poses a danger to the arresting officers

b. The search must be confined to areas where a person might be hiding

6. *New York v. Belton* (1981) established that the vehicle of a person who has been arrested can be searched without a warrant

F. Search in an emergency situation

1. In situations where police officers believe that there is probable cause but have no time to secure a warrant (e.g., if shots are being fired or a person is screaming), they may act on their own discretion

2. A warrantless search in the absence of a lawful arrest or consent is justified only in emergencies or *exigent circumstances* where probable cause exists and the search must be conducted immediately (*New York v. Quarles*, 1984)

3. The circumstances must include the following three conditions:

   a. There must be reason to believe a real emergency exists requiring immediate action to protect or preserve life or to prevent serious injury

   b. Any entry or search must not be motivated primarily by a wish to find evidence

   c. There must be a connection between the emergency and the area entered or searched

4. In *Mincey v. Arizona* (1978), the Supreme Court stated that the Fourth Amendment does not require police officers to delay a search in the course of an investigation if to do so would gravely endanger their lives or the lives of others

5. In *Brigham City, Utah v. Stuart* (2006), the Supreme Court ruled that law enforcement officers could enter a house without a warrant to render emergency assistance to an injured occupant or to protect an occupant from imminent injury

6. In *Michigan v. Fisher* (2009), the Court further clarified when officers may enter a home under the exigent circumstances exception to the warrant requirement by specifically identifying the *emergency aid requirement*:

   a. "The 'emergency aid exception' does not depend on the officers' subjective intent of the seriousness of the crime they are investigating"

   b. What matters is whether officers had "an objectively reasonable basis for believing that someone needs medical assistance or is in danger"

G. Warrantless searches of vehicles

1. The *Carroll* decision (*Carroll v. United States,* 1925) established that automobiles may be searched without a warrant if

    a. there is probable cause for the search
    b. the vehicle would be gone before a search warrant could be obtained

2. If probable cause does not exist, the officer may be able to obtain voluntary consent. The driver must be competent to give such consent, and silence is not consent. If at any time the driver rescinds consent, the search must cease

3. Officers also must know their state's laws regarding full searches of vehicles pursuant to issuing a traffic citation

    a. Pretext stops

        (1) The so-called *pretext stop* is overridden by an officer's probable cause to believe the motorist is, or is about to be, engaged in criminal activity
        (2) Probable cause trumps pretext

    b. Searches of passengers in a stopped vehicle

        (1) "Passengers' rights during vehicle stops often differ from those of drivers" (Rutledge, 2007f, p.70)
        (2) All passengers in private vehicles are detained at a stop
        (3) Passengers may be ordered out and kept from leaving
        (4) Passengers may be arrested for joint possession of contraband
        (5) Passengers' property and the vehicle may be searched incident to their arrest
        (6) "Passenger property exception" ruling, *Wyoming v. Houghton* (1999):

            (a) An officer may search an automobile passenger's belongings simply because the officer suspects the driver has done something wrong
            (b) However, in *Brendlin v. California* (2007), the Supreme Court reaffirmed what officers already knew—that they must have at least a *reasonable suspicion* of criminal activity to stop a vehicle

    c. Searches of vehicles incident to and contemporaneous with lawful arrests

        (1) *New York v. Belton* (1981) established that the vehicle of a person who has been arrested can be searched without a warrant

(2) *Belton* has since been limited by *Arizona v. Gant* (2009), in which the Supreme Court reduced law enforcement's authority to search the passenger compartment of a vehicle incident to arrest

(3) "The bright-line rule allowing automatic searches of vehicles incident to the arrest of an occupant has been narrowed to allow such a search only if the officer has a reasonable belief that the arrestee can gain access to the vehicle or that evidence of the crime of arrest will be found in the vehicle" (Judge, 2009, p.12)

(4) Although *Gant* restricts searches incident to arrest, it has no impact on the other warrant exceptions, such as consent, exigent circumstances and the motor vehicle exception (Myers, 2011)

(5) In *Thornton v. United States* (2004), the Supreme Court ruled that police can search the passenger compartment of a vehicle incident to arrest when the arrestee was approached after recently occupying that vehicle

d. Vehicle searches at roadblocks and checkpoints

(1) In *United States v. Martinez-Fuerte* (1976), the Supreme Court ruled that (immigration) checkpoints at the country's borders were constitutional because they served a national interest and that this interest outweighed the checkpoint's minimal intrusion on driver privacy

(2) The *functional equivalent doctrine* establishes that routine border searches are constitutional at places other than actual borders where travelers frequently enter or leave the country, including international airports

(3) In *Brown v. Texas* (1979), the Supreme Court created a *balancing test* (an evaluation of interests and factors) to determine the constitutionality of roadblocks, using three factors:

(a) The gravity of the public concerns served by establishing the roadblock

(b) The degree to which the roadblock is likely to succeed in serving the public interest

(c) The severity with which the roadblock interferes with individual liberty

(4) *Michigan v. Sitz* (1990) established that *sobriety checkpoints* to combat drunken driving were reasonable under the *Brown* balancing test if they met certain guidelines

(5) However, the Court ruled in *City of Indianapolis v. Edmond* (2000) that checkpoints for *drugs* are unconstitutional

(6) In *Illinois v. Lidster* (2004), the Court upheld the constitutionality of *informational checkpoints*

(7) In *United States v. Flores-Montano* (2004), the Court ruled that privacy interests do not apply to vehicles crossing the border

    e. Inventory searches

(1) *Chambers v. Maroney* (1970) established that a vehicle may be taken to headquarters to be searched

(2) Officers have the right to inventory vehicles if it is necessary to

(a) protect the owner's property

(b) protect the police from disputes and claims that property was stolen or damaged

(c) protect the police and public from danger

(d) determine the owner's identity

V. The Crime Scene Search

A. A successful crime scene search locates, identifies and preserves all evidence present

B. The goals of a search include

1. Establishing that a crime *was* committed and *what* the specific crime was
2. Establishing *when* the crime was committed
3. Identifying *who* committed the crime
4. Explaining *how* the crime was committed
5. Suggesting *why* the crime was committed

C. It is important that officers recognize the following:

1. A meticulous, properly conducted search usually results in the discovery of evidence
2. The security measures taken by the first officer at the scene determine whether evidence is discovered intact or after it has been altered or destroyed
3. During a search, do not change or contaminate physical evidence in any way, or it will be declared inadmissible
4. It is paramount to maintain the chain of custody of evidence from the initial discovery to the time of the trial

D. Organizing the crime scene search includes:

1. dividing duties, selecting a search pattern, assigning personnel and equipment, and giving instructions
2. determining the number of personnel needed, the type of search best suited for the area and the items most likely to be found

3. determining whether the scene was immediately secured and whether the scene is considered to be a *true,* or *uncontaminated, scene*

E. Physical evidence

1. Physical evidence ranges in size from very large objects to minute substance traces
2. Knowing what to search for is indispensable to an effective crime scene search
3. *Physical evidence* is anything material and relevant to the crime being investigated
4. The *"elephant-in-a-matchbox" doctrine* requires that searchers consider the probable size and shape of evidence they seek because, for example, large objects cannot be concealed in tiny areas

VI. Search Patterns

A. All search patterns have a common denominator: They are designed to systematically locate any evidence at a crime scene or at any other area where evidence might be found
B. Exterior searches

1. *Lane-search pattern*—partitions the area into lanes, using stakes and string
2. *Strip-search pattern*—if only one officer is available for the search, the pattern can be divided into lanes
3. *Grid-search pattern*—uses a modified grid
4. *Circle search*—begins at the center of an area to be searched and spreads out in ever-widening concentric circles
5. *Zone or sector-search pattern*—an area is divided into equal squares on a map of the same area

C. Interior searches

1. Most searches are interior searches
2. Interior searches go from the general to the specific
3. Process:

a. Start at an entry point
b. Search the floor first
c. Then search the walls
d. Then search the ceiling

D. General guidelines

1. In general, the precise pattern used is immaterial as long as the search is systematic
2. Finding evidence is no reason to stop a search. Continue searching until the entire area is covered

E. Plain-sense evidence

1. The most common type of plain-sense evidence is that seen by an officer

2. *Plain-view evidence*

    a. Anywhere officers have a right to be, they have a right to see—through the use of their unaided senses
    b. Unconcealed evidence seen by an officer engaged in a lawful activity is admissible in court
    c. An officer cannot use the plain-view doctrine to justify the seizure of an object that the warrant in use does not mention
    d. An officer also may seize evidence indicated by a sense other than sight
    e. Officers may seize any contraband they discover during a legal search
    f. Containers can be opened where their outward appearance reveals criminal contents (e.g., a kit of burglar tools or a gun case)

        (1) By their nature, they do not support a reasonable expectation of privacy because their contents can be inferred from their appearance

3. *Plain feel/touch evidence*

    a. The "plain feel/touch" exception is an extension of the plain-view exception.
    b. If a police officer lawfully pats down a suspect's outer clothing and feels an object that he or she *immediately* identifies as contraband, a warrantless seizure is justified (*Minnesota v. Dickerson*, 1993)

4. Plain smell

    a. Evidence may also be seized if an officer relies on a sense other than sight or touch
    b. If an odor reveals the presence of a seizable object, the object may be seized

5. Plain hearing

    a. Officers or undercover agents can position themselves in accessible locations where they can overhear criminal conversation without any extraordinary listening devices (such as wiretaps or parabolic microphones)
    b. Anything overheard can be used as evidence

VII.   Other Types of Investigatory Searches

A.   In addition to crime scene searches, officers may search buildings, trash or garbage cans, vehicles, suspects and dead bodies as they investigate criminal offenses

B.   Building searches

1.   "Building search and the entry into non-secured areas is one of the most intricate skills that are not routinely taught to police officers" (Oldham, 2006, p.73)

2.   Clear the fatal funnel (zone outside and inside the doorway) quickly

3.   When executing a warrant to search a building, officers should first familiarize themselves with the location and the past record of the person living there

4.   Do not treat the execution of a search warrant as routine. Plan for the worst-case scenario

5.   Have a plan before entering the building

6.   Keep light and weapons away from your body

7.   Officers may, for their own safety, detain occupants of the premises while a proper search is conducted

8.   Officers also may require residents to remain outside of their homes

9.   Officers should be aware of the ruling in *Kyllo v. United States* (2001), which held that thermal scanning of a private residence from outside the residence is a search

C.   Trash or garbage can searches

1.   In *California v. Greenwood* (1988), the Supreme Court ruled that containers left on public property are open to search by police without a warrant

2.   The most important factor in determining the legality of a warrantless trash inspection is the physical location of the retrieved trash. Police cannot trespass to gain access to the trash location

3.   Officers need to know if the trash is within the *curtilage* of the person's property, which is that part of the property that is not open to the public and that is reserved for the property owner

D.   Vehicle searches

1.   Remove occupants from the car or other vehicle

2.   Search the area around the vehicle

3.   Search the interior

4.   Take precautions to prevent contamination of evidence

E. Suspect searches

    1.   If the suspect has not been arrested, confine your search to a patdown or frisk for weapons

    2.   If the suspect has been arrested, make a complete body search for weapons and evidence

    3.   Under the Fourth Amendment, officers are permitted to handcuff, detain and question occupants when executing high-risk search warrants

        a. Before conducting any search, ask the suspect if he or she has anything that could get the officer into trouble, asking specifically about needles and blades

        b. When possible, search a suspect while a cover officer observes. If arresting the suspect, first handcuff and then search

        c. Every search should be done wearing protective gloves

    4.   Thorough search

        a. If you arrest a suspect, conduct a complete body search for both weapons and evidence

        b. Strip searches may be conducted only after an arrest and when the prisoner is in a secure facility

            (1)   Such searches should be conducted by individuals of the same gender as the suspect and in private and should follow written guidelines

            (2)   Cavity searches go beyond the normal strip search and must follow very strict departmental guidelines. Such searches should be conducted by medical personnel

    5.   Inhibitors to a thorough search:

        a. The presence of bodily fluids is one factor that may interfere with a complete search

        b. Officers also must be alert to suspects who may spit on or bite them

        c. Another inhibitor to thorough searches is a fear of needles

        d. Weather can also compromise the thoroughness of a search

F. Dead body searches

    1.   Searching a dead body should be done only after the coroner or medical examiner has arrived or given permission

    2.   Do *not* turn the body over to search for identification or other wounds or evidence. This causes major problems in documenting the body's original position

    3.   Search the dead body systematically and completely, including the immediate area around and under the body

G. Underwater searches

    1. Conditions beyond the control of the investigator may dictate what type of search is conducted

    2. Metal detectors are a necessity in underwater searches

VIII. Use of Dogs in a Search

A. A dog can be an invaluable resource to a patrol officer

B. Dogs can be trained to locate suspects, narcotics, explosives, cadavers and more.

C. Dogs "are good for bomb, chemical and drug detection; tracking both suspects and lost persons; and finding real and counterfeit money, land mines, people hiding, weapons, buried bodies or fire igniters/ accelerants in arson cases." (Falk, 2006, p.48)

D. Canines are a great force multiplier and a psychological advantage

IX. Warrant Checklist

A. No search warrant required

    1. No search (plain sense, open fields, abandoned property, private-party delivery, controlled delivery, exposed characteristics)

    2. Independent justification (consent, probation or parole, incident to arrest, officer safety, booking search, inventory)

    3. Exigent circumstances (rescue, protection of property, imminent destruction of evidence, fresh pursuit, escape prevention, public safety)

    4. Fleeing target (car, van, truck, RV, bus, boat, aircraft, etc.) with PC and lawful access

B. The courts also have identified several "special needs" exceptions

    1. These exceptions do not fit into other categories.

    2. Examples include school searches, searches of highly regulated businesses (e.g., firearms dealers, pawn shops and junkyards), employment and educational drug screening, and the immediate search for "evanescent" evidence (such as blood-alcohol content)

X. A Reminder

A. Jetmore (2007b, p.26) stresses, "Ability to skillfully document in writing facts and circumstances that lead to logical inferences and reasonable conclusions remains a professional requirement in criminal investigation. Excellent investigative work is negated and the guilty may walk free if the legal framework on which it was based can't be adequately explained"

B. The Fourth Amendment requires that officers' actions be *reasonable*: clearly outline every detail known to you at the time in your report so that the reasonability of your actions will be clear

XI. Summary

FORENSICS/ PHYSICAL EVIDENCE

OUTLINE

- Definitions
- Investigative Equipment
- Crime Scene Integrity and Contamination of Evidence
- Processing Evidence: Maintaining the Chain of Custody from Discovery to Disposal
- Frequently Examined Evidence
- Evidence Handling and Infectious Disease

Chapter 5
Forensics/Physical Evidence

Key Terms

- Advanced Fingerprint Information Technology (AFIT)
- associative evidence
- ballistics
- best evidence
- biometrics
- bore
- caliber
- cast
- chain of custody
- chain of evidence
- circumstantial evidence
- class characteristics
- competent evidence
- contamination
- corpus delicti
- corpus delicti evidence
- cross-contamination
- *Daubert* standard
- direct evidence
- DNA
- DNA profiling

- elimination prints
- evidence
- forensic science
- indirect evidence
- individual characteristics
- inkless fingerprint
- integrity of evidence
- latent fingerprints
- material evidence
- physical evidence
- plastic fingerprints
- *prima facie* evidence
- probative evidence
- proxy data
- relevant evidence
- rifling
- standard of comparison
- striations
- tool mark
- trace evidence
- visible fingerprints
- voiceprint

Learning Objectives
After reading this chapter, students should be able to

- Describe various methods of processing physical evidence.
- Determine what qualifies as evidence.
- Discuss common errors in collecting evidence.
- Identify evidence.

- Explain what should be recorded in crime scene notes.
- Describe various methods of packaging and transporting evidence to a department or a laboratory.
- Discuss methods of evidence storage.

(Continued)

• Describe how to ensure admissibility of physical evidence in court. • Describe methods of evidence disposal. • Identify the types of evidence most commonly found in criminal investigations and how to collect, identify and package each type. • Explain where fingerprints can be found and how they should be preserved. • Describe what can and cannot be determined from fingerprints, DNA, bloodstains and hairs. • Define DNA profiling. • Explain how the identification of blood and hair can be useful. • Describe where shoe and tire impressions can be found and how they should be preserved.	• Illustrate how to preserve tools that might have been used in the crime, as well as the marks they made. • Describe what a tool mark should be compared with during forensic analysis. • Explain how to mark and care for weapons used in crimes. • Describe how to preserve such things as glass fragments, soil samples, safe insulation material, rope, tapes, liquids and documents. • Identify the kind of evidence UV light can help discover. • Describe what evidence to collect in hit-and-run cases. • Explain what can be determined from human skeletal remains.

Internet Assignments

1. Ask students to use a search engine to locate the FBI *Handbook of Forensic Services.* Review the section on Crime Scene Safety and provide a two-page description of the issues raised by the section.

2. Have students explore the auction Web site of Property Room, which takes the burden of unclaimed property off police departments' hands. Have students categorize the types of evidence that are being auctioned. Does any of the evidence strike them as beyond what they would expect to be considered as physical evidence in a case? What are the pros and cons of disposing of evidence in this manner?

3. Have students review the following Web sites' information on DNA training or their own state's resources on DNA training for law enforcement or for prosecution or defense attorneys:

   • The DNA Initiative
   • Office of Justice Programs
   • Denver District Attorneys Office
   • Texas Department of Public Safety DNA Training

   Discuss as a class what police officers and crime scene investigators should know about DNA.

4. Ask students to go to the Arkansas State Crime Laboratory Web site and review the services they offer. Ask students to imagine: If they worked in this crime lab and had unlimited budgets, what additional services would they recommend the lab offer?

Class Assignment

Have students break into groups that are focused on the following topics:

- Hair evidence
- Fiber evidence
- Blood evidence
- Glass evidence
- Firearms evidence
- Fingerprint evidence
- Chemical analysis
- DNA evidence

Once you have arranged the groups, discuss the pros and cons of each topic as evidence.

Chapter Outline

I. Definitions

    A. Forensic science is "the application of scientific processes to solve legal problems most notably within the context of the criminal justice system" (Fantino, 2007, p.26)

       1. Criminal activity always removes something from the crime scene and leaves behind incriminating evidence

       2. Remnants of this transfer are called proxy data

    B. Types of evidence

       1. Best evidence, in the legal sense, is the original evidence

       2. Physical evidence is anything real (i.e., which has substance) that helps to establish the facts of a case

       3. Direct evidence establishes proof of a fact without any other evidence

       4. Indirect evidence merely *tends* to incriminate a person (e.g., a suspect's footprints found near the crime scene)

       5. Indirect evidence is also called circumstantial evidence

       6. Extremely small items, such as hair or fibers, are a subset of direct evidence called trace evidence

       7. Evidence established by law is called *prima facie* evidence

       8. Associative evidence links a suspect with a crime. Associative evidence includes fingerprints, footprints, bloodstains, hairs, and fibers

       9. Corpus delicti evidence establishes that a crime has been committed

      10. Probative evidence is vital to the investigation or prosecution of a case, tending to prove or actually proving guilt or innocence

11. Material evidence forms a substantive part of the case or has a legitimate and effective influence on the decision of the case
12. Relevant evidence applies to the matter in question
13. Competent evidence has been properly collected, identified, filed and continuously secured

II. Investigative Equipment

A. Equipment needed for each type of investigation will vary; however, investigators and officers need specialized equipment to properly process the various crime scenes. Examples would include cameras, chalk, containers, fingerprint kit, labels, magnifiers, measuring tape, notebooks, paper, pens and other equipment listed in the text

B. More expensive and elaborate equipment is also needed, such as more elaborate cameras and laptop computers

C. Selecting equipment

1. Work with other organizations to identify what is needed. It is helpful to contact other law enforcement agencies to determine what equipment they use and what they suggest for purchase
2. Select what you want to have for your organization. Investigators know best what is needed and what is needed by the organization

D. Equipment containers

1. Equipment may be stored in one or more containers. The equipment needs to be carefully cared for so that it will work when needed, and the purchase of specialized containers will help
2. The containers need to look professional. It is important that investigators make use of professional containers and equipment to create a consistent image

E. Transporting equipment

1. There are many possible ways to transport equipment to a crime scene from the use of a police car to a specially equipped vehicle
2. A mobile crime lab is generally a specially equipped van that contains the type of equipment needed to process most crime scenes

F. Training in equipment use

1. Most failures during use of equipment are because of lack of training given to those using it, rather than to any problem with the equipment
2. Crime scene investigators need to examine the scene carefully before entering it

III. Crime Scene Integrity and Contamination of Evidence

    A. The value of evidence is directly affected by what happens to it immediately following the crime

    B. Cordon off the crime scene

    C. Maintain evidence integrity

        1. Integrity of evidence refers to the requirement that any item introduced in court must be in the same condition as when it was found at the crime scene

        2. This is documented by the chain of evidence, also called the chain of custody: documentation of what has happened to the evidence from the time it was discovered until it is needed in court, including every person who has had custody

    D. Recalling Locard's principle of exchange, the very act of collecting evidence, no matter how carefully done, will result in a postcrime transfer of material—contamination

    E. The value of evidence may be lost because of improper collection, handling or identification

IV. Processing Evidence: Maintaining the Chain of Custody from Discovery to Disposal

    A. Discovering or recognizing evidence

        1. To determine what is evidence, first consider the apparent crime. Then look for any objects unrelated or foreign to the scene, unusual in location or number, or damaged or broken or whose relation to other objects suggests a pattern that fits the crime

        2. Sometimes it is difficult to recognize items as evidence. Investigators need to consider the type and nature of the crime and carefully examine what items are in the area of the crime scene

            a. Plain-view evidence can be seized legally

            b. Recall also that the Brady rule requires law enforcement to gather all evidence that helps establish guilt *or* innocence

        3. A standard of comparison is an object, measure or model with which evidence is compared to determine whether both came from the same source

        4. Forensic light sources (FLSs), which work on the principle of ultraviolet fluorescence, infrared luminescence or laser light, can make evidence visible that is not otherwise detectable to the naked eye, such as latent prints, body fluids and even altered signatures

            a. Ultraviolet (UV) light is the invisible energy at the violet end of the color spectrum that causes substances to emit visible light, commonly called *fluorescence*

        b.   Lasers can also assist in investigations through trajectory analysis, measurement and evidence collection

        c.   TracER stands for Trace Evidence Recovery

B.   Collecting, marking and identifying evidence

    1.   Some of the common errors in collecting evidence include

        a.   Not collecting enough of the sample

        b.   Not obtaining standards of comparison

        c.   Not maintaining the integrity of the evidence

    2.   Mark or identify each item of evidence in a way that can be recognized later. Indicate the date and case number as well as your personal identifying mark or initials. Record in your notes the date and time of collection, where the evidence was found and by whom, the case number, a description of the item and who took custody

C.   Packaging and preserving evidence: Package each item separately in a durable container to maintain the integrity of evidence

D.   Transporting evidence

    1.   Personal delivery, registered mail, insured parcel post, air express, Federal Express and United Parcel Service are legal ways to transport evidence

    2.   Always specify that the person receiving the evidence is to sign for it

E.   Protecting and storing evidence

    1.   Storage must be secure and free from pests, insects and excessive heat or moisture

    2.   Property management

        a.   Managing the growing mass of evidence is becoming increasingly challenging because there is a growing need for more storage space to accommodate the seemingly exponential increase in the quantity of evidence that must be stored for longer periods of time, as scientific advances in DNA technology have caused many state legislatures to extend or eliminate their statutes of limitation

        b.   A major crime scene investigation might generate more than 200 pieces of evidence

        c.   The amount of property that must be tracked and stored in metropolitan departments is typically 100,000 to 400,000 or more items

        d.   Automated systems, barcodes, handheld computers and portable printers are helping manage evidence and property

F. Exhibiting evidence in court

    1. To ensure admissibility of evidence in court, be able to

        a. identify the evidence as that found at the crime scene
        b. describe exactly where it was found
        c. establish its custody from discovery to the present
        d. voluntarily explain any changes that have occurred in the evidence

    2. *Frye* and *Daubert* cases

        a. Under *Frye v. United States* (1923), whether the science to process the evidence was acceptable under the "general acceptance" of the scientific community was a precondition to the admissibility of scientific evidence
        b. However, under *Daubert v. Merrell Dow Pharmaceuticals* (1993), which uses Federal Rules of Evidence rather than *Frye*, the material issue is that an expert's testimony must be both *reliable* and *relevant*. This is known as the two-pronged *Daubert* standard

G. Final disposition of evidence

    1. Legally disposing of evidence when the case is closed
    2. Evidence is either returned to the owner, auctioned or destroyed

V. Frequently Examined Evidence

A. Examining physical evidence often involves the use of biometrics, the statistical study of biological data
B. The labs themselves should be accredited
C. The lab also uses class and individual characteristics

    1. Class characteristics are the features that place an item into a specific category
    2. Individual characteristics are the features that distinguish one item from another of the same type

D. Fingerprints: At the end of each human finger, on the palm side, there is a unique arrangement of small lines called friction ridges. These ridges leave prints that are unique to the person

    1. Latent prints are not readily seen but can be developed through powders or chemicals. They are normally left on non-porous surfaces
    2. Visible fingerprints are made when fingers are dirty or stained. They occur primarily on glossy or light-colored surfaces and can be dusted and lifted
    3. Plastic fingerprints, one form of visible print, are impressions left in soft substances such as putty, grease, tar, butter or soft soap. These prints are photographed, not dusted

4. Dusting latent fingerprints: be careful not to use too much powder and thus over-process latent fingerprints
5. Lifting prints: use black lifters for light powders and light lifters for black powders
6. Chemical development of latent fingerprints: Use for unpainted wood, paper, cardboard or other absorbent surfaces
7. Other methods of lifting prints: Magnabrush techniques, laser technology, gelatin lifters and cyanoacrylate (superglue)

    a. Caution: Dusting for fingerprints can sometimes destroy parts of the prints.

    b. In addition, conventional fingerprinting methods may use liquids or vapors that might alter the prints

8. New technology: Microbeam X-ray fluorescence (MXRF) rapidly reveals a sample's elemental composition by irradiating the sample with a thin beam of X-rays that does not disturb the sample
9. Elimination prints: If fingerprint evidence is found, it is important to know whose prints "belong" at the scene
10. Inked prints: Standard procedure is to fingerprint all adults who have been arrested, either at the time of booking or at the time of release
11. Digital fingerprinting: Advances in computer technology are allowing digital fingerprinting to replace inked printing

    a. Inkless fingerprints that are stored in a database for rapid retrieval
    b. Automated fingerprint identification system (AFIS)
    c. Integrated Automated Fingerprint Identification System (IAFIS): developed by the FBI and Department of Homeland Security
    d. Fingerprint patterns, analysis and identification: Normally 12 matchable characteristics on a single fingerprint are required for positive identification

12. Fingerprint patterns, analysis and identification: arched, looped or whorled
13. Usefulness of fingerprints: positive evidence of identity
14. Admissibility in court
15. Other types of prints: palm, foot, lips, writer's edge (side of hand)

E. Voiceprints: a graphic record by a sound spectrograph of the energy patterns emitted by speech. Like fingerprints, no two voiceprints are alike

F.   Language analysis: The actual language is often an overlooked type of evidence. This evidence can be captured using digital recorders

1.   Excited utterances made by persons at a crime scene can, upon analysis, reveal the speaker's state-of-mind and may be admitted into testimony even if the person does not testify

2.   To qualify for this exception to the hearsay rule, the victim or witness must have seen an exciting or startling event and made the statement while still under the stress of the event. This is similar to the *res gestae* statement

3.   One area of language analysis involves psycholinguistics, the study of the mental processes involved in comprehending, producing and acquiring language

G.   Human DNA profiling: deoxyribonucleic acid (DNA) is the building block of chromosomes. This substance is individual to the specific person

1.   Genetic code can be used to create a genetic fingerprint to positively identify a person

a.   Except for identical twins, no two individuals have the same DNA structure

b.   DNA profiling uses material from which chromosomes are made to identify individuals positively

c.   Law enforcement should use DNA's full potential because the low cost per test today can also aid in solving high-volume crimes such as burglaries and car break-ins

2.   Collecting and preserving DNA evidence

a.   Collection is simple to conduct. The supplies are inexpensive. Processing time in the field is minimal. Standards are easily obtained

b.   Sterile, cotton-tipped applicator swabs, which are inexpensive, easily obtained and easy to carry and store, are used to collect four DNA samples by rubbing the inside surfaces of the cheeks thoroughly and then air-drying the swabs and placing them back into the original paper packaging or an envelope with sealed corners

c.   Plastic containers should not be used because they can retain moisture, which may damage the integrity of the DNA sample

d.   In some cases, DNA analysis has been rendered worthless by the defense's successful attack on the methods used to collect and store the evidence on which DNA analysis was performed

3.   DNA testing

a.   Two types of DNA are used in forensic analyses: nuclear DNA (nDNA) and mitochondrial DNA (mtDNA)

-       (1) Nuclear DNA (nDNA) from blood, semen, saliva, body tissues and hairs that have tissue at their root ends
-       (2) Mitochondrial DNA (mtDNA) from naturally shed hairs, hair fragments, bones and teeth

    b.   DNA analysis is difficult with a mixed profile sample (where DNA from more than one individual is in the sample)

-       (1) A new technique called Y-STR analysis is being used in such cases. It uses the Y chromosome as a male-specific identifier, and typing techniques are now available that develop profiles specific to the male contributor of the DNA
-       (2) A limitation of Y-STR analysis is that the DNA profile obtained will be identical for all males within the same paternal lineage

4.   Biogeographical ancestry DNA testing can be used to include or exclude certain people from an investigation based on their ancestry

    a.   Can suspects be identified by race with DNA?

    b.   Because DNA evidence has scientifically rigorous probabilities, the chances are far less than 1 in 10 billion for a full DNA profile from a single individual matching that of another individual

5.   DNA Database: Combined DNA Index System (CODIS):

    a.   Since its inception, more than 4.2 million forensic and convicted offender profiles have been entered into CODIS

    b.   The forensic index contains DNA profiles from crime scene evidence where the offender's identity is unknown

    c.   The offender index contains DNA profiles of individuals convicted of sex offenses and other violent crimes

6.   Backlog of DNA awaiting testing: More than 450,000 cases have not yet been entered in CODIS

7.   DNA admissibility in court: "Today a DNA match is virtually undisputable in court" (Ivy and Orput, 2007, p.30)

8.   Exoneration of incarcerated individuals: More than 200 convicts had been exonerated by 2007 after being convicted with wrongful misidentification

9.   Moral and ethical issues: The needs of the law enforcement community must be weighed with the public's interest in preserving its own civil liberties

H.   Blood and other body fluids: Blood and other body fluids, including semen and urine, can provide valuable information. Semen and saliva may be detected with fluorescent lights (FLS), and blood trails or blood "spatter" can also be useful as evidence. New software programs such as Backtrack can help analyze blood spatter patterns

I. Scent: Every person has a unique scent that cannot be masked or eliminated, not even by the most potent perfume. Scent can establish probable cause for an arrest

J. Hairs and fibers: Hairs and fibers can place an individual at the crime scene, especially in violent crimes in which evidence is generally transferred or exchanged. Secondary ion mass spectrometry (SIMS) chemicals can distinguish trace hair samples using consumer chemicals as identifiers. Although chemical colorants and other products commonly applied to hair can thwart microscopic analysis, SIMS is not affected by such substances and can capitalize on their presence to improve identification

K. Shoe and tire impressions: Tracks or marks left by shoes or tires can be specific to the shoe or tire

L. Bite marks: Bite marks can be found on the suspect or victim's body or on anything else placed in the mouth such as food

    1. Bite mark identification is based on the "supposed" individuality of teeth and is legally admissible in court, having endured a number of legal challenges

    2. Teeth may also be an excellent source of genomic DNA

    3. A forensic odontologist is recommended

M. Tools and tool marks: Tools are often used in the commission of a crime. They can be traced if broken parts are left behind or by marks caused by the use of the tool

N. Firearms and ammunition: Gunpowder tests, shot pattern tests and functional tests of a weapon can be made and compared

    1. Firearm evidence can include bullets, shell casings, slugs, shot pellets and gunshot residue including serial numbers, blood, fingerprints or other biological evidence

    2. A new bill in California requires that beginning in 2010, all semiautomatic handguns purchased have the ability to imprint identifying information on cartridges fired by the weapon, which could turn spent cartridges into potential evidence in civil and criminal cases

O. Glass: Glass can be used for transfer of evidence and to show where a piece of glass came from at the crime scene

    1. The Glass Evidence Reference Database contains more than 700 glass samples from manufacturers, distributors and vehicle junkyards and is a useful resource for investigators

    2. Although it cannot determine the source of an unknown piece of glass, the database can assess the relative frequency that two glass samples from different sources would have the same elemental profile

P. Soils and minerals: This circumstantial evidence can place a suspect at a crime scene

Q. Safe insulation: Safes contain insulation that can transfer to the suspect's clothing

R. Ropes, strings and tapes: These items can be compared, either by type or the cut ends

S. Drugs: Drug identification kits can be used to make a preliminary analysis of a suspicious substance, but a full analysis must be done at a laboratory

T. Weapons of mass destruction (WMDs) include nuclear weapons; radiological, biological or chemical agents; and explosives

    1. Testing matrixes include aerosols (or air), liquids, solids, surfaces and dermal samples

    2. At any WMD crime scene, however, the public's safety takes precedence over evidence collection

U. Documents: Typing, handwriting and printing can be compared

    1. Resource: Forensic Information System for Handwriting (FISH), which is maintained by the U.S. Secret Service

    2. This database merges federal and Interpol databases of genuine and counterfeit identification documents, such as passports, driver's licenses and credit cards

V. Digital evidence: The digital revolution and preponderance of electronic devices pervading everyday life, such as cell phones, pagers, personal digital assistants (PDAs), computers and global positioning systems (GPSs), has generated a new class of evidence and requirements for handling it

    1. Perhaps the greatest challenge in electronic crimes is the absence of geographic boundaries and the question of jurisdiction

    2. The first part of collecting evidence from a cell phone is the actual handling of the device. Dunnagan and Schroader (2006, p.47) suggest the following basic rules:

        a. Do not change the condition of the evidence. If it's off, leave it off; if it's on, leave it on

        b. Look for more devices. Remove any other potential points of evidence, which can include SIM cards, external media, power cables and data cables

        c. Make sure you have a search warrant before searching the device

        d. Return the device to a lab for proper processing

        e. Use forensically sound software and processing tools, and validate your evidence

    3. Only a person with training should analyze a cell phone

    4.   All cell phones leave a trail

    5.   Global positioning system chips built into cell phones allow authorities to track criminals as well as people in need of help

    6.   Each cell phone provider stores and maintains subscriber records, which include subscriber information, such as name, address and birth date, as well as call-detail records containing data regarding incoming and outgoing phone numbers and the towers that transmitted these calls

W.   Laundry and dry-cleaning marks: Many launderers and dry cleaners use specific marking systems. These can be used for comparisons and to find the business

X.   Paint: Paint colors and samples can lead to the identification of an automobile and can offer many leads

Y.   Skeletal remains: Laboratories can determine whether skeletal remains are animal or human. Dental comparisons and X-rays of old fractures are other important identifying features or individual characteristics

Z.   Wood: Wood comparisons are possible regarding the type of wood and origin

AA.   Other types of evidence: Prescription eyeglasses, broken buttons, glove prints and other personal evidence found at a crime scene can also be examined and compared

    1.   Investigators should learn to read "product DNA," the printed code that appears on nearly every manufactured, mass-produced item, because it can provide valuable leads

    2.   Other discarded items at a crime scene that may yield useful information include store and restaurant receipts, bank deposit slips, beverage containers, cigarette packages, membership and check-cashing cards, clothing manufacturer labels and laundry tags, and footwear

VI.   Evidence Handling and Infectious Disease

A.   Consider all body secretions as potential health hazards

B.   AIDS is not spread through casual contact such as touching an infected person or sharing equipment

C.   Tuberculosis (TB) is of greater concern

D.   MRSA is a staph infection that is resistant to most antibiotics. It is very infectious, severe and sometimes deadly

E.   Use "universal precautions" when collecting blood evidence and other bodily fluids

F.   Wash hands thoroughly with soap and water

G.   While processing the crime scene, constantly be alert for sharp objects, such as hypodermic needles and syringes

VII.   Summary

OBTAINING INFORMATION AND INTELLIGENCE

OUTLINE

Chapter 6
Obtaining Information and Intelligence

Key Terms

• admission	• interrogation
• adoptive admission	• interview
• beachheading	• leading question
• closed-ended question	• *Miranda* warning
• cognitive interview	• network
• complainant	• nonverbal communication
• confession	• open-ended question
• custodial arrest	• polygraph
• custodial interrogation	• public safety exception
• direct question	• rapport
• dying declaration	• sources-of-information file
• field interview	• statement
• in custody	• testimonial hearsay
• indirect question	• third degree
• informant	• waiver
• information age	

Learning Objectives
After reading this chapter, students should be able to

• Discuss what a sources-of-information file is and what it contains.	• Outline what two requirements are needed to obtain information.
• Explain the goal of interviewing and interrogation.	• Clarify the difference between direct and indirect questions, and when to use each.
• List the characteristics of an effective interviewer or interrogator.	• Describe techniques that are likely to assist recall as well as uncover lies.
• Discuss how to improve communication between the investigator, victims, witnesses or suspects.	• Explain when and in what order individuals are interviewed.
• Explain the emotional barriers to communication.	

(Continued)

<table>
<tr>
<td>

- Describe the various sources of information that are available to investigators.
- Discuss the basic approaches to use in questioning reluctant interviewees.
- Explain what the *Miranda* warning is and when to give it.
- Outline the two requirements of a place for conducting interrogations.
- Discuss what techniques to use in an interrogation.
- Explain what third-degree tactics are and describe their place in interrogation.

</td>
<td>

- Describe what restrictions are placed on obtaining a confession.
- Clarify what significance a confession has in an investigation.
- Discuss what to consider when questioning a juvenile.
- Explain what a polygraph is and what its role in investigation and the acceptability of its results in court are.
- Identify the differences between information and intelligence.

</td>
</tr>
</table>

Internet Assignments

1. Have students research the following topics:

    - FBI interviews of Arabs and Muslims
    - the USA PATRIOT Act

    Split the class into small groups. Have half of the groups discuss the FBI's interviews of Arabs and Muslims and the other half of the groups discuss the PATRIOT Act. Then have them compare, contrast and discuss the results from each side's perspective. How does *Miranda* factor into "inquisitive" interviews versus "interrogations"?

2. Have students explore the Web sites for the Law Enforcement National Data Exchange (N-DEx) and EJustice Solutions. What services does each provide that can assist police departments in obtaining information and intelligence? Have the students discuss commonalities and differences between these two Web sites and the organizations they represent.

3. Have students search the Web for information on *Miranda v. Arizona*. Who was Ernesto Miranda and why is his name linked to virtually every police interview or interrogation? Research Ernesto Miranda's personal history, including his family, criminal activity and ultimate fate. Research the case itself. What was the precise argument that led to the court's decision? Research and discuss challenges to the *Miranda* ruling. There are some who say it has outlived its usefulness and should be replaced, along with the exclusionary rule. Some argue that the *Miranda* ruling as well as the exclusionary rule should be tougher, not more lenient. Have your students debate the validity of these arguments.

4. Research both *Brewer v. Williams* and *Nix v. Williams*. Why did one man create the need for two separate key Supreme Court cases? Do your students agree or disagree with the Court's decisions?

Class Assignments

1. Have class members split into pairs and take turns playing the role of a victim and an investigator, then of a suspect and an interrogator, for a limited period of time. Afterward, have the class members discuss what they learned, both while playing the investigator/interrogator role and while observing their partner in it.

2. Have the class search the Internet for the case of Jose Medellín. Medellín was executed for the gang rape and murder of two young girls in Houston, Texas. The girls were 14 and 16 years old. Medellín argued, unsuccessfully, that he should not be executed because he had not been advised that he had the right to contact his country's consulate. (This requirement is different from the *Miranda* right to "counsel.") Medellín had been in prison for 15 years before finally being executed. Have the class review this issue and have a discussion on the following information:

   - The Vienna Convention on Consular Relations: Article 36 of the VCCR requires that foreign nationals who are arrested or detained must be given notice "without delay" of their right to have their embassy or consulate notified of that arrest. (Note the "without delay" requirement.)
   - The police must notify the embassy or consulate, which in turn can follow up on the case, if requested to do so by the foreign national who is in custody.
   - The notice to the consulate can be as simple as a fax, giving the person's name, the place of arrest and a brief description of the circumstances of the arrest or detention.
   - In June 2006 the U.S. Supreme Court ruled that foreign nationals who were *not notified* of their right to consular notification and access after an arrest *may not use the treaty violation to suppress evidence obtained in police interrogations* or belatedly raise legal challenges after trial (*Sanchez-Llamas v. Oregon* and later the Medellín case outlined above).
   - In March 2008 the Supreme Court further ruled that the decision of the International Court of Justice directing the United States to give "review and reconsideration" to the cases of 51 Mexican convicts on death row was not a binding domestic law and therefore could not be used to overcome state procedural default rules that barred further postconviction challenges(*Medellín v. Texas*). As a result Medellín was executed.

Chapter Outline

I. Sources of Information

    A. Three primary sources of information are available, in addition to physical evidence:

        1. Reports, records and databases, including those found on the Internet

        2. People who are not suspects in a crime but who know something about the crime or those involved

3.   suspects in the crime

B.   Sources-of-information file

    1.   So many sources of information exist and they often overlap
    2.   This file contains the name and location of people, organizations and records that may assist in a criminal investigation

C.   The information age

    1.   We are living in the information age, a period in which knowledge and information are increasing exponentially
    2.   Computerized information is much more available now to law enforcement entities, and the information can be accessed in the squad car almost immediately

D.   Reports, records and databases

    1.   Local resources

        a.   police department records, reports, files, etc.
        b.   laboratory and coroner's reports
        c.   banks, loan and credit companies, delivery services, hospitals, hotels and motels, personnel departments, etc.

            (1)   Inventory tracking systems
            (2)   Caller ID
            (3)   Pen registers
            (4)   Dialed number recorders (DNR)

    2.   State resources
    3.   Federal resources

        a.   U.S. Postal Office; Immigration and Naturalization Service; Social Security Administration; Federal Bureau of Investigation; Bureau of Alcohol, Tobacco, Firearms and Explosives; Drug Enforcement Administration
        b.   FBI's National Crime Information Center

E.   The Internet

    1.   Internet can be used to distribute photographs and details quickly
    2.   Web site of International Association of Chiefs of Police
    3.   Web site of FBI

F.   Victims, complainants and witnesses

    1.   Investigators should interview the victim(s), complainant(s) and witness(es)
    2.   Sometimes a search is needed to locate these individuals

3. Techniques to gain information

    a. The neighborhood canvass

    b. The knock and talk

    c. A caution: be aware that suspect and witness statements are not always reliable

G. Informants

1. An informant is anyone else who can provide information about a crime who has not been listed previously.

2. Investigators should be extremely careful in using such contacts

3. Confidential informants (CI)

    a. They are formally registered

    b. They are compensated by the department

    c. They supply information or perform a service

    d. Building trust is key in developing informants

4. Establishing reliability

    a. The investigator must be able to establish the reliability of the informant

    b. The investigator must establish the totality of circumstances necessary to establish probably cause

        (1) Corroborate as much of the informant's information as possible

        (2) Determine how, where, when and under what circumstances the informant obtained the information

        (3) Provide or reveal statements informants made

        (4) Identify the informant if it is safe to do so

H. Suspects

1. A suspect is a person considered to be directly or indirectly connected with a crime, either through his or her own actions or by planning or directing it

2. Any suspicious persons should be questioned

3. A field interview is when questioning occurs spontaneously on the street

4. Keep a record of the field interview

5. Sometimes the investigator will choose to gather information from a suspect through undercover or surveillance officers or various types of listening devices

II. Interviewing and Interrogating

A. The ultimate goal of interviewing and interrogation is to determine the truth—that is, to identify those responsible for a crime and to clear the innocent of suspicion

B. Characteristics of an interviewer/interrogator:

    1. Adaptable and culturally adroit
    2. Self-controlled and patient
    3. Confident and optimistic
    4. Objective
    5. Sensitive to individual rights
    6. Knowledgeable about the elements of crimes

C. Communication can be enhanced by:

    1. Preparing in advance
    2. Obtaining information as soon after the incident as possible
    3. Being considerate and friendly
    4. Using a private setting
    5. Eliminating physical barriers
    6. Sitting rather than standing
    7. Encouraging conversation
    8. Asking simple questions one at a time
    9. Listening and observing

D. Barriers to communication include:

    1. Emotional barriers to communication

        a. Ingrained attitudes and prejudices
        b. Fear
        c. Anger or hostility
        d. The instinct for self-preservation

    2. Other barriers to communication

        a. Language barriers
        b. Individuals who are hearing impaired
        c. Individuals who have Alzheimer's
        d. Individuals who are mentally retarded

E. Effective questioning technique

    1. Two basic requirements for obtaining information are to

        a. listen
        b. observe

    2. Guidelines for effective questioning

        a. Ask one question at a time and keep your responses simple and direct
        b. Avoid questions that can be answered with yes or no
        c. Be positive in your approach
        d. Give the person time to answer

      e.   Listen to answers, but at the same time anticipate your next question

      f.   Watch your body language and tone of voice

      g.   Start the conversation on neutral territory

      h.   Tuck any tape recorder behind a portfolio or notepad, as the use of it can be frightening to anyone being interviewed

      i.   React to what you hear

      j.   As you move into difficult territory, slow down

      k.   Don't rush to fill silences

      l.   Pose the toughest questions simply, directly and with confidence

      m.   Establish professional demeanor and keep your role clear

3.   Types of questions: direct, indirect, closed-ended, open-ended and leading

      a.   *Direct question:* to the point; allows little possibility of misinterpretation

      b.   *Indirect question:* disguised; can be useful in eliciting details

      c.   *Closed-ended question:* can be answered "yes" or "no" or with another short, simple answer; this type is generally avoided

      d.   *Open-ended question:* gives the victim, witness or suspect the opportunity to provide a full response, allowing the investigator great insight into the person's knowledge and feelings

      e.   *Leading question:* prompts or leads a person to a specific response and often implies an answer

      f.   Ask *direct* questions and *open-ended* questions liberally; *leading* questions also can also a useful interrogation technique; use *indirect* and *closed-ended* questions sparingly

4.   Repetition

      a.   Repetition is an effective technique for improving recall and uncovering lies

      b.   Someone who is lying will either provide very inconsistent stories or will tell a story *exactly* the same way each time, as if it is well rehearsed

      c.   A truthful story will contain the same facts but be phrased differently each time it is retold

5.   Recording and videotaping interviews and interrogations

      a.   Some states require that interviews be recorded

      b.   Some states are videotaping interviews rather than recording them

        c.   Benefits of tapes

            (1)   Provides a verbatim account to verify accuracy of the report
            (2)   Frees the investigator from taking notes
            (3)   Allows the investigator to pay closer attention to the body language and nonverbal cues
            (4)   Allows investigators the chance to review the conversation as often as needed
            (5)   Ensures that detectives do not stray into third-degree tactics, take unethical lines of questioning or engage in any conduct that violates the rights of those being questioned

        d.   Criticisms of mandatory recording policies

            (1)   Such techniques might deter confessions
            (2)   Some people might refuse to speak freely

III.   The Interview

   A.   Interview witnesses separately if possible and in this order:

      1.   victim or complainant
      2.   eyewitnesses
      3.   people who did not actually see the crime but who have relevant information

   B.   Advance planning

      1.   Review reports about the case
      2.   Learn as much as possible about the person you are going to question
      3.   Know which questions you need answers to
      4.   Have a plan of approach to likely responses

   C.   Selecting the time and place

      1.   Sometimes there is no time to decide where and when
      2.   Witnesses are best able to recall details immediately after an incident
      3.   They are less likely to embellish or exaggerate because others present can be asked to verify the information
      4.   Witnesses can be separated so they cannot compare information
      5.   Reluctance to give the police information is usually not so strong immediately after a crime

   D.   Beginning the interview

      1.   Very important to the success
      2.   Make your initial contact friendly but professional

3. Begin by identifying yourself and showing your credentials
4. Then ask a general question about the person's knowledge of the crime

E. Establishing rapport

1. Rapport is the most critical factor in any interview
2. Rapport is an understanding between individuals created by genuine interest and concern
3. Find a way to motivate every witness to talk with you and answer your questions
4. Careful listening enhances rapport

F. Networking an interview

1. A network is a body of personal contacts that can further one's career
2. Networks can also establish relationships between people and their beliefs
3. Officers need to understand the networks in their jurisdictions

G. Reluctant interviewees

1. Appeal to a reluctant interviewee's reason or emotion
2. Use reason to determine why the person refuses to cooperate, and explain the problems that result when people who know about a crime do not cooperate with investigators
3. The emotional approach addresses negative feelings; you can increase these emotions or simply acknowledge them

H. The cognitive interview

1. This type of interview tries to get the interviewee to recall the scene mentally by using simple mnemonic techniques aimed at encouraging focused retrieval
2. For this, you need a secluded, quiet place free of distractions
3. You need to encourage a subject to speak slowly
4. The interviewer

   a. Helps the interviewee reconstruct the circumstances
   b. Encourages the interviewee to report everything
   c. Asks the interviewee to relate the events in a different order or to change perspective

5. Drawbacks to this approach: the amount of time it takes and the need for a controlled environment

I. Testimonial hearsay

1. Police reports should differentiate between statements that resulted from structured questions and those that did not

2. If an interview yields substantial information, a statement should be obtained

J. Statements

1. A statement is a legal narrative description of events related to a crime
2. The statement includes identification of the person, his or her account of the incident and a clause stating that the information was given voluntarily

K. Closing the interview

1. Thank the person for cooperating
2. If you have established good rapport, that person will probably cooperate with you later if needed

IV. The Interrogation

A. It is critical to ensure that you do not violate a suspect's constitutional rights in an interview, so that the information you obtain will be admissible in court
B. The *Miranda* warning

1. The Miranda warning informs suspects of their Fifth Amendment rights and it must be given to every suspect who is interrogated while in custody
2. When *Miranda* does not apply

   a. It does not apply to voluntary or unsolicited spontaneous statements, admissions or confessions
   b. It is not required during identification procedures such as fingerprinting, taking voice or handwriting exemplars or conducting a lineup or sobriety tests
   c. It is not required during routine booking questions, during brief on-the-scene questioning or during brief investigatory questioning during a temporary detention such as a *Terry* stop
   c. It is not required during roadside questioning following a routine traffic stop
   d. It is not required by probation officers questioning those on probation
   e. It is not required during questioning by a private citizen who is not an agent of the government

3. Waiving the rights

   a. A suspect may waive the rights granted by *Miranda* but must do so intelligently and knowingly

73

        b.   A waiver is accompanied by a written or witnessed oral statement that the waiver was voluntary

        c.   Silence is not a waiver

    4.   The effects of *Miranda*

        a.   The basic intent of the *Miranda* decision is to guarantee the rights of the accused

        b.   The practical effect is to ensure that confessions are obtained without duress or coercion

    5.   *Miranda* challenged

C.   The "question first" or "beachheading" technique

    1.   Example: an officer questions a custodial suspect without giving the *Miranda* warnings and obtains incriminating statements; the officer then gives the warning, gets a waiver and repeats the interrogation to obtain the same statement

    2.   In *Missouri v. Seibert* (2004) the Court found this technique unconstitutional

D.   The interplay of the Fourth and Fifth Amendments

    1.   In *New York v. Quarles* (1984) the Court ruled on the public safety exception to the *Miranda* warning requirement

    2.   This means that in this case the need to have the suspect talk (an exigent circumstance) took precedence over the requirement that the defendant be read his rights

E.   Right to counsel under the Fifth and Sixth Amendments

F.   Foreign nationals, the Vienna Convention Treaty and diplomatic immunity

G.   Selecting the time and place

    1.   Conduct interrogations in a place that is private and free from interruptions

    2.   Ideal conditions exist at the police station, where privacy and interruptions can be controlled

H.   Starting the interrogation

    1.   Provide time for the anxiety to increase

    2.   As you enter, show that you are in command, but do not display arrogance

    3.   Determine your interrogation technique: increase or decrease the suspect's anxiety

    4.   Show your identification, introduce yourself, state the purpose of the interrogation, give the *Miranda* warning

5.   Do not overlook body language or nonverbal communication that may indicate deception, anger or indifference

I.   Establishing rapport
J.   Approaches to interrogation

1.   Inquiring indirectly or directly
2.   Forcing responses
3.   Deflating or inflating the ego
4.   Minimizing or maximizing the crime
5.   Projecting the blame
6.   Rationalizing
7.   Combining approaches

K.   Using persuasion during interrogation

1.   Persuasive techniques

a.   Make sure the suspect is comfortable
b.   Acknowledge that problem exists, but first suspect needs to be informed of his rights
c.   Suggest that the suspect probably already knows all about these rights and ask him to tell what he knows, then compliment him on his knowledge
d.   This builds rapport
e.   Next, encourage suspect to tell his side of the story in detail, then review the account step by step
f.   Begin a "virtual monologue about robbery," describing how no one starts out planning a life of crime but some fall into a criminal pattern that leads either to getting shot and killed or to spending a lifetime in prison
g.   Next suggest the suspect can avoid this fate only by breaking this pattern and that the first step is to admit that it exists
h.   Add that a person's life should not be judged by one mistake, nor should that person's life be wasted by a refusal to admit that mistake
i.   Finish by talking about the fairness of the criminal justice system, and how judges are likely to go easier on suspects who indicate remorse
j.   Point out that intelligent people recognize when it is in their best interest to admit a mistake

2.   Investigative questionnaires

a.   An alternative to a face-to-face interrogation is the Crime Questionnaire
b.   This is a document with 21 questions that test for truth and deception
c.   It can be used in conjunction with a polygraph or in situations where a polygraph cannot be used

d. Supporters of this method believe the questionnaire shows "considerable accuracy" in predicting guilt or innocence

L. Ethics and the use of deception

1. Although law enforcement officers are expected to be honest, the Supreme Court has recognized that their duties may require limited officially sanctioned deception during a criminal investigation
2. Several cases support officer use of deception
3. Interrogatory deception may include

a. Claiming to possess evidence that does not really exist
b. Making promises
c. Misrepresenting the seriousness of the offense
d. Misrepresenting identity (for example, pretending to be a cellmate or a reporter)
e. Using the "good cop/bad cop" routine

4. Some interrogation techniques, even if not illegal, may be unethical

M. Third-degree tactics

1. These include use of physical force; threats of force; or other physical, mental or psychological abuse to induce a suspect to confess to a crime
2. They are illegal
3. Any information so obtained, including confessions, is inadmissible in court

N. Admissions and confessions

1. An admission contains some information concerning the elements of a crime but falls short of a full confession
2. A confession is information supporting the elements of a crime given by a person involved in committing it
3. A confession can be oral or handwritten, but it must be given of the suspect's free will and not in response to fear, threats, promises or rewards
4. A confession is only one part of an investigation. Corroborate it by independent evidence
5. An adoptive admission occurs when someone else makes a statement in a person's presence and under circumstances where it would be logical to expect the person to make a denial if the statement falsely implicated him, but he does not deny the allegations

V. Questioning Children and Juveniles

A. Special considerations exist when questioning children and juveniles

B. Obtain parental permission before questioning a youth

C. Often juveniles will not feel comfortable being honest if their parents are present

D. Do not use a youth as an informant unless the parents know the situation

E. Many juveniles put on airs in front of their friends

F. Juveniles may have definite opinions about the police

G. Do not underrate young people's intelligence or cleverness; they are often excellent observers with good memories

H. If a juvenile confesses to a crime, bring in the parents and have the youth repeat the confession to them; they will see that the information is voluntary

VI. Evaluating and Corroborating Information

A. Do not accept information obtained from interviews and interrogations at face value because often the information provided to the police is only partially truthful

B. Corroborate or disprove statements made during questioning

C. To break a pat story, ask questions that require slightly different answers and that will alter memorized responses

VII. Scientific Aids to Obtaining and Evaluating Information

A. The polygraph and voice stress tests

1. The polygraph scientifically measures respiration and depth of breathing, as well as changes in the skin's electrical resistance, blood pressure and pulse rate

2. The polygraph is used to verify the truth, not as a substitute for investigating and questioning.

3. Although the results are not presently admissible in court, any confession obtained as a result of a polygraph test is admissible

B. Hypnosis and truth serums

1. These are supplementary tools to investigation, not used as shortcuts

2. Hypnosis

a. Physically induces a trancelike condition in which the person loses consciousness but responds to a hypnotist's suggestions

b. Used with crime victims and witnesses to crimes, not with suspects

c. Court guidelines for using testimony gained from hypnosis require that a trained professional perform it and that the professional be independent of, rather than responsible to, the prosecution

        3.   Truth serums

            a.   Fast-acting barbiturates of the type used to produce sleep at the approximate level of surgical anesthesia

            b.   Not used extensively by the police because the accuracy of the information obtained with them is questionable

            c.   Courts do not officially recognize them or their reliability, nor do they admit the results as evidence

VIII.   Use of Psychics and Profilers

        A.   Psychics: Although controversial, some agencies are willing to consider any possible lead or source of information, including psychics, in criminal investigations

        B.   Profilers: Effective profiling relies on the profiler's ability to combine investigative experience, training in forensic and behavioral sciences, and information about the characteristics of known offenders

IX.   Sharing Information

        A.   "Substantial obstacles" that prevent police agencies from sharing information include competing local systems, incompatible data formats, issues of who controls the data, security questions, cost and training time and resources

        B.   Global Justice XML Data Model (GJSCM) has become the national standard

        C.   National Criminal Intelligence Sharing Plan (NCISP)

        D.   OneDOJ

        E.   Law Enforcement National Data Exchange (N-DEx)

X.   Information versus Intelligence

        A.   Information or data is not intelligence; information plus analysis is intelligence

        B.   Fusion centers: used to exchange information and intelligence; merge data from many sources

        C.   Intelligence-led policing model

XI.   Summary

IDENTIFYING AND ARRESTING SUSPECTS

OUTLINE

Chapter 7
Identifying and Arresting Suspects

Key Terms

- arrest
- bugging
- close tail
- cover
- criminal profiling
- de facto arrest
- entrapment
- excessive force
- field identification
- fixed surveillance
- force
- geographic profiling
- loose tail
- open tail
- plant
- pretextual traffic stops
- psychological profiling
- racial profiling
- raid
- reasonable force
- rough tail
- show-up identification
- solvability factors
- stakeout
- subject
- surveillance
- surveillant
- tail
- tight tail
- undercover
- wiretapping

Learning Objectives
After reading this chapter, students should be able to

- Define and compare the differences between field identifications and show-up identifications.
- Discuss what rights a suspect has during field (show-up) identification and know what case established these rights.
- Describe how a suspect is developed.
- Relate how to assist witnesses in describing a suspect or a vehicle.
- Clarify when mug shots are used.
- Describe the four basic means of identifying a suspect.
- Explain what photographic identification processes are and how to use them properly.

- Explain how a proper lineup is created and how it is used.
- Define the legal rights suspects have regarding participation in a lineup and relate which cases established these rights.
- Describe whether it is advisable to have the same person make both a photographic and lineup identification.
- Describe when surveillance is used and what the objectives are.
- Define the different types of surveillances.

(Continued)

• Explain when wiretapping is legal and identify the precedent case. • Describe the objectives of undercover assignments and what precautions should be taken when going undercover. • Describe the objectives of a police raid. • Clarify how the police establish the legal requirements for staging a raid. • Discuss the precautions that should be taken when conducting a raid.	• Define when a lawful arrest can be made. • Identify the probable cause that must exist for believing that a suspect has committed a crime. • Define what constitutes an arrest. • Describe how officers leave themselves open to civil liability when making arrests. • Clarify when and how much force is justified when making an arrest.

Internet Assignments

1. Have students search the case of *Tennessee v. Garner* (1985). The case is readily available in both written and audio formats. Have them read or listen to the case and be familiar with the facts and legal decision. Have students discuss both the majority opinion and the dissenting opinion.

    Since the case of *Tennessee v. Garner* involved the use of force against an unarmed youth, have the students discuss whether or not there would be a time to use deadly force against an "unarmed" suspect, based on the provision of the case.
2. Technology continues to develop new forms of nonlethal or less-than-lethal weapons. Some examples include the TigerLight Non-Lethal Defense System and the PepperBall FlashLauncher. Have students or groups of students select a commercially offered nonlethal weapon and describe its capabilities, its innovations and the pros and cons of its use.
3. Have students search the Web for law enforcement technology. Have the class discuss the variety of contemporary applications using technology in investigations.

Class Assignments

1. Have students read the case of *Saucier v. Katz*, 533 U.S. 194 (2001). Have the class split into two groups. One group should argue the use-of-force continuum as valid, and the other group should argue the "objectively reasonable" test.
2. Research the case of *Scott v. Harris* (2007). The court ruled that Harris was culpable because, by initiating a high-speed chase that left him a quadriplegic, he had placed himself and others in danger.

    After reviewing *Scott v. Harris*, split the class into the following groups:

    •   Majority decision
    •   Minority decision
    •   Police officers

- Citizen groups
- Parents of children killed in police pursuits

Then have each group discuss the pros and cons of police pursuits, including ramming and the PIT maneuver.

Chapter Outline

I. Identifying Suspects at the Scene

   A. Identification by driver's license: The REAL ID Act requires states to take new steps to verify the identity of applicants before issuing driver's licenses and other ID cards
   B. Mobile identification technology: use of Reality Mobile's Reality Vision software
   C. Biometric identification: facial recognition systems
   D. Field identification or show-up identification

      1. This is on-the-scene identification of a suspect by a victim of or witness to a crime
      2. Must be made within a short time after the crime was committed
      3. *United States v. Ash, Jr.* (1973) established that a suspect does not have the right to have counsel present at a field identification

II. Developing Suspects

   A. If a suspect is not at the scene and not apprehended nearby, you must develop a suspect
   B. Means of developing suspects include:

      1. Victims and witnesses: Help witnesses describe suspects and vehicles by asking very specific questions and using an identification diagram
      2. Mug shots: Have victims and witnesses view mug shots if you believe a suspect has a police record
      3. Composite drawings and sketches: Identi-Kit version 6.0
      4. Modus operandi (MO) information
      5. Psychological or criminal profiling and geographic profiling

         a. Psychological or criminal profiling attempts to identify an individual's mental, emotional and psychological characteristics
         b. Profiles are developed primarily for violent acts such as homicides, sadistic crimes, sex crimes, arson without apparent motive and crimes of serial or ritual sequence
         c. Geographic profiling can be helpful in identifying suspects who commit multiple crimes (serial criminals)
         d. Geographic profiling is based on everyone having a pattern to their lives, particularly in relation to the geographical areas they frequent

        e.   GPS photomapping can be an excellent tool in helping investigators spatially piece together clues and evidence that are spread out over a relatively large area

   6.   Racial profiling

        a.   Racial profiling occurs when an officer singles out and focuses on an individual as a suspect based solely on that person's race, excluding legitimate factors such as behavior

        b.   It is important to distinguish between *profiling* (legitimate) as a policing technique and the politically charged term *racial profiling* (not legitimate)

        c.   Another viable alternative to racial profiling is "building a case"

   7.   Tracking

        a.   Forensic tracking is the science of locating, retaining and interpreting footprint and tire tread impressions to solve criminal cases

        b.   Material for tracking comes from several sources

           (1)   Footprints
           (2)   Tire tracks
           (3)   Other impressions

   8.   Other identification aids

        a.   Newspaper photos
        b.   Video
        c.   News films
        d.   Yearbook photos
        e.   Dental and orthopedic records
        f.   Facial reconstruction

   9.   Information in police files and files of other agencies

        a.   Police records on solved crimes and on suspects involved in certain types of crimes
        b.   Police files on suspects
        c.   Field-interview cards

III.   Locating Suspects

   A.   Many information sources used to develop a suspect can also help to locate the suspect

   B.   Potential methods for locating a suspect include:

       1.   Telephoning other investigative agencies
       2.   Inquiring around a suspect's last known address

3. Checking the address on a prison release form
4. Questioning relatives
5. Checking with utility companies
6. Checking with other contacts

IV. Identifying Suspects

A. Suspects can be identified through field or show-up identification, mug shots, photographic identification or lineups

1. Photographic identification

a. Use when you have a good idea of who committed a crime but the suspect is not in custody or when a fair lineup cannot be conducted
b. Tell witnesses they need not identify anyone from the photographs
c. A suspect does not have the right to a lawyer if a photographic lineup is used (*United States v. Ash, Jr.,* 1973)
d. The Supreme Court decision in *Manson v. Brathwaite* (1977) approved the showing of a single picture in specific circumstances (see text)

2. Lineup identification

a. Use when the suspect is in custody
b. Use at least five individuals of comparable race, height, weight, age and general appearance
c. Ask all individuals in lineup to perform the same actions or speak the same words
d. Instruct those viewing the lineup that they need not make an identification
e. A virtual human computer program called "Officer Garcia" has been designed to conduct photo lineups according to established guidelines
f. Suspects may refuse to participate in a lineup, but such refusals can be used against them in court (*Schmerber v. California,* 1966)
g. Suspects have a Sixth Amendment right to have an attorney present during a lineup
h. The Wade-Gilbert rule refers to the requirement of providing counsel to a suspect in a lineup that occurs after indictment; if suspect waives the right to counsel, get the waiver in writing

B. Avoid having the same person make both photographic and lineup identification; if the same person makes both photographic and lineup identification, do not conduct both within a short time

V.   Surveillance, Undercover Assignments and Raids: The Last Resort

A.   Surveillance, undercover assignments and raids are used only when normal methods of continuing the investigation fail to produce results

B.   These techniques are expensive and potentially dangerous and are not routinely used

VI.   Surveillance

A.   The objective of surveillance is to obtain information about people, their associates and their activities that may help to solve a criminal case or to protect witnesses

B.   Surveillance can help do the following:

1.   Gain information required for building a criminal complaint
2.   Determine an informant's loyalty
3.   Verify a witness's statement about a crime
4.   Gain information required for obtaining a search or arrest warrant
5.   Gain information necessary for interrogation of a suspect
6.   Identify a suspect's associates
7.   Observe members of terrorist organizations
8.   Find a person wanted for a crime
9.   Observe criminal activities in progress
10.   Make a legal arrest
11.   Apprehend a criminal in the act of committing a crime
12.   Prevent a crime
13.   Recover stolen property
14.   Protect witnesses

C.   The surveillant is the plainclothes investigator who makes the observation

D.   The subject is who or what is being observed

1.   It can be a person, place, property, vehicle, group of people, organization or object
2.   People under surveillance are usually suspects in a crime or their associates
3.   Surveillance of places generally involves a location where a crime is expected to be committed

E.   Types of surveillance

1.   The type of surveillance used depends on the subject and the objective of the surveillance
2.   Types of surveillance include stationary (fixed, plant or stakeout) and moving (tight or close, loose, rough, on foot or by vehicle)

F.   Avoiding detection

    1.   Criminals are often suspicious of stakeouts or of being followed and may send someone to scout the area to see whether anybody has staked out their residence or their vehicle

    2.   Anticipate and plan for such activities

G.   Surveillance equipment

    1.   Includes binoculars, telescopes, night-vision equipment, video systems, body wires, costumes and disguises

    2.   GPS technology is also being used

H.   Aerial surveillance

    1.   May provide information about areas inaccessible to foot or vehicle surveillance

    2.   Photographs taken from navigable air space, usually 1,000 feet, do not violate privacy regulations

I.   Visual/video surveillance

    1.   High-crime areas, such as locations commonly used for illegal drug sales, are increasingly being monitored by 24-hour surveillance cameras mounted on utility poles, buildings and other strategic vantage points

    2.   Automated license plate recognition (ALPR) technology

    3.   Through-the-wall-surveillance (TWS)

    4.   Backscatter X-ray devices

    5.   Department of Justice and the International Association of Chiefs of Police have developed three Regional Forensic Video Analysis Labs

J.   Audio or electronic surveillance

    1.   "Bugging" or wiretapping

    2.   Pen registers, trap-and-trace devices and content interceptions are most common

    3.   Electronic surveillance and wiretapping are considered forms of search and are therefore permitted only with probable cause and a court order (*Katz v. United States*, 1967)

    4.   Acoustic surveillance systems are being developed (e.g., gunshot location technology such as the SpotShotter Gunshot Location System, or GLS)

    5.   The courts have held that no expectation of privacy exists in prison cells or in interrogation rooms

K.   Surveillance and the Constitution

    1.   Of most importance is the balance between acting without violating suspects' constitutional rights and the need for law enforcement to do its job of protecting society

2. In *Kyllo v. United States* (2001), the Supreme Court held that thermal imaging of a house was a search and required a warrant

3. The use of a GPS device to monitor a vehicle's travel activity is not a search and does not intrude on a person's reasonable expectation of privacy, according to the Seventh Circuit Court in *United States v. Garcia* (2007)

4. Use of ALPR technology is not a search and requires no warrant

5. X-ray devices, like thermal imaging, require a warrant if they are to be used in a search capacity

VII. Undercover Assignments

A. The objective of an undercover assignment may be to gain a person's confidence or to infiltrate an organization or group by using an assumed identity and to thereby obtain information or evidence connecting the subject with criminal activity

B. Undercover assignments can be designed to

1. Obtain evidence for prosecution

2. Obtain leads into criminal activities

3. Check the reliability of witnesses or informants

4. Gain information about premises for use later in conducting a raid or an arrest

5. Check the security of a person in a highly sensitive position

6. Obtain information on or evidence against subversive groups

C. Precautions for undercover agents:

1. Write no notes the suspect can read

2. Carry no identification other than the cover ID

3. Ensure that any communication with headquarters is covert

4. Do not suggest, plan, initiate or participate in criminal activity

D. Entrapment

1. Entrapment occurs only when the criminal conduct was "the product of the creative activity" of law enforcement officials

2. *Sorrells v. United States* (1932): "the conception and planning of an offense by an officer, and his procurement of its commission by one who would not have perpetrated it except for the trickery, persuasion or fraud of the officer"

E. Sting operations

1. According to Newman (2007), all sting operations contain four basic elements:

a. an opportunity or enticement to commit a crime, either created or exploited by police

      b. a targeted likely offender or group of offenders for a particular crime type

      c. an undercover or hidden police officer or surrogate or some form of deception

      d. a "gotcha" climax when the operation ends with arrests

    2. Benefits of sting operations

    3. Downside of sting operations

VIII. Raids

    A. The objectives of a raid are to recover stolen property, seize evidence or arrest a suspect

    B. A raid must be the result of a hot pursuit or be under the authority of a no-knock arrest or search warrant

    C. Planning a raid

    D. Executing a raid

    E. Precautions in conducting raids

      1. Ensure that the raid is legal

      2. Plan carefully

      3. Assign adequate personnel and equipment

      4. Thoroughly brief every member of the raiding party

      5. Be aware of the possibility of surreptitious surveillance devices at the raid site

    F. SWAT teams

IX. Legal Arrests

    A. Police officers are authorized to make an arrest

      1. for any crime committed in their presence

      2. for a felony (or a misdemeanor, in some states) not committed in their presence, if they have probable cause to believe the person committed the crime

      3. under the authority of an arrest warrant

    B. Probable cause for believing the suspect committed a crime must be established *before* a lawful arrest can be made

    C. If your intent is to make an arrest and you inform the suspect of this intent and then restrict the suspect's right to go free, you have made an arrest

    D. Residential entry after outdoors arrest is unconstitutional (*James v. Louisiana*, 1965)

    E. Arresting a group of companions: okay with probable cause under *Maryland v. Pringle* (2003) when all suspects deny possession

F.　Off-duty arrests

　　1.　Every department needs a policy that allows off-duty officers to make arrests. A suggested policy for off-duty arrests requires officers to

　　　　a.　be within the legal jurisdiction of their agency
　　　　b.　not be personally involved
　　　　c.　perceive an immediate need for preventing crime or arresting a suspect
　　　　d.　possess the proper identification

X.　Avoiding Civil Liability When Making Arrests

A.　Officers leave themselves open to lawsuits in several areas related to arrests, including false arrests, excessive force, shootings and wrongful death
B.　False arrest
C.　Use of force

　　1.　When making an arrest, use only as much force as is necessary to overcome any resistance and gain compliance
　　2.　*Graham v. Connor* (1989) established five factors to evaluate alleged cases of excessive force:

　　　　a.　the severity of the crime
　　　　b.　whether the suspect posed an immediate threat to the officer or others
　　　　c.　whether the circumstances were tense, uncertain and rapidly evolving
　　　　d.　whether the suspect was attempting to evade arrest by flight
　　　　e.　whether the suspect was actively resisting arrest

　　3.　Use-of-force policies and continuums

D.　Less-lethal weapons

　　1.　"Less-lethal does not imply never-lethal. Munitions fired from most less-lethal weapons can cause death if vital areas are struck: head, eyes, throat and possibly the upper abdomen" (Page, 2007, p. 144)
　　2.　There are six basic options for controlling someone with non-lethal force/control

　　　　a.　Verbal/visual management of the scene
　　　　b.　Empty-hand control
　　　　c.　Restraints
　　　　d.　Aerosols
　　　　e.　Electronic control devices (ECDs)
　　　　f.　Impact weapons

E.   Restraints

1.   Handcuffs
2.   Aerosols, such as TigerLight
3.   Impact weapons, such as the PepperBall FlashLauncher
4.   Controlled electronic devices (CEDs or ECDs), such as TASERs
5.   Other less-lethal options, such as capture nets or acoustical weapons

F.   Use of deadly force

1.   The use of a deadly weapon is carefully defined by state laws and department policy
2.   The landmark case on use of deadly force is *Tennessee v. Garner* (1985)
3.   "21-foot rule" in using deadly force states that a knife-wielding attacker could be as far away as 21 feet and still stab the officer before he could effectively fire his handgun
4.   "Ramming" (intentional collision of a law enforcement officer's vehicle with another) in pursuit as use of force: In *Scott v. Harris* (2007), the court concluded the suspect was liable, not the police
5.   In-custody death: excited delirium
6.   Use of force and the mentally ill
7.   Suicide by police

G.   Use-of-force reports

XI.   Summary

DEATH INVESTIGATIONS

OUTLINE

Chapter 8
Death Investigations

Key Terms

• adipocere	• lustmurder
• algormortis	• malicious intent
• asphyxiation	• manslaughter
• autoerotic asphyxiation	• mass murder
• clearance rate	• mummification
• criminal homicide	• murder
• criminal negligence	• non criminal homicide
• defense wounds	• postmortem artifact
• equivocal death	• postmortem lividity
• excusable homicide	• premeditation
• expressive violence	• rigor mortis
• first-degree murder	• second-degree murder
• heat of passion	• serial murder
• hesitation wounds	• suicide
• homicide	• suicide by police
• instrumental violence	• third-degree murder
• involuntary manslaughter	• toxicology
• justifiable homicide	• voluntary manslaughter
• livormortis	

Learning Objectives
After reading this chapter, students should be able to

• Identify a basic requirement in a homicide investigation.	• Identify the first priority in a homicide investigation.
• Outline the four categories of death.	• Describe how to establish that death has occurred.
• Define and classify homicide, murder and manslaughter.	• Explain what physical evidence is usually found in homicides.
• Explain what degrees of murder are frequently specified.	• Outline what information and evidence can be obtained from a victim.
• Describe how excusable and justifiable homicide differ.	• Explain how to identify an unknown homicide victim.
• Explain the significance of premeditation.	• Report the different factors that can aid in estimating time of death.
• Explain the special challenges presented by a homicide investigation.	

(Continued)

• Explain the effect water has on a dead body. • Outline the information provided by the medical examiner or coroner. • Describe the most frequent causes of unnatural death and how to determine whether a death is a suicide or a homicide.	• Explain why it is important to determine a motive in homicide investigations. • Outline the similarities that exist between school and workplace mass murders. • Describe how the conventional wisdom about homicide has changed in some departments.

Internet Assignments

1. Have students visit the St. Louis (Missouri) Regional Crime Commission Web site, where individuals can provide anonymous tips regarding unsolved homicides. Ask students to describe how the Web site works and how the police work with this information. Have them also discuss the possible pros and cons of this type of Web site.

2. Have students go to the FBI Web site at and perform a search on the word "murder." Ask them to select three cases from the results provided and discuss what they might learn by examining the body of the victim.

Class Assignments

1. Have students discuss the issues that would confront a homicide investigator in the following cases:

   • A farmer has found a greatly decomposed body in one of his fields. While plowing the field for the first time in two years, he ran over the body and the plow brought the body to the surface.

   • A male, aged 20 to 40, has been found in an alley in the bar area of town. There is no obvious cause of death. The body was found when a janitor came out of a bar at approximately 4:00 A.M. When the officers arrived at the scene they checked for signs of life and canceled the ambulance. At that time, according to the responding officer, the body was warm to the touch, about 90 degrees. Based on what appear to be scuff marks, it is possible that the body was dragged into the alley.

   • A female, aged approximately 15 to 25, has been found in a fraternity bedroom. The victim is lying on her side on the bed. The responding officers have learned that the fraternity had a party the night before and that she was one of the students at the party. The bedroom is a mess, but this might or might not indicate a struggle, as other rooms in the same hallway are also disordered. However, some of the bed covers are on the floor, which may indicate that something out of the ordinary went on. There is no visible blood in the room.

2. Split the class into five groups and assign one of the following topics for each group:

- Latest crime rates according to the FBI's *Uniform Crime Reporting Handbook*
- Latest crime information according to the FBI's National Incident-Based Reporting System (NIBRS)
- Calculation of homicide figures: FBI's *Uniform Crime Reporting Handbook*
- Difference between arrest rates and crime rates: National Institute of Justice, Bureau of Justice Statistics (BJS)
- Local state, county or city crime statistics for a matching period (latest crime data if possible)

Once the groups have read and discussed their topics, have the groups report on what they have found and highlight and explain the differences between the information sources. Also, they may notice that it can be difficult to locate accurate and recent crime rates for some states, counties or cities. Why is this so?

Chapter Outline

I. Classification of Deaths

    A.   Natural causes of death include heart attacks, strokes, fatal diseases, pneumonia, sudden crib deaths and old age

    B.   Accidental death causes include falling; drowning; unintentionally taking too many pills or ingesting a poisonous substance; entanglement in industrial or farm machinery; or involvement in an automobile, boat, train, bus or plane crash.

    C.   Suicide

        1.   Suicide is defined as the intentional taking of one's own life

        2.   Suicide can be committed by shooting, stabbing, poisoning, burning, asphyxiating or ingesting drugs or poisons

    D.   Homicide

        1.   Homicide is the killing of one person by another

        2.   Homicide includes the taking of life by another person or by an agency, such as a government

        3.   Homicides are classified as follows:

            a.   Criminal homicide (felonious)

                (1) Murder (first-, second- or third-degree) is defined as the killing of another human being with malice aforethought

                    (a)   First-degree murder requires premeditation and is intentional, or while committing or attempting to commit a felony

       (b)   Second-degree murder is intentional but not premeditated

       (c)   Third-degree murder is neither intentional nor premeditated, but the result of an imminently dangerous act

   (2) Manslaughter is defined as the unlawful killing of another person with no prior malice

       (a)   Voluntary manslaughter is intentional homicide caused by intense passion resulting from adequate provocation

       (b)   Involuntary manslaughter is unintentional homicide caused by criminal (culpable) negligence

  b.   Non criminal homicide (non felonious)

   (1) Excusable homicide is the unintentional, truly accidental killing of another person

   (2) Justifiable homicide is killing another person under authorization of the law

II. Elements of the Crime

A. Causing the death of another human

1. If a death certificate is not available, the investigator must locate witnesses to testify that they saw the body of the person allegedly killed by the suspect
2. Otherwise, death is proven by circumstantial evidence
3. It is often difficult to prove the cause of death

B. Premeditation

1. Premeditation is the consideration, planning or preparation for an act, no matter how briefly, before committing it
2. Premeditation is the element of first-degree murder that sets it apart from all other classifications

C. Intent to effect the death of another person

1. Intent is a required element of most categories of criminal homicide. Evidence must show that the crime was intentional, not accidental
2. Malicious intent, an element of first- and second-degree murder, implies ill will, wickedness or cruelty
3. *Intent* and *premeditation* are not the same. Premeditation is not a requirement of intent. Most crimes of passion involve intent but not premeditation or malicious intent

D. Adequately provoked intent resulting from heat of passion

1. This element is the alternative to premeditation. It assumes that the act was committed when the suspect suddenly became extremely emotional, thus precluding premeditation
2. Heat of passion results from extremely volatile arguments between two people, from seeing a wife or family member raped, from a sudden discovery of adultery or from seeing a brutal assault being committed against a close friend or family member

E. While committing or attempting to commit a felony

1. In some states, a charge of first-degree murder does not require that the murder was committed with premeditation if the victim died as a result of acts committed while the suspect was engaged in a felony such as rape, robbery or arson
2. Proof of the elements of the felony must be established

F. While committing or attempting to commit a crime not a felony

1. Death may result from an act committed by a suspect engaged in a nonfelonious crime
2. In such cases, the death can be charged as either third-degree murder or voluntary manslaughter, depending on the state in which the offense occurs

G. Culpable negligence or depravity

1. The act and the way it is committed establish this element
2. The act must be so dangerous that any prudent person would see death of a person as a possible consequence
3. A person causing a death while depraved and committing acts evident of such depravity is guilty of third-degree murder

H. Negligence

1. A fine line separates this element from the preceding element
2. Some states make no distinction, classifying both in a separate category of criminal negligence
3. Where separate categories exist, this lesser degree of negligence involves creating a situation that results in an unreasonable risk of death or great bodily harm

III. Challenges in Investigation

A. Challenges include:

1. pressure by the media and the public
2. the difficulty of establishing that a crime has been committed
3. identifying the victim
4. establishing the cause and time of death

IV. Equivocal Death

    A. Equivocal death investigations are situations that are open to interpretation

        1. Cause may be homicide, suicide or accidental death
        2. Intentionally vague facts
        3. Staged crime scene

            a. *Posing* refers to positioning of the body only
            b. *Staging* refers to manipulation of the scene around the body in addition to posing of the body

        4. Sudden, unexplained infant death (SUID)

    B. Sudden in-custody deaths (SICD)

        1. These cases typically involve suspects who have been restrained for some time, during which they enter a state of medical crisis and die
        2. Excited delirium may be a cause
        3. Thorough but objective investigation is critical

V. Suicide

    A. Suicide often presents as a homicide. Investigators should keep in mind that more Americans die by suicide than by homicide

    B. Warning signs displayed by someone contemplating suicide:

        1. Observable signs of serious depression

            a. Unrelenting low mood
            b. Pessimism
            c. Hopelessness
            d. Desperation
            e. Anxiety, psychic pain and inner tension
            f. Withdrawal
            g. Sleep problems

        2. Increased alcohol and/or other drug use
        3. Recent impulsiveness and taking unnecessary risks
        4. Threatening suicide or expressing a strong wish to die
        5. Making a plan

            a. Giving away prized possessions
            b. Sudden or impulsive purchase of a firearm
            c. Obtaining other means of killing oneself such as poisons or medications

        6. Unexpected rage or anger

C. Suicide by police

1. Refers to a situation in which a person decides he or she wants to die but does not want to pull the trigger

2. Profilers indicate that such subjects often

    a. have a poor self-image
    b. feel a sense of guilt for harm they have caused
    c. talk about death and express a desire to be with deceased loved ones
    d. speak often of a higher being
    e. are aggressively confrontational with police
    f. possess an unloaded or nonfunctioning (toy) gun

3. Other issues that may indicate suicidal motivations may include:

    a. Financial concerns
    b. Divorce or serious relationship issues
    c. Loss of a job or retirement
    d. Being investigated
    e. Health problems

D. Suicide of police officers

1. Each year, as many officers kill themselves (about 300) as are killed by criminals in the line of duty, making suicide the most lethal factor in a police officer's line of work

2. Exact statistics vary, but police officers have a much greater chance of killing themselves than of dying in the line of duty and are much more likely to kill themselves than are other municipal workers

3. Contributing factors are alcohol, family issues and the breakup of relationships

4. Post-traumatic stress disorder (PTSD) can also contribute to depression, various forms of addiction, and can lead to suicide

5. About 97 percent of officer suicides involve their own duty weapon

6. Any officer's death requires a thorough investigation

VI. Preliminary Investigation of Homicide

A. "The homicide crime scene is, without a doubt, the most important crime scene to which a police officer or investigator will be called upon to respond" (Geberth, 2006, p.140)

B. The primary goals of the investigation are:

1. To establish whether a human death was caused by the criminal act or omission

2. To determine who caused the death

C. After ensuring the safety of the scene, the priority is to give emergency aid to the victim if he or she is still alive or to determine that death has occurred

D. The investigators must document everything they can about the scene, including:

1. detaining and identifying everyone present
2. obtaining brief statements from each
3. maintaining control of the scene and everyone present
4. listing all officers present upon the investigator's arrival and throughout the investigation
5. recording the presence of all other personnel at the scene (medical personnel, coroner, family members)

E. Determining that death has occurred

1. Medically, death is determined by the cessation of three vital functions: heartbeat, respiration and brain activity
2. Signs of death include lack of breathing, lack of heartbeat, lack of flushing of the fingernail bed when pressure is applied to the nail and then released and failure of the eyelids to close after being gently lifted

F. Securing and documenting the scene

1. The homicide scene must be secured, photographed and sketched
2. All evidence must be obtained, identified and properly preserved
3. Physical evidence can be found on the body, at the scene or on the suspect
4. Physical evidence in a homicide includes a weapon, a body, blood, hairs and fibers

G. Collecting and moving the body

1. Move the body carefully
2. Lift the body a few inches off the surface and slide a sheet under it to catch any evidence that may fall while transporting the body to the vehicle
3. Itemize other possessions and send them along with the body to the morgue for later release to the family if they are not evidence
4. Although you may use a body bag, first wrap the body in a clean, white sheet. Evidence on the body that falls off is much easier to see on a sheet. The sheet also absorbs moisture

H. The focus of the homicide investigation

1. Identify the victim
2. Establish the time of death

3. Establish the cause of and the method used to produce death
4. Develop a suspect
5. Fact-finding capsule might guide homicide investigations:

    a. Specificity

    b. Element of surprise

    c. Haste

VII. The Homicide Victim

  A. The victim's background provides information about whether the death was an accident, suicide or homicide. If a homicide, the background often provides leads to a suspect. Evidence on the victim's body can also provide important leads

  B. Discovering the victim

    1. In some cases, no body is present
    2. When searching for human remains, investigators can use technologies such as

      a. ground-penetrating radar
      b. magnetometers
      c. metal detectors and infrared thermography, which can distinguish between hidden new and old gravesites faster and more accurately than can other techniques

    3. Additionally, cadaver-search canines have proven effective

  C. Identifying the victim

    1. Once a body is found, it must be identified
    2. Homicide victims are identified by

      a. Immediate family members, relatives, friends or acquaintances
      b. Personal effects, fingerprints, DNA analysis and dental and skeletal studies
      c. Clothing and laundry marks
      d. Missing person files

    3. Investigations involving unidentified human remains often require the involvement of experts from a variety of scientific fields. Team members should consist of

      a. a medical examiner
      b. a forensic anthropologist, to provide information on gender, height, race and age
      c. a forensic odontologist, to provide an age range

        d. a forensic osteologist, to determine if there is evidence of bone trauma

        e. a forensic entomologist, to provide information on the location and approximate time of death

4. Identifying the mass fatalities resulting from the September 11, 2001, attacks presented the greatest forensic challenge in this country's history. A balance had to be struck between speed and accuracy

5. Cases involving unidentified human remains can be extremely challenging for criminal investigators, and these cases often intersect with missing person cases

6. NIJ launched the National Missing and Unidentified Persons (NamUs) Initiative in 2007. It brings together two existing programs and their online databases

        a. identifyUs.org, which contains data on unidentified human remains

        b. Findthemissing.org, which provides information about missing persons

7. For an unknown victim, record a complete description and take photographs if possible

8. After the victim has been identified, the homicide investigator must establish the time of death, typically with the help of the medical examiner or coroner

VIII. Estimating the Time of Death (ToD)

    A. In many homicides, there is a delay between the commission of the crime and the discovery of the body, sometimes only minutes, other times years

    B. The period between death and corpse discovery is called the postmortem interval (PMI)

    C. The time of death relates directly to whether the suspect could have been at the scene of the crime and to the sequence of multiple deaths

    D. Both the investigator and the medical examiner/coroner are responsible for estimating the time of death

    E. Factors that help in estimating the time of death are

       1. body temperature
       2. rigor mortis
       3. postmortem lividity (livor)
       4. eye appearance
       5. stomach contents
       6. stage of decomposition
       7. evidence suggesting a change in the victim's normal routine

F.   Recent death

1. A time of death that is less than one-half hour before examination is normally the easiest determination to make
2. Indications that death occurred in this time frame are:

    a. body is still warm
    b. mucous membranes are still moist but drying
    c. blood is still moist but drying
    d. pupils have begun to dilate
    e. in fair-skinned people, the skin is becoming pale (this characteristic of recent death becomes less discernible as skin pigmentation increases)

G.   Death that occurred one-half hour to 4 days prior

1. Indications that death occurred in this time frame are:

    a. mucous membranes and any blood from the wounds are dry
    b. there are skin blisters and skin slippage
    c. the body is slightly pink
    d. body temperature has dropped
    e. rigor mortis and postmortem lividity are present
    f. pupils are restricted and cloudy

2. Body temperature

    a. Algor mortis refers to the postmortem cooling process of the body and can be extremely helpful in homicide investigations
    b. Body temperature drops 2 to 3 degrees in the first hour after death and 1 to 1.5 degrees for each subsequent hour until 18 hours

3. Rigor mortis

    a. The body is limp after death until rigor mortis sets in
    b. Rigor mortis is a Latin term that literally translates to "stiffness of death"
    c. Rigor mortis is a stiffening of the joints of the body after death because of partial skeletal muscle contraction
    d. Rigor mortis appears as a stiffening of muscles several hours after death, with maximum stiffness occurring 12 to 24 hours after death. Rigor then begins to disappear and is generally gone 3 days postmortem

4. Postmortem lividity

    a. When the heart stops beating at death, the blood no longer circulates and gravity drains the blood to the body's lowest levels

      b. This causes a dark blue or purple discoloration of the body called postmortem lividity or livor mortis

      c. Postmortem lividity starts one-half to 3 hours after death and is congealed in the capillaries in 4 to 5 hours. Maximum lividity occurs within 10 to 12 hours

      d. The location of lividity can indicate whether a body was moved after death

  5. Examination of the eyes

      a. The appearance of the eyes also assists in estimating the time of death. After death, eye muscle tone lessens and tends to disappear. The pupils tend to dilate

      b. A partial restriction of the pupil occurs in about 7 hours. In 12 hours, the cornea appears cloudy

  6. Examination of stomach contents

      a. Although the stomach contents must be examined during the medical examination, the investigator can provide important information for the examiner

      b. Determine when and what the victim last ate. If any vomit is present, preserve it as evidence and submit it for examination

H. Many days after death

  1. It is more difficult to estimate the ToD if death occurred several days before discovery of the body

  2. The cadaver is bloated, lividity is darkened, the abdomen is greenish, blisters are filled with gas and a distinct odor is present

  3. The medical examiner makes a rough estimate of time of death based on the body's state of decomposition

  4. If the body is in a hot, moist location, a soapy appearance called adipocere develops

  5. Complete dehydration of all body tissues results in mummification

  6. The presence on the body of insect eggs, their stage of development and the life cycle of the species, as well as various stages of vegetation on or near the body, also provide information about the time of death

  7. Breakthroughs are being made in determining time of death, based on the progressive breakdown of biological compounds found in the human body

I. Effects of water

  1. Bodies immersed in water for some time undergo changes that help investigators determine whether the drowning was accidental or a homicide

2. A postmortem artifact is an injury occurring after death from another source

3. A dead body usually sinks in water and remains immersed for 8 to 10 days in warm water or 2 to 3 weeks in cold water. It then rises to the surface unless restricted. The outer skin loosens in 5 to 6 days, and the nails separate in 2 to 3 weeks

4. Several factors can alert an investigator to whether a drowning is a suicide, an accident or a homicide

   a. Body placement
   b. Lividity and rigor mortis
   c. The victim's eyes

5. The medical examination also determines whether the person was alive or dead at the time the body was immersed in water. This provides evidence to support homicide, suicide or accidental death

6. Diatoms and algal material can help forensic biologists determine the time of death for bodies found in water, as well as whether the person was drowned

J. Factors suggesting a change in the victim's routine

   1. Determining all such facts helps estimate the ToD
   2. These facts can also corroborate the estimate based on physical findings

IX. The Medical Examination or Autopsy

   A. After the preliminary investigation, the body is taken to the morgue for an autopsy, a term derived from the Greek *autopsia*, meaning "to see for oneself"

   B. The main purpose of the coroner's or medical examiner's (ME's) office is to determine the cause and manner of death

   C. The medical examination provides legal evidence related to the cause and time of death and to the presence of drugs or alcohol

   D. Exhuming a body for medical examination

      1. It is not common to exhume a body. Usually this is done to determine whether the cause of death stated on the death certificate is valid

      2. Exhuming a body requires adherence to strict legal procedures to prevent later civil action by relatives

      3. Present at the lid opening at the morgue are the coroner, police, family, undertaker and pathologist

X.   Unnatural Causes of Death and Method Used

A. Among the most common causes of unnatural death are gunshot wounds; stabbing and cutting wounds; blows from blunt objects; asphyxia induced by choking, drowning, smothering, hanging, strangulation, gases or poisons; poisoning and drug overdose; burning; explosions, electrocution and lightning; drugs; and vehicles

B. Gunshot wounds

1. Suicide indicators:

a.   Gun held against the skin
b.   Wound in mouth or in the right temple if victim is right-handed, and in the left temple if left-handed
c.   Not shot through clothing, unless shot in the chest
d.   Weapon present, especially if tightly held in the hand

2. Murder indicators:

a.   Gun fired from more than a few inches away
b.   Angle or location that rules out self-infliction
c.   Shot through clothing
d.   No weapon present

C. Stabbing and cutting wounds

1. Stab wounds

a.   Caused by thrusting actions
b.   Defense wounds result when the victim attempts to ward off the attacker

2. Cutting wounds

a.   With cutting wounds, external bleeding is generally the cause of death
b.   Hesitation wounds can be observed in areas where the main wound occurs, and are caused by attempts to build up enough nerve to make the fatal wound

3. Suicide indicators:

a.   Hesitation wounds
b.   Wounds under clothing
c.   Weapon present, especially if tightly clutched
d.   Usually wounds at throat, wrists, or ankles
e.   Seldom disfigurement
f.   Body not moved

4. Murder indicators:

    a. Defense wounds
    b. Wounds through clothing
    c. No weapon present
    d. Usually injuries to vital organs
    e. Disfigurement
    f. Body moved

D. Blows from blunt objects

E. Asphyxia

1. Asphyxiation results when the body tissues and the brain receive insufficient oxygen to support the red blood cells
2. In asphyxiation deaths, most cases of choking, drowning and smothering are accidental; most cases of hanging are suicides; most cases of strangulation are homicide
3. Asphyxia deaths result from many causes, including:

    a. Choking
    b. Drowning
    c. Smothering
    d. Hanging
    e. Strangulation
    f. Poisons, chemicals and overdoses of sleeping pills
    g. Autoerotic asphyxiation: Indicators of accidental death during autoerotic practices include:

        (1) Nude or sexually exposed victim
        (2) Evidence of solo sexual activity
        (3) Mirrors placed to observe the ritual
        (4) Evidence of masturbation and presence of such items as tissues or towels for cleanup
        (5) Presence of sexual fantasy aids or sexually stimulating paraphernalia
        (6) Presence of bondage

F. Other types of autoerotic death

1. In several documented cases, an act of risky solitary sexual behavior went further than anticipated, leading to accidental death
2. Such fatalities have involved electrocution, crushing, sepsis following perforation of the bowel and accidental self-impalement

G. Poisoning: Poisoning deaths can be accidental, suicide or homicide

1. Poisoning, one of the oldest methods of murder, can occur from an overwhelming dose that causes immediate death or from small doses that accumulate over time and cause death

2. Poisons can be injected into the blood or muscles, inhaled as gases, absorbed through the skin surface, taken in foods or liquids, or inserted into the rectum or vagina
3. Perpetrators of homicidal poisonings are often employed in the medical or care giving fields
4. Homicidal poisoning can be accomplished with any one of thousands of substances, but some are far more common than others
5. Among the most commonly used poisons is arsenic, known as the King of Poisons and the Poison of Kings
6. Cyanide, also commonly used, is a favorite in mass homicides, suicides and politically motivated killings
7. Strychnine, given in large enough doses, produces "a dramatic and horrifying death with the victim's body frozen in mid-convulsion, eyes wide open" (Steck-Flynn, 2007, pp.121–124)
8. Experts in toxicology (the study of poisons) can determine the type of poison, the amount ingested, the approximate time ingested and the effect on the body
9. Investigators should ask the following questions to help determine if a homicidal poisoning has occurred:

   a. Was the death sudden?
   b. Is there a caregiver who has been associated with other illnesses or death?
   c. Did the victim receive medical treatment and appear to recover only to die later?
   d. Did the caregiver have access to restricted drugs or other chemicals?
   e. Was the victim isolated by the caregiver? Did the caregiver position him- or herself to be the only one with access to the victim's food or medications?
   f. Was there a history of infidelity of either the victim or spouse?
   g. Is there a history of the deaths of more than one child?

H. Burning: Most deaths by burning are accidental

   1. A death resulting from burns received in a fire caused by arson is classified as homicide
   2. People sometimes try to disguise homicide by burning the victim's body

I. Explosions, electrocution and lightning: Most deaths caused by explosions, electrocution and lightning are accidental

   1. Explosives can cause death from the direct tearing force of the blast, from a shock wave or from the victim being blown off the top of a structure or against an object with enough force to cause death. Such deaths are usually accidental

2. Electrocution paralyzes the heart muscle, causing rapid death. Nearly all electrocution deaths are accidental

J. Drugs: Many studies have documented the relationship between drugs and homicide and the prominent role drugs play in homicide events

1. Different categories of drug-related homicides include:

a. deadly disputes involving individuals high on drugs (no organized drug or gang affiliation)

b. deaths caused during the commission of economically motivated crimes, such as robbery, in the offender's effort to get money to buy drugs

c. homicides associated with the systemic violence surrounding the drug business itself

(1) Hits on traffickers, dealers or buyers (may be gang related)

(2) Assassinations of law enforcement officers or others fighting drug trafficking

(3) Killing of innocent bystanders in drug-related disputes

2. The victim-offender relationship (VOR) requires an understanding of the difference between *expressive* and *instrumental* violence

a. *Expressive violence* stems from hurt feelings, anger or rage

b. *Instrumental violence* is goal-directed predatory behavior used to exert control

K. Vehicles: In 2005, motor vehicle traffic crashes were the leading cause of death for every age 3 through 6 and 8 through 34

1. Vehicular homicide can result from

a. reckless driving

b. driving under the influence

c. other circumstances where a driver's failure to obey the rules of the road, either intentionally or negligently, leads to the death of another person

2. Aggressive driving and road rage can escalate to a case of vehicular homicide

XI.   Witnesses

    A. Witnesses may know and name a suspect, or they may have seen the suspect or vehicle

    B. Often, however, there are no witnesses, and information must be sought from family members, neighbors and associates

XII.   Suspects

    A. Determining the suspects

       1. Suspect may be arrested at the crime scene
       2. If suspect is known but not at the scene, disseminate the description
       3. If suspect is not known, identification becomes a priority
       4. Any number of suspects may be identified

    B. Determine the motive for a killing because it provides leads to suspects and strong circumstantial evidence against a suspect

    C. Mass murder: occurs when multiple victims are killed in a single incident by one or a few suspects

       1. Mass familicides
       2. September 11, 2001
       3. shooting of U.S. Representative Gabrielle Giffords and others at a mall on January 8, 2011
       4. felony-related mass murder, such as killing of eyewitnesses during a robbery or a group of participants at a drug buy
       5. school shootings and attacks at the workplace.

          a. Similarities between school and workplace murders include the perpetrators' profiles, the targets, the means and the motivation

       6. Killers often take their own lives at the end of the shooting rampage, so motives are unclear

    D. Serial killing: the killing of three or more separate victims, with a "cooling off" period between the killings

       1. Some serial killers in the United States are Henry Lucas, Gary Ridgeway, Ted Bundy, John Wayne Gacey, Jeffrey Dahmer and Andrew Cunanan
       2. Investigating a murder committed by a serial killer may initially seem the same as investigating any other homicide
       3. Investigators should consider reporting the crime to the FBI's National Center for the Analysis of Violent Crime (NCVAC) which provides a profiling program, research, development, training and the Violent Criminal Apprehension Program (VICAP)

4. Because of improved information sharing, inter jurisdictional communication and media coverage, some homicide investigations that begin as single-incident investigations may now have the potential to develop into serial killing investigations
5. DNA evidence and understanding the psychology of serial killings will aid the investigator

E. Lust murder: a sex-related homicide involving a sadistic, deviant assault, in which the killer depersonalizes the victim, sexually mutilates the body and may displace body parts

1. Two types of lust murderers are often described, organized and disorganized

   a. Organized offender: usually of above-average intelligence, methodical and cunning; socially skilled and tricks victims into situations in which he can torture and then murder them
   b. Disorganized offender: usually of below-average intelligence, has no car and is a loner who acts on impulse

2. Both the organized and the disorganized offenders usually murder victims from their own geographic area
3. The murders involve fantasy, ritual, fetishes and symbolism
4. Both types of murderers both usually leave some sort of physical evidence

XIII. The Declining Clearance Rate

A. *Clearance rate* is the term used to define the quantity of cases removed from active investigation; it represents the ratio of crimes resolved to the number of crimes reported
B. Crimes are either *cleared, closed* or *solved* (terms are used interchangeably)

   1. A case can either be cleared by arrest or by exceptional means
   2. Examples of exceptional clearance include death of the offender (e.g., suicide or justifiably killed by law enforcement or citizen); victim's refusal to cooperate with the prosecution after the offender has been identified; and denial of extradition because the offender committed a crime in another jurisdiction and is being prosecuted for that offense

C. National clearance rate for homicide is highest of all the serious crimes, but homicides clearances have declined dramatically over the past few decades

   1. 94% clearance rate in 1961
   2. Study from 2008 shows that more recently, the clearance percentage is in the low-to mid-60s

3. In 2009, 66.6 percent of murders were cleared by arrest or by exceptional means
4. Some possible reasons for the decline: an increase in stranger-to-stranger homicides, which are difficult to solve; an increase in gang-related offenses that turn fatal; community and witness intimidation; and reductions in witness cooperation
5. Police departments also report an increasing number of "petty arguments" and incidents of "disrespect" that lead to homicides and an increase in the reentry of prisoners (650,000 per year) into communities
6. Backlogs and heavy caseloads in crime labs and coroners' offices may reduce investigative effectiveness
7. Increases in illegal immigration from countries where residents fear and do not trust the local police decrease the police department's effectiveness within these communities
8. The growth of "Thug Culture" and "Stop Snitch in'" campaigns reduces witness cooperation

D. A critical factor in clearing homicides is time, as cases become harder to solve the longer it takes to make an arrest

E. Aspects of the offense associated with likelihood of clearing a case

1. Homicide circumstances: felony-related homicides are more difficult to clear than those with other circumstances
2. Weapons: homicides committed with weapons that bring the offender and victim into contact with one another have an increased likelihood of being cleared
3. Location: homicides committed in residences have an increased likelihood of being cleared

F. Law enforcement actions affecting clearance

1. Initial response

   a. The first officer on the scene immediately notifies the homicide unit, the medical examiner's office and the crime lab
   b. The first officer on the scene immediately secures the area and attempts to locate witnesses
   c. The detective assigned to the case arrives at the scene within 30 minutes of being notified

2. Actions of detectives

   a. Three or four detectives, instead of one or two, were assigned to the case

    b. The detectives took detailed notes describing the crime scene, including measurements

    c. Detectives followed up on all information provided by witnesses

    d. At least one detective assigned to the case attended the postmortem examination

  3. Other police actions

    a. A computer check using the local criminal justice information system was conducted on the suspect or on any guns found

    b. A witness interviewed at the crime scene provided valuable evidence such as information about circumstances of the death or the perpetrator's motivation, an identification of the suspect or victim, or the whereabouts of the suspect

    c. Witnesses, friends, acquaintances and neighbors of the victim were interviewed

    d. The medical examiner prepared a body chart of the victim and it was included in the case file

    e. The attending physician and medical personnel were interviewed

    f. Confidential informants provided information

    g. Many departments use a homicide case review solvability chart to determine which cases to focus on

G. 10 most common errors in death investigations

  1. Improper response to the scene
  2. Failure to protect the crime scene
  3. Not handling suspicious deaths as homicides
  4. Responding with a preconceived notion
  5. Failure to take sufficient photos
  6. Failure to manage the process (maintaining chain of custody and proper documentation)
  7. Failure to evaluate victimology
  8. Failure to conduct effective canvass
  9. Failure to work as a team
  10. Command interference or inappropriate action

H. Impact of unsolved homicides

XIV. Cold Cases

A. The point at which a case is moved to the cold case shelf varies from agency to agency, depending on the number of cases and the staff available

B. Reasons to reopen a cold case: physical evidence has been well preserved, witnesses may become more cooperative over time, physical evidence can be reexamined using newly developed technology such as AFIT, CODIS or VICAP

C. Volunteer cold case squads: use of local retired investigators

D. Benefits of a cold case unit: "Case clearance rates increase, guilty parties are brought to justice, innocent parties are exonerated, victims' survivors get a measure of relief, and investigators benefit from the personal satisfaction associated with solving cold cases" (Cronin et al., 2007, p.116)

XV. Death Notification

A. Officers must be prepared for a wide range of emotional and physical reactions people may have upon hearing of a death

B. "Notification should be done in person, in pairs, in private, in plain language, and in time. Avoid words such as *passed on, expired*. And make notification before the family sees it on the news" (Page, 2008, p.20)

C. Notifying the family of an officer who has been killed is even more difficult. Officers should consider the following points:

1. Who should be notified after a line-of-duty death? Include address and relationship to officer

2. Are there any special circumstances to be aware of, such as a survivor's heart condition?

3. Is there a clergy preference?

4. Is there a family friend who can provide support?

XVI. Strategies for Reducing Homicide

A. Two trends are changing reactive view

1. Crime analysis shows that homicide is greatest for young people in core, inner-city neighborhoods and is often related to drugs, guns and gangs

2. Emergence of community policing and a problem-solving approach to crime in which homicide is viewed as part of the larger, more general problem of violence

B. The conventional wisdom about homicide has changed in some departments from viewing it as a series of unconnected, uncontrollable episodes to seeing it as part of the larger, general problem of violence, which can be addressed proactively

XVII. A Case Study

A. The "Moon berry Pond Murder" of James Mixon

B. Lessons learned by the Miami-Dade homicide unit investigating the murder

113

1. Work as a team: having two interviews going at the same time led to success
2. Avoid gender prejudice: women can kill too
3. Stay attuned to subtle clues

XVIII. Summary

ASSAULT, DOMESTIC VIOLENCE, STALKING AND ELDER ABUSE

OUTLINE

Chapter 9
Assault, Domestic Violence, Stalking and Elder Abuse

Key Terms

• aggravated assault	• femicide
• assault	• full faith and credit
• battery	• indicator crimes
• cyberstalking	• *in loco parentis*
• domestic violence	• simple assault
• elder abuse	• stake in conformity
• felonious assault	• stalking

Learning Objectives
After reading this chapter, students should be able to

• Define what constitutes assault.	• Describe what evidence is likely to be at the scene of an assault.
• Compare how simple assault differs from aggravated assault.	• Explain what offenses might be categorized as separate crimes, to aid in data collection.
• Explain when force is legal.	
• Articulate the elements of simple assault, aggravated (felonious) assault and attempted assault.	• Define what constitutes domestic violence.
• Describe what special challenges are posed by an assault investigation.	• Explain what constitutes stalking.
• Compare how to prove the elements of both simple and aggravated assault.	• Describe what constitutes elder abuse, and how prevalent elder abuse is.

Internet Assignments

1. Have students review the American Bar Association (ABA) Web site and answer the following questions, either individually in written form or during a class discussion:

   - What does the ABA recommend for victims of domestic violence?
   - Are there any differences between what the ABA recommends and what your text recommends?

2. A variety of organizations are dedicated to victims of domestic violence; however, although elder abuse is clearly on the rise, there are not as many organizations focused on victims of elder abuse. Divide the class into two groups. Have one group search the Internet for Web sites offering support for victims of domestic violence, and have the other group search for Web sites offering support to families and individuals who have suffered from elder abuse. After each group of students presents their findings to the class, initiate a conversation about the differences between these two types of abuse victims and why availability of support services for them differs.

Class Assignment

Have class members discuss issues of domestic violence and how best to respond to the following case:

A male who seems tired and disoriented is found wandering along a side street. The officer brings the male to the police station in order to determine the best course of action. The male is informed that he is not under arrest, just that the officer is taking him to the department so that he can be more comfortable. On the way to the station and at the station, the male recounts being assaulted by his wife. He states that he has hit her once or twice during their marriage, but has "only slapped her." He says that he has not had any recent altercations with her, but that earlier today, while he was in bed, she hit him over the head repeatedly with a hard object that he believes may have been a metal cooking pan. He says that he remembers very little between the time of this assault and the time he was picked up by the officer on the street.

His story has some unusual aspects and seems to run counter to a number of trends observed in domestic violence. However, this does not necessarily mean that the events described by the man did not occur. What actions would you take as the officer in this case?

Chapter Outline

I.   Assault: An Overview

   A.   Assault is unlawfully threatening to harm another person, actually harming another person or attempting unsuccessfully to do so

B. In most revised state statutes, the term *assault* is synonymous with *battery*, or the two terms have been joined in a single crime termed *assault*. Some states, however, still have separate statutory offenses of assault and battery

II. Classification

A. Simple assault is intentionally causing another person to fear immediate bodily harm or death or intentionally inflicting or attempting to inflict bodily harm on the person

B. Aggravated or felonious assault is an unlawful attack by one person on another to inflict severe bodily injury

C. NCVS data indicates a victimization rate of 17.1 per 1,000 persons age 12 or older in 2009, a decline from the rate of 20.7 in 2006. The rate was 11.3 for simple assault and 3.2 for aggravated assault. FBI data shows 806,843 aggravated assaults in 2009. The rate was estimated at 262.8 offenses per 100,000 inhabitants. The Office for Victims of Crime reports that one person is assaulted every 39.1 seconds. The clearance rate for aggravated assault was 56.8 percent in 2009

D. Officers assaulted: The FBI reports that in 2009, 57,268 officers were assaulted while performing their duties, at a rate of 10.3 per 100 officers: 32.6 percent were assaulted responding to disturbance calls (family quarrels, bar fights, etc.); 12.7 percent were handling, transporting or maintaining custody of prisoners; and 9.6 percent were performing traffic stops

E. Legal force

1. Physical force may be used legally in certain instances
2. In specified instances, teachers, people operating public conveyances and law enforcement officers can legally use reasonable physical force
3. Teachers have the authority of *in loco parentis* ("in the place of the parent") in many states
4. Force used in self-defense is justifiable

III. Elements of the Crime

A. Elements of the crime of simple assault

1. Intent to do bodily harm to another
2. Present ability to commit the act
3. Commission of an overt act toward carrying out the intention

B. Elements of the crime of aggravated or felonious assault

1. Intent to do bodily harm to another
2. Present ability to commit the act
3. Commission of an overt act toward carrying out the intention

    4.   The intentionally inflicted bodily injury must have resulted in *one* of the following:

        a. high probability of death
        b. serious, permanent disfigurement
        c. permanent or protracted loss or impairment of body members or organ or other severe bodily harm

C.   Attempted assault

    1   Attempted aggravated assault is also a crime in many states
    2.   If the suspect intended to assault someone but was prevented from doing so for some reason, it is still a punishable offense categorized as "unlawful attempt to commit assault"
    3.   Requires proof of intent along with some overt act toward committing the crime

IV.   Special Challenges in Investigation

A.   Special challenges in assault investigations include:

    1.   distinguishing the victim from the suspect
    2.   determining whether the matter is civil or criminal
    3.   determining whether the act was intentional or accidental

B.   It may be difficult to obtain a complaint against a simple assault
C.   Responding to simple assault calls may be dangerous for responding officers

V.   The Preliminary Investigation

A.   At a minimum, officers arriving on the scene of an assault should:

    1.   have backup either with them or on the way until the scene is secure
    2.   control and disarm those involved in the altercation
    3.   provide medical aid to injured people
    4.   separate suspects and victims
    5.   protect the crime scene
    6.   give the *Miranda* warning if applicable
    7.   obtain preliminary statements
    8.   photograph evidence
    9.   collect and preserve evidence
   10.   reconstruct the crime

B.   Proving the elements of assault

    1.   Establish the intent to cause injury by determining the events that led up to the assault

2.   Establish the severity of the injury inflicted by the assault by taking photographs and describing all injuries in your notes

3.   Establish whether a dangerous weapon was used by determining the means of attack and the exact weapon used

C.   Evidence in assault investigations

1.   Physical evidence in an assault case includes photographs of injuries, clothing of the victim or suspect, weapons, broken objects, bloodstains, hairs, fibers and other signs of an altercation

2.   For data collection, special categories of assault are domestic violence, stalking and elder abuse

VI.   Investigating Domestic Violence

A.   Domestic violence is a pattern of behaviors involving physical, sexual, economic and emotional abuse, alone or in combination, often by an intimate partner and often to establish and maintain power and control over the other partner

B.   History of domestic violence: from male privilege to criminal act

1.   Police interventions in domestic violence cases have changed from treating wife assault as a matter most appropriately addressed privately within the family to regarding it as a crime appropriate for criminal justice intervention

2.   By 2000, approximately 50 percent of domestic violence cases resulted in arrests

C.   The cycle of violence

1.   Tension-building stage
2.   Acute battering episode
3.   Honeymoon

D.   Types of assault and weapons used

1.   Four types of assault

   a.   Physical violence
   b.   Sexual violence
   c.   Threats of physical or sexual violence
   d.   Psychological/emotional violence

2.   Females more likely than males to use a weapon
3.   Women are twice as likely as men to use a knife or other sharp object
4.   Women are three times more likely than men to use a blunt object

E.   Prevalence of domestic violence and its victims

1.   Domestic violence is found at all socioeconomic levels across all racial demographics
2.   The OVC "Crime Clock" shows that one woman is victimized by an intimate partner every 52 seconds, one man is victimized every 3.5 minutes and one child is reported abused or neglected every 34.9 seconds
3.   Much domestic violence goes unreported
4.   Women as abusers

   a.   Women who assaulted their male partners were more likely to avoid arrest
   b.   Four decision points:

      (1)   the decision to file charges (versus rejection for insufficient evidence)
      (2)   the decision to file as a felony (versus a misdemeanor or probation violation)
      (3)   the decision to dismiss for insufficient evidence (versus full prosecution)
      (4)   the decision to reduce felony charges to a misdemeanor or violation of parole

   c.   A study found suspect gender to be statistically significant in all four outcomes, in favoring female over male suspects, suggesting that frequently female intimate violence perpetrators are viewed more as victims than offenders

5.   Same-sex domestic violence

   a.   Dynamics are similar to those of opposite-sex domestic violence in many respects
   b.   When the law enforcement response to domestic violence incidents involving heterosexual and same-sex couples is compared, the couples receive similar treatment
   c.   Same-sex victims are rarely afforded the same protection as heterosexuals

6.   When the abuser is a police officer

   a.   Research suggests that domestic abuse may occur more often in police families than among the general public
   b.   When the abuser is a police officer, special challenges exist
   c.   A federal law, known as the Lautenberg Act, was passed in 1996 prohibiting anyone, including a police officer, who has been convicted of a qualifying misdemeanor domestic violence offense from owning or using a firearm or possessing ammunition

F.   Predicators and precipitators of domestic violence

1.   History of family violence
2.   Indicator crimes
3.   Animal cruelty: Seventy-five percent of women entering shelters are pet owners; of those women, 71 percent said their abuser had either injured or killed their family pet
4.   Presence of firearms
5.   Unemployment of the batterer
6.   Estrangement, where the victim has moved out of the previously shared residence

G.   Police response

1.   Computers in patrol vehicles and use of real-time response software enable a premises and individual records check as part of preliminary investigation, enhancing the safety of the officers arriving on the scene
2.   Domestic disputes are the most dangerous calls that officers respond to; FBI Uniform Crime Reports show response to domestic assault is the single largest category for officer assaults
3.   Officers should always respond with a backup or two, separate people for the interviews, impound all firearms at the scene and never drop their guard just because they are dealing with a homosexual or lesbian couple
4.   Evidence in domestic violence cases includes:

a.   recording of 911 call
b.   photographs of any injuries
c.   photographs of the scene
d.   damaged clothing or other property
e.   weapons used
f.   prior police reports
g.   medical reports
h.   victim's statements
i.   suspect's statements
j.   statements from neighbors or other witnesses

5.   To arrest or not?

a.   Many states and police departments have a mandatory arrest policy for domestic abuse
b.   Alternatives to arrest may be better in specific circumstances
c.   Officers should not base their decisions regarding arrest on their perception of the willingness of the victim or witnesses to testify
d.   The victim need not sign a complaint
e.   Dual arrest policies allow officers to arrest both parties when injuries to both sides are observed

f. A dual arrest policy does not preclude the single arrest of the primary aggressor only, if the officer is able to make that determination. Factors to consider in making this assessment include:

(1) prior domestic violence involving either person
(2) relative seriousness of the injuries inflicted on each person involved
(3) potential for future injury
(4) whether one of the alleged batteries was committed in self-defense
(5) any other factor that helps the officer decide which person was the primary physical aggressor

g. Specialized domestic violence units may be a positive approach

6. Police nonresponse

a. Several studies have examined whether the police response to domestic violence calls does in fact receive a lower priority than other crime calls
b. The results generally show an increasingly high priority being placed on such calls

H. Effectiveness of various interventions

1. Results of studies that have examined the effectiveness of batterer intervention programs (BIPs) suggest that perhaps the most significant factor in the rehabilitation of a batterer is the offender's stake in conformity, a constellation of variables that, in effect, comprise "what an offender has to lose," such as marital status, residential stability or employment
2. Studies show strong support for the continued emphasis on interagency (and community) coordinated responses to intimate partner abuse
3. It is equally important to help victims

I. Restraining orders

1. The Violence Against Women Act of 1994 assigns full faith and credit to valid orders of protection, meaning that an order issued anywhere in the country is legally binding and enforceable nationwide
2. Some studies have found that women who seek restraining orders are well aware of their potential ineffectiveness
3. A new Massachusetts law requires an offender who violates a domestic order of protection to wear a global positioning system (GPS) monitoring device

J.   Legislation

    1.   Mandatory arrest laws
    2.   Restrictions on firearms

K.   Avoiding lawsuits

    1.   Failure to respond appropriately to domestic violence can result in serious financial liability to local governments
    2.   Lawsuits include failure of the police to protect victims, particularly when there have been restraining orders issued (*Thurman v. City of Torrington,* 1984)

VII.   Investigating Stalking

A.   Stalking, which is a crime of power and control, is the willful or intentional commission of a series of acts that would cause a reasonable person to fear death or serious bodily injury and that, in fact, does place the victim in fear of death or serious bodily injury
B.   Stalking often leads to homicide: Statistics on femicide, the murder of a woman, indicate that the majority of femicide victims had been stalked by the person who killed them
C.   Types of stalking: intimate or former intimate stalking, acquaintance stalking and stranger stalking
D.   A set of typologies for stalkers, presented by the NCVC, cover three types: the simple obsessional, the love obsessional and the erotomanic
E.   Cyberstalking is defined by the Department of Justice as the repeated use of the Internet, e-mail or other digital electronic communications devices to stalk another person
F.   Legislation and department policies: Although legislation makes stalking a specific crime and empowers law enforcement to combat the offense, a great deal of variation and subjectivity exists among the states' legal definitions of stalking
G.   Police response

    1.   The traditional law enforcement response to stalkers has been to encourage victims to obtain court-issued restraining orders; but unfortunately, such orders are often ineffective
    2.   Law enforcement faces a unique challenge in addressing and investigating stalking incidents for many reasons

        a.   Lack of clear definitions of stalking or of the elements constituting the crime
        b.   Stalking behaviors are complex and varied
        c.   There is no standard psychological profile of stalkers to assist investigators

        d.   When stalkers also commit domestic violence, investigations are likely to focus on the violence rather than the stalking

        e.   Stalkers often cross state or tribal lines to monitor, harass or commit violence against victims

        f.   Stalkers are not easily deterred

        g.   Ensuring victim safety is difficult

3. Investigators should conduct a technology risk assessment with the victim

4. Investigators should assess the threat to determine the credibility and overall capability of the stalker to actually carry out his or her expressed intent to cause harm

5. Victims must be instructed how to document, either in writing or with a video or audio recording, their emotional and physical reactions to each stalking act; this is called a "stalking log"

6. There is a strong connection between stalking and domestic violence. The FBI's NCAVC can help investigators assess an offender's potential for violence. The NCAVC recommends considering the following:

        a.   Threats to kill

        b.   Access to or recent acquisition of weapons

        c.   Violations of protective orders

        d.   Prior physical violence against the victim or others, including pets

        e.   Substance abuse

        f.   Location of violence (private versus public setting)

        g.   Status of the victim-offender relationship

        h.   Surveillance of the victim and "chance" meetings

        i.   Mental illness

        j.   Prior intimacy between victim and offender

        k.   Fantasy—homicidal or suicidal ideation

        l.   Obsessive jealousy

        m. Desperation

        n.   Blaming the victim for personal problems

        o.   Loss of power or control

7. Officers should make a concerted effort to talk to the stalker

VIII. Investigating Elder Abuse

A. Elder abuse has been defined as "intentional or neglectful acts by a caregiver or 'trusted' individual that lead to, or may lead to, harm of a vulnerable elder" (National Center on Elder Abuse)

B. Types of elder abuse

1. Physical abuse
2. Neglect
3. Emotional or psychological abuse
4. Verbal abuse and threats
5. Financial abuse and exploitation
6. Sexual abuse
7. Abandonment

C. Self-neglect—a refusal or failure to provide oneself with adequate food, water, clothing, shelter, personal hygiene, medication (when indicated) and safety precautions—is also considered elder abuse
D. Potential abusers of the elderly are family members, hired caregivers (in home or in a nursing home) and professional con artists
E. Definition in the text: Elder abuse is the physical and emotional abuse, financial exploitation and general neglect of the elderly
F. Financial abuse and exploitation of the elderly, which is an area of growing concern, falls into two categories:

1. fraud committed by strangers

2. exploitation by relatives and caregivers

G. Prevalence and nature of elder abuse

1. Between 1 and 2 million Americans age 65 or older have suffered elder abuse
2. The OVC Crime Clock reports that one elderly person is victimized every 4.2 minutes, in a 2009 study
3. Research indicates that fewer than 20 percent of cases of elder abuse are reported
4. The extent of elder abuse is currently unknown

H. Signs of physical abuse of the elderly

1. Signs investigators should be aware of

a. Injury incompatible with the given explanation
b. Burns
c. Cuts, pinch marks, scratches, lacerations or puncture wounds
d. Bruises, welts or discolorations
e. Dehydration or other malnourishment without illness-related causes, unexplained weight loss
f. Pallor, sunken eyes or cheeks
g. Eye injury
h. Soiled clothing or bedding
i. Lack of bandages on injuries or stitches where needed, or evidence of unset bone fractures

      j.   Injuries hidden under the breasts or on the other areas of the body normally covered by clothing

      k.   Frequent use of the emergency room or clinic

2.   Law enforcement officers should consider the following questions:

      a.   Has anyone at home ever hurt you?

      b.   Has anyone ever scolded or threatened you?

      c.   Have you ever signed any documents that you didn't understand?

      d.   Are you often alone?

      e.   Are you afraid of anyone at home?

      f.   Has anyone ever touched you without your consent?

      g.   Has anyone ever made you do things you didn't want to?

I.   Signs of financial abuse and exploitation of the elderly

1.   A recent acquaintance expresses an interest in finances, promises to provide care or ingratiates him- or herself with the elder

2.   A relative or caregiver has no visible means of support or is overtly interested in the elder's financial affairs

3.   A relative or caregiver expresses concern over the cost of caring for the elder, or is reluctant to spend money for needed medical treatment

4.   The utility and other bills are not being paid

5.   The elder's placement, care or possessions are inconsistent with the size of his or her estate

6.   A relative or caregiver isolates the elder, makes excuses when friends or family call or visit and does not give the elder the messages

7.   A relative or caregiver gives implausible explanations about finances, and the elder is unaware of or unable to explain the arrangements made

8.   Checking account and credit card statements are sent to a relative or caregiver and are not accessible to the elder

9.   At the bank, the elder is accompanied by a relative or caregiver who refuses to let the elder speak for him- or herself, or the elder appears nervous or afraid of the person accompanying him or her

10.   The elder is concerned or confused about "missing money"

11.   There are suspicious signatures on the elder's checks, or the elder signs the checks and another party fills in the payee and amount sections

12.   There is an unusual amount of banking activity, particularly just after joint accounts are set up or someone new starts helping with the elder's finances

13. A will, power of attorney or other legal document is drafted, but the elder does not understand its implications

J. Risk factors for elder abuse

1. The NCEA lists several risk factors associated with elder abuse:
   a. domestic violence grown old
   b. personal problems of the abuser, especially in the case of adult children
   c. caregiver stress
   d. personal characteristics of the elder (dementia, disruptive behaviors, problematic personality traits)
   e. the cycle of violence

2. Domestic violence is a learned problem-solving behavior transmitted from one generation to the next

K. Police response

1. The following investigative techniques have been suggested:

   a. Police should be patient with victims, who may be embarrassed, scared or forgetful
   b. For physical abuse cases, investigators should take good photographs both during the first response and several days later
   c. For financial crimes, investigators should collect anything that looks like evidence, including financial records
   d. For neglect cases, police should take a comprehensive video of the kitchen, bathrooms, bedrooms and other living areas
   e. Police should make creative arrests to get suspects out of the house and run all suspects for warrants, criminal histories, probation and parole violations, gang membership and DOJ hits

2. Investigators should observe the general condition of the residence when arriving to investigate an elder abuse complaint
3. Once inside, investigators should carefully observe the general conditions and interview the alleged victim, being aware that nonverbal cues are as important as verbal ones
4. Investigators should look for the tell-tale clues, such as whether the suspected perpetrator is hanging around and refusing to leave the senior alone to answer questions, or whether the potential victim is looking the officer in the eye and answering direct questions

5. One critical aspect of an investigation of physical elder abuse is to determine if bruising is the result of an accident or of abuse
6. Findings from NIJ-funded research projects help caretakers, medical personnel, Adult Protective Services agencies and law enforcement officers recognize abuse indicators—known as forensic markers—to help distinguish between injuries caused by mistreatment and those that are the result of accidents, illnesses or aging
7. NIJ-funded researchers also examined data from the deaths of elderly residents in long-term care facilities to identify potential markers of abuse

    a. Physical condition/quality of care
    b. Facility characteristics
    c. Inconsistencies
    d. Staff behaviors

L. Reducing elder abuse

1. Advise senior contacts to remain active in some type of community group (church, social, neighborhood)
2. Provide information about the services and resource centers in neighborhoods
3. Use Triad, a cooperative effort of the International Association of Chiefs of Police (IACP), AARP (formerly the American Association of Retired Persons) and the National Sheriffs' Association (NSA)

IX. Summary

SEX OFFENSES

OUTLINE

- Investigating Obscene Telephone Calls and Texts
- Investigating Prostitution
- Investigating Human Trafficking
- Classification of Sex Offenses
- Rape/Sexual Assault
- The Police Response
- The Victim's Medical Examination
- Blind Reporting
- Interviewing the Victim
- Follow-Up Investigation
- Interviewing Witnesses
- Sex Offenders
- Taking a Suspect into Custody and Interrogation
- Coordination with Other Agencies
- Prosecution of Rape and Statutory Charges
- Civil Commitment of Sex Offenders after Sentences Served
- Sex Offender Registry and Notification

Chapter 10
Sex Offenses

Key Terms

- bigamy
- blind reporting
- child molestation
- cunnilingus
- date rape
- digital penetration
- exhibitionists
- fellatio
- forcible rape
- incest
- indecent exposure
- intimate parts
- oral copulation

- pedophile
- penetration
- prostitution
- rape
- Rohypnol
- sadist
- sadomasochistic abuse
- sexual contact
- sexual penetration
- sexually explicit conduct
- sodomy
- statutory rape
- voyeurism

Learning Objectives
After reading this chapter, students should be able to

- Identify the key distinction between human trafficking and human smuggling.
- Describe how sex offenses are classified.
- Define the elements of rape and how it is classified.
- Identify the elements of sexual assault.
- Outline the special challenges that exist in investigating sex offenses.
- Explain what modus operandi factors are important in investigating a sexual assault.
- Describe what type of evidence is often obtained in sex offense investigations.

- Explain what evidence to seek in date rape cases.
- Define blind reporting and its advantages.
- Identify agencies that can assist in a sexual assault investigation.
- Clarify what is generally required to obtain a conviction in sexual assault cases.
- Explain whether recent laws have reduced or increased the penalties for sexual assault and why.
- Define which three federal statutes form the basis for sex offender registries.

Internet Assignments

1. Have students research and report on the date rape case involving Andrew Luster, heir to the Max Factor fortune. Luster was convicted of drugging women with GHB and videotaping his sexual assaults while the victims were unconscious.

2. Ask the class to research the sex offender registries that are available online for their state, city of residence, home town or other locations. You may want to assign them different cities or states in order to have a variety of samples. Have students discuss their findings in class, and initiate a conversation regarding the benefits and concerns of such online registries.

3. Have the class research Megan's Law and the Jacob Wetterling Act to familiarize themselves with the circumstances of the cases that led to each law. Have them conduct Web research to learn how local law enforcement practices are affected by these laws.

Class Assignments

1. Have the class discuss the different issues that may arise in cases involving:

   - A male victim of sexual assault
   - Juvenile victims of sexual assault
   - Older victims of sexual assault (65 and over)

2. Have students tell you what the local names are for common "club" or predatory drugs. This can be done as an anonymous exercise by having them hand in a written list of the names. Have a local drug expert from the police department or a DEA agent visit the class and describe local drug activity and law enforcement efforts to combat it.

3. Have the class discuss the pros and cons of the following question: Are sex offenders being unfairly stigmatized by the registration process and the ability of citizens to access personalized information on registered sex offenders via Internet databases?

Chapter Outline

I. Investigating Obscene Telephone Calls and Texts

   A. Making obscene telephone calls is a crime and can be a form of harassing stalking behavior
   B. The calls may or may not be of a sexual nature, but the procedures for investigating either would be the same

II.   Investigating Prostitution

    A.   Prostitution—soliciting sexual intercourse for pay—raises several concerns, including personal safety concerns, public health concerns and quality-of-life concerns

    B.   Of particular concern is the practice of enticing very young girls into prostitution. The Mann Act attempts to prevent such actions

    C.   Prostitutes may have the highest homicide rate of any group of women studied thus far, and a significant number of prostitute homicides remain unsolved

    D.   Single versus serial murders of prostitutes

        1.   Serial murderers differ from single murderers in three areas— sexual aggression, deviant sexual interests and active sexual fantasies

        2.   Serial killers engaged more frequently in planning activities, ritualistic behaviors, body mutilation and removal of body parts

III.   Investigating Human Trafficking

    A.   The Thirteenth Amendment to the U.S. Constitution, ratified in 1865, prohibits slavery or involuntary servitude

    B.   Human trafficking

        1.   Global phenomenon that involves obtaining or maintaining the labor or services of another through force, fraud or coercion in violation of an individual's human rights

        2.   Generates billions of dollars in profit each year; one of the world's fastest-growing criminal activities, operating on the same scale as the illegal trade of guns and drugs

        3.   Yields $9.5 billion a year in global profits, of which $3.5 billion is generated in the United States

        4.   As many as 12.3 million people are trafficked per year internationally; 80 percent are women and girls, and as many as half are minors

        5.   The Trafficking Victims Protection Act (TVPA) was passed in 2000 to address the problem of trafficking in persons and to provide for protection and assistance for victims, prosecution of offenders and prevention efforts internationally

        6.   Trafficking victims are often lured by the promise of better living conditions and good job opportunities, with adults and children being trafficked for commercial sex or forced labor

        7.   Trafficking is an underreported crime, and many cases go undiscovered

C. Trafficking versus smuggling

1. The key distinction lies in the individual's freedom of choice
2. Smuggling occurs when someone is paid to assist another in the illegal crossing of borders
3. Human trafficking occurs when someone is forced into a situation of exploitation and their freedom is taken away

D. Myths and misconceptions of human trafficking

1. The victim knew what he or she was getting into
2. The victim committed unlawful acts
3. The victim was paid for services
4. The victim had freedom of movement
5. There were opportunities to escape but the victim didn't
6. Trafficking involves the crossing of borders
7. U.S. citizens can't be trafficked
8. The trafficker's actions are culturally appropriate
9. It can't be trafficking when the trafficker and victim are related or married

E. Challenges to law enforcement

1. Human trafficking presents many challenges

    a. It involves movement from one jurisdiction to another
    b. It is difficult to identify and later convict offenders because trafficking comprises multiple crimes to prosecute
    c. There is a low tendency of victims to report crimes
    d. It is difficult to identify victims and perpetrators of the crime
    e. It is difficult to get victims and witnesses who are in the country illegally to cooperate in investigations and prosecutions
    f. Trafficking victims are often unable to communicate in English

2. The T visa, now available under federal law, allows important witnesses or victims to remain in the United States to testify against human traffickers and their criminal enterprises

IV. Classification of Sex Offenses

A. Sex offenses include:

1. Bigamy
2. Child molestation
3. Incest
4. Indecent exposure
5. Prostitution
6. Sodomy
7. Rape (sexual assault)

B. Terminology commonly used when investigating sex offenses includes:

1. Cunnilingus
2. Digital penetration
3. Fellatio
4. Intimate parts
5. Oral copulation
6. Penetration
7. Sadomasochistic abuse
8. Sexual contact
9. Sexual penetration
10. Sexually explicit conduct

V. Rape/Sexual Assault

A. Forcible rape is sexual intercourse against a person's will by the use or threat of force

B. Statutory rape is sexual intercourse with a minor, with or without consent

C. An estimated 18 to 20 million women and almost three million men in the United States have been forcibly raped at some time in their lives

D. Results from the National Violence Against Women Survey (NVAWS) indicate that more than 300,000 women and 93,000 men are raped every year in the United States

E. According to the Uniform Crime Reports, there were an estimated 88,097 forcible rapes reported to law enforcement in 2009, which was a 2.6 percent decrease from 2008

F. The rate of forcible rapes in 2009 was estimated at 56.6 offenses per 100,000 female inhabitants

G. The clearance rate for forcible rape was 41.2 percent in 2009

H. Elements of the crime of rape or sexual assault commonly include:

1. an act of sexual intercourse
2. with a person other than a spouse
3. committed without the consent of the victim
4. against the victim's will and by force

I. Challenges to investigation

1. Special challenges to investigating rape include:

a. the sensitive nature of the offense
b. social attitudes
c. the victim's horror or embarrassment

2. A rape investigation requires great sensitivity

VI. The Police Response

A. As soon as you arrive at the scene, announce yourself clearly to allay fears the victim may have that the suspect is returning

B.   Explain to the victim what is being done for her safety. If the rape has just occurred, if there are serious injuries or if it appears the victim is in shock, call for an ambulance

C.   Protect the crime scene and broadcast a description of the assailant, means and direction of flight, and the time and exact location of the assault

D.   Establish a command post away from the scene to divert attention from the address of the victim and to preserve the scene

E.   At a minimum, officers on the scene should:

1.   Record their arrival time
2.   Determine the victim's location and condition, and request an ambulance if needed
3.   Obtain identification of the suspect if possible
4.   Determine whether the suspect is at the scene
5.   Protect the crime scene
6.   Identify and separate witnesses. Obtain valid identification from them and then obtain preliminary statements
7.   Initiate crime broadcast if applicable

F.   Information to obtain

1.   If a suspect is arrested at or near the scene, conduct a field identification
2.   If much time has elapsed between the offense and the report, use other means of identification
3.   If the victim knows the assailant, obtain the suspect's name, address, complete description and the nature of the relationship with victim
4.   Then obtain arrest and search warrants
5.   If the suspect is unknown to the victim, check modus operandi (MO) files and have the victim look at photo files on sex offenders
6.   MO factors important in investigating sex offenses include type of offense, words spoken, use of a weapon, actual method of attack, time of day, type of location and victim's age

G.   Physical evidence

1.   Evidence in a rape case consists of:

   a.   stained or torn clothing
   b.   scratches, bruises or cuts
   c.   evidence of a struggle
   d.   semen and bloodstains

2. Such evidence shows the amount of force that occurred, establishes that a sex act was performed and links the act with the suspect

3. Because such evidence deteriorates rapidly, obtain it as soon as possible

4. Try to determine how the offender gained access to the victim

5. There also may be primary, secondary or multiple scenes

6. Preserve physical evidence by securing the scene, ensuring the safety of the victim and witnesses

7. A log of all persons at the scene is important, including emergency personnel

8. Medical personnel should be asked to help preserve evidence, such as carrying a stretcher around pools of liquid on the ground or floor

9. The victim's clothing can be placed in a clean paper evidence bag and sealed

10. Maintain the chain of custody where evidence on the victim is concerned by accompanying the victim to the hospital

11. Don't allow civilians or family members access to the scene

H. Investigating date rape

1. Date rape, also known as acquaintance rape, is a type of sexual assault in which the victim knows the suspect

2. Frequently drugs, including alcohol, are involved in such cases; this renders the victims physically helpless, unable to refuse sex and unable to remember what happened

3. The National Women's Health Center suggests that the preferred term is "drug-facilitated sexual assault"

4. Additional evidence in date rape cases may include the presence of alcohol, drugs or both in the victim's system

5. The three most common date rape drugs are

a. Rohypnol, which is a Schedule IV drug under the Controlled Substances Act and illegal to manufacture, sell, possess or use in the United States

b. Gamma hydroxybutyric acid (GHB)

c. Ketamine, a white powder, which is classified as a Schedule III non-narcotic drug under the Controlled Substances Act and is legal in the United States as an injectable, short-acting anesthetic commonly used by veterinarians

6. Another date rape drug is Ecstasy, or MDMA (3,4 methylenedioxymethamphetamine), which is a Schedule I drug under the Controlled Substances Act with no currently accepted medical use in the United States

7. The Drug-Induced Rape Prevention and Punishment Act was signed in 1996, allowing courts to impose prison sentences of as long as 20 years to anyone who distributes a controlled substance, such as Rohypnol, to another person with the intent to commit a crime of violence, including rape

VII. The Victim's Medical Examination

A. The rape victim should have a medical examination as soon as possible to establish injuries, to determine whether intercourse occurred and to protect against venereal disease and pregnancy
B. Many hospitals have formed specially trained units of physicians and nurses to deal specifically with sexual assaults; one such program is the Sexual Assault Nurse Examiners (SANE) program
C. The victim should be asked to sign a release form that authorizes the medical facility to provide police a copy of the examination record; hospital reports may be introduced as evidence even if a police officer was not present during the examination
D. The victim is reimbursed for medical examination costs in jurisdictions that have victim compensation laws; in other states, local or state health agencies may cover the costs
E. Rape remains a seriously underreported and recurring crime, which leads to a repeating cycle: No report of the crime leads to no collection of time-sensitive evidence, so there is little opportunity to prosecute the crime. No investigation occurs, so perpetrators are free to offend again
F. The Violence Against Women Act (VAWA) was reauthorized in 2005 and included a provision so that victims of sexual assault could receive a forensic medical exam at no cost
G. Investigators working sex offenses need to be aware that a softer response is often needed for victims of this crime compared with other crimes

VIII. Blind Reporting

A. Blind reporting allows sexual assault victims to retain their anonymity and confidentiality while sharing critical information with law enforcement; it also permits victims to gather legal information from law enforcement without having to commit immediately to an investigation
B. The success of blind reporting hinges on whether trust can be established between the victim and the investigator
C. Six steps law enforcement agencies can take to develop an effective blind reporting system are:

1. Establish and uphold a policy of victim confidentiality
2. Allow victims to disclose as much or as little information as they wish

3. Accept the information whenever victims might offer it—a delay of disclosure is not an indicator of the validity of the statement

4. Develop procedures and forms to facilitate anonymous information from third parties (e.g., examiners)

5. Clarify options with victims for future contact—where, how and under what circumstances they may be contacted by the law enforcement agency

6. Maintain blind reports in separate files from official complaints to prevent inappropriate use

IX. Interviewing the Victim

A. Basic guidelines for victim interviews:

1. Attempt to establish rapport by using sympathetic body language

2. Explain the necessity for asking sensitive questions

3. Attempt to reinforce the victim's emotional well-being, but also obtain facts

4. Both uniformed and investigative personnel, male and female, can help the victim cooperate if they are understanding and supportive

5. Treat the victim with care, concern and understanding

6. Assume that the sexual assault is real unless facts ultimately prove otherwise

7. Determine the location of the interview, and conduct the interview privately

8. Make a complete report of the victim's appearance and behavior, and take photographs to supplement your notes

9. Necessary information to gather includes the victim's name, age, home address, work address, telephone number(s) and any prior relationship with the offender (if the offender is known)

10. Obtain a detailed account of the crime, including the suspect's actions and statements, special characteristics or oddities and any unusual sexual behaviors

11. Determine exactly where and how the attack occurred

12. Determine the exact details of resistance

13. Establish lack of consent

14. Obtain the names of any witnesses

15. Obtain as much information as possible about the suspect

B. Establishing the behavioral profile in sex offense cases

    1. Interview the victim about the rapist's behavior, analyze that behavior to ascertain the motivation underlying the assault and compile a profile of the individual likely to have committed the crime

    2. Three types of rapist behavior

        a. Physical (use of force)
        b. Verbal
        c. Sexual

    3. Three common approaches

        a. Con
        b. Blitz
        c. Surprise

    4. Four common methods of maintaining control

        a. Mere presence
        b. Verbal threats
        c. Display of a weapon
        d. Use of physical force

    5. Four levels of physical force

        a. Minimal
        b. Moderate
        c. Excessive
        d. Brutal

    6. Ask about the offender's verbal behavior (as well as the victim's verbal behavior), about any changes in the offender's behavior and about the offender's experience level

C. Ending the victim interview

    1. Explain available victim assistance services, such as Sexual Offense Services (SOS)

    2. Arrange for relatives, friends or personnel from a rape crisis center to help the victim

    3. Explain what will happen next in the criminal justice system

X. Follow-Up Investigation

A. Interview the victim again in 2 to 5 days to obtain further information and compare the statements

B. Be aware that many prosecutors discourage conducting follow-up interview with sexual assault victims

XI.   Interviewing Witnesses

    A.   Locate witnesses as soon as possible, and obtain their contact information

    B.   Determine whether a relationship exists between the witness and the victim or the offender

    C.   Determine exactly what the witness saw and heard

XII.   Sex Offenders

    A.   Suspects fall into two general classifications: those who know the victim and those who are known sex offenders

    B.   Sexual sadists become more sexually excited the more the victim suffers

    C.   Rapists can be categorized as motivated by either power or anger, and each category is divided into two subcategories

    D.   Many rapists are opportunist sexual predators, and commit their acts because they can

    E.   No personality or physical type can be automatically eliminated as a sex offender

    F.   Significance of fantasy in sexual assaults

        1.   Fantasy is strongly associated with sexual assault

        2.   Search warrant applications should include a list of the materials officers would expect to recover from an offender who indulged in sexual fantasies

        3.   Sexual sadists may be obsessed with keeping trophies and recordings of the assaults; this will determine details for any search warrant applications as well

XIII.   Taking a Suspect into Custody and Interrogation

    A.   If a suspect is apprehended at the scene, record any spontaneous statements made by the suspect and photograph him

    B.   Do not allow communication among suspect, victim and witness

    C.   Remove the suspect from the scene as soon as possible

    D.   When interrogating sex offenders, obtain as much information as possible, yet remain nonjudgmental. Interview the suspect last

    E.   Build rapport with the suspect, and then ask him to tell his side of the story

    F.   Attempt to gain the suspect's confidence

    G.   Keep the possible charged offenses in mind and prepare questions to elicit supporting information

XIV.   Coordination with Other Agencies

   A.   A number of other agencies and individuals assist in handling rape cases

   B.   Rape cases often involve cooperation with medical personnel, social workers, rape crisis center personnel and the news media

XV.   Prosecution of Rape and Statutory Charges

   A.   Few criminal cases are as difficult to prosecute as rape, at least under older laws. Despite changes in the law, it is virtually impossible to obtain a conviction on the victim's testimony alone

   B.   Conviction in sexual assault cases requires

      1.   Medical evidence
      2.   Physical evidence such as torn clothing
      3.   Evidence of injuries
      4.   A complaint that is reported reasonably close to the time of the assault

   C.   Testimony about the victim's previous sexual conduct is not admissible unless

      1.   The victim has had prior sexual relations with the defendant
      2.   There is evidence of venereal disease or pregnancy resulting from the assault
      3.   Circumstances suggest that consent occurred within the calendar year
      4.   The victim has not told the truth or has filed a false report

   D.   Many recent laws have reduced the penalties for sexual assault, which should lead to more convictions

   E.   False reports

      1.   Victims make false reports of sexual assault for a number of reasons, including getting revenge on former lovers, covering up a pregnancy or getting attention
      2.   Victims may file a false report as a way of defending against a lapse in judgment
      3.   The credibility of rape reports is probably questioned more frequently than that of any other felony report
      4.   If the victim admits orally or in writing that her story was false, close the case

XVI.   Civil Commitment of Sex Offenders after Sentences Served

   A.   Because sex offenders have a high recidivism rate following their release from jail or prison, many have called for legislation that allows for the civil commitment of sex offenders upon completion of the sentence

B. Sex offender civil commitment (SOCC) has been enacted in 16 states amid widespread controversy

XVII. Sex Offender Registry and Notification

A. Because of the highly mobile nature of today's society, it is increasingly difficult to monitor these offenders as they move from jurisdiction to jurisdiction, changing their names and appearances along the way. Nonetheless, state and national sex offender registries have proliferated in recent years, as mandated by law

B. The evolution of sex offender registries can be traced to a trilogy of federal statutes

   1. The Jacob Wetterling Act

      a. Jacob Wetterling, 11 years old, was abducted in October 1989 near his home in rural Minnesota and has never been found

      b. The Jacob Wetterling Crimes against Children and Sexually Violent Offender Registration Act was enacted as part of President Bill Clinton's 1994 Crime Act

      c. It required states to establish registration systems for convicted child molesters and other sexually violent offenders

   2. Megan's Law

      a. Megan Kanka, 7 years old, was raped and murdered by a convicted sex offender who lived across the street from Megan's family with two other released sex offenders

      b. Megan's Law, signed by President Clinton in 1996, amends the Jacob Wetterling Act in two ways

         (1) It requires states to release any relevant information about registered sex offenders necessary to maintain and protect public safety

         (2) It allows disclosure of information collected under a state registration program for any purpose permitted under the laws of the state

   3. The Pam Lychner Act

      a. Named for a victims' rights advocate killed in a plane crash in July 1996

      b. Called the Pam Lychner Sexual Offender Tracking and Identification Act, it directed the FBI to establish a national sex offender database

      c. The permanent National Sex Offender Registry File is part of the FBI's National Crime Information Center (NCIC) and includes fingerprint and photo images of registered offenders

C.   In 2006, the Adam Walsh Child Protection and Safety Act was signed into law. Title I of the act was the Sex Offender Registration and Notification Act (SORNA), establishing comprehensive standards for sex offender registration and notification

D.   As of July 2006, all 50 states are included in the National Sex Offender Public Registry (NSOPR) Web site, which incorporates real-time public data on sex offenders around the country, allowing citizens to view registries outside their own states

E.   The challenge is to balance the communities' rights to access public information with the protections provided to convicted offenders

F.   The three basic objections to notification laws center around punishment, privacy and due process issues

    a.   National Association of Criminal Defense Lawyers (NACDL) asserts, "It's a fiction to say that this is a civil matter when this is, in fact, an extension of the criminal punishment" (VanderHart, 2008)

    b.   However, in April 1998, the Supreme Court rejected constitutional challenges that claimed that the laws' notification requirements represented an unconstitutional added punishment

G.   Sex offender registration and notification have more supporters than opponents

H.   In many jurisdictions, residents are now able to access a registry online, enter their zip codes and obtain information on sex offenders living in their area

I.   Some jurisdictions are tracking such offenders through the use of global positioning systems (GPS) or other electronic monitoring devices

J.   Another effort to track released sex offenders is to screen them against motor vehicle databases when they apply for or renew a driver's license

XVIII.   Summary

CRIMES AGAINST CHILDREN

OUTLINE

Chapter 11
Crimes against Children

Key Terms

- chicken hawk
- emotional abuse
- exploitation
- hebephile
- kidnapping
- lewdness
- maltreatment
- mandated reporters
- minor
- misoped
- molestation
- Munchausen syndrome
- Munchausen by proxy syndrome (MBPS)
- neglect
- osteogenesis imperfecta (OI)
- pedophile
- physical abuse
- sexting
- sexual abuse
- sexual exploitation
- sexual seduction
- sudden infant death syndrome (SIDS)
- temporary custody without hearing

Learning Objectives
After reading this chapter, students should be able to

- Describe the crimes that are frequently committed against children.
- Identify the four common types of maltreatment.
- Explain the most common form of child maltreatment and how serious it is.
- Identify the biggest single cause of death of young children.
- Discuss the effects of child abuse.
- Identify the two leading causes of child abuse.
- Describe the three components typically included in child abuse/neglect laws.
- Explain the challenges involved in investigating crimes against children.
- Clarify when a child should be taken into protective custody.
- Discuss which factors to consider in interviewing child victims.
- Determine whether children are generally truthful when talking about abuse.
- Describe who usually reports crimes against children.
- Explain what types of evidence are important in child neglect or abuse cases.
- Identify what things can indicate child neglect or abuse.
- Describe the types of sex rings that exist in the United States related to child abuse and sexual exploitation.
- Explain how a pedophile might typically react to being discovered.
- Describe what the Child Protection Act involves.

(Continued)

• Describe the three law enforcement approaches that are models to combat child sexual exploitation. • Discuss the challenges presented by a missing child report.	• Identify the most common type of child abduction. • Define the AMBER Alert program. • Discuss how crimes against children can be prevented.

Internet Assignments

1. Have students navigate to the U.S. Department of Health and Human Services Web resources on child abuse and neglect at the Child Welfare Information Gateway. Have them select three of the major topics on this site relating to child abuse and neglect and write a brief synopsis of each. Sample topics include:

   • Definitions of child abuse and neglect
   • Identification of child abuse and neglect
   • Prevalence of child abuse and neglect
   • Characteristics of perpetrators
   • Types of child abuse and neglect
   • Risk and protective factors
   • Impact of child abuse and neglect
   • Child fatalities

2. The text refers to many agencies and online organizations that have been developed to raise awareness of child abuse and to prevent crimes against children. Have the students each choose one online resource to research and present to the class. Students should pay attention to the mission of the organization, the information and services it offers, the audience to whom the Web site is directed and how successfully the Web site is organized. Examples of Web sites students may research include, but are not limited to:

   • The Virginia Community Policing Institute
   • Operation: Blue Ridge Thunder
   • AMBER Alert
   • The CyberTipline
   • A Child Is Missing

Class Assignments

1. Have the class discuss the methods they might use to differentiate between a possible child abuse or molestation case and a child neglect case.
2. Have students research and create a list of local resources that can help with child endangerment issues.

Chapter Outline

I.   Maltreatment of Children: Neglect and Abuse

A.   Maltreatment, which means to treat roughly or abuse, exists in many forms and along a continuum of severity and chronicity

B.   Definitions of the various types of maltreatment vary from state to state and even locality to locality, but all are based on minimum standards set by federal law

C.   The federal Child Abuse Prevention and Treatment Act (CAPTA), as amended by the Keeping Children and Families Safe Act of 2003, defines child abuse and neglect as

1.   Any recent act or failure to act on the part of a parent or care-taker which results in death, serious harm, serious physical or emotional harm, sexual abuse or exploitation; or

2.   An act or failure to act that presents an imminent risk of serious harm

D.   The four common types of maltreatment are neglect, physical abuse, emotional abuse and sexual abuse

1.   Neglect is the failure to meet a child's basic needs, including housing, food, clothing, education and access to medical care

a.   This is the most common form of child maltreatment and may be fatal

b.   Often the families from which neglected children come are poor and disorganized, and they have no set routine for family activity

c.   The family unit is often fragmented by death, divorce or the incarceration or desertion of parents

2.   Physical abuse refers to beating, whipping, burning or otherwise inflicting physical harm upon a child. Child abuse has been identified as the biggest single cause of death of young children

3.   Emotional abuse refers to causing fear or feelings of unworthiness in children by such means as locking them in closets, ignoring them or constantly belittling them

4.   Sexual abuse includes sexually molesting a child, performing sexual acts with a child and statutory rape and seduction.

a.   Sexual seduction means ordinary sexual intercourse, anal intercourse, cunnilingus or fellatio committed by a nonminor with a consenting minor

b.   Lewdness means touching a minor to arouse, appeal to or gratify the perpetrator's sexual desires. The touching may be done by the perpetrator or by the minor under the perpetrator's direction

c.   Molestation, which is a broader term referring to any act motivated by unnatural or abnormal sexual interest in minors that would reasonably be expected to disturb, irritate or offend the victim, may or may not involve touching of the victim

II.   The Extent of the Problem

A.   According to the Office for Victims of Crime, one child is reported abused or neglected every 34.9 seconds ("Crime Clock," 2009)

B.   The National Child Abuse and Neglect Data System (NCANDS), a federally sponsored effort that collects and analyzes data on child abuse and neglect and prepares an annual report, reported that during the federal fiscal year 2009:

1.   An estimated 3.3 million referrals were received by Child Protection Services (CPO)

2.   These referrals involved the alleged maltreatment of approximately 6.0 million children

3.   These figures translate into more than 510,000 substantiated or indicated cases of reported child maltreatment in a single year

C.   In 2009, among the children confirmed as victims by CPS agencies:

1.   Victims in the age group of birth to 1 year had the highest rate of victimization at 20.6 per 1,000 children

2.   Victimization was split between the sexes with boys accounting for 48.2 percent and girls accounting for 51.1 percent

3.   Eighty-seven percent were of three races or ethnicities: African American, Hispanic and White

4.   Neglect was the most common form of child maltreatment

III.   Children as Victims of Violent Crime

A.   Data from the National Survey of Children's Exposure to Violence (NatSCEV) in 2009 revealed that in the previous 12 months:

1.   Nearly half of the children and adolescents (46.3 percent) had been assaulted at least once

2.   More than 1 in 10 (10.2%) had been injured in an assault

3.   1 in 4 (24.6%) had been victims of robbery, vandalism or theft

4.   1 in 10 (10.2%) suffered maltreatment, including physical and emotional abuse, neglect or a family abduction

5.   1 in 16 (6.1%) had been sexually victimized

6.   More than 1 in 4 (25.3%) had witnessed a violent act

7.   Approximately 1 in 10 (9.8%) had observed one family member assault another

B. Child fatalities: During 2009,

1. An estimated 1,770 children died because of child abuse or neglect
2. The overall rate of child fatalities was 2.34 deaths per 100,000 children
3. Four-fifths (80.8%) of the children who died because of child abuse and neglect were younger than 4 years old
4. Infant boys had the highest rate of fatalities, at 2.36 deaths per 100,000 boys of the same age in the national population
5. Infant girls had a rate of 2.12 deaths per 100,000 girls of the same age
6. One-third (35.8%) of child fatalities were attributed to neglect exclusively
7. One-third (36.7%) of child fatalities were caused by multiple maltreatment types

C. Child abuse has been identified as the biggest single cause of death of young children
D. Child fatalities may be underreported, perhaps by 50 to 60 percent

IV. The Effects of Child Abuse and Neglect

A. Child abuse and neglect can result in serious and permanent damage

1. Physical damage
2. Emotionial damage

B. Research has also examined the potential correlation between childhood maltreatment and the likelihood of criminality and arrest later in life
C. Another likely effect of child abuse is that as an adult, the former victim frequently becomes a perpetrator of child abuse, thereby creating a vicious circle call the intergenerational transmission of violence

V. Risk Factors for Child Maltreatment

A. Parents or caretakers commit most emotional and physical child abuse
B. Certain risk factors have been found to contribute to increased chance of child maltreatment:

1. Children younger than 4 years of age
2. Special needs that may increase caregiver burden
3. Parents' lack of understanding of children's needs, child development and parenting skills
4. Parents' history of child maltreatment in family of origin
5. Substance abuse and/or mental health issues including depression in the family

6. Parental characteristics such as young age, low education, single parenthood, large number of dependent children and low income
7. Nonbiological, transient caregivers in the home
8. Parental thoughts and emotions that tend to support or justify maltreatment behaviors
9. Social isolation
10. Family disorganization, dissolution and violence, including intimate partner violence
11. Parenting stress, poor parent-child relationships and negative interactions
12. Community violence
13. Concentrated neighborhood disadvantage

VI. Child Abuse and Neglect Laws

    A. Typically child abuse/neglect laws have three components:

        1. Criminal definitions and penalties
        2. A mandate to report suspected cases
        3. Civil process for removing the child from the abusive or neglectful environment

    B. Federal legislation

        1. The Federal Child Abuse Prevention and Treatment Act passed in 1974 and was amended in 1978 and again in 2003

            a. Any of the following elements constitutes a crime: "The physical or mental injury, sexual abuse or exploitation, negligent treatment, or maltreatment of a child under the age of 18, by a person who is responsible for the child's welfare under circumstances that indicate the child's health or welfare is harmed or threatened"
            b. Federal courts have also ruled that parents are free to strike children because "the custody, care and nurture of the child resides first in the parents"
            c. This fundamental right to "nurture" has been supplanted by the Supreme Court with the "care, custody and management" of one's child (*Santosky v. Kramer*, 1982)
            d. Current laws often protect parents, and convictions for child abuse are difficult to obtain because of circumstantial evidence, the lack of witnesses, the husband-wife privilege and the fact that an adult's testimony often is enough to establish reasonable doubt

        2. The Child Abuse Prevention and Enforcement Act (2000) made more funds available for child abuse and neglect enforcement and prevention initiatives

3. The Adam Walsh Child Protection and Safety Act (2006) is aimed at tracking sex crime offenders and subjecting them to stiff, mandatory minimum sentences

C. State laws

1. Since the 1960s, every state has enacted child abuse and neglect laws
2. On the whole, states offer a bit more protection to children by statute than does the federal government
3. Legal definitions vary from state to state

VII. Case Processing

A. Most child abuse and neglect cases enter the child welfare system through CPS agencies
B. The term *child protective services* generally refers to services provided by an agency authorized to act on behalf of a child when parents are unable or unwilling to do so
C. CPS may provide protective custody of a child outside the home or provide protective supervision of the child within the family unit at any point until a case is closed or dismissed

VIII. Challenges in Investigating Maltreatment Cases

A. Challenges in investigating crimes against children include the need to protect the child from further harm, the possibility of parental involvement, the need to collaborate with other agencies, the difficulty of interviewing children and credibility concerns

B. Protecting the child

1. If the possibility of present or continued danger to the child exists, the child must be removed into protective custody
2. Temporary custody without hearing usually means for 48 hours
3. Factors that would justify placing a child in protective custody include:

   a. The child's age or physical or mental condition makes the child incapable of self-protection
   b. The home's physical environment poses an immediate threat to the child
   c. The child needs immediate medical or psychiatric care, and the parents refuse to get it
   d. The parents cannot or will not provide for the child's basic needs
   e. Maltreatment in the home could permanently damage the child physically or emotionally
   f. The parents may abandon the child

C. The need to involve other agencies: the multidisciplinary team approach

    1. Another challenge facing law enforcement is the need to collaborate with various social services, child welfare and health agencies to more effectively handle child abuse cases

    2. A multidisciplinary team (MDT) consists of professionals who work together to ensure an effective response to reports of child abuse and neglect

    3. Several national programs can assist in investigating abandoned or abducted children

        a. The National Children Identification Program provides fingerprint and DNA collection kits to parents.

        b. This identifying information can be provided to law enforcement authorities if needed

    4. The media can help when speed of information dissemination is critical

D. Difficulty in interviewing children

    1. Limited vocabulary of very young children

    2. Development of ability to feel shame, embarrassment and fearin older children

    3. When interviewing children, officers should consider the child's age, ability to describe what happened and the potential for retaliation by the suspect against a child who "tells"

    4. Children have short attention spans

E. Credibility concerns

    1. In most child abuse cases, children tell the truth to the best of their ability

    2. Children frequently lie to get out of trouble, but they seldom lie to get into trouble

    3. A child's motivation for lying may be revenge, efforts to avoid school or parental disapproval, efforts to cover up for other disapproved behavior or, in the case of sexual abuse, an attempt to explain a pregnancy or to obtain an abortion at state expense

IX. The Initial Report

A. Most reports of child neglect or abuse are made by third parties such as teachers, physicians, neighbors, siblings or parents. Seldom does the victim report the offense

B. Mandated reporters includes teachers, school authorities, child care personnel, camp personnel, clergy, physicians, dentists, chiropractors, nurses, psychologists, medical assistants, attorneys and social workers

C. Such a report may be made to the welfare department, the juvenile court or the local police
D. In most states, action must be taken on a report within a specified time, frequently 3 days

X. The Police Response

A. Interviewing abused children

1. Interviewing children requires special skills
2. Often several interviews are necessary to get a complete statement
3. Conduct the interview in private, in the child's or a friend's home or in a small room at a hospital or police station
4. Do not have a family member present. If necessary, have a family member seated out of the child's view to avoid influencing the interview
5. Investigators must maintain rapport
6. Make the child feel comfortable
7. Ask simple, direct, open-ended questions and avoid asking "why" questions
8. Use cognitive interview techniques
9. Do not put words into the child's mouth
10. It may be helpful to use drawing or anatomical dolls to assist the children in describing what happened

B. To assess the child's credibility and competence, use the following criteria:

1. Does the child describe acts or experiences to which a child of his or her age would not normally have been exposed?
2. Does the child describe circumstances and characteristics typical of a sexual assault?
3. How and under what circumstances did the child tell? What were the child's exact words?
4. How many times has the child given the history, and how consistent is it regarding the basic facts of the assault?
5. How much spontaneous information does the child provide? How much prompting is required?
6. Can the child define the difference between the truth and a lie?

C. A program called "Finding Words" trains officers in conducting child interviews and specifically teaches rapport, anatomy identification, touch inquiry, abuse scenarios and closure protocols

1. Building rapport is the critical first step in interviewing children
2. Anatomical identification then follows, using anatomically correct dolls to establish the names a child victim uses for various body parts

3. Good touch, bad touch can be done with the dolls
4. The abuse scenario gives trainees a fictitious abuse report and asks them to construct a plan to interview the victim
5. Finding closure

D. A sample protocol is provided in the text for investigating reports of sexual and physical abuse of children. The excerpt is from the Boulder City (Nevada) Police Department's protocol

XI. Evidence

A. Evidence in child neglect or abuse cases includes the surroundings, the home conditions, clothing, bruises or other body injuries, the medical examination report and other observations
B. Photographs may be the best way to document child abuse and neglect
C. Additional types of evidence that may be obtained in sexual assault cases include photographs, torn clothing, ropes or tapes and trace evidence such as the hair of the offender and the victim and, in some instances, semen
D. Indicators of neglect and abuse may be physical or behavioral or both
E. Neglect indicators:

1. Physical indicators: frequent hunger, poor hygiene, inappropriate dress, consistent lack of supervision, unattended physical problems or medical needs and abandonment
2. Behavioral indicators: begging, stealing (especially food), extending school days by arriving early or leaving late, constant fatigue, listlessness or falling asleep in school, poor performance in school, truancy, alcohol or drug abuse, aggressive behavior, delinquency and stating no one is at home to care for them

F. Emotional abuse indicators:

1. Physical indicators: speech disorders, lags in physical development, general failure to thrive
2. Behavioral indicators: habit disorders, conduct disorders, being physically or emotionally abusive toward others, being persistently disruptive in social settings, sleep disorders, inhibitions in play, obsessions, compulsions, phobias, hypochondria, behavioral extremes, attempted suicide

G. Physical abuse indicators

1. Physical indicators: unexplained bruises or welts, burns, fractures, lacerations, abrasions

2. Behavioral indicators: being wary of adults, being apprehensive when other children cry, extreme aggressiveness or withdrawal, being frightened of parents, being afraid to go home

3. Parental indicators: contradictory explanations for a child's injury; attempts to conceal a child's injury; routine use of harsh, unreasonable discipline; poor impulse control

H. Sexual abuse indicators

    1. Physical indicators: difficulty urinating and irritation, bruising or tearing around the genital or rectal areas; in preteens, venereal disease and pregnancy

    2. Behavioral indicators: unwillingness to change clothes for or participate in physical education classes; withdrawal, fantasy or infantile behavior; bizarre sexual behavior, sexual sophistication beyond the child's age or unusual behavior or knowledge of sex; poor peer relationships; delinquency or running away; reports of being sexually assaulted

    3. Parental indicators: jealousy and overprotectiveness of child

XII. The Suspect

A. Most sexual abuse is committed by persons known to the child

B. Data from the Children's Bureau shows that in 2009:

    1. More than 80 percent of perpetrators of child abuse and neglect were parents

    2. Another 6.3 percent were other relatives of the victim

    3. 4.3 percent were unmarried partners of parents

    4. Women comprised a larger percentage of all perpetrators than men, 53.8 percent compared with 44.4 percent

    5. Nearly 75 percent (73.2 percent) of all perpetrators were younger than age 40

C. The parent as suspect

    1. Munchausen syndrome and Munchausen by proxy syndrome

        a. Munchausen syndrome involves self-induced or self-inflicted injuries

        b. Munchausen by proxy syndrome (MBPS) is a form of child abuse in which a parent or adult caregiver deliberately provides false medical histories, manufactures evidence and causes medical distress in a child

    2. Osteogenesis imperfecta (OI)

        a. A genetic disorder characterized by bones that break easily, often from little or no apparent cause

b. False accusations of child abuse may occur in families with children who have milder forms of OI and/or in whom OI has not previously been diagnosed

3. Sudden infant death syndrome (SIDS)

a. SIDS is a diagnosis by exclusion and is the most frequently determined cause of sudden unexplained infant death (SUID)

b. It is often confused with child abuse

4. Investigating child fatalities

a. Tough questions must be asked to grieving parents or care-givers so the investigator may determine whether the fatality results from an unknown medical condition, an accident or a criminal act

b. The text provides a list of potential witnesses and other information sources

c. The text provides a list of tips and reminders for investiga-tors working possible child fatality cases

d. Successful investigations hinge on three factors

(1) Effectively conducted, well-documented interviews of witnesses

(2) Thorough background checks on every witness and suspect involved in the case

(3) Competent interrogation of the suspect(s)

C. Sex crimes by other children

1. An increasing number of child sex crimes are being committed by other children

2. Some child sex abusers were molested themselves

3. Do not automatically dismiss reports of children committing sex crimes against other children

D. The nonparent suspect

1. Perpetrators other than parents have included babysitters, camp counselors, school personnel, clergy and others

2. Habitual child sex abusers, whether they operate as loners or as part of a sex ring, have been classified into three types:

a. Misoped: the person who hates children, has sex with them and then brutally murders them

b. Hebephile: a person who selects high school–age youths as his or her sex victims

159

      c.   Pedophile: an adult who has either heterosexual or homosexual preferences for young boys or girls of a specific, limited age range; sometimes referred to as a chicken hawk; the most common habitual child sex abuser

XIII.   The Pedophile

    A.   Pedophiles are typically, but not always, white males
    B.   The FBI's Behavioral Science Services Unit identifies and categorizes two types of child predators:

        1.   Situational typology
        2.   Preferential typology

    C.   Pedophiles may obtain and collect photographs of their child victims; maintain diaries of their sexual encounters; collect books, magazines and newspapers on the subject of sexual activity with children; collect lists of people who have similar sexual interests; be members of sex rings

    D.   Child sexual abuse rings

        1.   Adults are usually the dominant leaders, organizers and operators of sex rings
        2.   Many ringleaders use their occupation as the major access route to the child victims
        3.   Sometimes rings are formed by an adult targeting a specific child
        4.   The adult's status in the neighborhood sometimes helps legitimize his or her presence with the children and their parents
        5.   Investigators should be aware of three types of sex rings: solo, transition and syndicated. Certain cults are also involved in the sexual abuse of children

            a.   Solo sex rings are organized primarily by the age of the child. This type of offender prefers to have multiple children as sex objects
            b.   In transition sex rings, experiences are exchanged. Photographs of children and sexual services may be traded or sold
            c.   Syndicated sex rings are well-structured organizations that recruit children, produce pornography, deliver direct sexual services and establish an extensive network of customers

    E.   Ritualistic abuse by satanic cults

        1.   Cults are groups that use rituals or ceremonial acts to draw their members together into a certain belief system

2. When the rituals of a group involve crimes, including child sexual abuse, they become a problem for law enforcement

F. Victimology

1. A bond often develops between offender and victims
2. Children and teens are the perfect victims in that they are often naïve and trusting, and often desire material things
3. Pedophile ring operators are skilled at gaining the continued cooperation and control of their victims through well-planned seduction; they also are skilled at recognizing and temporarily filling the emotional and physical needs of children

G. Offender reactions

1. When the pedophile is discovered, certain reactions are pre-dictable
2. Pedophiles' reactions to being discovered usually begin with complete denial and then progress to minimizing the acts, justifying the acts and blaming the victims. If all else fails, they may claim to be sick

XIV. Commercial Sexual Exploitation

A. Exploitation refers to taking unfair advantage of children or using them illegally. This includes using children in pornography and prostitution. At the federal level, child abuse statutes pertain mainly to exploitation, but they also set forth important definitions that apply to any type of child abuse

B. Sexual exploitation was defined in Public Law 95–225 (1978)

C. Pornography

1. Child pornography is highly developed into an organized, multimillion-dollar industry
2. The Child Protection Act (1984) prohibits child pornography and greatly increases the penalties for adults who engage in it
3. An emerging challenge in the area of child pornography is sexting, sending or posting a nude picture of oneself to another person through the Internet, using a cell phone to transmit the image

D. Internet sex crimes against children

1. Advances in computer technology and the expansion of the Internet have created an entirely new global forum in which sex offenders can access potential victims and distribute or trade child pornography, network with other child abuse perpetrators, promote child sexual tourism and traffic children

2. Online technology has given rise to new terminology used in the investigation of crimes involving this medium:

    a. online victimization
    b. sexual solicitation
    c. aggressive sexual solicitation
    d. unwanted exposure to sexual materials

3. Internet sex crimes against minors can be categorized in three mutually exclusive groups:

    a. Internet crimes against identified victims involving Internet-related sexual assaults and other sex crimes, such as the production of child pornography committed against identified victims
    b. Internet solicitations unknowingly to undercover law enforcement officers posing as minors that involved no identified victims
    c. The possession, distribution or trading of Internet child pornography by offenders who did not use the Internet to sexually exploit identified victims or unknowingly solicit undercover investigators

4. Online predators use chat rooms and newsgroups or bulletin boards to meet their victims
5. The Child Protection and Sexual Predator Punishment Act (1998) prohibits contacting a minor via the Internet to engage in illegal sexual activity and punishes those who knowingly send obscenity to children
6. Several initiatives are aimed at protecting children in cyberspace:

    a. The Office of Juvenile Justice and Delinquency Prevention (OJJDP) funds the Internet Crimes against Children (ICAC) Task Force
    b. The National Center for Missing and Exploited Children (NCMEC) has a congressionally mandated Cyberline, a reporting mechanism for child sexual exploitation
    c. Project Safe Childhood (PSC) empowers federal, state and local law enforcement officers with tools needed to investigate cybercrimes against children

E. Models to combat child sexual exploitation

1. Special task forces
2. Strike forces
3. Law enforcement network

F. Federal agencies working against child pornography

    1. Several federal agencies are involved in combating child pornography:

        a. FBI's Crimes against Children (CAC) unit
        b. U.S. Customs Service
        c. Customs CyberSmuggling Center (C3)

    2. The Innocent Images National Initiative
    3. Internet Crimes against Children Task Forces
    4. CyberTipline

G. International initiatives

    1. In 1996, the First World Congress against Commercial Exploitation of Children adopted a Declaration and Agenda for Action calling upon states to

        a. accord higher priority and adequate resources to action against the commercial exploitation of children
        b. promote stronger cooperation between states and all sectors of society to strengthen families
        c. criminalize, condemn and penalize offenders while ensuring victims are not penalized
        d. review and revise laws, policies, programs, and practices
        e. enforce laws, policies and programs

    2. INTERPOL has established a Standing Working Party (SWP) on Offenses against Minors that seeks to improve international cooperation in preventing and combating child pornography and other forms of child sexual exploitation

H. Prostitution of juveniles

    1. International rings and interstate crime operations traffic young girls to faraway places, promising them employment and money
    2. Runaway and homeless youths are recruited by pimps or engage in "survival sex"
    3. Drug dealers get youths addicted, and then force them to prostitute themselves to receive drugs or have a place to stay
    4. Some parents have advertised and prostituted their children over the Internet
    5. Often the trafficking of children precedes their involvement in prostitution

I. Trafficking of children

   1. Human trafficking often involves school-age children, particularly those not living with their parents, who are vulnerable to coerced labor exploitation, domestic servitude or commercial sexual exploitation

   2. The average age of entry into prostitution is 12 to 14 years old

XV. Missing Children: Runaway or Abducted?

A. A special challenge in cases where a child is reported missing is to determine whether the child has run away or been abducted

B. Runaway children

   1. Many runaways are insecure, depressed, unhappy and impulsive with low self-esteem. Typical runaways report conflict with parents; alienation from them; rejection and hostile control; lack of warmth, affection and parental support

   2. Running away may compound their problems. Many runaways become streetwise and turn to drugs, crime, prostitution or other illegal activities

   3. For 21 percent of the 1.7 million runaway/thrownaway youths, their episode involved physical or sexual abuse at home before leaving or fear of such abuse upon their return

   4. Other problems reported included parental drug and/or alcohol abuse, mental health problems within the family and domestic violence between the parents

C. Abducted children

   1. Abducted children are often kidnapped. Kidnapping is taking someone away by force, often for ransom

   2. The most frequent type of child abduction is parental abduction, often by a parent who has lost custody

D. Investigating a missing child report

   1. First steps:

      a. Verify child is missing
      b. Verify child's custody status
      c. Conduct search of surrounding areas
      d. Evaluate contents and appearance of child's room
      e. Obtain photographs and videotapes of missing child
      f. Enter the missing child into the NCIC Missing Persons File and report it to the NCMEC

2.   Runaways

    a.   Check agency records for recent contact with the child
    b.   Review school records and interview teachers, school personnel and classmates; check contents of the school locker
    c.   Determine whether the child is endangered

3.   Abductions

    a.   Criminal charges against parents: Unlawful Flight to Avoid Prosecution Statute
    b.   More complicated when suspect-parent leaves the country with the child
    c.   Seek assistance of national resources and specialized services, such as the AMBER Alert plan

E.   The AMBER Alert plan

1.   A voluntary partnership between law enforcement and broadcasters to activate an urgent bulletin in the most serious child abduction cases
2.   Created in the Dallas–Fort Worth region in 1996 in response to the death of 9-year-old Amber Hagerman, who was abducted while riding her bicycle in Arlington, Texas, and then brutally murdered
3.   All 50 states now have statewide AMBER Alert plans
4.   The program has helped rescue more than 540 children nationwide

F.   Beyond AMBER alerts

1.   Law enforcement agencies should consider technologies to supplement the AMBER Alert program, such as e-mails to law enforcement agencies, a call to a cell phone, a fax blast, an Internet pop-up window or the A Child Is Missing system

    a.   Whatever system is used, it must be able to be implemented and accessed quickly, as time is of the essence in such cases
    b.   If an abductor is going to murder a child, 74 percent of the time he or she will do so within the first three hours

2.   A child abduction response team (CART)

    a.   The mission of a CART is to bring expert resources to child abduction cases quickly
    b.   Such a team typically consists of seasoned, experienced officers from around the region, each with a preplanned response related to that officer's field of expertise

     c.   Such teams might also include mounted patrol, ATVs, heli-copters and K-9s—whatever resources are readily available

    G.   Additional resources available

        1.   The Missing and Exploited Children's Program provides training and technical assistance to law enforcement, and it conducts research

        2.   The Team HOPE helps families of missing children handle the day-to-day issues of coping by linking victim-parents with experienced and trained parent volunteers who have gone through the experience of having a missing child

XVI.   Children as Witnesses in Court

    A.   Courts have altered some court procedures to accommodate children:

        1.   Some courts give preference to those cases by placing them ahead of other cases

        2.   Some courts permit videotaping child interviews

        3.   Courts are limiting privileges for repeated medical and psychological examinations of children

        4.   To reduce the number of times the child must face the accused, the courts are allowing testimony concerning observations of the child by another person who is not a witness, allowing the child to remain in another room during the trial and/or using videotape

        5.   Some courts remove the accused from the courtroom during the child's testimony

    B.   Many of these changes in rules and procedures are being challenged

    C.   Some studies have provided evidence that courtroom testimony is not always the best way to elicit accurate information from children

XVII. Preventing Crimes against Children

    A.   The text provides a list of signs that a child may be at risk of victimization, particularly by online predators

    B.   Crimes against children may be prevented by educating them about potential danger and by keeping the channels of communication open

    C.   Digital technology is allowing police to become more effective in preventing and handling crimes against children

XVIII. Summary

ROBBERY

OUTLINE

Chapter 12
Robbery

Key Terms

• bait money • carjacking • dye pack	• robbery • Stockholm syndrome

Learning Objectives
After reading this chapter, students should be able to

• Define robbery. • Classify robberies. • Define home invaders. • Define carjacking. • List the types of robbery in which the FBI and state officials become involved. • Identify the elements of the crime of robbery. • Describe the factors to consider in responding to a robbery-in-progress call.	• Explain the special challenges that are posed by a robbery investigation. • Explain how to prove each element of robbery. • Identify what descriptive information is needed to identify suspects and vehicles. • Describe the modus operandi information to obtain in a robbery case. • Identify what physical evidence can link a suspect with a robbery.

Internet Assignments

1. Have students search the Internet for suggestions from security firms and consultants about how bank employees and other business employees should respond in the case of a robbery. Ask students to review the major points made and determine if the suggestions offered differ from what law enforcement officers are trained to do in responding to robberies.

2. Have students search the Web for information on ALPR, GIS and Video Surveillance for the police. Have students choose one technology—either one of these or another they've discovered in their search—and report on how this technology can help police in tracking both criminals and their vehicles.

Class Assignments

1. Describe the following cases to the class and then break the class into groups, asking students to develop suggestions for the investigation of the listed cases.

    A. Three of the fifteen convenience stores in your community have been robbed within the last month, all between 11:00 P.M. and midnight. The same suspect, who was captured on security videotape in two of the robberies but wears a ski mask over his face, is apparently responsible for each. His modus operandi is to enter the store when it is empty, point a gun (revolver) at the clerk and demand all the money in the cash register. The suspect speaks with a stutter and had difficulty getting the words out in one of the robberies. The clerks each say that they smelled alcohol on the suspect. What would you do?

    B. A 24-hour restaurant has been robbed. Shots were fired and one person was shot in the arm. Local business owners are worried and the local newspaper has carried front-page articles each day for the past five days. The only evidence so far is a woolen cap that was found a block away from the store and appears similar to one worn by the robber. Some witnesses claim that the suspect seemed very nervous, and that the shots were fired when the person who was shot made a move toward the suspect. No other information exists. What would you do?

    C. During the past week, every evening at approximately 7:00 P.M., a person on a bicycle has ridden up to a different pedestrian, pointed a knife at the individual, demanded the pedestrian's money and wallet, then ridden away. In each case, the suspect has tossed the wallet on the sidewalk not far from the scene, several times in sight of the victim. The suspect has worn gloves in each case. The robberies have occurred in different parts of town and do not display a consistent pattern as to location at this point. The suspect is male and wears a bike helmet, glasses and bike pants, as well as bike shoes of the type that snap into the peddles of the bike. He is of small build and slight stature and seems to be between 20 and 30 years of age. What would you do?

2. Have students search the Web for information on the Stockholm syndrome. In particular, have them look for Stockholm syndrome, Patty Hearst and Elizabeth Smart. After students have reviewed the three searches, have them break into three groups to discuss the impact of the Stockholm syndrome on each case. What were some commonalities? Were there opportunities for Elizabeth Smart or Patty Hearst to escape?

Chapter Outline

I. Robbery: An Overview

    A.   Robbery is one of the three most violent crimes against the person; only homicide and rape are considered more traumatic to a victim

    B.   Robbery data

        1.   According to the FBI Uniform Crime Reports, there were an estimated 408,217 robberies in the nation in 2009, an 8.0 percent decrease from the 2008 estimate

        2.   Data from the National Crime Victims Survey (NCVS) reports a much higher incidence of robberies—533,790 in 2009, at a rate of 2.1 per 1,000 households

        3.   Other facts about robbery reported in *Crime in the United States 2006* include:

            a.   Robbery accounted for 31.0 percent of all violent crimes in 2009

            b.   The clearance rate for robbery was 28.2 percent in 2009

            c.   By location type, most robberies (42.8 percent) were committed on streets or highways

            d.   The average dollar value of property stolen per robbery offense was $1,244

            e.   By location type, bank robbery had the highest average dollar value taken—$4,029 per offense

            f.   Losses estimated at $508 million were attributed to robberies during 2009

            g.   Firearms were used in 42.6 percent of robberies for which the UCR program received data

        4.   This crime poses a definite hazard to law enforcement officers: "According to the FBI, the number one reason why officers are killed and or assaulted while off duty is intervening in or being the victim of a robbery or robbery attempt" (Rayburn, 2007, p.56)

    C.   Robbery is the felonious taking of another's property, either directly from the person or in that person's presence, through force or intimidation

    D.   Characteristics of robberies:

        1.   Most robbers carry a weapon

        2.   Most robbers make an oral demand for the desired money or property; some robbers present a note rather than speaking

        3.   Most robberies do not result in personal injury

        4.   Hostages are held in some robberies and are used as collateral or protection by robbers

        5.   Robbers use various ruses to get themselves into position for the crime

6. Most robberies are committed by men
7. Most robbers are usually serial criminals and may commit 15 to 25 robberies or more before being apprehended
8. Most robberies are committed by strangers rather than acquaintances
9. Most robberies are committed with the use of stolen cars, stolen motor-vehicle license plates or both
10. Most robberies are committed by two or more people working together
11. The offender lives within 100 miles of the robbery
12. Robberies committed by a lone perpetrator tend to involve lone victims and are apt to be crimes of opportunity
13. Youths committing robberies tend to operate in groups and to use strong-arm tactics more frequently than do adults
14. Less physical evidence is normally found after robberies than in other violent crimes
15. They take much less time than other crimes
16. Middle-aged and older people tend to be the victims

II. Classification

A. Robberies are classified as residential, commercial, street or vehicle driver
B. Residential robberies

1. May occur in hotel or motel rooms, garages, elevators or private homes
2. One type of robber is the home invader. Home invaders are typically young Asian gang members who travel across the country robbing Asian families, especially Asian business owners

C. Commercial robberies

1. Convenience stores, loan companies, jewelry stores, liquor stores, gasoline or service stations and bars are common targets
2. Drugstores may be targeted as a source of narcotics as well as cash
3. Commercial robberies occur most frequently toward the end of the week between 6 P.M. and 4 A.M.
4. Stores with few employees on duty and poor visibility from the street are the most likely targets
5. Many commercial robberies are committed by individuals with criminal records
6. Many robbers of convenience stores are on drugs or rob to pay for drugs, and the majority of convenience store robbers report being under the influence of an intoxicant when they committed their crime
7. Convenience stores that are robbed once are likely to be robbed again

8. About 8 percent of convenience stores account for more than 50 percent of convenience store robberies

9. OSHA lists these recommendations for deterring workplace violence in late-night retail establishments:

   a. Keep the cash-register cash balance low
   b. Provide good lighting outside and inside the store
   c. Elevate the cash-register area so the clerk has better viewing ability and is in sight of passersby

D. Street robberies

1. Most frequently committed in public streets and sidewalks and in alleys and parking lots
2. Street robberies are frequently committed at night and in dimly lit areas
3. Most are committed with a weapon, but some are strong-arm robberies, in which physical force is the weapon
4. The crime is often characterized by its speed and surprise
5. Because most street robberies yield little money, the robber often commits several robberies in one night
6. Victim is often unable to identify the suspect
7. Illegal immigrants are particularly vulnerable

E. Vehicle-driver robberies

1. Drivers of taxis, buses, delivery and messenger vehicles, armored vehicles and personal cars are frequent targets

   a. "Driving a taxi is one of the most dangerous professions" (Petrocelli, 2007a, p.22)

2. Armored-car robberies are usually well planned by professional, heavily armed robbers and involve large amounts of money

   a. In 2010, according to the FBI, there were 48 armored carrier incidents with more than $12.6 million in loot taken, most as cash. A little more than 12 percent of the loot was recovered

3. Drivers of personal cars are often approached in parking lots or at red lights in less-traveled areas

F. Carjacking

1. Carjackings often occur at gas stations, ATMs, car washes, parking lots, shopping centers, convenience stores, restaurants, mass transit stations and intersections requiring drivers to come to a stop
2. Carjacking, a category of robbery, is the taking of a motor vehicle by force or threat of force. The FBI may investigate the crime

3. This type of robbery now covers all types of motor vehicles. The stolen vehicle is then used as in the conventional crime of vehicle theft: for resale, resale of parts, joyriding or use in committing another crime

4. Theories for the sudden increase in carjacking include:

   a. Because of alarms and protective devices on vehicles, it is easier than stealing a vehicle by traditional means
   b. Status is involved in the criminal subculture
   c. Certain groups of young people use it as a way to enhance their image with their cohorts

5. Guidelines to those reporting a carjacking:

   a. Describe the event
   b. Describe the attacker
   c. Describe the attacker's vehicle
   d. Give only that information you absolutely remember—if you are not sure, don't guess

6. The Anti-Car Theft Act (1992) made armed carjacking a federal offense. Automakers must engrave a 17-digit vehicle identification number on 24 parts of every new car

G. Bank robbery

   1. Bank robberies are within the jurisdiction of the FBI, the state and the community in which the crime occurred and are jointly investigated
   2. Technological innovations in searchable video surveillance helps catch robbers with the use of tools such as facial recognition and advanced video searching capabilities
   3. Bank robberies may be committed by rank amateurs as well as habitual criminals. Amateurs are usually more dangerous because they are not as familiar with weapons and often are nervous and fearful
   4. Robbers may appear to act alone inside the bank but most have a getaway car with lookouts posted nearby
   5. The number of branch robberies has increased with the number of branch banks, many of which are housed in storefront offices and outlying shopping centers, thus providing quick entrance to and exit from the robbery scene
   6. Deterrents:

      a. Adding clerks is not necessarily a deterrent, because a person with a gun has the advantage regardless of the number of clerks

        b.   Adding bulletproof glass around the cashier may increase the incidence of hostage taking. This problem has been reduced in some banks by enclosing and securing the bank's administrative areas

        c.   Bait money is U.S. currency with recorded serial numbers placed at each teller position

        d.   A dye pack is a bundle of currency containing a colored dye and tear gas that is activated when the robber crosses an electromagnetic field at the exit

    7.   ATM robberies

        a.   Most ATM robberies are committed by a lone, armed offender acting against a lone victim

        b.   Most ATM robberies occur at night in dimly lit areas, but can occur at any time of the day

III.   Elements of the Crime: Robbery

    A.   Some states have only one degree of robbery; others have multiple degrees; in most state statutes common elements exist

    B.   The elements of the crime of robbery are:

        1.   the wrongful taking of personal property

        2.   from the person or in the person's presence

        3.   against the person's will by force or threat of force

IV.   Responding to a Robbery-in-Progress Call

    A.   When responding to a robbery-in-progress call:

        1.   Proceed as rapidly as possible, but use extreme caution

        2.   Assume that the robber is at the scene, unless otherwise advised

        3.   Be prepared for gunfire

        4.   Look for and immobilize any getaway vehicle you discover

        5.   Avoid a hostage situation if possible

        6.   Make an immediate arrest if the suspect is at the scene

    B.   Automatic license plate recognition (ALPR) systems can be of great assistance in identifying a stolen vehicle that might be serving as a getaway car

V.   Hostage Situations

    A.   The priorities in a hostage situation are to:

        1.   Preserve life

        2.   Apprehend the hostage taker

        3.   Recover or protect property

B. Direct assault should be considered only if there has already been a killing or if further negotiations would be useless
C. The average length of hostage situations is approximately 12 hours
D. To successfully resolve a hostage situation, special weapons and tactics (SWAT) teams and crisis negotiation teams (CNTs) need to work together
E. Usually there is no need to rush and proceed with direct contact. Passage of time can:

   1. Provide the opportunity for face-to-face contact with the hostage taker
   2. Allow the negotiator to attempt to establish a trustful rapport
   3. Permit mental, emotional and physical fatigue to operate against a hostage taker
   4. Increase the hostage taker's needs for food, water, sleep and elimination
   5. Increase the possibility of the hostage taker's reducing demands to reasonable compliance levels
   6. Allow hostage-escape possibilities to occur
   7. Provide for more rational thinking, in contrast to the emotionalism usually present during the initial stage of the crime
   8. Lessen the hostage taker's anxiety and reduce his or her adrenalin flow, allowing more rational negotiations
   9. Allow for important intelligence gathering concerning the hostage taker, hostages, layout, protection barriers and needed police reinforcement

F. One disadvantage of the passage of time is that it could possibly foster the Stockholm syndrome, which occurs when hostages report that they have no ill feelings toward the hostage takers and, further, they feared the police more than they feared their captors
G. Negotiation

   1. Negotiator should have street knowledge and experience with hostage incidents
   2. In some cases, a trained clinical psychologist may be called to the scene, not as a negotiator but as a consultant regarding possible behavioral deviations of the hostage taker
   3. Face-to-face negotiations are ideal because they provide the best opportunity for gathering knowledge about and personally observing the hostage taker's reactions
   4. Negotiable items may include food and drink (but not liquor, unless it is known that liquor would lessen the hostage taker's anxieties rather than increase them), money, media access and reduced penalties
   5. Transportation is generally not negotiable because of the difficulty in monitoring and controlling the situation

6. Police departments should establish policies regarding hostage negotiations in advance. A general rule, however, is that nothing should be granted to a hostage taker unless something is received in return

7. A wounded suspect presents an especially dangerous situation

VI. The Preliminary Investigation and Special Challenges

A. Three major problems occur in dealing with robberies:

1. Robberies are usually not reported until the offenders have left the scene

2. The rapidity of the crime makes it difficult to obtain good descriptions or positive identification from victims and witnesses

3. The items taken, usually currency, are difficult to identify

B. Officers often arrive at the scene just after the suspect has fled

C. After taking care of emergencies, broadcast initial information about the suspect, the getaway vehicle and the direction of travel

D. Conduct an immediate canvass of the neighborhood because the suspect may be hiding nearby

E. Robbery usually leaves victims and witnesses feeling vulnerable and fearful, making it difficult for them to give accurate descriptions and details of what occurred. Be patient

VII. Proving the Elements of the Offense

A. Know the elements of robbery in your jurisdiction

B. Most states have three elements for the crime of robbery:

1. Was personal property wrongfully taken?

a. Determine the legal owner of the property taken. Describe completely the property and its value

2. Was property taken from the person or the person's presence?

a. Record the exact words, gestures, motions or actions the robber used to gain control of the property

3. Was property taken against the person's will by force or the threat of force?

a. Obtain a complete description of the robber's words, actions and any weapon used or threatened to be used

C. Record in your notes descriptions of any injuries to the victim or witnesses. Photograph the injuries if possible

VIII. The Complete Investigation

    A. Most robberies are solved through prompt actions by the victim, witnesses and the police patrolling the immediate area or by police at checkpoints

    B. Identifying the suspect: Obtain information about the suspect's general appearance, clothing, disguises, weapon and vehicle

    C. Establishing the modus operandi:

        1. Type of robbery
        2. Time (day and hour)
        3. Method of attack (real or threatened)
        4. Weapon
        5. Number of robbers
        6. Voice and words
        7. Vehicle used
        8. Peculiarities
        9. Object sought

    D. Physical evidence that can connect a suspect with a robbery includes fingerprints, DNA, shoe prints, tire prints, restraining devices, discarded garments, fibers and hairs, a note and the stolen property

    E. Mapping robbery has proven successful, since robbery is inherently serial

IX. False Robbery Reports

    A. Investigators need to rule out the probability that a robbery report is false

    B. Indicators of a false report include:

        1. Unusual delay in reporting the offense
        2. Amount of the loss not fitting the victim's apparent financial status
        3. Lack of correspondence with the physical evidence
        4. Improbable events
        5. Exceptionally detailed or exceptionally vague description of the offender
        6. Lack of cooperation

X. Summary

BURGLARY

OUTLINE

- Burglary versus Robbery
- Classification
- Elements of the Crime: Burglary
- Establishing the Severity of the Burglary
- Elements of the Crime: Possession of Burglary Tools
- The Burglar
- Responding to a Burglary Call
- The Preliminary Investigation
- Determining Entry into Structures
- Determining Entry into Safes and Vaults
- Obtaining Physical Evidence
- Modus Operandi Factors
- Effective Case Management
- Recovering Stolen Property
- The Offense of Receiving Stolen Goods
- Preventing Burglary

Chapter 13
Burglary

Key Terms

• blowing a safe • burglary • burning a safe • chopping a safe • commercial burglary • crime prevention through environmental design (CPTED) • dragging a safe • fence • hit-and-run burglary • peeling a safe	• presumptive evidence • pulling a safe • punching a safe • residential burglary • routine activity theory • safe • smash and grab • target hardening • vault • verified response policy

Learning Objectives
After reading this chapter, students should be able to

• Define burglary. • Identify the basic difference between burglary and robbery. • Explain the two basic classifications of burglary. • Identify three elements that are present in laws defining burglary. • Describe what additional elements can be included in burglary. • Explain what determines the severity of a burglary. • Identify the elements of the crime of possession of burglary tools. • Explain how to proceed to a burglary scene and what to do on arrival.	• Describe the most frequent means of entry to commit burglary. • Explain how safes are broken into. • Describe what physical evidence is often found at a burglary scene. • Identify what modus operandi factors are important in burglary. • Explain where to search for stolen property. • Define the elements of the offense of receiving stolen goods. • Describe what measures may be taken to prevent burglary.

Internet Assignment

Have students perform a Web search for burglary prevention suggestions. Ask them to compare the content of at least two sites with the text and determine what is missing from the text and/or the Web sites. Have students compile a list of suggestions for law enforcement officers based on what they read.

Class Assignment

Ask students to analyze each of the burglary cases listed below and have them indicate what actions they would take.

a.   A 35-year-old male has been arrested by patrol officers. He was caught breaking into a place of business that appeared to be deserted. However, the owner happened to be in the back office, where he had fallen asleep going over the accounts after work. The owner took a baseball bat to the suspect, knocking him out. The suspect had glass cutters, wore gloves and carried a briefcase. What type of burglar is this suspect? What actions should be taken?

b.   A 54-year-old female was arrested outside of a business when a silent alarm went off, alerting an officer in the area. He found her prying at a side door using a crowbar. While it is unusual that a female rather than a male has been arrested for this crime, should the investigators handle this case any differently? What actions should be taken?

c.   A 19-year-old male was arrested during a response to a home burglary in an upper-income area of the community. The youth is from a neighboring community but attends college in the town. The officers have to chase the suspect on foot and wrestle him to the ground to arrest him. He is defiant, has asked for an attorney and claims that the officers beat him up when they arrested him. There have been a series of burglaries in the area, but each with a slightly different MO. What actions should the investigators take with this individual and the case?

Chapter Outline

I.   Burglary versus Robbery

   A.   Burglary

      1.   Burglary is the unlawful entry of a structure to commit a crime
      2.   The word *burglar* comes from the German words *burg,* meaning "house," and *laron,* meaning "thief"; thus the meaning "house thief"
      3.   According to the FBI, an estimated 2,199,125 burglary offenses occurred throughout the nation during 2009, a decrease of 1.3 percent from 2008
      4.   Burglary offenses made up 23.6 percent of all property crimes reported in 2009
      5.   Of these, law enforcement cleared 12.5 percent by arrest or exceptional means
      6.   Burglary offenses cost victims an estimated $4 billion in lost property, with the average dollar loss per burglary being $2,096
      7.   Although the number of burglaries in 2009 had increased by 7.2 percent from 2000, this crime has shown a general decline over the past three decades

8. Several reasons for the overall 30-year decline in burglaries include improvements in locks and burglar alarm technology, as well as the growing use of private security

B. Burglary versus Robbery

1. Burglary differs from robbery in that burglars are covert, seeking to remain unseen, whereas robbers confront their victims directly
2. Burglary is a crime against property; robbery is a crime against a person
3. Most burglaries are not solved at the crime scene but through subsequent investigation

II. Classification

A. Residential burglaries

1. Residential burglaries occur in buildings, structures or attachments that can be used as dwellings, even if unoccupied at the time

a. Nearly three-fourths of all burglaries are residential burglaries (72.6 percent in 2009)
b. Of these, nearly half took place during the day

2. The routine-activity theory proposes that crime results from the simultaneous existence of three elements:

a. the presence of likely or motivated offenders
b. the presence of suitable targets
c. an absence of guardians to prevent the crime

B. Burglary at single-family house construction sites

1. The two primary reasons for burglary at single-family house construction sites is the high cost of construction materials and lax builder practices
2. Amateur opportunists and professional thieves alike take advantage of unprotected construction sites

C. Commercial burglaries

1. A commercial burglary is one that involves churches, schools, barns, public buildings, shops, offices, stores, factories, warehouses, stables, ships or railroad cars
2. In contrast to residential burglaries, most commercial burglaries take place after-hours, either at night (58.7 percent at nightaccording to the FBI) or on weekends, whenever the establishment is closed
3. Commercial burglaries are often committed by two or more people

III. Elements of the Crime: Burglary

    A.   Although burglary laws vary from state to state, statutes of all states include three key elements:

        1.   Entering a structure

            a.   Breaking into a window and taking items from the window display is called a smash and grab

            b.   Entry also includes remaining in a store until after closing time and then committing a burglary

        2.   Without the consent of the person in possession

            a.   Entering a *public* place is done with consent unless consent has been expressly withdrawn

            b.   The hours for legal entry usually are posted on public buildings

        3.   With intent to commit a crime

            a.   Regardless of whether the burglary is planned well in advance or committed on the spur of the moment, intent must be shown

            b.   When the first two elements are present, the third is often presumed present; that is, if a person enters a structure without the owner's consent, the presumption is that it is to commit a crime, usually larceny or a sex offense

    B.   Elements of burglary can also include breaking into the dwelling of another during the nighttime

        1.   Breaking into

            a.   Actual "breaking" is a matter of interpretation. Any force used during a burglary to enter or leave the structure, even if a door or window is partly opened or closed, constitutes breaking

            b.   Breaking and entering is strong presumptive evidence that a crime is intended. That is, it provides a reasonable basis for belief

        2.   The dwelling of another

            a.   Some states still require that the structure broken into be a dwelling, that is, a structure suitable for sheltering people

            b.   This remnant from common law restricts burglary to residential burglaries

3. During the nighttime

    a. Common law also specified that burglary occur under the cover of darkness, an element still retained in some state statutes.

    b. *Nighttime* is defined as the period from sunset to sunrise as specified by official weather charts

IV. Establishing the Severity of the Burglary

A. Most burglary laws increase the crime's severity if the burglar possesses a weapon or an explosive

B. A burglary's severity is determined by:

    1. the presence of dangerous devices in the burglar's possession, or

    2. the value of the property stolen

V. Elements of the Crime: Possession of Burglary Tools

A. A companion crime to burglary is possession of burglary tools, an offense separate from burglary

B. The charge of possession of burglary tools can be made even if a burglary has not been committed if circumstances indicate that the tools were intended for use in a burglary

C. Elements of the crime of possessing burglary tools include possessing any device, explosive or other instrumentality, with intent to use or permit its use to commit burglary

D. Burglary tools include:

    1. Nitroglycerin or other explosives

    2. Any engine, machine, tool, implement, chemical or substance designed for the cutting or burning open of buildings or protective containers

    3. A large number of automobile keys, portable key cutters, codes and key blanks

    4. Slam pullers and bump keys

E. Many people, especially mechanics and carpenters, have tools that might be used in a burglary in their car or on their person, so circumstances must clearly show intent to use or allow their use in committing a crime

VI. The Burglar

A. Most amateur burglars are between the ages of 15 and 25. They are unskilled, and usually steal radios, televisions, cash and other portable property

B. Most professional burglars are 25 to 55 years of age. They usually steal furs, jewelry and more valuable items and have been trained by other professional burglars

VII.   Responding to a Burglary Call

    A.   Proceed to a burglary scene quietly. Be observant and cautious at the scene

    B.   Search the premises inside and outside for the burglar

    C.   False burglar alarms

        1.   Data from the U.S. Justice Department indicates that 96 percent of all burglar alarm activations are false

        2.   Some law enforcement agencies have implemented a verified response policy, meaning that they will not respond to a burglary alarm unless criminal activity is first confirmed through either an onsite security officer or some method of electronic surveillance, such as closed-circuit television

        3.   An aggressive form of verified response is Enhanced Call Verification (ECV), which requires that a minimum of two phone calls be made from the alarm monitoring center, to assess whether user error activated the alarm

        4.   Another approach that departments are taking is to use an escalating series of fines and fees for police dispatch when the alarm turns out to be false

        5.   False alarms are a waste of time for responding officers, and more importantly, they may cause officers to be caught off guard when a genuine alarm occurs

VIII.   The Preliminary Investigation

    A.   The preliminary investigation is most critical

    B.   Preliminary investigation of residential burglaries should include the following steps as a minimum:

        1.   Contact the resident(s)

        2.   Establish points and methods of entry and exit

        3.   Collect and preserve evidence

        4.   Determine the type and amount of loss, with complete descriptions

        5.   Describe the MO

        6.   Check for recent callers such as friends of children, salespeople and maintenance people

        7.   Canvass the neighborhood for witnesses, evidence, discarded stolen articles and so on

    C.   Preliminary investigation of commercial burglaries should include the following steps as a minimum:

        1.   Contact the owner

        2.   Protect the scene from intrusion by the owner, the public and others

        3.   Establish the point and method of entry and exit

        4.   Locate, collect and preserve possible evidence

        5.   Narrow the time frame of the crime

6.   Determine the type and amount of loss
7.   Determine who closed the establishment, who was present at the time of the crime and who had keys to the establishment
8.   Describe the MO
9.   Identify employees' friends, maintenance people and any possible disgruntled employees or customers
10.   Rule out a faked or staged burglary for insurance purposes

D.   Fake burglaries

1.   Do not overlook the possibility of faked burglaries, especially in commercial burglaries
2.   Check the owner's financial status

IX.   Determining Entry into Structures

A.   Jimmying is the most common method of entry used in burglaries
B.   The hit-and-run burglary, also called "smash and grab," is most frequently committed by younger, inexperienced burglars
C.   Burglars use "code grabbers" to record and replicate the electronic signal emitted from an automatic garage door opener and use it to gain access to a house that way

X.   Determining Entry into Safes and Vaults

A.   A safe is semi portable strongbox with a combination lock. The size of the safe or lock does not necessarily correlate with its security
B.   A vault is a stationary room of reinforced concrete, often steel lined, with a combination lock
C.   Safes and vaults are entered illegally by punching, peeling, chopping, pulling, blowing and burning. Sometime burglars simply haul the safe away

1.   Punching: the dial is sheared from the safe door, exposing the safe mechanism spindle
2.   Peeling: a hole is drilled in a corner of the safe, and then enlarged using other drills until the narrow end of a jimmy can be inserted into the hole to pry the door partially open
3.   Chopping: a heavy instrument is used to chop a hole in the bottom of the safe large enough to remove the contents
4.   Pulling (also called dragging): a V plate is inserted over the dial and then tightened until the dial and spindle are pulled out. This method works on many older safes but not on newer ones
5.   Blowing: a hole is drilled in the safe near the locking bar area, or cotton is pushed into an area of the safe door crack, and nitroglycerin is put on the cotton, which is then exploded. This method is noisy and dangerous and is rarely used
6.   Burning: the use of a portable safecracking tool called a burning bar that burns a hole into the safe

D. Modern safes are more resistant to all of these methods because they do not have spindles and cannot be punched, peeled or pulled. Safes of newer steel alloys are highly resistant to burning and drilling

XI. Obtaining Physical Evidence

A. Most burglars are convicted on circumstantial evidence. Any physical evidence at the burglary scene is of utmost importance

B. Physical evidence at a burglary scene includes fingerprints, footprints, tire prints, tools, tool marks, broken glass, paint chips, safe insulation, explosive residue and personal possessions

C. DNA is also becoming important in burglary investigations. If a burglar gets cut breaking into a structure, he or she may leave blood behind that can be analyzed for DNA, perhaps linking the burglary to others

XII. Modus Operandi Factors

A. Important factors of the MO include the time, type of victim, type of premises, point and means of entry, type of property taken and any peculiarities of the offense

B. MO factors can tie several burglaries to one suspect

C. Check the MO with local files, talk to other officers, inquire at other agencies within a 100-mile radius and discuss the case at area investigation meetings

XIII. Effective Case Management

A. Because burglary is predominantly a serial crime, the serial burglar should be the primary target of the burglary unit

B. Using the computer's search capabilities, information retrieval is fast and simple

C. Effective case management recognizes the mobility of burglars and makes assignments based on MO rather than geographical location

D. The rise in narcotics and other prescription drug thefts from pharmacies has led to the creation of a new national database called Rx Pattern Analysis Tracking Robberies and Other Losses (RxPATROL)

XIV. Recovering Stolen Property

A. Stolen property is disposed of in many ways. Some burglars may sell items on the street, to pawnshops or to others, such as people who deal in stolen goods. For anonymity, Internet auction sites are very popular as a method of unloading stolen property

B. Check with pawnshops, secondhand stores, flea markets, online auction sites and informants for leads in recovering stolen property

C. Recovering stolen property and returning it to the rightful owner is aided by Operation Identification programs

D. Technology innovation: JustStolen.net is a Web site where people can register the name, model, serial number, photos and other details of their valued property

XV.   The Offense of Receiving Stolen Goods

    A.   A go-between who receives stolen goods for resale is referred to as a fence

    B.   The elements of the offense are receiving, buying or concealing stolen or illegally obtained goods, knowing them to be stolen or otherwise illegally obtained

    C.   Sting operations

        1.   The police legally establish a fencing operation to catch individuals who purchase stolen goods for resale

        2.   The shop is run for two to three months and then discontinued

        3.   Arrest warrants are then issued for those implicated during the store's operation

XVI.   Preventing Burglary

    A.   Premises that are burglarized are likely to be burglarized again

    B.   Homes without security systems are about three times more likely to be broke into than are homes with security systems

    C.   Target hardening, also known as crime prevention through environmental design (CPTED), involves altering the physical characteristics of property to make it less attractive to criminals

    D.   Measures to deter burglaries include:

        1.   Install adequate locks, striker plates and doorframes

        2.   Install adequate indoor and outdoor lighting

        3.   Provide clearly visible addresses

        4.   Eliminate bushes or other obstructions to windows

        5.   Secure any skylights or air vents over 96 square inches

        6.   Install burglarproof sidelight window glass beside doors

        7.   Install a burglar alarm

        8.   Keep dogs on the premises

XVII.   Summary

LARCENY/THEFT, FRAUD AND WHITE-COLLAR CRIME

OUTLINE

Chapter 14
Larceny/Theft, Fraud and White-Collar Crime

Key Terms

- confidence game
- corporate crime
- cramming
- economic crime
- embezzlement
- flaggers
- floor-release limit
- fluffing
- forgery
- fraud
- goods
- gouging
- grand larceny
- holder
- identity theft
- integration
- jamming
- larceny/theft
- layering

- leakage
- long-con games
- money laundering
- parallel proceedings
- petty larceny
- placement
- poaching
- Ponzi scheme
- property
- property flipping
- short-con games
- shrinkage
- slamming
- sliding
- smurfing
- structuring
- white-collar crime
- zero floor release

Learning Objectives
After reading this chapter, students should be able to

- Differentiate larceny from burglary and robbery.
- Describe the elements of larceny/theft.
- Compare the two major categories of larceny and describe how to determine them.
- Describe what legally must be done with found property.
- Define the common types of larceny.
- Discuss whether a shoplifter must leave the premises before being apprehended.

- Explain when the FBI would become involved in a larceny/theft investigation.
- Define what fraud is and how it differs from larceny/theft.
- Discuss the common means of committing fraud.
- Clarify the common types of check fraud.
- Explain what the elements of the crime of larceny by debit or credit card are.

(Continued)

• Describe what form of larceny/theft headed the FTC's top 10 consumer fraud complaints in 2006. • Define white-collar crime and explain what offenses are often included in this crime category. • Discuss the FBI's two-pronged approach to investigating money laundering.	• Describe the main problems in prosecuting environmental crime. • Explain how the monetary loss value of certain thefts, frauds or other economic crimes influences which agency has jurisdiction over a criminal investigation.

Internet Assignments

1. Have students search the FBI's Web site for its Art Theft Program. Ask students to review the Web site and write a short report about new trends in art theft, including new methods of theft, new types of art thieves, types of art that seem to be increasingly targeted for theft and new methods for preventing art theft.
2. Have students search the Internet for examples of white-collar crime committed in the United States. Resources might include news agencies and consumer protection Web sites. Are any additional methods being employed beyond what is described in the text? Are the agencies involved in investigating and prosecuting any different from those described in the text?
3. Ask students to visit the FTC Bureau of Consumer Protection Web site. Have the students report on the mission of the Bureau and present a sampling of issues that are addressed on the Web site. Examples might include medical identity theft, free trial offers and mortgage marketplace information, to name a few.

Class Assignments

1. Divide the class into groups and assign each group one specific type of theft (mail theft, credit card theft, art theft, etc.) discussed in the text. Ask each group to list the actions they would take as an investigator to solve the problem of their particular theft type if the same offender were committing it in more than one jurisdiction.
2. Have students bring in a recent newspaper or magazine article on a recent local larceny or theft case. Try to make them as local as possible. Have students swap the materials, write a brief synopsis of the case as a crime report and then discuss what the most important elements of the case are and how they would write a report for prosecution. What areas would be important?

    If possible, obtain the local police officer's report on a similar case (deleting confidential information) to demonstrate the differences between a news account and actual crime reports and arrest reports.

Chapter Outline

I.   Larceny/Theft: An Overview

A.   Larceny/theft is the unlawful taking, carrying, leading or driving away of property from the possession of another. It is committed though the cunning, skill and criminal design of the professional thief or as a crime of opportunity committed by the rank amateur

B.   Both larceny and burglary are crimes against property, but larceny, unlike burglary, does not involve illegally entering a structure. Larceny differs from robbery in that no force or threat of force is involved

C.   National statistics

1.   Reported larceny/thefts exceed the combined total of all other Index crimes. Data from the FBI indicates that two-thirds of all property crimes in 2009 were larceny/thefts

2.   An estimated 6.3 million thefts occurred nationwide, a 4.0 percent decrease from 2008 and a 9.2 percent decrease from 2000. The Office for Victims of Crime's "Crime Clock" (2009) reports that one home is victimized by theft every 4.8 seconds

3.   The National Crime Victimization Survey (NCVS) reported 113,210 personal thefts (pickpocketing, purse snatching) in 2009, at a rate of 0.5 per 1,000 households, and 11,709,830 other thefts, at a rate of 95.7 per 1,000 households

4.   The average value of property stolen was $864 per offense, for an estimated $5.5 billion in lost property in 2009

5.   Nationwide, law enforcement cleared 21.5 percent of all reported larceny/thefts in 2009

6.   Typically, there must be either interstate involvement and/or a loss exceeding a minimum financial threshold of $250,000 for federal investigators to take the case

II. Elements of the Crime: Larceny/Theft

A.   The basic elements of the crime of larceny/theft are similar in the statutes of every state. These elements are the felonious stealing, taking, carrying, leading or driving away of another's personal goods or property, valued above (grand) or below (petty) a specified amount, with the intent to permanently deprive the owner of the property or goods

B.   Felonious stealing, taking, carrying, leading or driving away

1.   This element requires an unlawful, wrongful or felonious removal of the property; that is, the property is removed by any manner of stealing

C. The personal goods or property of another

    1. *Goods* or *property* refers to all forms of tangible property, real or personal

    2. *Another* refers to an individual, a government, a corporation or an organization

D. Of a value above or below a specified amount

    1. Value determines whether the offense is grand or petty larceny

    2. Value refers to the market value at the time of the theft

    3. Value is determined by replacement cost, legitimate market value, value listed in government property catalogs, fair market value or reasonable estimates

E. With the intent to permanently deprive the owner of the property or goods

    1. Intent either exists at the time the property was taken or is formed afterward

    2. Intent is usually the most difficult element to prove

    3. Ownership can be established through documents of purchase, statements describing how the property was possessed, the length of time of possession and details of the delegation of care and control to another by the true owner

III. Classification of Larceny/Theft

A. Grand larceny

    1. A felony

    2. Usually more than $100

B. Petty larceny

    1. A misdemeanor

    2. Usually less than $100

IV. Found Property

A. In most states, taking found property with the intent to keep or sell it is a crime

B. Although the finder has possession of the property, it is not legal possession

    1. Thieves apprehended with stolen property often claim to have found it—an invalid excuse

    2. A reasonable effort must be made to find the owner of the property

    3. If the owner is not located after reasonable attempts are made to do so and after a time specified by law, the finder of the property can legally retain possession of it

V. The Preliminary Investigation

    A. Investigating larceny/theft is similar to investigating a burglary, except that in a larceny/theft even less physical evidence is available because no illegal or forcible entry occurred

    B. Physical evidence might include empty cartons or containers, empty hangers, objects left at the scene, footprints and fingerprints

VI. Types of Larceny/Theft

    A. Common types of larceny are pocket picking and purse snatching; bicycle theft; theft from motor vehicles; mail theft; retail shrinkage, including employee theft, shoplifting and organized retail crime; and jewelry theft

    B. Pickpockets and purse snatchers

        1. Difficult to apprehend because the victim must identify the thief

        2. These thieves use force if necessary but generally rely instead on their skills of deviousness and stealth to avoid the use of force and evade identification

        3. These types of thefts are sometimes called *distraction thefts* because of how the offender gains access to the victim's property. The two necessary elements of this crime are a distraction followed by an extraction, the actual theft

        4. Purse snatching may be a larceny/theft or a robbery depending on whether force is used

        5. As a general rule, investigators should determine whether the victim experienced any sensation of force being used because any force, no matter how slight, would satisfy the element of robbery

    C. Bicycle theft

        1. As bicycles have increased in popularity, so has bicycle theft. More than 1.5 million bicycles, worth an estimated $200 million, are stolen each year in the United States

        2. Almost 50 percent of all stolen bicycles are recovered every year by law enforcement, but only 5 percent are returned to their owners because most bikes are unregistered

        3. Bicycles are most frequently stolen from schoolyards, college campuses, sidewalk parking racks, driveways and residential yards

        4. Juveniles are responsible for the majority of thefts, although some professional bike theft rings operate interstate, even exporting stolen bicycles out of the country. A juvenile apprehended for a single theft can be prosecuted, especially with a prior record of similar or other offenses

5. In some bicycle thefts, the crime is grand larceny because of the high value of the stolen bike

6. A single bike theft is best investigated by the patrol force. Determine the bicycle's value and have the owner sign a complaint

7. Bike thefts are entered into the police computer system. Patrol officers are given a bike "hot sheet" similar to that for stolen vehicles and periodically check bike racks at parks, schools and business areas against this sheet

8. Bikes are sometimes reported stolen to defraud insurance companies. Even if the bike is recovered, the owner has already collected its value, and there will seldom be a prosecution

9. Large numbers of thefts in a short time may indicate an interstate ring has moved into the community

10. Identification of bicycles is difficult because of

   a. failure to have a registration system or to use one that exists
   b. the complex method of providing serial numbers
   c. the fact that stolen bikes are often altered, dismantled, repainted and resold

D. Theft from motor vehicles

   1. Though largely unreported, these thefts still account for at least one-third of all larcenies reported to police
   2. Thefts from cars usually involve a small amount of property value, but put a large strain on police resources

E. Mail theft

   1. Thieves may target mailboxes because many households receive government assistance checks, credit card applications or credit cards. Additionally, millions of people leave their bills, accompanied by checks, for pickup in their mailboxes
   2. Thieves known as *flaggers* go around neighborhoods targeting mailboxes with their flags up, searching for envelopes containing checks and other forms of payment. Thieves may also raid the large blue mailboxes
   3. Mail theft is a felony-level federal offense and is investigated by the U.S. Postal Service (USPS) Postal Inspectors. In 2010 USPS Postal Inspectors arrested more than 6,000 mail theft suspects

F. Retail shrinkage: employee theft, shoplifting and organized retail crime

   1. *Shrinkage* refers to the unexplained or unauthorized loss of inventory, merchandise, cash or any other asset from a retail establishment because of employee theft, shoplifting, organized retail crime, administrative errors and vendor fraud

    a.   According to the *2009 National Retail Security Survey,* retail losses were $33.5 billion or 1.44 percent of sales, a decrease from the 1.51 percent reported in 2008

    b.   According to the survey, most retail shrinkage—an estimated $14.4 billion—was caused by employee theft, representing almost half the losses

    c.   Shoplifting accounted for $11.7 billion of shrinkage, more than one-third of losses (35 percent)

    d.   Other losses were from administrative errors ($4.9 billion and 14.5 percent of shrinkage) and vendor fraud ($1.3 billion and 3.8 percent of shrinkage)

    e.   The survey also found that organized retail crime (ORC) was gaining more awareness within the retail industry

2.   Employee theft: Most any retail company's shrinkage is more generally due to internal employee theft rather than shoplifting by outsiders

3.   Shoplifting, also known as *boosting,* involves taking items from retail stores without paying for them

    a.   It is usually committed by potential customers in the store during normal business hours

    b.   It does *not* include thefts from warehouses, factories or other retail outlets or thefts by employees

    c.   Shoplifting is rising at many retail chains, and the prime cause is the sputtering economy. In the past, much of shoplifting was done to support a drug habit, but in the current economy, everyday items, such as groceries, are being stolen

4.   Elements of larceny by shoplifting

    a.   Intentionally taking or carrying away, transferring, stealing, concealing or retaining possession of merchandise or altering the price of the merchandise

    b.   Without the consent of the merchant

    c.   With intent to permanently deprive the merchant of possession or of the full purchase price

    d.   Altering the price of an item is considered larceny

    e.   It is usually not required that the person leave the premises with the stolen item before apprehension

    f.   Shoplifting can be either petty or grand larceny, a misdemeanor or a felony, depending on the value of the property

5. Organized retail crime (ORC)

    a. The National Retail Federation (NRF) defines ORC as the theft/fraud activity conducted with the intent to convert illegally obtained merchandise, cargo, cash or cash equivalent into financial gain (no personal use) when these elements are present:

        (1) Theft/fraud is multiples of items
        (2) Theft/fraud is conducted

            (a) over multiple occurrences
            (b) and/or in multiple stores
            (c) and/or in multiple jurisdictions
            (d) by two or more persons or by an individual acting in dual roles (booster and fence)

    b. ORC is a relatively low-risk, high-reward crime conducted by fairly sophisticated and skilled groups of criminals
    c. The thefts usually involve specific small, high-priced items that have a high resale value on the black market
    d. Once an item is boosted, it can be converted into cash through one of three primary avenues:

        (1) fenced at a physical location (pawnshop or flea market) for roughly 30 percent of the original value
        (2) e-Fenced (listed and sold online through auction sites or other Web pages) for as much as 70 percent of retail value
        (3) fraudulently refunded by returning the merchandise to a retail store for 100 percent of the retail value plus tax (if applicable)

    e. A Web-based national database called the Law Enforcement Retail Partnership Network, or LERPnet, is a public-private partnership between the National Retail Federation, the Retail Industry Leaders Association and the FBI that will be used to analyze, track and prevent activities by these criminal networks

G. Jewelry theft

1. According to the FBI, the jewelry industry loses more than $100 million each year to jewelry and gem theft
2. Most often stolen by sophisticated professional thieves, jewelry is also the target of armed robbers and burglars
3. Always inform the FBI of jewel thefts, even without immediate evidence of interstate operation

4. Since 1992, the FBI's Jewelry and Gem (JAG) Program has helped local law enforcement investigators by providing a sophisticated and multijurisdictional response to these types of thefts

H. Art theft

1. The FBI estimates losses as high as $6 billion annually
2. The FBI's National Stolen Art File (NSAF) provides a computerized index of stolen art and cultural property
3. Thefts of valuable art should be reported to the FBI and to the International Criminal Police Organization (INTERPOL)

I. Numismatic theft: coins, metals and paper money

1. Coin collections are typically stolen during commercial and residential burglaries
2. The increasing demand for copper and rising resale market prices have fueled copper thefts that cost industries across the country nearly $1 billion in 2006

J. Agricultural theft

1. Timber
2. Cactus
3. Livestock
4. Farm equipment and chemicals

K. Fish and wildlife theft

1. Poaching is illegally taking or possessing fish, game or other wildlife
2. Game wardens and conservation officers may help in investigating fish and wildlife theft

L. Cargo theft

1. Increasing popularity of cargo theft: low risk (few thieves are apprehended, prosecuted or incarcerated), and extremely profitable
2. The FBI proposes that cargo theft causes an estimated $30 billion in losses each year
3. Leakage is the illegal or unauthorized removal of cargo from the supply chain (compare with shrinkage in retail industry)
4. A national 2011 survey of retailers found that almost half (49.6 percent) were victims of cargo theft during the previous 12 months
5. Drivers may be hijacked en route or targeted at commercial truck stops; drivers also may be part of the theft crew itself

6. Numerous challenges face cargo theft investigators, including:

   a. The lack of respect or seriousness historically given to the issue
   b. The mobility of cargo thieves

VII. Proving the Elements of the Crime

A. To prove the felonious stealing, taking, carrying, leading or driving away of property, you must gather enough evidence to prove that the property is missing—not simply misplaced
B. Intent to permanently deprive the owner of the property is shown by the suspect's selling, concealing, hiding or pawning the property, or converting it to personal use
C. Intent is proven by a motive of revenge, possession under circumstances of concealment, denial of possession where possession is proven or flight from normal residence

VIII. Fraud

A. Fraud is an intentional deception to cause a person to give up property or some lawful right. Fraud differs from theft in that fraud uses deceit rather than stealth to obtain goods illegally
B. Fraud includes confidence games, real estate fraud, insurance fraud, health care fraud, mass marketing fraud, mail fraud and fraud committed through counterfeiting or the use of checks or debit/credit cards. An increasingly serious and pervasive type of fraud is identity theft
C. If the value amount involved does not meet or exceed a minimum monetary threshold, the federal government may opt not to become involved in the case, leaving local jurisdictions to deal with many of these types of crimes

D. Confidence games

   1. A confidence game obtains money or property by a trick, device or swindle that takes advantage of a victim's trust in the swindler
   2. Short-con games take the victims for whatever money they have with them at the time of the action
   3. Long-con games are usually for higher stakes
   4. The FBI maintains a confidence artist file to assist in locating such susp1ects as well as a general appearance file of con artists
   5. The FBI assists in investigating violations that occur on interstate conveyances. If the swindle exceeds $5,000, the FBI has jurisdiction under the Interstate Stolen Property Act

6. Other scams

   a. Online auction sites are becoming used more frequently to perpetuate scams

   b. Easy-credit scams

   c. Bogus prize offers

   d. Phony home repairs

   e. Travel scams

   f. Cyber-scams

E. Real estate and mortgage fraud

1. Common mortgage fraud schemes include equity skimming, property flipping, air loans, foreclosure schemes, loan modification, builder bailouts, inflated appraisals, nominee loans/straw buyers and silent seconds

2. Equity skimming schemes involve use of corporate shell companies, corporate identity theft and use of bankruptcy/foreclosure to dupe homeowners and investors

3. In property flipping, the offender buys a property near its estimated market value, artificially inflates the property value through a false appraisal and then resells (flips the property) for a greatly increased price. Although property flipping per se is not illegal, it often involves mortgage fraud, which is illegal

4. Air loans involve a nonexistent property loan where there is usually no collateral

5. Foreclosure schemes involve perpetrators misleading homeowners at risk of foreclosure or already in foreclosure into believing they can save their homes in exchange for a transfer of the deed and up-front fees. The perpetrator then either remortgages the property or pockets the fees

6. Loan modification scams purport to help homeowners who are delinquent in their mortgage payments and on the verge of losing their home renegotiate the terms of their loan with the lender, but the scammers demand large up-front fees and either negotiate unfavorable terms or do not negotiate at all, with the result being the homeowners ultimately lose their homes

7. Inflated appraisals involves an appraiser acting in collusion with a borrower and providing a misleading appraisal report to the lender

8. Nominee loans/straw buyers conceal the identity of the borrower through use of a nominee who allows the borrower to use the nominee's name and credit history to apply for a loan

9. In the silent second, the buyer of a property borrows the down payment from the seller through the issuance of a nondisclosed second mortgage. The primary lender believes the borrower has invested his or her own money as the down payment, when in fact, it is borrowed

F.   Insurance fraud

   1.   The most prevalent type of insurance fraud involves premium diversion by insurance agents and brokers, where customers' payments are pocketed for personal gain instead of being sent to the policy underwriter
   2.   Scams run by unauthorized, unregistered and unlicensed agents involve collecting premiums for nonexistent policies
   3.   Another type involves worker's compensation, in which the con operator collects a premium without providing any legitimate protection against claims
   4.   In 2009, the FBI investigated 152 insurance fraud cases, which led to 43 indictments/information, 22 arrests and the convictions of 42 insurance fraud criminals

G.   Health care fraud

   1.   Medicare and Medicaid are the most visible programs affected by such fraud
   2.   One of the most serious trends observed involves the increased number of medical professionals willing to risk patient harm in their fraud schemes, which can include unnecessary surgeries, dilution of cancer and other lifesaving drugs and fraudulent lab tests

H.   Mass marketing fraud

   1.   Frauds that exploit mass-communication media, such as telemarketing, mass mailings and the Internet
   2.   Although these fraud schemes take a variety of forms, they have in common use of false and/or deceptive representations to induce potential victims to make advance fee-type payments to fraud perpetrators
   3.   Telemarketing fraud and other types of fraud using the telephone have proliferated, and the victims are predominantly the elderly
   4.   Frauds involving cell phones and personal communication services (PCS) are growing problems:

      a.   Grabbing
      b.   Slamming
      c.   Cramming
      d.   Gouging
      e.   Sliding
      f.   Jamming
      g.   Fluffing

I.   Mail fraud: perpetuating scams through the mail

    1.   If mail fraud is suspected, police officers should contact the postal inspector through their local post office

    2.   Postal authorities can assist in investigating if the scheme uses the mails to obtain victims or to transport profits from crime

J.   Counterfeiting

    1.   INTERPOL's Counterfeits and Security Documents Branch (CSDB) has established programs that provide forensic support, operational assistance and technical databases to help federal and local investigators in counterfeit currency cases

    2.   Counterfeit identification documents: It is fairly easy for a perpetrator to make fake identification documents, a crime that can yield a large profit

    3.   Commercial counterfeiting

        a.   Trademark counterfeiting: the illegal production of cheap "knock-offs" of well-known pricier products, such as Rolex watches, Gucci handbags or Mont Blanc fountain pens

        b.   Copyright piracy: making for trade or sale unauthorized copies of copyrighted material, including print and sound media

K.   Check fraud

    1.   Common types of check fraud are issuing insufficient-fund or worthless checks and committing forgery

    2.   Insufficient- or nonsufficient-fund check: falls into one of two categories:

        a.   accidental: generally not prosecuted

        b.   intentional: intent to defraud, a prosecutable offense

    3.   Issuing a worthless check occurs when the issuer does not intend the check to be paid

    4.   Forgery is signing someone else's name to a document with the intent to defraud. It is also forgery to alter the amount on a check or to change the name of the payee

    5.   The FBI maintains a National Fraudulent Check File to help track and identify professional check passers

L.   Debit and credit card fraud

    1.   Debit card: also called a check card; refers to a card presented to a merchant exactly as a credit card would be, with the amount instantly credited before verification of the existence of funds is established

2. Credit card: refers to any credit plate, charge plate, courtesy card or other ID card or device used to obtain a cash advance, a loan or credit or to purchase or lease property or services on the issuer's credit or that of the holder

3. The holder is the person to whom such a card is issued and who agrees to pay obligations arising from its use

4. The Department of Justice refers to debit and credit cards as *access devices*

5. Losses from debit and credit card fraud are in the billions annually, with U.S. businesses absorbing $3.2 billion in losses in 2007 from online credit card fraud alone, a figure that excludes fraudulent purchases made from retail stores

6. Credit cards used for fraud are often obtained by people involved in other types of crime such as mugging, robbery, burglary, pickpocketing, purse snatching and prostitution

7. Credit cards may also be obtained through fraudulent applications or by manufacturing counterfeit cards

8. The elements of the crime of larceny by debit or credit card include:

    a. Possessing a credit card obtained by theft or fraud
    b. By which services or goods are obtained
    c. Through unauthorized signing of the cardholder's name

9. The criminal using a card illegally must operate under the floor-release limit to avoid having a clerk check the card's validity. The floor-release limit is the maximum dollar amount that may be paid with a charge card without getting authorization from the central office unless the business assumes liability for any loss

10. Zero floor release means that all credit card transactions much be checked

11. Some merchants and businesspeople commit credit card fraud themselves

M. Identity theft

1. Identity theft, currently the fastest growing crime in the country, can wreak enormous havoc on a person's credit and financial security. Identity theft can be defined as:

    a. the unauthorized use or attempted use of existing credit cards
    b. the unauthorized use or attempted use of other existing accounts such as checking accounts
    c. the misuse of personal information to obtain new accounts or loans, or to commit other crimes
    d. or any combination of the preceding

2. An estimated 9 million or more incidents each year, and approximately one in four people in the United States will fall victim to identity theft at some point in their lives

3. By 2008 the number of identity theft victims in the United States had climbed to 9.9 million, an increase of 22 percent over the 2007 figure

4. Identity theft became a federal crime in the United States in 1998 with the passage of the Identity Theft Assumption and Deterrence Act. Most states have passed identity theft legislation, but the laws vary from state to state

5. Identity theft topped the list of consumer complaints made to the FTC in 2006, totaling nearly $50 billion in losses

6. Thieves steal identities through dumpster diving, skimming (using a special storage device when processing a card), completing a change of address form to divert billing statements to another location, "old-fashioned" stealing and phishing

   a. Phishing involves tricking consumers into replying to an e-mail or accessing a Web site that appears to be associated with a legitimate business but is actually a carefully concocted hoax intended to strip consumers of personal identifying information that can be used for criminal purposes

   b. A Gartner survey showed that phishing attacks escalated in 2007 with more than $3 billion lost to these attacks

   c. Debit cards were the financial instruments targeted most often by fraudsters

7. Identity theft went to a new level when one company tried to steal $23 million by pretending to be another company in 2007

8. Tools of the identity thief's trade: blank checks, laminating machines, laptop computers, typewriters, color scanners and copiers, and skimming devices

9. Collaborative efforts

   a. The President's Task Force on Identity Theft (established 2006): provides a coordinated approach among government agencies to combat identity theft

   b. Law enforcement benefits by forming partnerships with the Federal Trade Commission (FTC), the National White Collar Crime Commission (NW3C), the Postal Inspection Service, the Secret Service and the FBI

IX.   White-Collar Crime

A.   White-collar crime, also called economic or corporate crime, involves illegal acts characterized by fraud, concealment or a violation of trust and does not depend on the actual or threatened use of physical force or violence

B.   White-collar or economic crime includes (1) securities and commodities fraud; (2) insurance fraud; (3) health care and medical fraud; (4) telemarketing fraud; (5) credit card and check fraud; (6) consumer fraud, illegal competition and deceptive practices; (7) bankruptcy fraud; (8) computer-related fraud; (9) bank fraud, embezzlement and pilferage; (10) bribes, kickbacks and payoffs; (11) money laundering; (12) election law violations; (13) corruption of public officials; (14) copyright violations; (15) computer crimes; (16) environmental crimes; and (17) receiving stolen property

C.   Much white-collar crime is never reported because it involves top-level executives at organizations who do not want their reputations damaged

D.   Corporate fraud

1.   Corporate fraud may include falsification of financial information; self-dealing by insiders such as insider trading and kickbacks; fraud in connection with an otherwise legitimately operated mutual or hedge fund; and obstruction of justice designed to conceal such criminal conduct

E.   Money laundering

1.   Converting illegally earned (dirty) cash to one or more alternative (clean) forms to conceal its illegal origin and true ownership

2.   Federal statutes prohibit money laundering

3.   The basic process of laundering money includes:

a.   Placement of the funds into the legitimate U.S. market. Common methods include:

(1)   Creating shell corporations or fake cash-intensive businesses

(2)   Smurfing, more technically known as structuring, whereby large amounts of cash are broken into increments of less than $10,000 to avoid federal reporting requirements, and deposited into various bank accounts

b.   Layering, where the money is cleaned by moving it around through a series of elaborate transactions, often involving offshore bank accounts and international business companies. These transactions aim to obscure the connection between the money and the criminal group

   c. Integration, where criminals repatriate their money through seemingly legitimate business transactions

  4. The FBI's proactive, two-pronged approach to investigating money laundering includes:

   a. Prong 1: Investigating the underlying criminal activity. If there is no criminal activity, or specified unlawful activity that generates illicit proceeds, then there can be no money laundering

   b. Prong 2: A parallel financial investigation to uncover the financial infrastructure of the criminal organization. This involves following the money, discerning how it flows through an organization and what steps are taken to conceal, disguise or hide the proceeds

 F. Embezzlement

  1. Embezzlement is the fraudulent appropriation of property by a person to whom it has been entrusted

  2. Embezzlement includes:

   a. Committing petty theft over time
   b. "Kiting" accounts receivable, in which a check is written on an account that does not have enough funds to cover the check amount
   c. Overextending credit and cash returns
   d. Falsifying accounts payable records
   e. Falsifying information put into computers, which is a highly sophisticated crime

  3. Business, industries, banks and other financial institutions are victims
  4. Losses may be discovered by accident, by careful audit, by inspection of records or property, by the embezzler's abnormal behavior, by a sudden increase in the embezzler's standard of living or by the embezzler's disappearance from employment
  5. Bank embezzlement is jointly investigated by the local police and the FBI

 G. Environmental crime

  1. The most common environmental crimes prosecuted in the United States involve illegal waste disposal or dumping
  2. Hazardous wastes are the most frequently involved substances in such offenses
  3. Other substances often involved include used tires and waste oil

4.   EPA's list of signs of possible environmental violations:

    a.   Containers or drums that appear to be abandoned, especially if they are corroded or leaking

    b.   Dead fish in streams or waterways, especially if the water appears to contain foreign substances (e.g., detergent, bleach or chemicals) or has a strange color

    c.   Dead animals alongside a riverbank or in a field

    d.   Discolored or stressed, dying plant life

    e.   Foul-smelling or oddly colored substance discharged onto the ground or into a stream or waterway

    f.   Visible sheens on the ground or in the water

    g.   Foul-smelling or strange-looking emissions into the air

    h.   Stains around drains, sinks, toilets or other wastewater outlets

    i.   Pipes or valves that appear to allow the bypass of wastewater treatment systems

    j.   Pipes or valves that would allow for discharge from a plant that appear hidden

    k.   Building demolition that may involve illegal removal of asbestos or other hazardous materials

5.   Investigating possible environmental crimes

    a.   Local law enforcement plays an important role in protecting the environment

    b.   Main problems in investigating

        (1)   Understanding the numerous laws regarding what constitutes environmental crime

        (2)   It is often considered a civil matter

        (3)   Collaborating with civil regulatory agencies

    c.   Convictions and harsh penalties for crimes against the environment send a message to companies and individuals that local police actively monitor and enforce compliance with environmental laws

    d.   Premeditation or malice is not required to prove an environmental crime. All that must be proved was that an act that violated the law was done knowingly rather than by mistake

    e.   Criminal prosecution of environmental crimes is often most successful using parallel proceedings, that is, pursuing civil and criminal sanctions at the same time

6. Trafficking in wildlife and organized crime

    a. An often-overlooked environmental crime is the international wildlife trade, estimated to be worth billions of dollars per year, including hundreds of millions of plant and animal specimens

    b. Investigating wildlife crime may result in apprehending organized crime rings

    c. Indicators that may reveal the involvement of organized crime in illicit wildlife trafficking: detailed planning, significant financial support, use or threat of violence, international management of shipments, sophisticated forgery and alteration of permits and certifications, well-armed participants with the latest weapons and the opportunity for massive profits

X. A Final Note about Jurisdiction

    A. Many types of theft and fraud are of an interjurisdictional nature; sometimes a single crime will violate local, state and federal laws.

    B. Investigators must be aware that even though a crime may fall under federal jurisdiction, such as a theft of federally insured monies, that fact alone does not dictate whether another agency will assume responsibility for the investigation; other factors, including the monetary value of the loss, will play a role in determining who is assigned the case

    C. Jurisdictional issues are a reality in many cases involving theft, fraud and other economic crimes

    D. Investigators must be aware of monetary thresholds that must be surpassed for a case to elevate to a federal investigation

XI. Summary

MOTOR VEHICLE THEFT

OUTLINE

- Motor Vehicle Identification
- Classification of Motor Vehicle Theft
- Elements of the Crime
- Motor Vehicle Embezzlement
- The Preliminary Investigation
- Insurance Fraud
- Vehicle Cloning
- Cooperating Agencies in Motor Vehicle Theft
- Recognizing a Stolen Motor Vehicle or an Unauthorized Driver
- Recovering an Abandoned or Stolen Motor Vehicle
- Combating Motor Vehicle Theft
- Preventing Auto Theft
- Thefts of Trucks, Construction Vehicles, Aircraft and Other Motorized Vehicles

Chapter 15
Motor Vehicle Theft

Key Terms

• chop shop • Dyer Act • motor vehicle	• telematic technology • vehicle identification number (VIN)

Learning Objectives
After reading this chapter, students should be able to

• Explain what a VIN is and why it is important. • Identify the five major categories of motor vehicle theft. • Discuss the elements of the crime of unauthorized use of a motor vehicle. • Explain what types of vehicles are considered "motor vehicles." • Define embezzlement of a motor vehicle.	• Explain how the Dyer Act assists in motor vehicle theft investigations. • Discuss why false reports of auto theft are sometimes made. • Identify what two agencies can help investigate motor vehicle theft. • Describe how to improve effective-ness in recognizing stolen vehicles. • Discuss how to help prevent motor vehicle theft.

Internet Assignments

1. Have students search the National Highway Traffic Safety Administration Website for information about vehicle theft, theft prevention and related topics. Ask them to summarize the information they find and present it to the class in groups.
2. Ask the class to do some research specifically on technological innovations that can prevent auto theft and facilitate the recovery of stolen vehicles, such as LoJack. What are the benefits of these systems? What drawbacks might there be?

Class Assignment

Ask the students to analyze the following case in class and make suggestions to resolve it:

• There have been a series of thefts of expensive convertibles in the community. The thefts are occurring during the day. No witnesses or victims have any suspect information. In one incident, the owner unknowingly observed his car being driven away, but did not realize it was his own convertible until he reached his garage to find it gone. None of the cars have been recovered. Cars are not stolen on days when there is snow on the ground. At one scene, officers found some type of debris that was consistent with parts of a convertible top. What actions would you take as an investigator?

Chapter Outline

I.   Motor Vehicle Identification

    A.   The vehicle identification number (VIN) is the primary nonduplicated, serialized number assigned by a manufacturer to each vehicle made. This number is critical in motor vehicle theft investigation because it identifies the specific vehicle in question

    B.   The VIN of a vehicle is the automotive equivalent of human DNA

    C.   VINs for vehicles manufactured between 1958 and 1970 may have 11 numbers and letters or fewer, while all automobiles manufactured in North America since 1971 contain a series of 17 numbers and letters

    D.   Example of a VIN number: **1F1CY62X1YK555888**

        1.   **1** = Nation or origin
        2.   **F** = Manufacturer symbol
        3.   **1** = Make
        4.   **C** = Restraint
        5.   **Y** = Car line
        6.   **62** = Body type
        7.   **X** = Engine symbol
        8.   **1** = Check digit
        9.   **Y** = Model year
        10.   **K** = Assembly plant
        11.   **555888** = Sequential production number

    E.   The Motor Vehicle Theft Law Enforcement Act of 1984 requires manufacturers to place the 17-digit VIN on 14 specified component parts

II.   Classification of Motor Vehicle Theft

    A.   Motor vehicle theft is classified based on the motive of the offender

    B.   Joyriding

        1.   Joyrider is generally a younger person who steals for thrills and excitement
        2.   Stolen vehicles are often found where young people congregate

    C.   Transportation

        1.   Can involve a joyrider, but more apt to involve a transient, hitchhiker or runaway
        2.   A vehicle stolen for transportation is kept longer than one stolen for joyriding

D. Commission of another crime

1. Automobiles are used in most serious crimes
2. Stolen cars are used in committing other crimes to escape detection at the crime scene and to avoid being identified by witnesses
3. A stolen motor vehicle driven by a criminal is 150 to 200 times more likely to be in an accident than is a vehicle driven by a noncriminal

E. Gang initiation

1. Occasionally a vehicle is stolen as part of a gang initiation
2. Vehicles may also be stolen to be used as part of "putting in work" for the gang (i.e., doing something for the benefit of the gang)

F. Stripping for parts and accessories

1. Many vehicles are stolen by juveniles and young adults who strip them for parts and accessories to sell
2. Airbag theft

   a. Airbags are a primary accessory on the black market for stolen vehicle parts
   b. Approximately 50,000 airbags are stolen each year, resulting in an annual loss of more than $50 million for vehicle owners and insurers

3. Stealing for chop shops

   a. A chop shop is a business, usually a body shop, that disassembles stolen autos and sells the parts
   b. The vehicle may triple in value when sold for parts

G. Reselling

1. Committed by professional thieves who take an unattended vehicle, with or without the keys, and drive it away
2. Car is altered by repainting, changing seat covers, repairing existing damage, altering the engine number
3. Many stolen cars are exported for resale in other countries, most commonly Central and South America

III. Elements of the Crime

A. Most car thieves are prosecuted for unauthorized use rather than theft because proof that the thief intended to permanently deprive the owner of the vehicle is often difficult to establish

B. The elements of the crime for unauthorized use of a motor vehicle are:

1. Intentionally taking or driving

   a. Intent is described in state laws as "with intent to permanently or temporarily deprive the owner of title or possession" or "with intent to steal"

      b.   Intent can be inferred from the act of taking or driving, being observed taking or driving or being apprehended while taking or driving

      c.   Laws often include as culpable any person who voluntarily rides in a vehicle knowing it is stolen

2.   A motor vehicle

      a.   Motor vehicle is not restricted to automobiles; it includes any self-propelled device for moving people or property or pulling implements, whether operated on land, on water or in the air

      b.   Motor vehicles include automobiles, trucks, buses, motorcycles, motor scooters, mopeds, snowmobiles, vans, self-propelled watercraft and aircraft

      c.   Homemade motor vehicles are also included

3.   Without the consent of the owner or the owner's authorized agent

      a.   Legitimate ownership of motor vehicles exists when the vehicle is in the factory being manufactured, when it is being sold by an authorized dealership or when it is owned by a private person, company or corporation

      b.   *Owner* and *true owner* are not necessarily the same. For example, the true owner can be a lending agency that retains title until the loan is paid

C.   Interstate transportation

1.   The Dyer Act made interstate transportation of a stolen vehicle a federal crime and allowed for federal help in prosecuting such cases

2.   The Dyer Act was amended in 1945 to include aircraft, and it is now the Interstate Transportation of Stolen Motor Vehicles Act

3.   The elements of the crime of interstate transportation are:

      a.   The motor vehicle was stolen

      b.   It was transported in interstate or foreign commerce

      c.   The person transporting or causing it to be transported knew it was stolen

      d.   The person receiving, concealing, selling or bartering it knew it was stolen

4.   The crime may be prosecuted in any state through which the vehicle passed

5.   Intent is not required

IV.   Motor Vehicle Embezzlement

A.   This most frequently occurs when a new or used-car agency permits a prospective buyer to try out a vehicle for a specific time, and the person decides to convert the vehicle to personal use and does not return it

B.   It can also occur under rental or lease agreements or when private persons let someone test-drive a vehicle that is for sale

C.   Motor vehicle embezzlement exists if the person who took the vehicle initially had consent and then exceeded the terms of that consent

V.   The Preliminary Investigation

A.   When a motor vehicle theft is reported, initial information obtained by police includes the time, date and location of the theft; the make, model and color of the vehicle; the state of issue of the license plate; the license plate number; the direction of travel; a description of any suspect; and the complainant's present location

B.   False motor vehicle theft reports are often filed when a car has been taken by a family member or misplaced in a parking lot, when the driver wants to cover up for an accident or crime committed with the vehicle or when the driver wants to provide an alibi for being late for some commitment

C.   Recovered vehicles must be examined for usable latent prints and other physical evidence

D.   Computerized police files can assist in searching for suspects

E.   Investigators must be familiar with the tools and methods commonly used to commit vehicle theft, including car openers, rake and pick guns, tryout keys, impact tools, keyway decoders, modified vise grips, tubular pick locks, modified screwdrivers and hot wiring

VI. Insurance Fraud

A.   Vehicle insurance fraud is a major economic crime that affects every premium payer through increased insurance rates

B.   Many police departments facilitate insurance fraud by allowing car theft reports to be phoned in or by taking them "over the counter" at the police station and then never investigating the reports

C.   To avoid this situation, law enforcement agencies should investigate all auto theft reports and not discount the possibility that the "victim" is actually committing insurance fraud

VII. Vehicle Cloning

A.   Vehicle cloning is a crime in which stolen vehicles assume the identity of legally owned or "nonstolen" vehicles of a similar make and model

B.   Criminals apply counterfeit labels, plates, stickers and titles to these stolen cars, making them appear legitimate. The nonstolen vehicles can be actively registered or titled in another state or country, resulting in multiple vehicles having the same VIN being simultaneously regis- tered or titled—but, of course, only the nonstolen vehicles are legiti- mate. The rest are fakes, or clones

C.   High-end luxury cars are the usual targets of cloning

D.   Conservative U.S. vehicle cloning profits are estimated to exceed more than $12 million annually, with an average net of $30,000 per cloned vehicle

E. Compounding the cloning problem is the fact that many cloned vehicles are used for illegal operations

VIII. Cooperating Agencies in Motor Vehicle Theft

A. FBI's National Crime Information Center (NCIC)
B. National Insurance Crime Bureau (NICB)
C. National Vehicle Identification Program (NVIP)

IX. Recognizing a Stolen Motor Vehicle or an Unauthorized Driver

A. Keep a list of stolen vehicles or a "hot sheet" in your car
B. Develop a checking system to rapidly determine whether a suspicious vehicle is stolen
C. Learn the common characteristics of stolen vehicles and car thieves

1. Potential car thieves on foot usually appear nervous
2. Drivers of a stolen vehicle tend to make sudden jerks or stops, drive without lights or excessively fast or slow, wear gloves in hot weather and attempt to avoid or outrun a squad car
3. Juveniles account for some 16 percent of stolen vehicles, so it makes sense to take a second glance at stature and youthful appearances of drivers
4. One license plate when two are required, or two when one is required—or no plates at all
5. Double or triple plates with one on top of the other
6. Old set of plates with new screws, wired-on plates, altered numbers, dirty plates on a clean car or clean plates on a dirty car, differing front and rear plate numbers, plates bent to conceal a number, upside-down or hanging plates and homemade cardboard plates are all suspicious

D. Take time to check suspicious persons and vehicles
E. Learn how to question suspicious drivers and occupants

1. Observe their behavior, watching for signs of nervousness, hesitancy in answers, over-politeness and indications that the driver does not know the vehicle
2. Request the driver's license and vehicle registration papers for identification
3. Ask questions about the car (year, make and model, mileage)
4. Look in the car for suspicious materials that may have been used to break into the car

F. Parked cars may have been stolen if debris under the car indicates it has been in the same place for a long time
G. Fridays and Saturdays are the busiest car theft days

X. Recovering an Abandoned or Stolen Motor Vehicle

   A. Most stolen vehicles are recovered, and most of them within 48 hours
   B. If you suspect the vehicle was used in another crime, take it to a garage or lock and seal it with evidence tape, then notify proper authorities
   C. Technology is facilitating the recovery of stolen vehicles; for example, LoJack has developed a system with a homing device that can be placed on a car

XI. Combating Motor Vehicle Theft

   A. Police departments are using several strategies to combat rising auto theft levels:

      1. Setting up sting operations and using bait cars
      2. Providing officers with auto theft training
      3. Coordinating efforts across jurisdictional lines
      4. Instituting anti–car theft campaigns
      5. Increasing penalties for stealing vehicles

   B. In areas where police have made special efforts to educate the public and to assign extra squads to patrol high-auto-theft areas, auto theft has significantly decreased

   C. License plates

      1. Something as low-tech as a license plate can often be used to identify and capture auto thieves
      2. New technology includes automatic license plate recognition (ALPR) systems
      3. Plate Scan is one of the leaders in ALPR

   D. Routine activities and motor vehicle theft

      1. The routine activity approach to crime suggests that the daily, routine activities of populations influence the availability of targets of crime
      2. Bait cars

         a. A bait car is a model of vehicle with a high theft rate that is selected and placed in a high crime area; officers then simply sit back and wait for the vehicle to be stolen
         b. Bait cars can be enhanced using telematic technology, which transfers data between a remote vehicle and a host computer

   E. Border area auto theft

      1. According to the NICB, many of the top metropolitan areas for vehicle theft are in or near ports or the Mexican or Canadian borders
      2. There is no international border for this highly mobile crime

F.   Theft of patrol cars

1.   Police vehicles are also vulnerable to thieves
2.   Technology answers: break-light kill switch, secure-idle system

XII.   Preventing Auto Theft

A.   Numerous motor vehicle thefts can be prevented by effective educational campaigns and by installing antitheft devices in vehicles during manufacture
B.   The NCIB Web site suggests a four-layered approach to combat auto theft:

1.   Common sense
2.   Visible and audible warning devices
3.   Immobilizing devices
4.   Tracing devices

XIII.   Thefts of Trucks, Construction Vehicles, Aircraft and Other Motorized Vehicles

A.   Trucks and trailers: These are usually stolen by professional thieves, although they are also stolen for parts
B.   Construction vehicles and equipment

1.   Heavy equipment theft is a growing problem, with approximately 13,452 thefts reported in 2009
2.   National surveys suggest that the total cost of heavy equipment theft could be as much as $1 billion each year in the U.S. alone
3.   The National Equipment Register (NER)

a.   24/7 access to specialist NER operators who will offer expert advice on equipment identification, PIN locations and other identification techniques
b.   24/7 searches of the NER database online via a toll-free number (866-FIND-PIN)
c.   24/7 access to millions of ownership records through NER operators
d.   Additional online investigation tools such as PIN location information
e.   Local and national training programs

4.   The NER offers the following "red flags" as theft indicators:

a.   Transport

(1)   Equipment being transported late at night or on weekends or holidays
(2)   Hauled equipment that is being moved in a hurry and therefore lacks the proper tie-downs, over-width/over-weight signs or lights

(3) Equipment being hauled on trucks not designed to haul such equipment

(4) Equipment being hauled with buckets in the up position or booms not lowered

(5) New equipment on old transport

(6) The labels/markings on a piece of equipment do not match those of the unit carrying or hauling it

b. Use and location

(1) Equipment in an unsecured location that has not been moved for some time

(2) The type of equipment does not suit the location or use

c. Equipment and markings

(1) Equipment with missing PIN plates

(2) Equipment that has been entirely repainted or that has decals removed or painted over

(3) Manufacturer decals or model number stickers do not match the piece of equipment to which they are affixed

(4) A commercially manufactured trailer with registration plates reflecting a homemade trailer (certain states only)

d. Price: Equipment that is being offered, or has been purchased, at a price well below market value

C. Recreational vehicles

D. Motorized boats and jet skis

E. Snowmobiles

F. Motorcycles, motor scooters and mopeds

G. Aircraft

1. Aircraft identification consists of a highly visible *N* identification number painted on the fuselage

2. After the September 11, 2001, attacks, security of aircraft has become more of a priority

3. The Aircraft Owners and Pilots Association (AOPA) has provided a list of suspicious activities that pilots and aircraft owners should report

XIV. Summary

ARSON, BOMBS AND EXPLOSSIVES

OUTLINE

Chapter 16
Arson, Bombs and Explosives

Key Terms

• accelerants	• disrupters
• administrative warrant	• fire triangle
• aggravated arson	• igniters
• alligatoring	• line of demarcation
• arson	• simple arson
• burn indicators	• spalling
• crazing	• strikers
• depth of char	• trailer

Learning Objectives
After reading this chapter, students should be able to

• Describe how fires are classified.	• Identify the common igniters that are used in arson.
• Explain what presumption is made when investigating fires.	• Describe common burn indicators.
• Identify the elements of arson.	• Describe how to determine a fire's point of origin.
• Define aggravated and simple arson.	• Explain how fires normally burn.
• Detail what degrees of arson the Model Arson Law establishes.	• Describe what factors indicate the likelihood of arson.
• Explain who is responsible for detecting and investigating arson.	• Discuss when administrative and criminal warrants are issued.
• Describe what special challenges exist in investigating arson.	• Explain when a warrant is needed for investigating a fire scene and identify the precedent case.
• Explain what the fire triangle is and why it is important in arson investigations.	• Make a checklist of what to look for when investigating suspected arson of a vehicle.
• Discuss what accelerants are and which are most commonly used in arson.	• Identify what to pay special attention to when investigating explosions and bombings.

Internet Assignments

1. Have students go to the Insurance Committee for Arson Control Web site and review its suggestions for arson control. Ask students to write a report summarizing three major points made by the Web site.

2. Have students search the local district attorney and police or sheriff's Web sites for recent statistics on arson cases. What trends can students find of prosecution and conviction rates for arson, and do the local statistics match those trends? Have students consider methods to improve the arrest and prosecution statistics.

3. Have students search the Internet for these cases:

   - Oklahoma City bomber: Timothy McVeigh
   - Unabomber: Theodore Kaczynski
   - Atlanta Olympic and Abortion Clinic bomber: Eric Rudolph
   - Mad Bomber: George Metesky
   - Courthouse Bomber: Donny Love

   Have them prepare a brief report on each of these bombers, listing the motive, intent and types of devices for each.

Class Assignments

1. Have students search the Internet for these "famous" fires:

   - Iroquois Theater fire, Chicago, Illinois, December 30, 1903
   - Cocoanut Grove nightclub fire, Boston, Massachusetts, November 28, 1942
   - Station nightclub fire, West Warwick, Rhode Island, February 20, 2003

   After they have reviewed the information on these fires, have students discuss the lessons learned, and perhaps those not learned, from these deadly fires.

2. Ask class members to discuss how they would handle the following cases:

   - The fire department has responded to a grass fire in a vacant field behind a school. They believe that several preteens may have accidentally started a fire while playing with matches, and the fire department has asked for help with the investigation.
   - An apartment on the fifth floor of a six-story apartment complex has been partially gutted by fire. The incident has not been definitely established as a case of arson, but two suspicious indicators exist. First, after the fire the apartment residents received an anonymous phone call from a person who claimed that the fire was deliberately set. Also, the fire seems to have had two points of origin. A faint trail appears on the remnants of the living-room carpet, but it is hard to discern because of the fire damage to the carpet fibers.
   - Following the burning of a small commercial building a week ago, the fire investigators have received an analysis of a charred floorboard that indicates the presence of accelerant on the board. The building is about 60 years old, in a middling state of repair and has housed a number of different businesses over the years.

Chapter Outline

I. Classification of Fires

    A.   A natural fire is one caused without direct human action or intervention

    B.   An accidental fire is not intentional

    C.   An incendiary fire (arson) is ignited intentionally and maliciously under circumstances in which the person knows that the fire should not be set

    D.   A fire of undetermined origin is one in which there is no evidence to indicate whether the fire was natural, accidental or incendiary; the cause simply cannot be proven to an acceptable level of certainty

    E.   Fires are presumed natural or accidental unless proven otherwise

    F.   The prosecution has the burden of proving that a fire is not accidental or natural

II. Elements of the Crime: Arson

    A.   The elements of the crime of arson include

        1.   Willful, malicious burning of a building or property

            a.   *Willful* means "intentional"

            b.   *Malicious* denotes a vindictive desire to harm others

            c.   *Burning* is the prime element in the corpus delicti

        2.   Of another or of one's own to defraud

            a.   The motive for burning another's property can range from revenge to economic gain

            b.   The burning of one's own property, however, is almost always to defraud

        3.   Or causing to be burned, or aiding, counseling or procuring such burning

            a.   A person who hires a professional (a "torch") to commit arson is also guilty of the crime

            b.   Seek evidence connecting this person with the actual arsonist

    B.   Attempted arson is also a crime in most states

III.   Classification of Arson

   A.   Aggravated arson

         1.   Intentionally destroying or damaging a dwelling or other property by means of fire or explosives or other infernal device
         2.   Creating an imminent danger to life or great bodily harm, which risk was known or reasonably foreseeable to the suspect

   B.   Simple arson: Intentional destruction by fire or explosives that does not create imminent danger to life or risk of great bodily harm
   C.   Attempted arson

         1.   Elements include the intent to set a fire and some preparation to commit the crime
         2.   The intent is normally specific, and the act must be overt

   D.   Setting negligent fires: Causing a fire to burn or to get out of control through culpable negligence
   E.   Model Arson Law: written and promoted in the 1920s by the NFPA; used by many states that do not classify fires as aggravated or simple but instead specify four degrees of arson:

         1.   First-degree: burning of dwellings
         2.   Second-degree: burning of buildings other than dwellings
         3.   Third-degree: burning of other property
         4.   Fourth-degree: attempting to burn building or property

IV.   The Arsonist

   A.   The typical adult male arsonist has been reared in a broken or unstable home, has an extensive criminal history, is below average intelligence, lacks marital ties, is socially maladjusted or a loner, is unemployed or working in an unskilled position and is intoxicated at the time he sets the fire
   B.   Female arsonists usually burn their own property, and rarely that of an employer, neighbor or associate; they are often self-destructive, mentally defective, older, lonely and unhappy, and often have some psychotic problems, primarily schizophrenia
   C.   Juvenile fireplay/firesetting: Arson has a higher rate of juvenile involvement than any other Index crime; according to the FBI's UCR, more than half of those arrested for arson are under age 18

         1.   Majority of those arrested for arson are White males (FBI's UCR)
         2.   *Fireplay* conveys a low level of intent to inflict harm and an absence of malice; rather, it involves curiosity and fascination
         3.   *Firesetting* is "decidedly different" and involves malice and intent to inflict harm

4. Juvenile firesetters are often divided into four categories:

    a. Curiosity/experimental
    b. Troubled/crisis
    c. Delinquent/criminal
    d. Pathological/emotionally disturbed

D. Motivation

1. Revenge, spite and jealousy
2. Vandalism and malicious mischief
3. Crime concealment and diversionary tactics
4. Profit and insurance fraud

    a. Profit can be to secure employment: a firefighter, security guard or police officer might set fires to obtain a job
    b. "Vanity" arsonists are called strikers: firefighters who set fires and respond to the alarm, receiving attention and praise at "playing the hero"

5. Intimidation, extortion and sabotage
6. Psychiatric afflictions, pyromania, alcoholism and mental retardation
7. Several studies reveal revenge as the most common motive, although many arson investigators believe that insurance fraud is the most prevalent motive
8. Professional torches, or arsonists for hire, are extremely difficult to identify because they have no apparent link to the fire

V. Police and Fire Department Cooperation

A. In many jurisdictions, arson is a joint investigation, with the fire department determining origin and cause, and the law enforcement agency handling the criminal investigation. Insurance investigators and utility companies may also become involved
B. Many police departments give arson a low priority, believing the fire department should investigate; however, many fire departments do not train their personnel to investigate arson
C. Logic suggests that the fire department should work to detect arson and determine the fire's point of origin and probable cause, whereas the police department should investigate arson and prepare the case for prosecution
D. Fire department expertise and role

1. Expertise: Smoke and fire conditions, detecting arson evidence and determining the origin and cause
2. Role: Fire investigation and arson detection, not arson investigation

E. Police department expertise and role

    1. Expertise: Investigating crimes, including knowing possible arson suspects; interviewing witnesses; interrogating suspects; having contacts with informants and arrest power

    2. Role: Apprehending criminals

F. Coordinating efforts: need for joint command/coordination

    1. Best choice is to have a full-time arson squad; next best arrangement is to have a well-trained arson investigator from local jurisdictions or the state fire marshal's office

    2. Cross-training between fire and police is one way to help police and firefighters work together and understand each other's roles

VI. Other Sources of Assistance in Investigating Arson

A. Bureau of Alcohol, Tobacco, Firearms and Explosives (ATF)

B. News media

C. Insurance companies

D. Arson task forces

    1. Detecting arson

    2. Reducing the number of arsons and deliberately set fires

    3. Developing a preventive program

E. Importance of the dispatcher

    1. Emergency dispatchers are often a fire investigator's first link to solving what may turn out to be a difficult fire investigation

    2. Often and without realizing it, the person answering the 911 call for help may be speaking to the person responsible for starting the fire

VII. Special Challenges in Investigation

A. Coordinating efforts with the fire department and others

B. Determining whether a crime has in fact been committed

C. Finding physical evidence, most of which is destroyed by the fire

D. Finding witnesses

E. Determining whether the victim is a suspect

VIII. Responding to the Scene

A. While approaching a fire scene, first responders should observe, mentally note and, when time permits, record in their notes a variety of observations

B. Responders should note:

    1. The presence, location and conditions of victims and witnesses

    2. Vehicles leaving the scene, bystanders and unusual activities near the scene

3. Flame and smoke conditions
4. Type of occupancy, use and condition of the structure
5. Conditions surrounding the scene
6. Weather conditions
7. Fire-suppression techniques used, including ventilation, forcible entry and utility shutoff measures
8. Status of fire alarms, security alarms and sprinklers

IX. The Preliminary Investigation

A. The fire triangle

1. The fire triangle consists of three elements necessary for a substance to burn: air, fuel and heat. In arson, one or more of these elements is usually present in abnormal amounts for the structure
2. Extra amounts of *air* or oxygen can result from opened windows or doors, etc.
3. *Fuel* can be added by piling up newspapers, excelsior or other combustible materials
4. Gasoline, kerosene and other accelerants add sufficient *heat* to the fire to cause the desired destruction after it has been ignited

B. Arson indicators

1. Accelerants

   a. Evidence of accelerants, substances that promote combustion, especially gasoline, is a primary form of physical evidence at an arson scene
   b. Look for residues of liquid fire accelerants on floors, carpets and soil because the liquid accelerants run to the lowest level
   c. *Olfactory detection,* the sensitivity of the human nose to gasoline vapor, is ineffective if the odor is masked by another strong odor, such as that of burned debris
   d. *Catalytic combustion detectors,* commonly known as *sniffers, combustible gas indicators, explosimeters* or *vapor detectors,* are the most common type of flammable vapor detectors used by arson investigators
   e. Fire accelerants are the most frequent type of evidence submitted to laboratories for analysis (80 percent)

2. Igniters

   a. Igniters are substances or devices used to start fires
   b. Common igniters include matches; candles; cigars; cigarettes; cigarette lighters; electrical, mechanical and chemical devices; and explosives

226

3. Burn indicators

   a. Burn indicators are visible evidence of the effects of heating or partial burning; they indicate various aspects of a fire such as rate of development, temperature, duration, time of occurrence, presence of flammable liquids and points of origin

   b. Common burn indicators include alligatoring, crazing, the depth of char, lines of demarcation, sagged furniture springs and spalling

   c. Alligatoring: Checking of charred wood that gives it the appearance of alligator skin; large, rolling blisters indicate rapid, intense heat, while small, flat alligatoring indicates slow, less intense heat

   d. Crazing: Formation of irregular cracks in glass caused by rapid, intense heat, possibly caused by a fire accelerant

   e. Depth of char: How deeply wood is burned indicates the length of burn and the fire's point of origin. Use a ruler to measure depth of char

   f. Line of demarcation: A boundary between charred and uncharred material. A puddle-shaped line of demarcation on floors or rugs can indicate use of a liquid fire accelerant. In a cross section of wood, a sharp, distinct line of demarcation indicates a rapid, intense fire

   g. Sagged furniture springs usually occur when a fire originates inside the cushions of upholstered furniture or when a fire is intensified by an accelerant

   h. Spalling: Breaking off of surface pieces of concrete or brick due to intense heat; brown stains around the spall indicate use of an accelerant

4. Point of origin is established by finding the area with the deepest char, alligatoring and usually the greatest destruction. More than one point of origin indicates arson. The more extensive the destruction, the more difficult it is to determine the fire's point of origin

5. Burning pattern

   a. Fires normally burn upward, not outward. They are drawn toward ventilation and follow fuel paths

   b. Given adequate ventilation, a fire will burn upward. If a door or window is open, it will be drawn toward that opening

   c. If the arsonist places a path of flammable liquid, the fire will follow that path, known as a trailer. The char marks will follow the trailer's path

6. Appearance of collapsed walls

7. Smoke color

    a. Blue smoke results from burning alcohol

    b. White smoke results from burning vegetable compounds, hay or phosphorous

    c. Yellow or brownish yellow smoke results from film, nitric acid, sulfur, hydrochloric acid or smokeless gunpowder

    d. Black smoke results from petroleum or petroleum products

C. Summary of arson indicators: Arson is likely in fires that

    1. Have more than one point of origin

    2. Deviate from normal burning patterns

    3. Show evidence of trailers

    4. Show evidence of accelerants

    5. Produce odors or smoke of a color associated with substances not normally present at the scene

    6. Indicate that an abnormal amount of air, fuel or heat was present

    7. Reveal evidence of incendiary igniters at the point of origin

D. Photographing and videotaping an arson fire

    1. Pictures of a fire in progress show the smoke's color and its origination as well as the size of the fire at different points and times

    2. Pictures taken of people at the fire scene might reveal the presence of a known arsonist or show a person who repeatedly appears in photos taken at fires and is therefore an arson suspect

    3. After the fire, take enough pictures to show the entire scene in detail

E. Physical evidence

    1. Preserving evidence is a major problem because much of the evidence is very fragile

    2. An important step in an arson investigation is identifying potential accelerants at a fire scene

F. Use of K-9s in arson investigations

    1. Detecting accelerants at fire scenes

    2. Searching crowd for possible suspect

    3. Searching suspect's clothing and vehicle for accelerants

    4. Searching areas for accelerant containers

G. Evidence on a suspect

H. Observing unusual circumstances

I. Interviewing the owner/victim, witnesses and firefighters

X.   Search Warrants and Fire Investigations

    A.   Entry to fight a fire requires no warrant

        1.   Once in the building, fire officials may remain a reasonable time to investigate the cause of the blaze

        2.   After a reasonable time, an administrative warrant is needed, as established in *Michigan v. Tyler* (1978)

    B.   Administrative warrant: Issued when it is necessary for a government agent to search the premises to determine the fire's cause and origin

        1.   The scope of the search must be limited to determining the cause and origin

        2.   If evidence of a crime/arson is discovered, a criminal warrant is required to continue the search

    C.   Criminal warrant: Issued on probable cause when the premises yield evidence of a crime

    D.   The Court established guidelines for arson investigators in *Michigan v. Clifford* (1984)

    E.   In *Coolidge v. New Hampshire* (1971), the Court held that evidence of criminal activity discovered during a search with a valid administrative warrant may be seized under the plain-view doctrine

    F.   Guidelines on the current legal status of searches conducted during fire investigations include:

        1.   Warrants are not required when an authorized individual consents to the search

        2.   Warrants are not required when investigators enter under "exigent circumstances" (e.g., while firefighters are extinguishing the blaze or conducting overhaul)

        3.   Warrants are required if the premises are subject to a "reasonable expectation of privacy"

        4.   Evidence of a crime discovered during an administrative search may be seized if in plain view

        5.   Once evidence of arson is discovered, the cause and origin of the fire are assumed to be known; a criminal warrant is required to continue the search

        6.   When in doubt, obtain a warrant

XI.   Final Safety and Legal Considerations

    A.   Entering a building can be dangerous, both from a safety perspective and a legal standpoint; it requires some advanced preparation

    B.   Before entering fire-damaged property:

        1.   Obtain either consent from the legal owner or a search warrant

        2.   Turn off utilities

        3.   Have the structure inspected and ventilated

4. Bring a partner
5. Put on safety boots, protective eyewear and a hard hat
6. Wash your boots with detergent to eliminate cross contamination

XII. Investigating Vehicle Arson

A. Look for evidence of accelerants
B. Determine whether the vehicle is insured, since it is seldom arson if there is no insurance

XIII. Prosecuting Arsonists

A. Some studies indicate that considerably more than 90 percent of arsonists go unpunished, probably because arson is most often committed without the benefit of witnesses
B. Most arson cases involve only circumstantial evidence
C. Prosecutors may choose not to prosecute such cases

XIV. Preventing Arson

A. Six key risk factors for arson:

1. Abandoned properties
2. Negative-equity properties
3. Properties whose gas and/or electric were shut off
4. Sites of prior-year fires
5. Gang locales
6. Known drug hot spots

B. With accurate predictions, officers can be stationed close to and be more observant of targeted zones

XV. Bombings and Explosions

A. Most explosive incidents in the United States fall into one of five classes:

1. Juvenile/experimentation
2. Recovered military ordnance/commercial explosives
3. Emotionally disturbed persons
4. Criminal actions
5. Terrorist or extremist activity

B. Motives for bombing include vandalism, revenge and protest
C. Common types of bombs referred to as improvised explosive devices (IEDs) or homemade bombs:

1. Dry ice
2. Mailbox bomb
3. Car bomb

4.   Nail bomb
5.   Pipe bomb

D.   Other types of explosives

    1.   Liquid explosives such as TATP (triacetone triperoxide)
    2.   Vehicle-born improvised explosive devices (VBIED)

E.   Terrorists have long used cellular phones to trigger IEDs, although other remote control devices are also used
F.   Examples of recent bombs and bombers

    1.   1993, World Trade Center in New York
    2.   1995, Murrah Federal Building in Oklahoma City
    3.   2001, World Trade Center and the Pentagon
    4.   Unabomber, Ted Kaczynski, 1978–1995 attacks
    5.   Eric Rudolph, late 1990s, nail-laden bombs at Summer Olympics and abortion clinics and nightclubs
    6.   2002, Luke Helder, 18 pipe bombs in rural mailboxes

XVI.   Responding to a Bomb Threat

A.   Officers should not approach a bomb threat call with a nonchalant attitude; it could be fatal
B.   Searchers must pay attention to unattended bags, boxes or briefcases, as well as trash cans, ashtrays and flower pots
C.   If a bomb is found, responding officers should contact a specially trained bomb squad to handle the situation from that point; responding officers do not deal with explosives
D.   If a bomb is found, the most important rule in handling suspect packages is to NOT TOUCH the package. The area should be cleared to a 300-foot radius, emergency personnel should be alerted and all radios should be turned off
E.   Methods of explosives detection: Often additional tools are needed to help responding officers determine if an explosive threat truly exists; some methods are low-tech, while other techniques employ highly advanced equipment and technology

    1.   K-9s: used to detect explosives
    2.   Stationary technology used in detecting explosives

        a.   Airports and cargo terminals use X-ray and computed axial tomography (CAT) equipment to scan large numbers of items and people
        b.   Law enforcement also must rely on "sniffer" technology. A sniffer detection device is an instrument that takes in a sample of air, processes it through a detector and then identifies and calculates the approximate quantities of explosive material in the air sample

3.   Robots are used in bomb threat responses

    a.   Robots can be equipped with disrupters, devices that use gunpowder to fire a jet of water or a projectile at a particular component of an explosive to make it safe

    b.   Other features of bomb robots include portable X-ray machines and devices to remotely cut open a car door

XVII.   The Bomb Scene Investigation

    A.   If there has been an explosion, investigators should:

    1.   Ensure that a search for secondary explosive devices has been conducted

    2.   Ensure that the scene has been secured, that a perimeter and staging areas for the investigation have been established and that all personnel have been advised of the need to prevent contaminating the scene

    3.   Ensure that the chain of custody is initiated for evidence that may have been previously collected

    4.   Establish procedures to document personnel entering and exiting the scene

    5.   Establish and document procedures for evidence collection, control and chain of custody

    6.   Make sure safety is of prime concern throughout the investigation

    B.   When investigating explosions and bombings, pay special attention to fragments of the explosive device as well as to powder present at the scene

    C.   Raising awareness

    D.   Importance of the team approach

XVIII. Summary

COMPUTER CRIME

OUTLINE

Chapter 17
Computer Crime

Key Terms

• adware	• logic bomb
• computer crime	• malware
• computer virus	• pharming
• cracker	• phishing
• cybercrime	• phreaking
• cyberterrorism	• piracy
• data remanence	• port scanning
• denial of service	• script kiddie
• domain name	• skimming
• dynamic IP address	• sniffing
• e-crime	• spam
• encryption	• spoofing
• firewall	• spyware
• hacker	• static IP address
• hacktivism	• steganography
• hardware disabler	• Trojan horse
• imaging	• URL
• Internet Protocol (IP) address	• worm
• ISP	• zombie
• keystroke logging	

Learning Objectives
After reading this chapter, students should be able to

• Identify the two key characteristics of computer crime.	• Explain the basic tenet for first responders at a computer crime scene.
• Explain how computer crime can be categorized.	• Discuss how an investigator with a search warrant should execute it in a computer crime investigation.
• Describe the special challenges that are presented by computer-related crimes.	• Describe what forms electronic evidence and other computer crime evidence may take.
• Describe the common protocol for processing a crime scene involving electronic evidence.	

(Continued)

• Identify different precautions you should take when handling PC media. • Explain how electronic evidence should be stored. • Discuss whether "deleted" data are really deleted. • Explain whether most cybercrimes against businesses are committed by insiders or outsiders.	• Define how cybercriminals may be categorized. • Describe what motivates different types of cybercriminals. • Explain what approach is often required in investigating computer crime. • Discuss how computer crimes can be prevented.

Internet Assignments

1. Divide students into four groups. Have each group visit the Web site of one of the following organizations and present a detailed report to the class not only about what they learned from the site, but also about how well the site was developed, how current the information on it is, who created and maintains the site and why investigators should (or should not) rely on the information provided.

   • Electronic Evidence Information Center
   • National White-Collar Crime Center
   • Regional Computer Forensic Laboratory
   • FBI White-Collar Crime Center

2. Have students research online to find out what the latest forms of computer crime are and how these crimes have been perpetrated. Ask them to bring in examples of news stories that describe current cases, either newly reported or under investigation, that involve computer crime. As a class, discuss how law enforcement can proactively combat these recent developments in cybercrime.

Class Assignment

Assign students to groups and have them discuss these questions:

• What steps should a law enforcement agency take to start a computer crime unit?
• What steps should the agency take to reduce computer crime in its community?
• Where would the law enforcement agency find expertise in the field of computer crime that they could use to assist with investigations?

Chapter Outline

I.   The Scope and Cost of the Problem

   A.   The current hot crime tool is a personal computer linked to the Internet

      1.   Cybercrime has significant economic impacts and threatens U.S. national security interests

2. According to the Federal Trade Commission (FTC), nearly 9 million people are victims of identity theft annually, many of whom had information stolen from cyberspace

3. Computers are pervasive in the home, workplace and school. At the end of 2006, CTIA–The Wireless Association reported 302.9 million U.S. wireless subscribers, equivalent to 96 percent of the total U.S. population

4. Computer crimes are relatively easy to commit and difficult to detect

5. Most computer crimes are not prosecuted

B. The IC3 *2010 Internet Crime Report*

1. Internet Crime Complaint Center (IC3) is a partnership between the FBI and the National White-Collar Crime Center (NW3C) designed to serve as a clearinghouse for cybercrime data for law enforcement and regulatory agencies at the federal, state and local levels

2. The IC3 received 303,809 complaints in 2010, of which 121,710 were referred to law enforcement

3. Among the 2010 top ten complaint categories, nondelivery of payment or merchandise was the most reported offense, comprising 14.4 percent of referred crime complaints

4. Although auction fraud has historically topped the list of consumer complaints, reaching a high of 71.2 percent of all referrals in 2004, the steady decline in the number of reports of auction fraud and the concurrent rise and expansion of complaints in other categories indicate the growing diversification of crimes related to the Internet

5. Of the top ten countries reporting cybercrime victimization, the United States ranked first at 91.2 percent, followed by Canada (1.5 percent) and the United Kingdom (1.0 percent)

C. The 2010 Cyber Security Watch Survey

1. This survey is conducted jointly by *CSO Magazine*, the U.S. Secret Service, Carnegie Mellon University's Software Engineering Institute's CERT® Program and Deloitte

2. Of the organizations responding to the survey, 37 percent reported an increase in cyber security events during the previous 12 months; 14 percent reported a decrease; 34 percent experienced no change; and 16 percent were unsure of whether cyber security events increased or decreased

3. Fifty-five percent of participants reported they were more concerned about cyber security threats posed to their organization during the past 12 months compared with the prior 12 months; and 58 percent responded that they felt more prepared to deal with cyber security threats currently than they had been 12 months before

4. The survey found that the technologies considered most effective at detecting or countering cyber security events were stateful firewalls (86%), electronic access control systems (82%), traditional access controls (80%), password complexity (79%) and encryption (76%)

5. The least effective technologies were keystroke monitoring, biometrics and anomaly detection systems

D. The 2010/2011 CSI Computer Crime and Security Survey

1. Since 1995, the Computer Security Institute (CSI), with the help of the FBI, has conducted annual surveys of computer security practitioners in corporations, financial and medical institutions, universities and government agencies throughout the nation to analyze and assess the current state of computer network security

2. The percentage of respondents who have seen various kinds of attacks has generally dropped over time

3. Half of respondents this year said they'd suffered no security incidents

4. Most respondents have seen no evidence of "advanced persistent threat" attacks

5. Based on responses, what is needed is better visibility into networks, Web applications and endpoints

6. There are a growing number of highly sophisticated attacks. These attacks are more malign; more money is lost when an attack is successful, and more records are breached

7. Key findings of the 2010/2011 survey also included:

   a. Malware infection continued to be the most commonly seen attack, with 67.1 percent of respondents reporting it

   b. Respondents reported markedly fewer financial fraud incidents than in previous years, with only 8.7 percent saying they'd seen this type of incident during the covered period

   c. Of the approximately half of respondents who experienced at least one security incident in the previous year, fully 45.6 percent of them reported they'd been the subject of at least one targeted attack

   d. Fewer respondents than ever were willing to share specific information about dollar losses they incurred. Given this result, the report did not share specific dollar figures concerning average losses per respondent. It would appear, however, that average losses were very likely down from prior years

   e. Respondents said that regulatory compliance efforts had a positive effect on their security programs

   f. By and large, respondents did not believe that the activities of malicious insiders accounted for much of their losses because of cybercrime; 59.1 percent believed that no such losses resulted from malicious insiders. Only 39.5 percent could say that none of their losses resulted from nonmalicious insider actions

g.   Slightly over half (51.1%) of the group said that their organizations did not use cloud computing. Ten percent, however, said their organizations used cloud computing and had deployed cloud-specific security tools

II.   Terminology and Definitions

A.   Major definitions include:

1.   The FBI previously defined *computer crime* as "that which involves the addition, deletion, change or theft of information" (FBI)
2.   However, the Internet has become an increasingly common element among crimes committed via the computer and the FBI has refocused its efforts and created the Cyber Investigations unit
3.   *Cybercrime* has many definitions, but one that can be agreed upon is that cybercrime is part of the larger category of computer crime, a criminal act that is carried out using *cybertechnology* and takes place in *cyberspace*
4.   *Cybertechnology* is the spectrum of computing and information/ communication technologies, from individual computers to computer networks to the Internet
5.   *Cyberspace* is an intangible, virtual world existing in the network connections between two or more computers
6.   *Cybercrime* has also been referred to as *electronic crime*, or *e-crime*, describing any criminal violation in which a computer or electronic form or media is used in the commission of that crime

B.   The effective investigator must be familiar with basic computer terminology as well as with terms specifically related to computer crime:

1.   adware
2.   browser
3.   byte
4.   digital evidence
5.   disk drive
6.   electronic device
7.   electronic evidence
8.   encryption
9.   firewall
10. gigabyte (GB)
11. hacktivism
12. imaging
13. keystroke logging
14. kilobyte (KB)
15. logic bomb
16. malware
17. megabyte (MB)
18. network
19. phreaking

20. piracy
21. port scanning
22. removable media
23. script
24. skimming
25. sniffing
26. spyware
27. terabyte (TB)
28. Trojan horse
29. URL
30. virtual reality
31. zombie

C. Net versus Web: The Internet is a network of networks, while the Web is an abstract (imaginary) space of information

    1. On the Net, you find computers; on the Web, you find information
    2. Internet Protocol (IP) addresses: static IP addresses, dynamic IP addresses and ISPs
    3. Deciphering e-mail and Web addresses: domain name and Web address or Uniform Resource Locator (URL)

D. Social networking has opened a new forum in which people can interact and communicate

    1. Instant messaging (IM)
    2. Internet Relay Chat (IRC) environment offers worldwide communication

III. Classification and Types of Computer Crimes

A. Investigators should be familiar with the types of crimes that may involve computers. "Computers and other electronic media can be used to commit crimes, store evidence of crimes and provide information on suspects and victims" (*Best Practices*, 2010)

B. The U.S. Department of Justice has delineated three basic ways computers are being used criminally: computer as target, computer as tool and computer as incidental to an offense

    1. Computer as target

        a. Hacking

            (1) *Hacking* and *cracking* both refer to the act of gaining unauthorized access to a computer system
            (2) A *hacker* is one who intrudes for the challenge and status
            (3) A *cracker* is a hacker in the negative sense, someone who cracks software protection and removes it. A cracker deliberately, maliciously intrudes into a computer or network to cause damage

(4) A *script kiddie*, or *skiddie,* is a derogatory term used to describe a less talented hacker who must use scripts or programs created by others to carry out a cyberattack

(5) Many investigative agencies refer to these people simply as intruders or attackers

b. Viruses: A *computer virus* is a program that attacks, attaching itself to and becoming part of other executable programs

c. Worms, which are self-contained programs that travel from machine to machine across network connections, often clog networks and information systems as they spread; they are actually more powerful and destructive than computer viruses

d. Denial-of-service attacks

(1) A *denial-of-service* (DoS) attack disrupts or degrades a computer or network's Internet connection or e-mail service, thus interrupting the regular flow of data

(2) Using multiple agents to create a widespread interruption is a *distributed DoS,* or DDoS

e. Extortion: Cybercriminals may attempt to extort large sums of money from companies by threatening to or actually damaging the company's computers, network or Web presence; in these cases, the offense fits both categories of computer as *target* and as *tool*

2. Computer as tool

a. Fraud: Internet fraud can involve several other offenses, such as phishing, spamming and identity theft

b. *Phishing* is a method in which criminals misrepresent themselves as a trustworthy source to get victims to disclose personal, sensitive information that is then used by the criminals to commit fraud or other crimes

c. Reshipper schemes

d. Spam consists of unsolicited bulk e-mail messages, similar to junk mail and commonly commercial, and is less well known by its formal designation as unsolicited commercial e-mail (UCE)

(1) Spam is most often perceived by recipients as an annoyance and nothing more

(2) Sometimes, however, spam is distributed on such a massive scale, with such malicious or contentious content or with intent to defraud, that the spamming becomes criminal

(3)　Spam that leaves no question as to its illegality is that intended to phish, commit identity theft or otherwise extract sensitive information from a computer user with the ultimate goal of using such information to engage in criminal activity

e.　*Spoofing*, often considered synonymous with phishing, is acquiring unauthorized access to a computer or network through a message using an IP address that appears to be from a trusted host, in an attempt to commit identity theft

f.　*Pharming*: A cybercrime that is catching even the most cautious and experienced Internet users off guard

(1)　Involves hijacking a domain name to redirect online traffic away from a legitimate Web site toward a fake site, such as a bogus bank Web site

(2)　When a computer user types in the correct domain name of a legitimate site, if that site has been pharmed, the user will be unknowingly taken to the fraudulent site, where he or she may unwittingly reveal account numbers, passwords and other sensitive personal information that can be used for identity theft or other criminal endeavors

g.　Theft of intellectual property, which involves the pirating of proprietary information and copyrighted material, is rampant. Online piracy is allowing criminals around the globe to cash in on the lucrative black market of illegally copied and distributed software, movies, music and videos, and computer games

h.　Online child pornography and child sexual abuse

i.　*Cyberterrorism* is the premeditated, politically motivated attack against information, computer systems, computer programs and data that results in violence against noncombatant targets by subnational groups or clandestine agents

(1)　It also refers to using a computer system as a conduit for causing terror

(2)　Terrorists use global interconnectivity to communicate with each other and to commit crimes to fund their other nefarious activities

IV.　Special Challenges in Investigation

A.　Special challenges in investigating computer crime include:

1.　Victims' reluctance or failure to report such crimes
2.　The investigator's lack of training and the lack of understanding of computer crimes by others within the justice system
3.　The need for specialists and teamwork
4.　The fragility of the evidence
5.　Jurisdictional issues
6.　Determining the exact nature of the crime

       7.   Gathering evidence in a way that does not disrupt an organization's regular operation

  B.   Nonreporting of computer crimes

      1.   Law enforcement's ability to identify coordinated threats is directly tied to the amount of reporting that takes place

      2.   Victims of computer-related crimes are often unaware that a crime has been committed or have a reason for not reporting the crime to authorities

          a. The *2010 CyberSecurity Watch Survey* found that most e-crimes committed by insiders are handled internally without involving legal action or law enforcement (72 percent)

          b. Reasons included the damage level was insufficient to warrant prosecution (37 percent), a lack of evidence (35 percent) or the individuals responsible could not be identified (29 percent)

          c. The *CSI Survey* reports that the most common reason for not reporting e-crimes to law enforcement was a belief that law enforcement would be unable to help, followed by the belief that the incidents were too small or insignificant to report

  C.   Lack of investigator training

      1.   Cybercriminals are usually more technologically sophisticated and have more resources, more access to the newest technology and more time to devote than do investigators assigned to the cases

      2.   Law enforcement at all levels needs additional training in

          a. the unique requirements of computer crimes
          b. digital evidence
          c. identifying, marking and storing this evidence
          d. the capabilities of present private and state agencies to analyze this evidence
          e. the procedures for developing teams to conduct investigations of computer-related crimes

  D.   Need for specialists and teamwork

      1.   When forming a cybercrime unit, the areas to focus on are

          a. selecting the right personnel
          b. establishing a specific protocol to guide investigators
          c. providing the proper training for team members
          d. acquiring the necessary tools and equipment to do the job

      2.   Enlisting the aid of specialists is extremely critical considering the fragile nature of much computer crime evidence

E.   Fragility and sensitivity of evidence in computer crime

1.   "Digital evidence, by its very nature, is fragile and can be altered, damaged or destroyed by improper handling or examination. For these reasons special precautions should be taken to preserve this type of evidence. Failure to do so may render it unusable or lead to an inaccurate conclusion" (*Forensic Examination of Digital Evidence*, 2004)

2.   An officer responding to a computer crime may destroy digital evidence simply by turning a computer or other device on or off at the wrong time

F.   Jurisdictional issues

1.   The global reach of the Internet poses challenge in computer crime cases by introducing jurisdictional complications on top of an already complex area of criminal investigation

2.   The traditional concept of jurisdiction focuses almost exclusively on the territorial aspect of "where did the act take place?"

3.   Traditional territorial boundaries are often complicated in cybercrime cases, as the location of the acts must account for the location of the defendant and where the material originated (was uploaded from), any servers this information passed through, the location of computers where material was downloaded and the location of any effects this material may have set in motion

4.   In cases of international scope, it is necessary to determine whether the act is illegal in all of the countries involved

5.   Virtual child pornography, illegal in Canada and the European Union, was also declared illegal in the United States under the Child Pornography Prevention Act (CPPA) of 1996. However, the Supreme Court ruled in *Ashcroft v. Free Speech Coalition* (2002) that the portion of the CPPA prohibiting the production or distribution of such virtual pornography was overly broad and an unconstitutional infringement on the First Amendment right to freedom of speech

6.   A computer crime investigation may also involve domestic jurisdictional issues, between state and federal levels of jurisdiction as well as between states

7.   Another piece of the jurisdiction puzzle—one the courts have yet to reach consensus on—centers on whether cybercrime necessarily falls under federal jurisdiction because of the commerce clause and what is commonly referred to as the *nexus requirement*

V.   The Preliminary Investigation

A.   Because of the highly technical nature of computer crimes and the fragile nature of the evidence, officers must receive "first responder" training and have extensive knowledge of computers or seek the assistance of a computer expert

B.   First responders have a critical role in preserving the crime scene to protect the integrity of the evidence, because this is the point where such digital evidence is most vulnerable. They should follow the common protocol for processing a crime scene involving electronic evidence, which has the following 8 steps:

    1.   Secure and evaluate the crime scene

        a.   Recommended steps are:

            (1)   Follow departmental policy for securing crime scenes
            (2)   Immediately secure all electronic devices, including personal or portable devices
            (3)   Ensure that no unauthorized person has access to any electronic devices at the crime scene
            (4)   Refuse offers of help or technical assistance from any unauthorized persons
            (5)   Remove all persons from the crime scene or the immediate area from which evidence is to be collected
            (6   Ensure that the condition of any electronic device is not altered
            (7)   Leave a computer or electronic device off if it is already turned off

        b.   Follow the basic tenet for first responders at computer crime scenes by observing the ON/OFF rule: If it's on, leave it on; if it's off, leave it off

        c.   Preliminary interviews: The NIJ recommends the following information be obtained in the preliminary interviews:

            (1)   Names of all users of the computers and devices
            (2)   All computer and Internet user information
            (3)   All log-in names and user account names
            (4)   Purpose and uses of computers and devices
            (5)   All passwords
            (6)   Any automated applications in use
            (7)   Types of Internet access
            (8)   Any offsite storage
            (9)   Internet service provider
            (10)   Installed software documentation
            (11)   All e-mail accounts
            (12)   Security provisions in use
            (13)   Web mail account information
            (14)   Data access restrictions in place

(15) All instant message screen names

(16) All destructive devices or software in use

(17) MySpace, Facebook or other online social networking Web site account information

d. The investigator should attempt to assess the skill levels of the computer users involved because proficient users may conceal or destroy evidence by employing sophisticated techniques such as encryption or steganography

e. *Encryption* puts information in code and thus obscures a normally comprehensible message

f. *Steganography*, which is Greek for "hidden writing," aims to keep everyone except the intended recipient of a message oblivious to its very existence; this type of message often appears as some type of "cover" message

g. Before evidence can be collected, determine if it is necessary to obtain a warrant, because having a search warrant generally decreases the amount of resistance investigators face at the scene and increases the odds of successful prosecution should the case go to court

2. Obtain a search warrant, although searches also may be conducted by consent

a. If the suspect is unknown, this is not desirable because it could alert the person who committed the crime; in such cases, a search warrant must be obtained

b. Privacy issues surrounding some or all of the information contained in the digital evidence desired may pose a legal technicality. If the organization involved is the victim of the crime, its management normally grants permission

c. If the organization is not the victim, it may be necessary to obtain permission from individuals named in the evidentiary file, which could be an enormous task

d. It may be better to take the evidence to a court and obtain court permission if possible

e. Investigators may have both a consent search form and a search warrant, thus avoiding the possibility of destruction of evidence

f. Consent is better than a search warrant because it avoids the usual attack by the defense in search warrant cases

3. Recognize and identify evidence—traditional and digital

a. Electronic evidence is latent like fingerprints or DNA evidence; crosses jurisdictional borders quickly and easily; is easily altered, damaged or destroyed; and can be time-sensitive

      b.   Electronic devices, components and peripherals may also be collected as digital evidence; a list of such objects is given in the text

      c.   Investigators should remember that digital evidence may also contain physical evidence such as DNA, fingerprints or serology

4.   Document the crime scene and digital evidence

      a.   Observe and document the physical scene

      b.   Document the condition and location of the computer system

      c.   Identify and document related electronic components that will not be collected

      d.   Photograph the entire scene with 360-degree coverage if possible

      e.   Photograph the front and back of the computer, the monitor screen and other peripheral components connected to the computer

      f.   Indicators of a computer network include the presence of multiple computer systems; the presence of cables and connectors running between computers or central devices such as hubs; and information provided by those on the scene or by informants

5.   Collect and preserve physical and digital evidence

      a.   Investigators assigned to cybercrimes or other computer-related crimes must have ready certain tools and equipment commonly required in cases involving electronic evidence

          (1)   Investigators should check for a *hardware disabler*, a device designed to ensure a self-destruct sequence of any potential evidence. It may be present on or around a computer, with a remote power switch being the most prevalent of the disabler hardware devices. If a disabler is found, the disabler switch should be taped in the position in which it was found

          (2)   Digital evidence is often contained on disks, CDs, hard drives or any number of peripheral electronic devices. Other computer crime evidence may exist in the form of data reports, logs, programming or other printed information run from information in the computer. Latent prints may be found on the keyboard, mouse, power button or any other peripheral equipment near the computer

          (3)   Avoid contact with recording surfaces of computer tapes and disks. Never write on disk labels with a ballpoint pen or pencil or use paper clips or rubber bands with disks. To do so may destroy the data they contain

(4) Other nonelectronic evidence that may prove valuable to the investigation includes material found in the vicinity of the suspect computer system, such as handwritten notes, Post-It notes with passwords written on them, blank pads of paper with the indentations from previous pages torn off, hardware and software manuals, calendars and photographs

(5) Investigators should be aware that the chain-of-custody issues regarding data are additional to the chain-of-custody issues regarding the physical item

b. Collecting evidence from cyberspace: Most, if not all cybercrimes leave some type of cyber trail or e-print evidence

(1) If an investigator knows a suspect user's screen name, it can be linked to an identifiable IP address, which can provide such information as the suspect's billing address and log-in records, which can in turn lead to the location of the computer used, such as in a private residence, a public library or an Internet café

(2) After the desired target information is culled from the general ISP data records, the investigator needs a search warrant to delve further into a particular user's account information

(3) Understanding how to decipher e-mail headers is a necessary skill for cyber investigators

c. Mobile evidence on a mobile or cell phone system may be found on the communication equipment (the phone itself), the subscriber identity module (SIM), a fixed base station, switching network, the operation/maintenance system for the network and the customer management system; it may also be possible to retrieve deleted items

(1) Call data records (CDRs) obtained from the network service provider are also very valuable as evidence, for they can reveal the location of the mobile phone user every time a call is sent or received

(2) Because of its digital nature, mobile evidence must be handled carefully, yet few standards have been widely implemented regarding how best to collect such evidence

(3) A list is provided in the text for the proper seizure and preservation of mobile devices

6. Package, transport and store digital and other computer crime evidence

    a. Before electronic evidence is packaged, it must be properly documented, labeled, marked, photographed, video-recorded or sketched and inventoried

    b. All connections and connected devices should be labeled for easy reconfiguration of the system later

    c. All digital evidence should be packed in antistatic packaging and in a way that will prevent it from being bent, scratched or otherwise deformed

    d. When transporting computer evidence, investigators should keep digital evidence away from magnetic fields such as those produced by radio transmitters, speaker magnets and magnetic mount emergency lights

    e. Store electronic evidence in a secure area away from temperature and humidity extremes and protected from magnetic sources, moisture, dust and other harmful particles or contaminants

    f. Do not use plastic bags

    g. Also be aware of the time-sensitive nature of perishable data evidence

7. Submit digital evidence (e.g., hard drives) for analysis and data recovery

8. Document the investigation in an incident report

C. Crime-specific investigations: NIJ documents provide in-depth coverage

1. *Investigations Involving the Internet and Computer Networks* (2007) provides in-depth explanations of investigations involving e-mail; Web sites; instant message services and chat rooms; file sharing networks; network intrusion/denial of service; and bulletin boards, message boards and newsgroups

2. *Electronic Crime Scene Investigation* (2008) contains detailed discussions of electronic crime and digital evidence considerations by crime category: child abuse or exploitation; computer intrusion; counterfeiting; death investigation; domestic violence, threats and extortion; e-mail threats, harassment and stalking; gaming; identity theft; narcotics; online or economic fraud; prostitution; software piracy/telecommunication fraud; and terrorism. For those interested in these in-depth discussions, search the Internet by their titles

VI. Forensic Examination of Computer Evidence

A. Computer forensics carries the potential to benefit nearly every type of criminal investigation

B. Computer forensics can provide evidence of motivation, a chronology of events, insight into an offender's interests and activities and links among multiple offenders

C. Data analysis and recovery

1. Data recovery is a computer forensic technique that requires an extensive knowledge of computer technology and storage devices and an understanding of the laws of search and seizure and the rules of evidence

2. Although deleted files remain on the hard drive in a nonviewable format, their existence hidden from most computer users, the computer forensic expert knows where to look and how to make such files viewable again

3. *Data remanence* refers to the residual physical representation of data that have been erased

4. A qualified computer forensic analyst may be able to recover evidence of the copying of documents, whether to another computer on the network or to some removable storage device such as a flash drive; the printing of documents; the dates and times specific documents were created, accessed or modified; the type and amount of use a particular computer has had; Internet searches run from a computer; and more

VII. Legal Considerations in Collecting and Analyzing Computer Evidence

A. Investigators and forensic technicians must adhere to strict standards if the evidence is to be of value in the courtroom

1. Individuals must testify in court to the authenticity of the disks, CDs or printouts

2. The materials must be proven to be either the originals or valid substitutes in accordance with the best-evidence rule

3. Evidence must be tied to its source by a person qualified to testify about it

B. The Privacy Protection Act's (PPA) prohibition on use of a search warrant does not apply in the following circumstances *(Investigations Involving the Internet)*:

1. Materials searched for or seized are contraband, fruits or instrumentalities of the crime

2. There is reason to believe that the immediate seizure of such materials is necessary to prevent death or serious bodily injury

3. Probable cause exists to believe that the person possessing the materials has committed or is committing a criminal offense to which the materials relate

C. The NIJ cautions first responders seizing electronic devices that improper access of data stored within may violate provisions of certain federal laws, including the Electronic Communications Privacy Act

D. An evolving area of legal wrangling concerns copyright laws and investigative agencies that seize computers with an operating system installed on them, as most do. Operating systems, which are copyright protected, may not be copied without the author's (the software company's) expressed permission

VIII. Follow-Up Investigation

A. Developing suspects

    1. Most cybercrimes against businesses are committed by "outsiders"

        a. The *2010 CyberSecurity Watch Survey* reports that of the 53 percent of businesses that were victims of viruses, worms or other malicious codes, 41 percent were infiltrated by outsiders compared with 14 percent victimized by insiders

        b. Of the 32 percent of businesses victimized by illegal generation of spam, 26 percent fell victim to outsiders compared with 7 percent victimization by insiders

        c. Of the 41 percent of businesses victimized by spyware, 28 percent of the cases were committed by outsiders compared to 15 percent by insiders

    2. According to the FBI, a cybercriminal will likely fall into one of three categories:

        a. Crackers (hackers): Motivated by achieving prohibited access; inspired by boredom and the desire for intellectual challenge; no real damage done

        b. Vandals: Motivated to cause damage and as much harm as possible; are often disgruntled, either with their employer or with life and society in general

        c. Criminals: Motivated by economic gain; use espionage and fraud, among other tactics, to accomplish their goals

    3. According to the FBI, cybercriminals can generally be classified by their organization level:

        a. Most computer criminals, although commonly active in a social underground, commit their criminal acts alone

        b. A smaller percentage of cybercriminals will exist in organized groups, such as corporate spies and organized crime groups

    4. The *2010 Internet Crime Report* (2011) found the following:

        a. Perpetrators were predominantly male (75 percent) and more than half resided in one of the following states: California, Florida, New York, Texas or the District of Columbia

        b. Most reported perpetrators were from the United States

      c. A significant number of perpetrators also were located in the United Kingdom, Nigeria and Canada

      d. Most perpetrators were in contact with the complainant either through e-mail or via the Web

    B. Organized cybercrime groups

      1. A few hacker groups have been observed to have a Mafia-like hierarchy

      2. Particularly challenging are cases involving cybergangs that operate in countries with weak hacking laws and lax enforcement, such as Russia, eastern European countries and China

      3. An effective tactic being used to apprehend organized cyber-crime networks is undercover investigation and surveillance

    C. Undercover investigation and surveillance

      1. Covert investigation including ongoing surveillance operations is a method being used to gather evidence against cybercrime gangs

      2. Undercover tactics are also commonly used in cases of online child pornography and sexual exploitation

IX. Security of the Police Department's Computers

    A. Law enforcement officers should not overlook the possibility that their own computers may be accessed by criminals

    B. Any computer attached to a phone line is accessible by unauthorized people outside the department, even thousands of miles away on a different continent

    C. Ensuring the security of an agency's network should be a top priority

X. Legislation

    A. With the proliferation of online child pornography phishing and other crimes involving the computer, legislation efforts have been challenged to keep up with security safeguards

    B. The USA PATRIOT Act (2001) consists of more than 150 sections, many of which pertain to electronic communications and other areas of cybercrime investigation

    C. The PATRIOT Act also changed key features of existing National Security Letter (NSL) protocol

      1. NSLs are a type of subpoena issued in foreign counterintelligence and international terrorism investigations to obtain records under the statutory authority of the Electronic Communications Privacy Act (telephone and ISP records), the Right to Financial Privacy Act (financial institution records) and the Fair Credit Reporting Act (records from credit bureaus)

2. The PATRIOT Act expanded signature authority for NSLs to increase the efficiency and effectiveness of processing such subpoenas

3. The PATRIOT Act received a four-year extension in May 2011

D. Other federal statutes relevant to computer-related crimes include patent laws, espionage and sabotage laws, trade secret laws, the Copyright Act of 1976 and the Financial Privacy Act of 1978

E. Phishing schemes are likely to violate not only various existing state statutes on fraud and identity theft but also several federal criminal laws

F. Transmission of computer viruses and worms may be prosecuted under the federal provisions of the computer fraud and abuse statute relating to damage to computer systems and files

XI. The Investigative Team

A. Investigating computer crimes often requires a team approach

B. The investigative team is responsible for assigning all team personnel according to the specialties, including securing outside specialists if necessary; securing the crime scene area; obtaining search warrant applications; determining the specific hardware and software involved; searching for, obtaining, marking, preserving and storing evidence; obtaining necessary disks, printouts and other records; and preparing information for investigative reports

C. In most computer-related crimes, investigators seek assistance from the victim who owns the equipment, database processing technicians, auditors, highly trained computer experts or programmers and others

D. If necessary, the team should contact the manufacturer of the equipment, the consulting services of a private computer crime investigative agency or the technology resources found at local universities and other institutions of higher learning

E. To assist in combating increasing computer crimes, government and private businesses are developing computer crime teams similar to the FBI's kidnapping crime teams and the arson investigation specialist teams of the Bureau of Alcohol, Tobacco, Firearms and Explosives (ATF)

F. The FBI's Computer Analysis Response Team (CART) helps state and local law enforcement as well as federal agents

XII. Resources Available

A. Police agencies in many states are forming cooperative groups and providing training seminars on investigating computer crimes

B. The U.S. Department of Justice (DOJ) has developed the National Cybercrime Training Partnership (NCTP) with these purposes:

1. Developing and promoting a long-range strategy for high-tech police work, including interagency and interjurisdictional cooperation, information networking and technical training

2. Garnering public and political understanding of the problem and generating support for solutions

3. Serving as a proactive force to focus the momentum of the entire law enforcement community to ensure that proposed solutions are fully implemented

C. The IC3 provides to cybercrime victims a convenient, user-friendly reporting mechanism that notifies authorities of suspected violations

D. The Secret Service has established a nationwide network of Electronic Crimes Task Forces (ECTFs). The ECTF network brings together federal, state and local law enforcement, as well as prosecutors, private industry and academia, to prevent, detect, mitigate and provide aggressive investigation of attacks on the nation's financial and critical infrastructures. The Secret Service offers numerous services to its field agents as well

E. The Computer Crime and Intellectual Property Section of the DOJ maintains a Web cybercrime resource for law enforcement to help with preventing, detecting, investigating and prosecuting cybercrime

F. Other resources include the Computer Crime Research Center and the Electronic Evidence Information Center

G. Perverted Justice is an Internet-based organization whose volunteers pose as young kids and trawl the Internet for predators; founded in 2002, it has the resources to spend hundreds of hours on a single case, and volunteers have worked with police to collar more than 157 criminals

H. NetSmartz is an Internet safety and awareness program created by the National Center for Missing and Exploited Children, the Internet Crimes against Children Task Force and the Boys and Girls Clubs of America

XIII. Preventing Computer Crime

A. Computer crimes can be prevented by educating top management and employees and by instituting internal security precautions. Top management must make a commitment to defend against computer crime

B. The FBI's National Computer Crime Squad suggests the following procedures for computer users to institute, both before becoming a computer crime victim and after a violation has occurred:

1. Place a log-in banner to ensure that unauthorized users are warned that they may be subject to monitoring

2. Turn audit trails on

3. Consider keystroke-level monitoring if an adequate banner is displayed

4. Request trap and tracing from your local telephone company

5. Consider installing caller identification

6. Make backups of damaged or altered files

7. Maintain old backups to show the status of the original

8. Designate one person to secure potential evidence
9. Evidence can consist of tape backups and printouts. These should be initialed by the person obtaining the evidence. Evidence should be retained in a locked cabinet with access limited to one person
10. Keep a record of resources used to reestablish the system and locate the perpetrator

C. Another security measure is to use a paper shredder; and yet another technique that is gaining momentum is the use of biometrics

D. Businesses need to become more proactive. *CIO Magazine*, the FBI and the U.S. Secret Service have collaborated to produce guidelines on how businesses should plan for and respond to attacks on information systems, including viruses, hacks and other breaches

E. The U.S. Secret Service contends that law enforcement must take a proactive approach to cyberthreats and that prevention coupled with aggressive proactive investigations deliver the best outcome in the fight against cybercrime

F. National strategy to secure cyberspace

1. Besides individuals and companies, the entire U.S. population faces risk of victimization by cybercriminals because of our increasing reliance on information technology and the role computers play in many aspects of our daily lives
2. Cyberattacks on any part of this infrastructure could lead to tremendous loss of revenue and intellectual property and to loss of life

XIV. Summary

A Dual Threat: Drug-Related Crime and Organized Crime

OUTLINE

Chapter 18
A Dual Threat: Drug-Related Crime and Organized Crime

Key Terms

- analogs
- body packing
- bookmaking
- capital flight
- club drugs
- cook
- crack
- crank
- criminal enterprise
- depressant
- designer drugs
- drug addict
- Ecstasy
- excited delirium
- flashroll
- hallucinogen
- loan-sharking
- MDMA
- mules
- narcotic
- organized crime
- OTC drugs
- pharming
- raves
- reverse buy
- robotripping
- sinsemilla
- skittling
- sting
- tweaker
- victimless crime

Learning Objectives
After reading this chapter, students should be able to

- Discuss what act made it illegal to sell or use certain narcotics and dangerous drugs.
- Describe when it is illegal to use or sell narcotics or dangerous drugs.
- Explain how drugs are commonly classified.
- Describe what drugs are most commonly observed on the street, in the possession of users and seized in drug raids, and what the most frequent drug arrest is.
- Explain what the major legal evidence in prosecuting drug use and possession is.
- Describe what the major legal evidence in prosecuting drug sale and distribution is.
- Explain when an on-sight arrest can be made for a drug buy.
- Discuss what precautions to take in undercover drug buys and how to avoid a charge of entrapment.
- Explain what hazards exist in raiding a clandestine drug laboratory.
- Clarify what agency provides unified leadership in combating illegal drug activities and what its primary emphasis is.

(Continued)

• Describe what the key to reducing our nation's drug problem is. • Explain the distinctive characteristics of organized crime and its major activities. • Identify what organized crime activities are specifically made crimes by law.	• Outline what crimes organized crime is typically involved in. • Describe the investigator's primary role in dealing with the problem of organized crime. • Discuss what agencies cooperate in investigating organized crime.

Internet Assignments

1. Ask students to visit the Drug Enforcement Administration's Web site and review the recent major cases featured there. Have the students each provide a short written report in which they explain the primary focus of the operations as well as any commonalities they have been able to discern in terms of where the operations have developed, how the cases have been investigated and what issues have been involved.

2. Have the students choose one of the five specific organized crime groups outlined in the text: Italian, Asian, Latino, African and Russian. Ask the students to prepare a presentation to the class on their chosen group, including recent criminal activity that has been in the news.

Class Assignments

1. Divide the class into groups and ask them to discuss the following issues:

   • A highly organized group of drug sellers exists in your community. It is well managed and efficient at evading authorities. Previous attempts to infiltrate the organization using undercover officers or informants have ended in failure, and in one case the officer was in grave danger. What other tactics might be in order?

   • Drug sales have increased dramatically at two local high schools. What actions can local law enforcement take to reduce this problem?

   • What actions might a law enforcement agency take that would combine both enforcement and prevention of drug-related crime?

2. Have students go to the DEA Web site and research club drugs. After they have researched club drugs, ask students to engage in a group discussion to come up with more common "street" names that they have heard used to describe these types of drugs.

3. Have students research organized crime on the Internet. A good place to start would be the FBI's Website on organized crime. Have the class discuss local cases of various types of organized crime that have affected their communities. Ask a local police officer or federal investigator to come into the class to discuss local organized crime issues.

Chapter Outline

I.   The Threat of Drugs

    A.   Cocaine use was common in the United States by the 1880s

    B.   By the early 1900s, the situation was so bad, President Theodore Roosevelt pressed for antidrug legislation

    C.   In 1914, the federal government passed the Harrison Narcotics Act, which made the sale or use of certain drugs illegal

    D.   In 1937, under President Franklin Delano Roosevelt, marijuana became the last drug to be banned

    E.   After the 1960s and the Vietnam War, the drug "culture" had been created

    F.   The 1980s saw a turnaround in drug use: "Just say no to drugs"

II.   Seriousness and Extent of the Drug Problem

    A.   Today, an estimated 14.2 percent of Americans 12 and older have used illegal drugs in the previous 12 months

    B.   The DEA reports:

        1.   More young Americans die from drugs than from firearms, suicide or school violence

        2.   The use of illicit drugs and the abuse of prescription medication directly led to the deaths of 38,000 Americans in 2006

        3.   Substance abuse is the single largest contributor to crime in the United States

        4.   The most recent data estimate that drug abuse imposes a direct cost of $52 billion a year on our nation, with indirect costs of $128 billion

    C.   An increasing threat is posed by drug trafficking organizations (DTOs), complex entities with highly defined command-and-control structures that produce, transport or distribute large quantities of one or more illicit drugs

    D.   According to the *National Drug Threat Assessment* of 2010:

        1.   Wholesale-level DTOs, especially Mexican DTOs, constitute the greatest drug trafficking threat to the United States. These organizations derive tens of billions of dollars annually from the trafficking and abuse of illicit drugs and associated activities

        2.   The influence of Mexican DTOs, already the dominant wholesale drug traffickers in the United States, is still expanding, primarily in areas where the direct influence of Colombian DTOs is diminishing

        3.   Asian DTOs have expanded their influence nationally in recent years by trafficking MDMA and high-potency marijuana—drugs that do not put them in direct competition with Mexican, Colombian or Dominican DTOs

4.   Cuban DTOs and criminal groups are slowly expanding their drug trafficking activities beyond the Florida/Caribbean region, in part by partnering with Mexican DTOs

E.   Especially disturbing is the violence connected with the Mexican drug cartels, with drug violence from Mexico spilling into the United States, the brutality giving rise to formidable new problems for both countries (e.g., there have been a large number of kidnappings in Phoenix, Arizona, with 260 in 2007, 299 in 2008 and 267 in 2009)

F.   The drug problem remains a serious issue, as evidenced by data presented in *Monitoring the Future 2010 (MTF)*:

1.   American secondary school students and young adults show a level of involvement with *illicit drugs* that is among the highest in the world's industrialized nations

2.   *Heavy drinking* also remains widespread and troublesome, though it has been declining gradually

3.   In total, 29 percent of all 8th graders in 2010 have tried some *illicit drug* (including inhalants), and 11 percent, or 1 in 9, have tried *some illicit drug other than marijuana or inhalants*. Put another way, in an average 30-student classroom of 8th graders, about 9 have used some illicit drug other than marijuana including inhalants, and about 3 have used some illicit drug other than marijuana or inhalants

4.   The very large number of 8th graders who have already begun using the so-called "gateway drugs" (*tobacco, alcohol, inhalants and marijuana*) suggests that a substantial number are also at risk of proceeding further to such drugs as LSD, cocaine, amphetamines and heroin

III.   Legal Definitions

A.   Laws generally categorize drugs into five schedules of controlled substances, arranged by the degree of danger associated with the drug, with Schedule I drugs being the most dangerous

B.   It is illegal to possess or use narcotics or dangerous drugs without a prescription and to sell or distribute them without a license

C.   The laws also establish prohibited acts concerning the controlled substances and assign penalties in ratio to the drug's danger

D.   Specific laws vary by state (e.g., possessing a small amount of marijuana is a felony in some states, a misdemeanor in others and not a crime at all in a few states)

IV.   Identification and Classification of Controlled Drugs

A.   The sale of prescription drugs, the fastest-growing category of drugs being abused, has skyrocketed since 1990

B.   Identification via field testing can be tricky

    1.   Several brands of self-contained, single-use test kits are available that reduce the likelihood of user error and require very small samples

    2.   Officers must understand that field testing cannot be used to *establish* probable cause, only *confirm* it

    3.   Officers rely on several reference sources for identification: the *Physicians' Desk Reference* (PDR), the *Drug Identification Bible* or Web-based pill identifiers

C.   Drugs can be classified as depressants, stimulants, narcotics, hallucinogens, cannabis or inhalants

D.   Stimulants and depressants are controlled under the Drug Abuse Control Amendments to the Federal Food, Drug and Cosmetic Act (U.S. Code Title 21)

E.   The most commonly observed drugs on the street, in possession of users and seized in drug raids are cocaine, codeine, crack, heroin, marijuana, morphine and opium. Arrest for possession or use of marijuana is the most frequent drug arrest

F.   Powder cocaine and crack: *Crack*, also called *rock* or *crack rock*, is produced by mixing cocaine with baking soda and water, heating the solution and then drying and splitting the substance into chunks

    1.   Crack is much less expensive than cocaine and has 10 times the impact on the user

    2.   For the past two decades, the cocaine supply in the United States has been controlled by the Colombian Medellin and Cali mafias. The U.S.–Mexico border is the primary point of entry for cocaine into the United States

    3.   According to the *National Drug Threat Assessment* (2010), cocaine availability is decreasing sharply, with significantly decreased availability in 2009 as compared to 2006

    4.   Concern is rising, however, over indications that Colombian cocaine producers are increasing their use of a harmful cutting agent, levamisole

G.   Heroin, a commonly abused narcotic, is synthesized from morphine and is as much as 10 times more powerful in its effects

    1.   Heroin is physically addictive and relatively expensive

    2.   According to the *National Drug Threat Assessment* (2010), heroin remains widely available and that availability is increasing in some areas

H.   Marijuana is made from a plant in the genus *Cannabis* and is the most widely available and most commonly used illicit drug in the United States, with 25.8 million individuals age 12 and older (10.3 percent of the national population) reporting past year use

1. Marijuana is variously classified as a *narcotic*, a *depressant* and a *hallucinogen*
2. Marijuana is the most controversial of the illicit drugs, and a wide spectrum of opinion exists regarding its harmfulness; some think it should be legalized, while others think it is a very dangerous drug and that it is also a "gateway" drug
3. Some users lace marijuana with other substances, including PCP, cocaine and even embalming fluid, or formaldehyde
4. Mexican commercial-grade marijuana is the most common variety, but BC bud (from British Columbia) generally has a higher concentration of THC and thus greater potency
5. Large quantities of marijuana are being grown hydroponically indoors, often in abandoned barns or other buildings in rural areas; this homegrown marijuana, known as *sinsemilla*, has become extremely popular
6. A new type of synthetic marijuana is KS, or "spice," a mixture of herbs and spices sprayed with a synthetic compound chemically similar to THC

I. Methamphetamine (crank) is now firmly entrenched as a major U.S. drug problem that is only getting bigger

1. Meth is a highly addictive synthetic stimulant that looks like cocaine but is made from toxic chemicals
2. Concocting *crank*, a street name for meth, is relatively simple and inexpensive. A *tweaker* is a meth addict. A meth *cook* is someone who produces the drug
3. Meth abuse is a particular problem in rural communities, where most meth production occurs, because of the lack of resources available to address addiction and its side effects such as crime and child abuse
4. One of the main ingredients in the production of meth is pseudoephedrine, a powerful stimulant found in many OTC meditations; in 2005, Congress passed the Combat Methamphetamine Epidemic Act (aka CMEA), which encompasses new purchasing restrictions and standards along with new standards for storage, employee training and record keeping
5. A chemical additive, GloTell, can identify those who handle anhydrous ammonia fertilizer, a common ingredient in producing methamphetamine

J. *Club drugs* are those drugs commonly found at *raves*, dance parties that feature fast-paced, repetitive electronic music and light shows

1. *Ecstasy*: 3,4-Methylenedioxymethylamphetamine (*MDMA*)
2. Rohypnol
3. GHB: Gamma-hydroxybutyric acid
4. Ketamine
5. LSD (acid)

K. Prescription drug abuse has become a nationwide epidemic

1. Pain relievers, such as Vicodin, Percodan, Percocet and Oxy-Contin top the list of abused prescription drugs
2. Other commonly abused prescription drugs include tranquilizers such as Xanax and Valium, stimulants and Viagra
3. Marijuana, the illicit drug that has previously and pervasively been the most popular drug with teens, has lately taken a backseat to the nonmedical use of pain relievers
4. Prescription drug diversion occurs by faking, forging or altering a prescription; obtaining bogus prescriptions from criminal medical practitioners; or buying drugs diverted from health care facilities by personnel. Pharmacy thefts are increasing nationwide to feed the growing demand for prescription drugs
5. Law enforcement officers spend a significant amount of time investigating cases involving prescription fraud, many of which also involve insurance, Medicare or Medicaid fraud
6. OxyContin is a pain medication derived from opium with heroin-like effects that is used in treating pain related to cancer and other debilitating diseases; it is meant to be swallowed, but abusers chew it, melt it to inject intravenously or crush the tablet and snort it

L. Inhalants: the use of inhalants has increased during the past few years; methods used to inhale include sniffing or snorting, *huffing* and *bagging*

M. Khat (pronounced "cot") is a natural narcotic whose primary psychoactive ingredients are chemically similar to amphetamines

1. Khat is a relative newcomer to the U.S. drug scene but is well known in eastern African and southern Middle Eastern countries, some of which consider it a legitimate and quite profitable export
2. The rising use of khat in the United States appears to coincide with the increased numbers of immigrants coming from eastern African and Middle Eastern countries where the substance is legal, and many immigrants may be unaware of the illegal status of the drug in this country

N. Over-the-counter (OTC) drugs

1. Some teens are turning to legal OTC drugs for their highs, mistakenly assuming that if something is legal and readily available, it can't be dangerous, or at least not deadly
2. Drinking bottles of cough syrup, such as Robitussin DM, to get high is called *robotripping*
3. *Skittling*, so named because the pills resemble small, red pieces of Skittles candy, is ingesting high doses of Coricidin Cough and Cold ("Triple C") tablets

4. *Pharming* is rifling through the family medicine cabinet for pills, both OTC and prescription, combining everything in a bowl, scooping out and ingesting a handful, and waiting to see what happens. When groups of youth get together and combine their medicinal booty, it is called a *pharm party*

5. Because these drugs are legal, law enforcement requires a more proactive approach to the problem, such as educating youths and their parents and networking with professional organizations

O. Other narcotics and drugs

1. *Designer drugs* are created by adding to or omitting something from an existing drug; in many instances, the primary drug is not illegal

2. The illicit drugs are called *analogs* of the drug from which they are created (e.g., meperidine analog or mescaline analog)

V. Investigating Illegal Possession or Use of Controlled Substances

A. Recognizing the drug addict: drug-recognition experts

1. Congress has defined a *drug addict* as "any person who habitually uses any habit-forming narcotic drug so as to endanger the public morals, health, safety or welfare, or who is or has been so far addicted to the use of habit-forming narcotic drugs as to have lost the power of self-control with reference to the addiction"

2. Drug addiction is a progressive disease

3. Police officers are not always able to recognize drug-impaired individuals

4. Drug evaluation classification (DEC) programs, more commonly known as drug recognition expert (DRE) programs, have demonstrated international success in detecting and deterring drug-impaired driving

5. If an officer suspects a driver is impaired, the officer must assess the driver

a. Standard field sobriety tests are used first

b. If impairment is noticeable, subject is given a breath test

c. If blood alcohol reading is inconsistent with the perceived impairment, a DRE evaluates the individual's appearance, performance on psychological tests, eyes and vital signs

6. A pupilometer, a lightweight handheld binocular-type instrument that measures absolute pupil dynamics, allows officers to conduct sobriety checks in the field at a low cost

B. Physical evidence of possession or use of controlled substances

    1. The suspect's clothing may conceal drugs
    2. Drugs can be hidden in the hair, behind the ears, between the toes or attached to body parts with tape
    3. A strip search is usually conducted because drugs can be concealed in any body opening; this method of concealment is called *body packing*
    4. Objects in the suspect's possession can also contain drugs (e.g., packages, jewelry, lockets, pencil erasers) or apparatus or paraphernalia
    5. Officers should also check hiding places in vehicles, residences and buildings
    6. One of the first problems is to identify the suspected substance
    7. Physical evidence of possession or use of controlled substances includes the actual drugs, apparatus associated with their use, the suspect's appearance and behavior, and urine and blood tests

C. In-custody deaths: one serious problem that may be encountered in dealing with drug users is *excited delirium*, which may occur in people under the influence of an illicit stimulant substance or in people with a history of mental illness who are not taking their medication

    1. Occasionally a suspect in a drug case will attempt to hide or destroy evidence by ingesting it, which could lead to an in-custody overdose death
    2. Subjects have also been known to swallow entire packages or bags containing drugs, which results in their suffocating or choking to death
    3. According to one study, 53 percent of the people who die suddenly while in police custody have used illicit substances proximal to their collapse

VI. Investigating Illegal Sale and Distribution of Controlled Substances

A. Drug control must be directed toward the supplier, because addiction depends on drug availability
B. Drug users often become sellers to support their habits; many such individuals, called *mules,* sell or transport drugs for a regular dealer in return for being assured of a personal drug supply
C. The actual transfer of drugs from the seller to the buyer is the major legal evidence in prosecuting drug-sale cases
D. Challenges in investigating the illegal sale and distribution of drugs include:

    1. the evolving use of technology by drug traffickers and street dealers
    2. the wide variety of drugs
    3. the difficulty faced when trying to identify them under street conditions

    4.   the special types of searches often required to locate minute amounts of drugs that may be hidden ingeniously

    5.   finding drugs smuggled across national borders and identifying those who transport and distribute them

E.   Confidential informants are crucial to many law enforcement investigations, especially in the field of narcotics investigations; they:

    1.   can provide specific information that is not available from other sources

    2.   are often criminals themselves

    3.   are often vital to making on-sight arrests

F.   On-sight arrests

    1.   If you observe what appears to be a drug buy, you can make a warrantless arrest if you have probable cause; often, however, it is better to simply observe and gather information

    2.   Probable cause is established through knowledge of the suspect's criminal record, by observing other people making contact with the suspect and finding drugs on them, by knowing the suspect's past relationships with other drug users or sellers and through observing actions of the suspect that indicate a drug buy

G.   Surveillance

    1.   Some common indicators of residential drug trafficking are

        a.   a high volume of foot or vehicle traffic to and from a residence at late or unusual hours

        b.   periodic visitors who stay at the residence for very brief periods

        c.   altered property to maximize privacy

    2.   Surveillance officers must have patience because many planned drug buys necessitate a long period of surveillance before the actual sale, or bust, is made

H.   Undercover assignments: undercover investigations are used more routinely in drug cases than perhaps any other type of criminal investigation

    1.   Because street dealers are aware of the restrictions imposed on undercover agents, undercover narcotics officers have had to develop more convincing ways to fit into the drug culture; Narc-Scent Incorporated has developed new products to help officers gain street credibility by giving them the right smell

    2.   Planned buys usually involve working an undercover agent into a group selling or buying drugs or having an informant make the buy

a. Usually undercover agents are police officers of the investigating agency (in large cities) or of cooperative agencies on the same level of government in an exchange operation or a mutual-aid agreement that provides an exchange of narcotics officers

b. Undercover drug buys are carefully planned, witnessed and conducted so that no charge of entrapment can be made

c. The three things that dealers value the most are the drugs, the money the drugs can bring and their freedom to do business; the officer is in the middle of the triangle, and when the money—the *flashroll*—and the drugs are both present, the officer is in the most danger

d. Officers should make two or more buys to avoid the charge of entrapment

3. A *sting*, or a *reverse buy*, is a complex operation organized and implemented by undercover agents to apprehend drug dealers and buyers and to deter other users from making drug purchases at a certain location. Stings are labor intensive, complex and require officers to be well trained

I. A narcotics raid is another method used to apprehend narcotics dealers

1. Surveillance frequently provides enough information for obtaining a no-knock search or arrest warrant

2. The raid itself must be carried out forcefully and swiftly because drugs can easily be destroyed in seconds

3. Narcotics raids are often dangerous

J. Drug paraphernalia stores, or "head shops," sell products (e.g., pipes, syringes) that help the end user ingest drugs; "cut or vial stores," in contrast, sell adulterants, diluents and other "office supplies" used by drug organizations in measuring, separating, chemically altering and packaging mass quantities of drugs

K. Online drug dealers

1. Club drugs, prescription narcotics and ultra-pure forms of DXM, an ingredient found in OTC cough medication, can all be purchased online and shipped directly to the user's home—transactions that are extremely difficult for law enforcement to detect

2. Online drug dealers commonly try to disguise their activities by posting their available products as some type of legitimate substance

VII. Clandestine Drug Laboratories

A. Clandestine drug laboratories present physical, chemical and toxic hazards to law enforcement officers engaged in raids on the premises

B.   The production of meth involves ingredients such as strong acids and bases, flammable solvents and very explosive and poisonous chemicals

C.   Identifying a clandestine (clan) lab

    1.   From the outside:

        a.   Strong chemical odors
        b.   Blacked out or boarded up windows
        c.   Hoses sticking out through windows and doors
        d.   Dead vegetation from dumped chemical wastes
        e.   Exhaust fans running constantly
        f.   Disturbed ground or dead vegetation
        g.   Excessive traffic

    2.   On the inside:

        a.   Coffee grinders with white residue
        b.   Coffee filters with red stains
        c.   Large quantities of acetone, antifreeze, camping fuel, drain cleaner, lithium batteries, matches, plastic baggies, cold tablets or cough syrup containing the ingredient pseudoephedrine
        d.   An abundance of mixing containers such as Pyrex glassware, crock pots and other large pots
        e.   Strips of bed linen or cloth for filtering liquid drug mixtures
        f.   General clutter, disarray and filthy living conditions

D.   Entering a clandestine drug lab: only properly trained and certified personnel should proceed onto the site

    1.   Personnel entering a suspected meth lab should have a self-contained breathing apparatus and complete skin protection
    2.   The entry team faces the possibility of armed resistance as well as booby traps
    3.   Autonomous robotics can enhance officers' safety in investigating a suspected meth lab and be an important force multiplier
    4.   The assessment team deals with immediate hazards
    5.   The processing team identifies and collects evidence
    6.   Autonomous robots are being developed for making the first entry into hazardous surroundings such as meth labs

E.   Processing of clandestine drug labs requires taking photographs with identifying labels, completing a thorough inventory, collecting evidentiary samples and preparing chemicals and equipment for disposal

F.   Cleanup of clandestine drug labs: estimates suggest that for every pound of meth produced, as much as five pounds of waste are created

    1.   Such trash requires special handling and disposal, often at great expense

2.	The Comprehensive Methamphetamine Control Act (MCA) of 1996 allows the courts to order a defendant convicted of manufacturing methamphetamine to pay the cost of cleanup of the lab

VIII.	Indoor Marijuana Growing Operations

A.	Indoor growing operations are often indicated by an excessive use of electricity (stolen or legally acquired)
B.	If such a residence is identified, police may observe the type and amount of traffic to and from the house and, based on the combination of information involving electricity use and traffic, obtain a search warrant
C.	Many grow operations steal electricity by diverting power from a main supply line
D.	Inherent dangers associated with the high-energy needs of these indoor grow operations include the risk of electrocution; explosion and fire risks; and upper respiratory infections caused by mold that thrives in these high-humidity environments

IX.	Investigative Aids

A.	National Drug Pointer Index (NDPIX): a national database on drug trafficking to enhance agent and officer safety; eliminate duplication; increase information sharing and coordination; and minimize costs
B.	Canines are an effective force multiplier
C.	A special high-accuracy laser rangefinder developed for the U.S. Customs Service can find secret compartments that might contain drugs
D.	Flying "drones" for aerial surveillance

X.	Agency Cooperation

A.	The federal Drug Enforcement Administration (DEA) provides unified leadership in attacking narcotics trafficking and drug abuse
B.	The DEA's emphasis is on the source and distribution of illicit drugs rather than on arresting abusers
C.	The DEA emphasis is stopping the flow of drugs at their foreign sources, disrupting illicit domestic commerce at the highest levels of distribution and helping state and local police prevent the entry of illegal drugs into their communities
D.	The National Drug Intelligence Center (NDIC) also plays a vital role in providing police administrators and officers with the latest information on drug distribution patterns

XI.	Drug Asset Forfeitures

A.	The federal Comprehensive Crime Control Act of 1984 initiated procedures for asset forfeitures as a result of drug arrests

1.	The U.S. Congress gave final approval to the Civil Asset Forfeiture Reform Act of 2000, which lowered the burden of proof from "clear and convincing" to "a preponderance of the evidence"

2. The act also reduced the statute of limitations from 11 years to 5 years for a property owner to make a claim on the property

B. Assets used may be seized by the investigating agencies

C. Confiscating drug dealers' cash and property has been effective in reducing drug trafficking

D. Confiscated funds may be used only in police department antidrug efforts

E. A common defense to asset seizure is the *innocent owner defense*: If an owner can prove that he or she had no knowledge of the prohibited activity, the property is not subject to forfeiture

XII. Preventing Problems with Illegal Drugs: Community Partnerships

A. Tremendous national, state and local efforts are being directed to meeting the challenges of drug use and abuse in the United States

1. National drug czar
2. Federal funding through state agencies
3. Operation Weed and Seed—a national initiative
4. Local initiatives
5. State laws restricting sales of OTC drugs

B. Strategic crime-control partnerships with a range of third parties are more effective at disrupting drug problems than law-enforcement-only approaches

XIII. The National Drug Control Strategy

A. Drug arrests have nearly tripled since 1980, when the federal drug policy shifted to arresting and incarcerating users

B. Approximately 1.7 million people were arrested on drug charges in 2009, more than 50 percent of which involved the sale, distribution or possession of marijuana

C. In 2010, President Barack Obama pledged "to prevent drug use and addiction and to make treatment available for those who seek recovery"

D. The key to reducing our nation's drug problem is a three-pronged approach including prevention, treatment and law enforcement

XIV. Organized Crime: An Overview

A. The FBI defines *organized crime* as any group having some manner of a formalized structure and whose primary objective is to obtain money through illegal activities

B. A *criminal enterprise* is defined by the FBI as a group of individuals with an identified hierarchy, or comparable structure, engaged in significant criminal activity

C. Distinctive characteristics of organized crime include:

1. Definite organization and control
2. High-profit and continued-profit crimes
3. Singular control through force and threats
4. Protection through corruption

D. Other characteristics not as frequently mentioned in definitions of organized crime include restricted membership, being nonideological, specialization and code of secrecy

E. Organized crime functions through many forms of corruption and intimidation to create a *singular control* over specific goods and services that ultimately results in a monopoly

F. Organized crime flourishes most where *protection* from interference and prosecution exist

G. Organized crime is not a single entity controlled by one superpower

1. It does not exist only in metropolitan areas
2. It does not involve only activities such as narcotics, prostitution, racketeering and gambling; it is involved in virtually every area where profits are to be made, including legitimate businesses
3. Citizens are not isolated from organized crime

XV. Applicable Laws against Organized Crime

A. Acts that make it permissible to use circumstantial rather than direct evidence to enforce conspiracy violations: 1946 Hobbs Anti-Racketeering Act, the 1968 Omnibus Crime Control and Safe Streets Act, the RICO Act of 1970 and the Organized Crime Control Act of 1970

B. It is a prosecutable conspiracy to

1. acquire any enterprise with money obtained from illegal activity
2. acquire, maintain or control any enterprise by illegal means
3. use any enterprise to conduct illegal activity

C. These three areas that can be prosecuted were defined by Title 18 U.S. Code, Section 1962

XVI. Major Activities of Organized Crime

A. Organized crime is heavily involved in the so-called victimless crimes of gambling, drugs, pornography and prostitution, as well as fraud, loan-sharking, money laundering and infiltration of legitimate businesses

B. Federal crimes prosecutable under the RICO statute include bribery, sports bribery, counterfeiting, embezzlement of union funds, mail fraud, wire fraud, money laundering, obstruction of justice, murder for hire, drug trafficking, prostitution, sexual exploitation of children, alien smuggling, trafficking in counterfeit goods, theft from interstate shipment and interstate transportation of stolen property

C. State crimes chargeable under RICO include murder, kidnapping, gambling, arson, robbery, bribery, extortion and drug offenses

D. Organized crime bosses manipulate the business economy to their benefit. Such crimes as labor racketeering, unwelcome infiltration of unions, fencing stolen property, gambling, loan-sharking, drug trafficking, employment of illegal aliens and white-collar crimes of all types can signal syndicate involvement

E.   Victimless crimes are illegal activities in which all involved are willing participants

   1.   Such crimes include gambling, drug use, pornography and prostitution
   2.   Because there is no complainant, these crimes are difficult to investigate and to prosecute
   3.   *Bookmaking*—soliciting and accepting bets on any type of sporting event—is the most prevalent gambling operation

F.   *Loan sharking*—lending money at exorbitant interest rates—is supported initially by the profits from gambling operations
G.   Money-laundering and the infiltration of legitimate businesses: in recent years, organized crime has become increasingly involved in legitimate business. The vast profits from illegal activities are given legitimacy by being invested in legal business. This is another way of turning dirty money into clean money, or "laundering" it

XVII.   The Threat of Specific Organized Crime Groups

A.   Italian organized crime (IOC)

   1.   Four separate groups: the Sicilian Mafia; the Neapolitan Camorra; the 'Ndrangheta, or Calabrian Mafia; and Sacra Corona Unita, or "United Sacred Crown"
   2.   La Cosa Nostra (LCN)

      a.   Nationwide alliance of criminals with both familial and conspiratorial connections
      b.   Rooted in Italian organized crime, but an Americanized version of the "old school" mafias from Italy, separate and distinct from the other IOC groups
      c.   Estimated membership 1,100 nationwide, with the vast majority (roughly 80 percent) operating in the New York metropolitan area
      d.   Five crime families make up New York City's LCN: Bonanno, Colombo, Genovese, Gambino, Lucchese

B.   Asian organized crime (AOC)

   1.   Involved in murder, kidnapping, extortion, prostitution, pornography, loan-sharking, gambling, money laundering, alien smuggling, trafficking in heroin and methamphetamine, counterfeiting of computer and clothing products and various protection schemes
   2.   Often well run and hard to crack; use very fluid, mobile global networks of criminal associates
   3.   Asian criminal enterprises are classified as either traditional, such as the Yakuza and Triads, or nontraditional, such as ethnic Asian street gangs

4. Japanese organized crime is sometimes known as Boryokudan but is more commonly known as the Yakuza. A *gyangu* (Japanese gangster) is a member of the Yakuza (organized crime family) and is affiliated with the Yamaguchi-gumi (Japan's largest organized crime family) as a *boryokudan* (used primarily for muscle)

5. Triads are the oldest of the Chinese organized crime (COC) groups and engage in a wide range of criminal activities, including money laundering, drug trafficking, gambling, extortion, prostitution, loan-sharking, pornography, alien smuggling and numerous protection schemes

6. Vietnamese organized crime is generally one of two kinds: roving or local

   a. Roving bands travel from community to community, have a propensity for violence, have no permanent leaders or group loyalty, lack language and job skills and have no family in the United States

   b. Local groups tend to band together in a certain area of a specific community, have a charismatic leader, have a propensity for violence and tend to engage in extortion, illegal gambling and robbery

C. Latino organized crime

1. Cubans, Colombians, Mexicans, Dominicans and El Salvadorians are included

2. Heavily involved in drug trafficking

3. Because of Mexico's proximity to the United States, its organized crime groups are becoming an increasing threat to the United States and are among the fastest-growing gangs in the country

D. African organized crime

1. An emerging criminal threat facing law enforcement agencies worldwide and known to be operating in at least 80 other countries

2. African criminal enterprises have proliferated in the United States since the 1980s

3. Although some groups comprise members originating in Ghana and Liberia, by far the predominant nationality in African organized crime is Nigerian

E. Russian organized crime (aka Russian Mafia)

1. Since the collapse of the Soviet Union, Russian organized crime has gone international and poses a great threat to and challenge for U.S. justice

2. The FBI refers to these groups as Eurasian Organized Crime (EOC)

3. Members tend to be well educated

4. Focus on a wide range of frauds and scams, including insurance scams, securities and investment fraud, fuel oil scams and credit card scams

5.   Other activities: contract murders, kidnappings, business arson, transnational money laundering, traffic in women and children, traffic in such hazardous commodities as weapons and nuclear material smuggled out of their homeland

6.   EOC consists of hundreds of groups, all acting independently, with no formal hierarchy

7.   Most members are already hardened criminals, have military experience and are highly educated

XVIII.   Organized Crime and Corruption

A.   One of the greatest threats posed by organized crime is the corruption it engenders throughout the entire legal system

B.   Police are especially concerned about corruption in their own department

C.   Bribes of police officers can take many forms: outright offers of money, taking care of medical bills or providing free merchandise or free vacations

D.   Any police officer who is offered a bribe must report it immediately to a superior and then attempt to make an arrest that will involve the person making the offer as well as those responsible higher in the organization

XIX.   The Police Response

A.   The daily observations of local law enforcement officers provide vital information for investigating organized crimes. Report all suspicious activities and persons possibly associated with organized crime to the appropriate person or agency

B.   Report in writing all information pertaining to such activities, either immediately, if the activity involves an imminent meeting, or when time permits

C.   Information can arise from many sources, and seemingly unimportant details can fit into an overall picture that an intelligence unit is putting together

XX.   Agencies Cooperating in Investigating Organized Crime

A.   Organized crime strike forces coordinate all federal organized crime activities and work closely with state, county and municipal law enforcement agencies

B.   Other agencies that play important roles in investigating organized crime:

1.   FBI: often has a member on the strike forces

2.   Postal Inspection Service: in charge of mail fraud, embezzlements and other crimes involving material distributed through the mails

3.   U.S. Secret Service: investigates government checks and bonds as well as foreign securities

4. Department of Labor: investigates organized crime activities related to labor practices and pension funds
5. Securities and Exchange Commission: investigates organized crime activities in the purchase of securities
6. Internal Revenue Service: investigates violations of income tax laws

C. Organized crime investigations in the United States increasingly involve agencies from other countries

XXI. Methods to Combat Organized Crime

A. The enterprise theory of investigation (ETI) is a combined organized crime/drug strategy used by the FBI that focuses investigations and prosecutions on entire criminal enterprises rather than on individuals
B. Investigative aids

1. Electronic surveillance
2. Pen registers, which record the numbers dialed from a telephone by monitoring the electrical impulses of the numbers dialed

   a. These do not constitute a search under the meaning of the Fourth Amendment (*Smith v. Maryland,* 1979)
   b. Several state courts, however, have held that using a pen register *is* a search under the respective state statutes and that a warrant supported by probable cause *is* needed

3. The same situation exists for trap-and-trace devices, which reveal the telephone number of the source of all *incoming* calls to a particular number; their use may or may not require a warrant, depending on the specific state
4. Regional Information Sharing System (RISS): a multijurisdictional intelligence sharing system comprising nearly 5,000 local, state and federal agencies; helps investigators identify, target and remove criminal conspiracies and activities that reach across jurisdictional boundaries

C. Asset forfeitures: a program that allows law enforcement agencies to seize funds and property associated with criminal activity and effectively subjects criminals to 100 percent tax on their earnings

XXII. The Decline of Organized Crime?

A. It can be difficult to determine whether criminal events are the work of organized crime or of gangs
B. Following the 9/11 terrorist attacks, many of the law enforcement resources previously allocated to organized crime investigations have been redirected toward counterterrorism efforts, allowing a resurgence in organized crime activity throughout the country

XXIII. Summary

CRIMINAL ACTIVITIES OF GANGS AND OTHER DANGEROUS GROUPS

OUTLINE

Chapter 19
Criminal Activities of Gangs and Other Dangerous Groups

Key Terms

• Antichrist	• hate incidents
• Beelzebub	• incantation
• bias crime	• magick
• Black Mass	• moniker
• coven	• occult
• cult	• ritual
• flash mob	• ritualistic crime
• gang	• sabbat
• graffiti	• street gang
• Hand of Glory	• turf
• hate crime	

Learning Objectives
After reading this chapter, students should be able to

• Analyze whether the gang problem is increasing or decreasing.	• Explain two defense strategies that are commonly used by gang members' lawyers in court.
• Outline how to classify gangs.	• Articulate the primary motivation for bias or hate crimes, and identify who is most frequently targeted in such crimes.
• Describe the types of crimes gangs typically engage in.	
• Identify the first step in dealing with a gang problem.	
• Describe how to identify gang members.	• Discuss what a cult is, and explain a better way to refer to cults.
• Explain what kinds of records to keep on gangs.	• Describe what a ritualistic crime is.
• Discuss what special challenges are involved in investigating illegal activities of gangs.	• Explain what may be involved in ritualistic crime.
	• Identify indicators of ritualistic crimes.
• Describe what strategies have been used to combat a gang problem.	• Describe special challenges involved in investigating ritualistic crimes.

Internet Assignments

1.   Have students go to the Office of Juvenile Justice Delinquency Prevention's Gang Prevention Programs Web site, navigate to the Model Programs Guide and search programs for gang prevention. Ask students to review the information and provide a written report describing the steps they would take to coordinate the law enforcement response and investigations in their community with the services and programs mentioned on the site.

2.   Have the students research gangs on the Internet, particularly the FBI's Web site. Ask the students to write a definition of a gang. Then work together as a class to agree on a common definition.

3.   Have students research hate crimes and ritualistic crimes on the Internet. (References to several recent crimes may be found in the text.) Ask each student to choose an example of one such crime and present it to the class. Presentations should include the following elements: profile of perpetrator(s), motive, physical evidence, the investigative process and final outcome.

Class Assignments

1.   A small juvenile gang composed of no more than 15 members has been active in the community recently. Their members have been linked to drug sales, assaults, thefts and graffiti. The gang is multiracial and appears to be led by a slightly older person, who is about 20 years of age. What approach would you take to reduce or eliminate these gang problems?

2.   Have the class search for news articles or material on gangs that are either in or affiliated with local communities. As a class, discuss the different identifiable gangs in their local communities.

Chapter Outline

I.   The Threat of Gangs: An Overview

    A.   Belonging to a gang is *not* illegal in the United States
    B.   However, many activities that gangs engage in are illegal

II.   Gangs Defined

    A.   No single definition exists to describe a gang
    B.   One commonly accepted definition is that a *gang* is a group of individuals with a recognized name and symbol that forms an allegiance for a common purpose and to engage in continuous unlawful activity
    C.   The National Alliance of Gang Investigators' Associations (NAGIA) defines a *gang* as "a group or association of three or more persons with a common identifying sign, symbol or name who individually or collectively engage in criminal activity that creates an atmosphere of fear and intimidation" (2009)
    D.   Gang investigators must be aware that many states have legislatively enacted their own definitions of a *gang* that all local and state law enforcement agencies are mandated to follow

III. Extent of Gangs

A. By the late 1990s, every state and the District of Columbia reported gang activity

B. Gangs range in size from small groups to as many as several thousand. More than 90 percent of gangs have between 3 and 100 members, and only 4 percent have more than 100 members. The number of gangs in large cities ranges from 1,200 to 1,500

C. The 2009 National Gang Threat Assessment reported that at year-end 2008, an estimated one million gang members and more than 20,000 gangs were criminally active in the United States

D. The National Youth Gang Survey (NYGS) estimated 731,000 gang members belonging to 28,100 gangs in existence across the nation during 2009

E. Although the estimates differ, it is clear that gangs and gang-related crime are a serious threat to communities across the country

F. The number of gangs and gang members has remained relatively stable over the last few years, but gang-related crime is still a serious concern for law enforcement

G. Gang violence has become increasingly lethal

H. According to the NYGS, the three factors that most influence local gang violence are drug-related factors (73%), intergang conflict (61%) and a return of gang members to society from secure confinement, such as prison (50%)

I. As society in general has become more mobile, gangs and gang members have also increased their mobility, contributing to gang migration

IV. Why People Join Gangs

A. Recent research (2009) has revealed three common themes regarding why males and females join gangs

1. Neighborhood disadvantage
2. Having gang-involved family and friends
3. Parent-child relationship problems, such as neglect, lack of supervision and substance abuse and addiction

B. A lack of parental attachment is an important risk factor in adolescent gang membership

V. Types of Gangs

A. The National Gang Intelligence Center has identified three general types of gangs: street gangs, prison gangs and outlaw motorcycle gangs (OMGs)

B. Street gangs

1. A nominal definition of a *street gang* is "any durable, street-oriented youth group whose own identity includes involvement in illegal activity"

2. Within the street gang category, groups are classified as:

    a. *National-level street gangs:* highly organized and typically have several hundred to several thousand members nationwide who operate in multiple regions; may have cells in foreign countries; currently, 11 national-level street gangs have been identified in the United States

    b. *Regional-level street gangs:* typically organized with several hundred to several thousand members; may have some members in foreign countries and maintain ties to DTOs and other criminal groups operating in the United States; increasingly distribute drugs at the wholesale level; at least five regional-level street gangs have been identified in the United States

    c. *Local- or neighborhood-level street gangs:* mostly operate in a single location and usually range in membership from three to several hundred members; most engage in violence in conjunction with a variety of crimes, including retail-level drug distribution; these neighborhood-based groups pose a considerable challenge to local law enforcement and are a concern for federal law enforcement

3. Hybrid gangs are a new breed of increasingly violent street gangs appearing throughout the country in which several small groups, some of them rivals, band together into one larger gang; this new generation is singularly focused on making money from drugs, robbery and prostitution

C. Prison gangs

1. According to one expert, "Many of the most notorious and violent street gangs we now see across the nation had their beginnings in our nation's prisons and jails"

2. Another expert notes that, "In some cases, gang activity is tacitly encouraged [by prison officials] since it makes inmates easier to handle and a certain order rules the prison population"

D. Outlaw motorcycle gangs (OMGs)

1. Major gangs are Hell's Angels, Bandidos, Outlaws, Mongols and Pagans

2. OMG-related criminal activity poses a threat to public safety in local communities in which these gangs operate because of their wide-ranging criminal activity, propensity to use violence and ability to counter law enforcement efforts

3. Primary source of income for these gangs is drug trafficking, but also involved in murder, assault, kidnapping, prostitution, money laundering, weapons trafficking, intimidation, extortion, arson and smuggling

E. Female gang involvement

    1. Female gang involvement is increasing, and females are assuming greater responsibility in gang activities

    2. Traditionally, female gangs have received less attention from researchers and law enforcement

    3. A large percentage of law enforcement agencies were unable to provide quantitative data regarding female gang membership, which suggests that the issue of girls in gangs is "of lesser significance for law enforcement"

F. Gang members in the military

    1. Members of nearly every major street gang as well as some prison gangs and OMGs have been identified on both domestic and international military installations

    2. Deployments and military transfers have resulted in gang members, both service members and dependents/relatives, moving to new areas and establishing a gang presence

VI. Gang Culture, Membership and Organization

A. Three Rs of gang culture: reputation, respect and revenge

    1. Without question, the subcultural value that carries the highest value for all gang members is *respect*

    2. Disrespect inevitably leads to the third R—revenge

B. Gangs are essentially self-operated and self-governed. Some operate by consensus, but most have leaders and a sub-governing structure. Leadership may be single or dual

C. Status is generally obtained by joining the gang, but equal status within the gang once joined is not automatically guaranteed

D. Incremental increases in gang organization are related to increased involvement in offending and victimization

E. Symbols

    1. Clothing

    2. Hand signals

    3. Graffiti

    4. Tattoos

F. Turf and graffiti

    1. *Turf:* The *geographic* area of domination that gang members will defend to the death

    2. Gangs identify their turf through *graffiti*

G. Tattoos

    1. Used by some gangs, especially OMGs and Hispanic gangs

    2. They are meant to intimidate, show gang affiliation and indicate rank

VII.   Gang Activities

A.   Many gang activities are *not* illegal
B.   Gangs and crime

1.   The 2009 *National Gang Threat Assessment* reports that criminal gangs commit as much as 80 percent of the crime in many communities
2.   Gangs are increasingly associating with organized crime entities
3.   A *flash mob,* also called swarming, is an event when an entire gang, or a large portion of it, participates in an illegal activity
4.   In addition to drug dealing, gang members often engage in vandalism, arson, auto theft, shoplifting, shootings, stabbings, intimidation and other forms of violence
5.   Competing hypotheses are currently circulating to explain the relationship between gangs and crime:

a.   Facilitation model: gang membership facilitates or promotes drug involvement, which in turn facilitates or increases violence
b.   Selection model: gangs attract members who are already delinquent or criminally involved, and antisocial behaviors precede joining the gang
c.   Enhancement model: gangs attract those who are already delinquent or criminally involved, and membership in the gang further facilitates or enhances their preexisting antisocial behavior

C.   Gangs and drugs

1.   Gangs remain the primary distributors of drugs in the United States
2.   Gang membership facilitates drug use and promotes drug sales among the juveniles (2010 study)

D.   Gangs and violence

1.   Gangs rely on intimidation, force and violence to attain and maintain power and control over a territory
2.   Drug distribution has been found to be a major facilitator of violence
3.   Another study found that drug involvement was associated with gun-carrying behaviors, which increases the potential for violence

VIII.   Recognizing a Gang Problem

A.   The first step in dealing with a gang problem is to recognize it
B.   Warning signs of a gang problem: graffiti, obvious colors of clothing, tattoos, initiations, hand signals or handshakes, uncommon terms or phrases and a sudden change in behavior

C. After a gang problem has been recognized, the next step is to identify the gang members

IX. Identifying Gang Members

A. There are no consistent national criteria used to identify individual gang members

B. The Violent Gang and Terrorist Organizations File (VGTOF) defines a gang member as one who admits gang membership or meets any two of the following criteria:

1. Has been identified as a gang member by an individual of proven reliability

2. Has been identified as a gang member by an individual of unknown reliability, and that information has been corroborated in significant respects

3. Has been observed by law enforcement members to frequent a known gang's area, associate with known gang members or effect that gang's style of dress, tattoos, hand signals or symbols

4. Has been arrested on more than one occasion with known gang members consistent with gang activity

5. Has admitted membership in a gang at any time other than at the time of current arrest/incarceration

C. Gang members may be identified by their names, symbols (clothing and tattoos) and communication styles, including graffiti and sign language

D. Warning signs that an individual may be involved with a gang:

1. Admits to "hanging out" with kids in gangs

2. Shows an unusual interest in one or two particular colors of clothing or a particular logo

3. Has an unusual interest in gangster-influenced music, videos, movies or Web sites

4. Uses unusual hand signals to communicate with friends

5. Has specific drawings of gang symbols on schoolbooks, clothes, walls or tattoos

6. Has unexplained physical injuries (fighting-related bruises, injuries to hands/knuckles)

7. Has unexplained cash or goods, such as clothing or jewelry

8. Carries a weapon

9. Has been in trouble with the police

10. Exhibits negative changes in behavior

X. Records to Keep

A. Most common way to gather information about gangs is internal contacts with patrol officers and detectives, followed by internal departmental records and computerized files and then by review of offense reports

B. A gang file should be maintained with the following information:

1. Type of gang (street, motorcycle, etc.)
2. Ethnic composition
3. Number of active and associate members
4. Territory
5. Hideouts
6. Types of crimes usually committed
7. Method of operation
8. Choice of targets or victims
9. Leadership
10. Members known to be violent

C. Maintain records on gangs, gang members, monikers, photographs, vehicles and illegal activities. Cross-reference the records

1. A *gang member pointer file* cross-references the names of suspected gang members with the gang file
2. A *moniker file* connects suspected gang members' street names with their legal names. A *moniker* is the name gang members use among their peers and often during the commission of crimes
3. A *photograph file* is of great help in conducting photographic identification sessions
4. A *gang vehicle file* can be maintained; includes vehicle make, color, year, body type, license number, distinguishing features, known drivers and usual parking spots
5. An *illegal activities file* lists the gangs known to engage in the activities

XI. Investigating Illegal Gang Activity

A. Special challenges in investigating the illegal activities of gangs include the multitude of suspects and the unreliability or fear of witnesses

B. Anyone may be an "unofficial informant" and "cooperative witness"; every person contacted is a potential gang informant

C. The immediate area in which a crime occurs may yield much information, such as which gang controls the territory

D. Field interviews are "the bread and butter of any gang investigator"

1. When dealing with gang members, address their expectation of respect by maintaining a firm but fair attitude

2. When talking to a gang member about a significant matter, such as a crime or another gang member, hold your conversation where other gang members can neither see nor hear you

3. Isolate gang members suspected of a crime immediately so that they cannot collaborate on their "story"

4. Keep in mind that gang members will often attempt to discard any contraband they are carrying, such as weapons or drugs, when they see an officer approaching

E. Reading and responding to graffiti

1. Gangs use graffiti to send the following types of messages:

   a. To mark the gang's turf
   b. To disrespect a rival gang or gang member
   c. To memorialize a deceased gang member
   d. To make a statement
   e. To send a message
   f. To conduct business

2. To document graffiti evidence, take the following steps:

   a. Photograph it whole and in sections
   b. Analyze it while it is intact
   c. Remove it (paint over it, sandblast it, etc.)
   d. Archive the photo
   e. Record the colors used
   f. Record the gang "tag" names
   g. Record indicators of "beef" or violence
   h. Create an anti-graffiti program to cover over all graffiti

F. Technology innovations: Tracking Automated Graffiti Reporting System (TAGRS)

XII. Approaches to the Gang Problem

A. A three-pronged approach identified as the Comprehensive Community-Wide Gang Program Model, or the Spergel Model, addresses the gang problem using a balance of prevention, intervention and suppression strategies

B. Prevention aims at keeping youths from becoming gang members in the first place

1. Approaches include after-school activities, truancy and dropout prevention programs and job programs; these are strategies that disrupt gang recruiting efforts by keeping kids in prosocial activities and away from unstructured social environments

2. Primary prevention is directed at all youths living in communities where gangs are present

      3.   Some experts believe that prevention is the weakest link because the effort is going toward the 10 percent of kids who are already in gangs, not toward the 90 percent who aren't involved and who are getting beaten up by gang members

  C.   Intervention is directed at youths already involved in gangs, either as active members or close associates

      1.   This approach provides sanctions and services designed to push these juveniles out of and away from gangs; this strategy involves aggressive outreach and recruitment activity, and support services for gang-involved youths and their families that help youth make positive choices

      2.   This group of gang-involved youths make up a relatively large share of the population, typically range in age from 12 to 24 and are involved in significant levels of illegal activity but are not necessarily considered the more serious or chronic offenders

  D.   Suppression targets serious and chronic offenders, those hard-core members most embedded in the gang culture

      1.   This group comprises a relatively small proportion of the population, but they commit a disproportionately large share of crime and violence

      2.   Strategy involves both formal and informal social control procedures, such as close supervision and monitoring of gang-involved youth by the juvenile/criminal justice system and by community-based agencies, schools and grassroots groups

  E.   Civil gang injunctions (CGIs) and ordinances are legal tools used with urban gangs that focus on individuals and the locations of their routine activities

      1.   These injunction strategies target specific individuals who intimidate residents and cause other public nuisance issues, and restrict these gang members' activities within a specific geographic area

      2.   Injunctions and ordinances may be challenged as unconstitutional violations of freedom of speech, right of association and due process rights if they do not clearly delineate how officers may apply such orders

      3.   Tougher legislation is also being used as a gang control approach

XIII.   Collaborative Efforts: Gang Task Forces

  A.   Collaboration among law enforcement agencies can greatly enhance efforts to cope with the gang problem

  B.   Multiagency task forces bring together differing perspectives and focus human labor efforts and resources on a common goal, providing a more effective response to the issue of gangs

C. Partnerships with the community, parents and schools significantly increase the likelihood of a successful response

D. The OJJDP's Comprehensive Gang Model for a gang reduction program (GRP) is based on years of experimentation and research on gang prevention. The model's key distinguishing feature is a strategic planning process that empowers communities to assess their own gang problems and fashion a complement of antigang strategies and program activities

XIV. Prosecuting Gang-Related Crimes

A. "The gang investigator should form a close partnership with the gang prosecutor and each must be available to the other 24/7. This ensures critical input in the early stages of the case and the swift reaction to witness intimidation later" (Valdemar, 2010)

B. Some jurisdictions are seeing positive results by escalating the level of prosecution, particularly for higher level gang members

C. The two most often used defense strategies are pleas of diminished capacity and self-defense

D. Therefore officers should *document* whether the suspect was under the influence of alcohol or other drugs at the time of the crime

E. Officers should also *document* whether the suspect was threatened by the victim and could possibly have been acting in self-defense

XV. Federal Efforts to Combat the Gang Problem

A. National Gang Intelligence Center (NGIC): A multiagency effort that integrates the gang intelligence assets of federal, state and local law enforcement entities to serve as a centralized intelligence resource for gang information and analytical support

B. National Gang Targeting, Enforcement and Coordination Center (GangTECC): Aims "to help disrupt and dismantle the most significant and violent gangs in the United States"

C. In October 2009, the National Youth Gang Center (NYGC) merged with the National Gang Center (NGC). The current NGC provides a plethora of published research about gangs; descriptions of evidence-based, antigang programs; and links to tools, databases and other resources to assist in developing and implementing effective community-based gang prevention, intervention and suppression strategies

XVI. Bias and Hate Crime: An Overview

A. A *bias crime* or a *hate crime* is a traditional criminal act—such as murder, arson or vandalism—with the added element of bias; it is committed because of someone's actual or perceived membership in a particular group

B. Since 2000, the number of hate groups organized in the United States has increased by 54 percent, a surge fueled by fears of Latino immigration and, more recently, the election of the country's first African American president and the economic crisis

C. The Southern Poverty Law Center (SPLC) estimates that there are currently 1,002 known groups operating across the country, up from an estimated 888 groups in 2007

D. The FBI's Uniform Crime Report for 2009 indicates there were 6,604 hate incidents for that year, involving 7,789 offenses

XVII. Motivation for Hate Crime

A. Bias or hate crimes are motivated by bigotry and hatred against a specific group of people; race is usually the primary motivation for hate crimes, and African Americans are most often the victims

B. Groups most likely to be victims of hate crime are (in alphabetical order): African Americans, Arabs, Asians, gay males, Jews, Latinos, lesbians, Native Americans and White women in interracial relationships

C. A group often overlooked in discussions of hate crime is the homeless

D. Offenses

    1. Of the 7,789 hate crimes in 2009:

        a. 4,793 (61.5%) were crimes against persons
        b. 45.0% of these were intimidation
        c. 35.3% were simple assault
        d. 19.1% were aggravated assault
        e. 0.4% were murder (8 cases) and forcible rape (9 cases)
        f. 0.3% were other types of offenses

    2. Of the 2,970 hate crimes (38.1%) committed against property:

        a. 83.0% were destruction/damage/vandalism
        b. the remaining 17.0% were robbery, burglary, larceny-theft, motor vehicle theft, arson and other crimes

E. Offenders

    1. Of the 6,225 known offenders involved in hate crimes during 2009:

        a. 62.4% were White
        b. 18.5% were Black
        c. 7.3% were groups made up of individuals of various races
        d. 1.0% were American Indian/Alaskan Native
        e. 0.7% were Asian/Pacific Islander
        f. 10.2% were of unknown race

XVIII.   Hate Groups

    A.   The main hate groups in the United States are "skinheads," Christian Identity groups, the Ku Klux Klan, Black separatists, White supremacists and neo-Nazis

    B.   Several watchdog organizations such as the SPLC and the Anti-Defamation League track the size and activities of racist groups and are good resources for law enforcement

XIX.   The Police Response

    A.   Respond promptly to reports of hate crime, attempt to reduce the victims' fears and determine the exact type of prejudice involved

    B.   Ask the following questions to determine whether an incident was hate or bias motivated:

        1.   Was the victim a member of a targeted class and outnumbered?

        2.   Were the offenders from a different racial or ethnic group than the victim(s)?

        3.   Did the offender use biased language?

    C.   Always provide follow-up information to the victims

    D.   Include in the report the exact words or language used; the perpetrators' actions, symbols, colors and dress; any other identifying characteristics

    E.   Officers must differentiate between hate crimes and hate incidents

        1.   Hate incidents involve behaviors that, though motivated by bias against a victim's race, religion, ethnic/national origin, gender, age, disability or sexual orientation, are *not* criminal acts

        2.   Hostile or hateful speech or other disrespectful/discriminatory behavior may be motivated by bias but is not illegal

    F.   Reporting bias and hate crimes

        1.   The Hate Crime Statistics Act of 1990 requires the attorney general to collect data "about crimes that manifest evidence of prejudice based on race, religion, sexual orientation or ethnicity"

        2.   The responsibility for developing the procedures for implementing, collecting and managing hate crime data was delegated to the director of the FBI, who in turn assigned the tasks to the Uniform Crime Reporting (UCR) Program

        3.   In 2009 Congress further amended the Hate Crime Statistics Act with the passage of the Matthew Shepard and James Byrd, Jr. Hate Crime Prevention Act; this amendment includes the collection of data for crimes motivated by bias against a particular gender and gender identity, as well as for crimes committed by, and crimes directed against, juveniles

XX.   Efforts to Combat Bias and Hate Crimes

    A.   Two responses have been taken: legislation to expand the scope of the law and increase the severity of punishment for hate crimes, and more police focus on and fully investigating such crimes

    B.   Other efforts include community-based programs to increase awareness of and offer solutions to the problem of hate crime

    C.   Legislation

        1.   No national consensus exists about whether hate crimes should be a separate crime, and those supporting hate crime statues disagree about what should be included

        2.   States vary greatly in legislation related to hate crimes

        3.   The most common elements of hate crime legislation include:

            a.   Enhanced penalties

            b.   Criminal penalties for vandalism of religious institutions

            c.   Collection of data

    D.   Legislation must also keep up with the technology used to spread messages of hate. Despite such legislation, those who propagate messages of bigotry, intolerance and hatred claim they have a constitutionally protected right to do so, citing free speech, due process and equal protection challenges

XXI.   Ritualistic Crime: An Overview

    A.   A *cult* is a system of religious beliefs and rituals; it also refers to those who practice such beliefs

    B.   According to some estimates, 3,000 cults exist throughout the world, claiming a total estimated membership of more than 3 million people

    C.   A less negative term than *cult* is *new religious movement* (NRM)

        1.   Normally, NRMs have a charismatic leader who develops an idea that attracts people looking for fulfillment

        2.   The leader is usually self-appointed and claims the right of rule because of a supernatural power of appointment

        3.   NRM membership may include males and females, and there is normally no room for democratic participation

        4.   Leadership is most often exerted through fear and mysticism

XXII.   Terminology and Symbols of Cults

    A.   Among the terms law enforcement officers should be familiar with are:

        1.   *Antichrist*—the son of Satan

        2.   *Beelzebub*—powerful demon, right under Satan

        3.   *Coven*—group of witches or Satanists

        4.   *Hand of Glory*—the left hand of a person who has died

5. *Incantation*—verbal spell
6. *Magick*—the "glue" that binds occult groups, a supernatural act or force that causes a change in the environment
7. *Occult*—secret knowledge of supernormal powers
8. *Ritual*—prescribed form of religious or mystical ceremony
9. *Sabbat*—gathering of witches

B. Symbols

1. The *circle,* which symbolizes totality and wholeness and within which ceremonies are often performed
2. The *inverted cross,* which mocks the Christian cross
3. The *goat's head,* symbolizing the devil
4. The *heart,* symbolizing the center of life
5. The *hexagram* (six-pointed star), purported to protect and control demons
6. The *pentagram* (five-pointed star), representing the four elements of the earth surmounted by "the Spirit"
7. The *horned hand,* a hand signal of recognition used between members

C. Colors

1. Black—darkness, night, sorrow, evil, the devil
2. Blue—water, tears, sadness
3. Green—vegetation, nature, restfulness
4. Red—blood, physical life, energy, sexuality
5. White—cleanliness, purity, innocence, virginity
6. Yellow—perfection, wealth, glory, power

XXIII. The Nature of Ritualistic Crimes

A. A *ritualistic crime* is an unlawful act committed within the context of a ceremony. Investigate the crime, not the belief system
B. Like gangs, occult groups have three levels of activity: dabbling, serious involvement and criminal involvement
C. Ritualistic crimes include vandalism, destruction or theft of religious artifacts; desecration of cemeteries; the maiming, torturing or killing of animals and people; and the sexual abuse of children
D. The "Black Masses" of Satanism often incorporate religious articles stolen from churches; a *Black Mass* mocks the Christian ritual of communion by substituting blood and urine for the wine and feces for the bread
E. "Stoner" gangs consist of middle-class youths involved in drugs, alcohol and often Satanism; although stoners are not as apt to engage in the violent crimes associated with other street gangs, they may mutilate animals, rob graves and desecrate churches and human remains

XXIV.   Who Commits Ritualistic Crime?

    A.   People involved in the occult tend to be creative, imaginative, curious and daring, as well as intelligent and well-educated, although frequently underachievers. Although egocentric, they also have low self-esteem and have suffered peer rejection or persecution

    B.   A number of factors may lead an individual to occult involvement, including family alienation, insecurity and a quest for personal power; unfulfilled ambitions; a spiritual search for answers; idealism; nonconformity; adolescent rebellion; a desire for adventure and excitement; a need for attention and recognition; and a need to escape reality or the circumstances of his or her own birth

    C.   Types of perpetrators

        1.   Dabblers: Intermittently involved in the occult and have a strong, curious interest in supernatural belief systems

        2.   True believers: Committed to their religion and commit ritualistic crimes because the acts are required by their belief system

        3.   True criminals: Use the occult as an excuse to justify or rationalize their crimes

XXV.   Investigating Ritualistic Crimes

    A.   One challenge in investigating ritualistic crime is determining that an act is, in fact, motivated by a religious belief system, rather than by hate or bias

    B.   Signs of cult-related activity: if you suspect a ritualistic crime, list any of the items listed in the text in any search warrant

    C.   Indicators of ritualistic crimes: indicators that criminal activity may be cult related include symbols, candles, makeshift altars, bones, cult-related books, swords, daggers and chalices

    D.   Investigating animal deaths

        1.   Unusual circumstances surrounding animal deaths may be important indicators of satanic or cult activity

        2.   The following circumstances connected with dead animals should be noted:

            a.   no blood (the blood has been drained from the animal)
            b.   an inverted cross carved on the animal's chest
            c.   surgically removed head
            d.   intestines or other body organs removed

        3.   If a rash of missing-animal reports occurs, gather information on the kind of animals they are, when they disappeared and from what area

E.   Investigating homicides

1.   Occult murders are usually stabbings or cuttings—seldom are they gunshot wounds—and many victims are cult members or former members

2.   The murderer is typically a White male from a middle- to upper-class family with above-average intelligence and using some form of drug

3.   Guard against reacting emotionally when confronted with ritualistic crimes, for they tend to be emotionally and spiritually repulsive

4.   During postmortem examination, the stomach contents can be of great importance in determining what occurred just before death

5.   Most juries disbelieve seemingly outlandish charges of Satanism and human sacrifice, and most judges do not regard Satanism as a real problem; hence, most cases are dismissed

F.   Investigating satanic serial killings

1.   Serial killings may be linked to satanic-like rituals in the murder act itself as well as in the killer's behavior following the murder

2.   Serial killings frequently linked to Satanism include ritualistic overtones; conspiracy among satanic cult members of the Process group; Satanism as a justification for their bizarre antisocial behavior; satanic graffiti; obsession with AC/DC's *Highway to Hell* album

XXVI.   Special Challenges in Ritualistic Crime Investigations

A.   Special challenges involved in investigating ritualistic or cult-related crimes include separating the belief system from the illegal acts, the sensationalism that frequently accompanies such crimes and the "abnormal" personalities of some victims and suspects

XXVII.   Summary

TERRORISM AND HOMELAND SECURITY

OUTLINE

Chapter 20
Terrorism and Homeland Security

Key Terms

• asymmetric warfare	• hawala
• bioterrorism	• intifada
• contagion effect	• jihad
• cyberterrorism	• sleeper cell
• deconfliction	• technological terrorism
• ecoterrorism	• terrorism
• fusion center	

Learning Objectives
After reading this chapter, students should be able to

• Describe what most definitions of terrorism have in common.	• Describe how the USA PATRIOT Act enhances counterterrorism efforts by the United States.
• Describe what motivates most terrorist attacks.	• Identify the first line of defense against terrorism in the United States.
• Explain how the FBI classifies terrorist acts.	• Explain the three-tiered model of al-Qaeda terrorist attacks.
• Outline what groups are commonly identified as Islamic terrorist organizations.	• Identify a key to successfully combating terrorism.
• Discuss what domestic terrorist groups exist in the United States.	• Describe what the Law Enforcement Officers Safety Act authorizes.
• Describe the various methods terrorists may use.	• Identify two major concerns related to the war on terrorism.
• Explain what federal office was established as a result of 9/11.	• Discuss the balances that must be maintained in investigating terrorism.
• Identify the two lead agencies in combating terrorism.	

Internet Assignments

1. Have students review the public Web sites of the Central Intelligence Agency and the Department of Homeland Security for information on terrorism in the United States. Ask them to provide a written response to the following questions based on their review of these sites:

   • Which terrorist group or groups do you believe represent the greatest threat to the United States, and why? What methods would you be most concerned about them using?

   • Do the two sites present different points of view as to the danger levels that various groups pose to the United States? If so, summarize the different perspectives as well as their sources, and explain which you would consider to be the most authoritative.

2. Have students review the FBI's Web site for information on counterterrorism. Ask students to discuss events that have occurred since 9/11 that have demonstrated the constant need for both domestic and international oversight and monitoring of terrorist groups.

3. Have students visit the DHS Web site and review ongoing activities. Ask students discuss what's working and what isn't working with regard to homeland security.

4. Have students visit President Obama's Web site and report back to the class on the president's stance on terrorism.

Class Assignment

1. Break the class into several groups and have the groups discuss answers to the following questions:

   • Which community organizations, governmental agencies and other groups should be included in developing a community or hometown security plan?

   • A number of unmarried young men from the Middle East have moved into your community in recent months. What actions, if any, should be taken?

   • The Department of Homeland Security has notified you, as a member of the local police department, that a group of individuals who may be a sleeper cell for al-Qaeda have been making drawings and taking pictures of a major bridge in your community. What should you do?

Chapter Outline

I. Terrorism: An Overview

    A. Terrorism defined

        1. The Terrorism Research Center defines terrorism as "the use of force or violence against persons or property in violation of the criminal laws of the United States for purposes of intimidation, coercion or ransom"

2. The FBI's definition: "Terrorism is the unlawful use of force or violence against persons or property to intimidate or coerce a government, the civilian population, or any segment thereof, in furtherance of political or social objectives"

3. The U.S. Code Title 22 defines terrorism as the "premeditated, politically motivated violence perpetrated against noncombatant targets by subnational groups or clandestine agents, usually intended to influence an audience"

B. Most definitions of terrorism have common elements, including the systematic use of physical violence, either actual or threatened, against noncombatants to create a climate of fear to cause some religious, political or social change

C. Motivations for terrorism

1. Most terrorist acts result from dissatisfaction with a religious, political or social system or policy and frustration resulting from an inability to change it through acceptable, nonviolent means

2. Religious motives are seen in Islamic extremism

3. Political motives are seen in such elements as the Red Army Faction

4. Social motives are seen in single-issue groups such as those against abortion or active in animal rights or environmentalist movements

II. Classification of Terrorist Acts

A. The FBI categorizes terrorism in the United States as either domestic or international

B. Domestic terrorism

1. The FBI defines *domestic terrorism* as "the unlawful use, or threatened use, of force or violence by a group or individual based and operating entirely within the United States or its territories without foreign direction committed against persons or property to intimidate or coerce a government, the civilian population or any segment thereof, in furtherance of political or social objectives"

2. Examples of domestic terrorism include the bombing of the Alfred P. Murrah Federal Building and the pipe bomb explosions in the Centennial Olympic Park during the 1996 Summer Olympic Games in Atlanta

C. International terrorism

1. International terrorism is foreign based or directed by countries or groups outside the United States against the United States

2.   The FBI divides international terrorism into three categories:

    a.   Foreign state sponsors using terrorism as a tool of foreign policy

    b.   Formalized terrorist groups such as the Lebanese Hezbollah, the Egyptian al-Gamm'a al-Islamiyya, the Palestinian Harakat al-Muqawamah al-Islamiyyah (HAMAS) and Osama bin Laden's al-Qaeda

    c.   Loosely affiliated international radical extremists who have a variety of identities and travel freely in the United States, unknown to law enforcement or the government

3.   These international terrorist groups are likely to engage in what is often referred to as *asymmetric warfare*: combat in which a weaker group attacks a superior group not head-on but by targeting areas where the adversary least expects to be hit, causing great psychological shock, along with loss of life among random victims

4.   The number of attacks rose by almost 5 percent from 2009 to 2010, the number of deaths declined for a third consecutive year, dropping 12 percent from 2009

5.   The fewest incidents in 2010 were reported in the Western Hemisphere, where both attacks and deaths declined by roughly 25 percent

6.   In 2010 armed attacks continued to be the most prevalent form of attack; however bombings, the second most prevalent form of attack, were far more lethal, causing almost 70 percent of all deaths

7.   Although secular, political and anarchist groups committed some of the terrorism reported in 2010, the majority of worldwide terrorist attacks were perpetrated by religious extremists, with Sunni extremists accounting for nearly 60 percent of all attacks around the globe

8.   Muslims constituted the greatest number of terrorism victims in 2010

9.   These data help explain why much of the international antiterrorism effort is focused on radical Islamic groups and their jihadist ideology

    a.   Islamic jihad: several Middle Eastern groups go by this name

    b.   Although they have different ideas about how to go about their militant actions, they share a similar beginning born of the first intifada, or uprising, which was a spontaneous Palestinian revolt in Gaza and the West Bank against Israeli crackdowns on rioting

10. Islamic terrorist groups include:

   a. Hezbollah: literally the Party of God, a militia group and political party that first emerged in Lebanon following the Israeli invasion of that country in 1982
   b. HAMAS: a militant Palestinian Islamic movement in the West Bank and Gaza Strip dedicated to destroying Israel and creating an Islamic state in Palestine; founded in 1987
   c. Palestinian Islamic Jihad (PJJ), which emerged from Egypt; its founders were influenced by militant factions and disillusioned with Egypt's traditional Muslim Brotherhood; they moved into the Gaza Strip in the late 1970s; they want to create an Islamic state through military action
   d. Al-Aqsa Martyrs Brigade: formed in refugee camps in the West Bank; their terrorist operations are divided into six geographical areas, controlled by division commanders; they do not always follow the wishes of the command council, formerly led by the late Yasser Arafat
   e. Al-Qaeda: means "the base"; founded in the late 1980s by now-deceased bin Laden; a broad-based Islamic militant organization that openly declared jihad on the United States; Osama bin Laden was killed in May 2011 when President Obama authorized U.S. special forces to raid the compound in Pakistan

D. The threat and reality of terrorism

   1. *National Intelligence Estimate: The Terrorist Threat to the U.S. Homeland* (2007) is a report that uses *estimative language* based on analytical assessments and judgments.
   2. The *Estimate:*

      a. Judges that that United States will face a "persistent and evolving terrorist threat over the next three years"
      b. Suggests that international cooperation following 9/11 may wane and that al-Qaeda will "continue to enhance its capabilities to attack the Homeland through greater cooperation with regional terrorist groups"
      c. Projects that al-Qaeda will "continue to focus on prominent political, economic and infrastructure targets with the goal of producing mass casualties, visually dramatic destruction, significant economic aftershocks and/or fear among the U.S. population"
      d. Assesses that al-Qaeda will "continue to try to acquire and employ chemical, biological, radiological or nuclear material in attacks"
      e. Projects that other non-Muslim terrorist groups will probably conduct attacks in the next three years given their violent histories, but that this violence will be on a small scale

E. The dual threat: the United States must also protect its citizens from those among us who would like nothing better than to tear the country apart and recast it in their own image

III. Terrorist Groups in the United States

A. Domestic terrorist groups within the United States include White supremacists, Black supremacists, militia groups, other right-wing extremists, left-wing extremists, pro-life extremists, animal rights extremists and environmental extremists
B. White supremacists: Ku Klux Klan and Neo-Nazi groups
C. Black supremacists: Black Panther Party
D. The militia movement

1. Most are heavily armed
2. Members are commonly frustrated, overwhelmed and socially unable to cope with the modern world

E. Other right-wing extremists: the Brady Bill, the Ruby Ridge incident and the Waco incident rejuvenated the extreme right during the 1980s and have kept it active since then
F. Left-wing extremists: Believe in a Pro-Marxist stance that the rich must be brought down and the poor elevated; anarchists are the largest groups of supporters for this cause
G. Pro-life extremists

1. Many antiabortion advocates stay within the law in promoting their beliefs
2. The Army of God is an active terrorist organization that commits crimes ranging from arson to assault to assassination

H. Animal rights extremists

1. The Animal Liberation Front (ALF) is a clandestine decentralized group and one of the most active domestic terrorist assemblages
2. Its objective is to eliminate animal euthanasia and prevent the use of animals in scientific lab testing by "liberating" such caged animals
3. Arson, vandalism and other crimes are targeted at research labs, meat packing plants and furriers

I. Environmental extremists

1. *Ecoterrorism* seeks to inflict economic damage on those who profit from the destruction of the natural environment
2. Earth Liberation Front (ELF) often works with the ALF
3. Arson is a favorite weapon

IV.   Terrorists as Criminals

A.   Law enforcement agencies and officers trained to deal with traditional crimes are now focusing on apprehending individuals operating with different motivations, different objectives and much deadlier weapons than traditional criminals use

B.   Terrorists seek to cause wide-scale damage and inflict fear and may be less concerned with escape, making them very different from conventional criminals, who usually seek personal, financial or material gain and an escape route

C.   Traditional criminals are spontaneous, but terrorists go to great lengths preparing for their attacks

D.   When fighting terrorists, it's kill or be killed—not capture and convict

V.   Methods Used by Terrorists

A.   In addition to armed attacks, terrorists use arson, explosives and bombs; weapons of mass destruction (biological, chemical or nuclear agents); or technology

B.   Law enforcement agencies use the term *CBR* to include all potential terrorist threats that can have consequences for the health of large numbers of people: chemical agents (C), biological agents (B) and radiation exposure (R)

C.   Explosives and bombs: suspicious packages, vehicle bombs and suicide bombers

D.   Weapons of mass destruction (WMDs)

1.   Biological agents: *bioterrorism* involves dissemination of anthrax, botulism and smallpox as WMDs; the nation's food and water supplies are especially susceptible to bioterrorism

2.   Chemical agents: nerve agents, blood agents, choking agents and blistering agents

3.   Nuclear terrorism

4.   Detecting radiation and other bioterrorism agents

a.   Dosimeters
b.   *Electronic nose* technology
c.   Robotic detection and identification technology
d.   Global positioning systems (GPS)

5.   A WMD team: law enforcement agencies should select and train officers to form a WMD team to be ready if needed; members of the team must have adequate personal protective equipment (PPE)

E.   *Technological terrorism*

1.   *Technological terrorism* includes attacks *on* our technology as well as *by* technology

2. *Cyberterrorism* is defined by the FBI as "terrorism that initiates, or threatens to initiate, the exploitation of or attack on information systems"

VI. Funding Terrorism

A. Terrorist groups commonly collaborate with organized criminal groups to deal drugs, arms and, in some instances, people

B. *Narcoterrorism* refers to the use of terrorist tactics to support drug operations or the use of drug trade profits to finance terrorism

C. Many terrorist operations are financed by charitable groups and wealthy Arabs sympathetic to the group's cause

D. Fraud has become increasingly common among terrorists as a way to generate revenue and as a way to gain access to their targets

E. Money laundering

1. *Hawala* is an informal banking system based on trust and often bartering, common throughout the Middle East and used to transfer billions of dollars every year; no tax records or paper trails exist

2. Hawala allows money launderers to secretly hide and send money out of the country without detection

VII. The Federal Response to Terrorism

A. The Department of Homeland Security

1. Established as a result of 9/11, reorganizing the departments of the federal government

2. At the federal level, the FBI is the lead agency for responding to acts of domestic terrorism; the Federal Emergency Management Agency (FEMA) is the lead agency for consequence management (after an attack)

3. In April 2011, DHS Secretary Janet Napolitano announced that the five-tiered color-coded security advisory system that had been used since 2002 would be replaced by a two-level threat advisory:

a. Elevated threat: warns of a credible terrorist threat against the United States

b. Imminent threat: warns of a credible, specific and impending terrorist threat against the United States

4. Goals of the DHS:

a. Increase our ability to keep bad people out of the country

b. Keep bad things out of the country, increasing port security

c. Protect our infrastructure better

      d.   Continue to build a response capability with modern computer tools

      e.   Promote intelligence sharing, horizontally across the federal government and vertically with the local government

B.   The USA PATRIOT Act

    1.   The USA PATRIOT Act significantly improves the nation's counterterrorism efforts by

      a.   Allowing investigators to use the tools already available to investigate organized crime and drug trafficking

      b.   Facilitating information sharing and cooperation among government agencies so they can better "connect the dots"

      c.   Updating the law to reflect new technologies and new threats

      d.   Increasing the penalties for those who commit or support terrorist crimes

    2.   President Obama signed a 4-year extension of the USA PATRIOT Act on May 26, 2011, which includes three key provisions related to roving wiretaps, surveillance and searches of business records

    3.   Controversy over the USA PATRIOT Act: Some members of Congress and civil liberties groups say the act has given federal agents too much power to pursue suspected terrorists, threatening the civil rights and privacy of Americans

C.   The National Infrastructure Protection Plan (NIPP)

    1.   NIPP is a comprehensive risk management framework defining critical infrastructure protection roles and responsibilities of federal, state, local, tribal and private security partners

    2.   Its goal is to "Build a safer, more secure and more resilient America by enhancing protection of the nation's critical infrastructure and key resources (CIKR) to prevent, deter, neutralize or mitigate the effects of deliberate efforts by terrorists to destroy, incapacitate or exploit them; and to strengthen national preparedness, timely response and rapid recovery in the event of an attack, natural disaster or other emergency"

D.   Fusion centers

    1.   An initiative aimed at promoting and facilitating information and intelligence sharing among federal and local law enforcement agencies is the development of fusion centers throughout the country

2. A *fusion center* is a "collaborative effort of two or more agencies that provide resources, expertise and information to the center with the goal of maximizing their ability to detect, prevent, investigate and respond to criminal and terrorist activity"

3. There are 72 fusion centers operating throughout the country

4. However, general assessment of the centers is that they are a costly but largely ineffective weapon against terrorism. DHS has given states $380 million to set up the centers but they tend to gravitate to an "all-crimes and even broader all-hazards approach" rather than focusing on recognizing suspicious activity, patterns and people and using the information to prevent terrorist attacks

VIII. Hometown Security and Homeland Security

A. The IACP has identified five key principles that should form the basis for a national homeland security strategy:

1. All terrorism is local
2. Prevention is paramount
3. Hometown security is homeland security
4. Homeland security strategies must be coordinated nationally, not federally
5. Bottom-up engineering is important, involving the diversity of the state, tribal and local public safety communities in noncompetitive collaboration

B. The first line of defense against terrorism is the patrol officer in the field

IX. Investigating Possible Terrorist Activities

A. A major challenge in the war on terrorism is ensuring that individual officers remain vigilant and cognizant of their critical role in homeland security

B. Law enforcement officers should be aware of terrorist *indicators* such as negative rhetoric, excessive physical training, anti-American literature or a disregard for U.S. laws

C. Investigators should also be knowledgeable of vulnerable, valuable targets for a terrorist attack, which might include:

1. Any high-occupancy structure or any site where a significant number of lives are affected
2. A structure containing dangerous substances or articles
3. Any vital, high-use structure composing an infrastructure
4. A site of significant historical, symbolic, strategic, defensive or functional value to the nation, including structures holding highly sensitive, rare, historical or irreplaceable artifacts, documents or other such content

D. "Soft" targets—those that are relatively unguarded or difficult to guard—should not be overlooked. Examples include: shopping malls, subways, trains, sporting stadiums, theaters, schools, hospitals, restaurants, entertainment parks, compressed gas and oil storage areas, chemical plants, pharmaceutical companies and many others

E. The typical stages of a terrorist attack are research, planning and execution

    1. Research: includes surveillance, stakeouts and local inquiries

    2. Planning: usually conducted behind closed doors; average planning stage for international terrorists is 92 days

    3. Execution: the actual attack and possible escape, often carried out by a *sleeper cell*, a group of terrorists who blend into a community

F. The three-tiered model of al-Qaeda terrorist attacks consists of sleeper cells attacking in conjunction with the group's leaders in Afghanistan, sleeper cells attacking on their own apart from centralized command and individuals attacking with support from small cells

G. It is crucial that investigators identify members of sleeper cells within their community. Approaches include:

    1. Profiling

    2. Behavior pattern recognition (BPR)

    3. NYPD is using is different tactic, called Operation Nexus: having detectives visit scuba shops and hardware stores, talk to parking garage attendants and plastic surgeons, hotel managers and tool rental companies, bulk fuel dealers and trade schools

    4. Confidential informant reward programs established by the 1984 ACIT; award amount was increased by the PATRIOT Act to $250,000

H. Surveillance cameras as investigative tools

    1. London: Ring of Steel—a network of thousands of surveillance cameras that line London's intersections and neighborhoods

    2. NYC: Lower Manhattan Security Initiative has been implemented

X. Information Gathering and Intelligence Sharing

A. An important distinction differentiates information and intelligence, with intelligence broadening to become organized information

B. One way to understand this is to think of information as raw data; once that data has been placed through various filters, sieves and other analytical processes, the more meaningful or useful bits of data that are extracted are referred to as *intelligence*. The process of extracting intelligence from raw data is referred to as the *intelligence cycle*

C. The intelligence cycle:

1. Knowing the *intelligence requirements* needed for an investigation

2. *Planning and direction*, a function of the FBI

3. *Collecting raw information* from local, state and federal investigations

4. *Processing and exploiting* the raw information, that is, converting the collected information into a form usable for analysis

5. *Analysis and production*, converting the raw information into intelligence

6. *Dissemination* of intelligence to consumers, who make decisions based on the intelligence. These decisions may levy further requirements, thus continuing the intelligence cycle

D. Local networking modules developed among local, state and federal law enforcement agencies are the most effective way to discuss and share investigative and enforcement endeavors to combat terrorism

1. This networking module approach avoids compromising existing investigations or conducting conflicting cases

2. It should also have a built-in *deconfliction* protocol, which essentially means guidelines to avoid conflict

E. The National Criminal Intelligence Sharing Plan (NCISP)

1. Unites law enforcement agencies of all sizes and geographic locations in a national effort to prevent terrorism and criminal activity

2. Raises cooperation and communication among local, state and federal partners to an unprecedented level and thus strengthens the abilities of the justice community to detect threats and protect American lives and liberties

XI. Crucial Collaborations and Partnerships

A. A key to combating terrorism lies with the local police and the intelligence they can provide to federal authorities

B. Communication should be the number one priority in any terrorist-preparedness plan and is number one in collaboration among local, state and federal law enforcement agencies

C. Regional Information Sharing Systems (RISS) program: assists state and local agencies by sharing information and intelligence regarding terrorism

D. Limitations on information sharing have caused tensions in the past, as often information received by the FBI is classified. Rules of federal procedure and grand jury classified material are two other limitations to how much information can be shared

XII. Initiatives to Assist in the Fight against Terrorism

    A. The *FBI Intelligence Bulletin:* a weekly online publication containing information related to terrorism in the United States

    B. The Law Enforcement Officers Safety Act of 2004 (LEOSA): gives qualified active duty as well as qualified retired police officers the right to carry their firearms concealed in all 50 states

    C. Increased border security: the program requires visitors to submit to inkless finger scans and digital photographs, allowing Customs and Border Protection (CBP) officers to determine whether the person applying for entry is the same one who was issued a visa by the State Department

    D. Community Vulnerability Assessment Methodology (C-VAM)

    E. The National Memorial Institute for the Prevention of Terrorism

        1. Grew out of the desire of the survivors and families of the Murrah Federal Building bombing to have a living memorial in the form of an online, national network of best practices and lessons learned

        2. Since 2000, this nonpartisan, nonprofit organization, located in Oklahoma City, Oklahoma, has amassed the largest national open source collection of documents on counterterrorism and functions as a terrorism prevention training center for police officers and other first responders, investigators and intelligence analysts from throughout the country

    F. The National Center for Food Protection and Defense

        1. To reduce the vulnerability of the nation's food system to terrorist attack by contamination with biological, chemical or radiological agents at any point along the food supply chain

        2. To strengthen the food system's preparedness and resiliency to threats, disruption and attacks

        3. To mitigate the potentially catastrophic public health and economic effects of food system attacks

    G. The National Incident Management System (NIMS)

        1. On March 1, 2004, Secretary Ridge announced the approval of the country's first standardized management approach unifying federal, state and local governments for incident response

        2. NIMS establishes standardized incident management processes, protocols and procedures that all responders—federal, state, tribal and local—will use to coordinate and conduct response action

    H. Joint terrorism task forces (JTTFs):

        1. The FBI has joint terrorism task forces (JTTFs) in 106 cities throughout the country, including at least one in each of its 56 field offices

      2.   JTTFs are the nation's front line on terrorism and consist of small cells of highly trained, locally based investigators, analysts, linguists, special weapons and tactics (SWAT) experts and other specialists from dozens of U.S. law enforcement and intelligence agencies

      3.   In a JTTF, all investigators, whether FBI agents, other federal officers or state or local officers, are equal partners

      4.   Every investigator is assigned substantive cases and works from established FBI protocols for investigating terrorism, completing paperwork requirements and using data systems

XIII.   The Role of the Media in the War on Terrorism

    A.   According to the Terrorism Research Center, "Terrorism and the media have a symbiotic relationship. Without the media, terrorists would receive no exposure, their cause would go ignored and no climate of fear would be generated. Terrorism is futile without publicity, and the media generates much of this publicity"

    B.   Scholars have raised the question of the *contagion effect*, that is, coverage of terrorism inspires more terrorism, thus making terrorism, in effect, contagious

    C.   This controversial issue leads to discussions about censorship in the war on terrorism

XIV.   Concerns Related to the War on Terrorism

    A.   Two pressing concerns related to the "war on terrorism" are that civil liberties may be jeopardized and that people of Middle Eastern descent may be discriminated against or become victims of hate crimes

    B.   Concerns for civil rights

      1.   Civil libertarians are concerned that valued American freedoms will be sacrificed in the interest of national safety

      2.   A difficult challenge facing law enforcement is balancing the need to enhance security with the need to maintain freedom

    C.   Another concern is that some Americans may retaliate against innocent people of Middle Eastern descent, many of whom were either born in the United States or are naturalized citizens

      1.   Four obstacles to improved relations between police and Arab American communities have been identified:

         a.   Distrust between Arab American communities and law enforcement

         b.   Lack of cultural awareness among law enforcement officers

         c.   Language barriers

         d.   Concerns about immigration status and fear of deportation

2. Community policing efforts can do much to overcome these obstacles

XV. Community Policing and Homeland Security

A. Community policing is an important concept to adopt in efforts to prepare for and respond to acts of terrorism

B. Guidelines for departments wishing to mobilize their community in counterterrorism efforts:

1. Establish a liaison with DHS
2. Formulate a policy statement that will guide community mobilization efforts
3. Educate community members about the significant differences between reporting sought-after information (proper) and conducting covert investigations or other quasi-police actions (improper)
4. Emphasize the importance of reporting information without making assumptions about a person's guilt

C. Being proactive

1. It is far preferable to be proactive and interfere with an attack in the preparation stage than to be reactive and respond to an attack after the fact
2. Officers must be able to recognize the warning signs of terrorism-related surveillance and other preparatory acts, such as building explosives
3. Law enforcement officers who can recognize and act on these warning signs will make a valuable contribution to counterterrorism in the months and years ahead
4. Officers must keep their ears to the ground and establish a rapport with the various sources of information in their community, including storage facilities, religious groups, real estate agents, hotels and motels, colleges and universities, transportation centers and tourist attractions

XVI. Summary

PREPARING FOR AND PRESENTING CASES IN COURT

OUTLINE

Chapter 21
Preparing for and Presenting Cases in Court

Key Terms

- adversary system
- bench trial
- brackets
- Brady rule
- cross-examination
- de minimus communication
- direct examination
- discovery process
- exceptionally cleared

- expert witness
- impeach
- motion in limine
- rebuttal
- rule on witnesses
- subpoena
- surrebuttal
- the well
- witness sequestration rule

Learning Objectives
After reading this chapter, students should be able to

- Identify the most important rule to eradicate fear of testifying in court.
- Outline what to include in the final report.
- Describe the relative importance of the prosecutor in the court system.
- Explain why some cases are not prosecuted.
- Discuss how to prepare a case for court.
- Describe how to review a case.
- Explain what occurs during the pre-trial conference.
- Describe the usual sequence in a criminal trial.
- Clarify what the "win" is for an investigator who testifies in court.

- Explain what kinds of statements are inadmissible in court.
- Describe how to testify most effectively.
- Explain when to use notes while testifying.
- Describe what nonverbal elements can influence courtroom testimony positively and negatively.
- Discuss strategies that can make testifying in court more effective.
- Describe what defense attorney tactics to anticipate.
- Describe the key to testifying during cross-examination.
- Explain how to avoid objections to your testimony.

Internet Assignments

1. Have students research the role of the district attorney, particularly in their own county or state.
2. Have students search the Internet for information on how both prosecution and defense attorneys attempt to strategize to ensure they get the best juror for their side. What techniques are used? How successful have they been? Is this jury tampering? Why or why not?

Class Assignments

1. Break the class into groups and have them discuss the following questions:

   - What would make a strong case, as opposed to a weak case, against a suspect for burglary, based on both facts and the case file?
   - Why is nonverbal communication important when testifying to a jury, and what suggestions do students have for helping a testifying officer make a positive impression on a jury?

2. Break the class into groups. After a set preparation time, give each group five minutes to perform a mock investigator presentation with prosecution testimony and a defense cross-examination in front of the class.
3. Break the class into small groups, with one student representing district attorneys, one criminal defense lawyers and one the American Civil Liberties Union (ACLU). See what the groups can agree on after a short discussion about the priorities of public safety versus civil liberties of a defendant.

Chapter Outline

I.   The Final Report

    A.   The final report contains

        1.   The complaint
        2.   The preliminary investigation report
        3.   All follow-up, supplemental and progress reports
        4.   Statements, admissions and confessions
        5.   Laboratory reports
        6.   Photographs, sketches and drawings
        7.   A summary of all negative (exculpatory) evidence

    B.   The quality of the content and writing of the report influences its credibility
    C.   Prepare the report after a careful review of all information. Organize the facts logically

D. The complaint :

   1. Include a copy of the original complaint received by the police dispatcher and complaint desk
   2. Include the date and time of the complaint, location of the incident, brief details, times when officers were dispatched and the names of the officers assigned to the initial call

E. The preliminary investigation report: the report of the officer's initial investigation at the crime scene provides essential information about the time of arrival, lighting and weather conditions, observations at the scene and immediate and subsequent actions taken by officers responding to the call

F. Follow-up reports: assemble each contact and follow-up report in chronological order, presenting the sequence of the investigation and the pattern used to follow leads

   1. These reports contain the essential information gathered in proving the elements of the crime and in linking the crime to the suspect
   2. The reports can be in the form of progress notes

G. Statements, admissions and confessions: include the statements of all witnesses interviewed during the investigation

   1. If written statements were not obtained, report the results of oral interviews with witnesses
   2. Assemble all statements, admissions or confessions by suspects in a separate part of the report
   3. Include the reports of all polygraphs or other examinations used to determine the truth of statements, admissions or confessions

H. Laboratory reports: assemble laboratory results in one segment of the final report, and make recommendations regarding how these results relate to other areas of the report

I. Photographs, sketches and drawings: include photographs, sketches and drawings of the crime scene to show conditions when officers arrived and the available evidence

J. Summary of negative evidence: include a summary of all negative or exculpatory evidence developed during the investigation

   1. Statements of witnesses who claim the suspect was elsewhere at the time of the crime are sometimes proved false, but the prosecution must consider such statements and develop a defense
   2. If information exists that the suspect committed the crime but did so in self-defense or accidentally, state this in the report
   3. Include all recognizable weaknesses in proving the corpus delicti or the offender's identity

K.   Write the report clearly and accurately, as the quality of the final report influences its credibility; also, arrange the material in a logical sequence and a convenient format

II.   The Role of the Prosecutor

A.   The prosecutor is the gatekeeper of the court system, determining which cases are prosecuted and which are not
B.   On a daily basis, the prosecutor is the only official who works with all actors of the criminal justice system
C.   The prosecutor is the most powerful official in the court system
D.   At the county level, the prosecutor, or district attorney (DA), is the chief law enforcement official
E.   At the federal level, the prosecutor is called the U.S. attorney, a position appointed by the president, approved by Congress and confirmed by the Senate

1.   Federal prosecutors' offices commonly have staff investigators and are in frequent contact with other federal investigative agencies, such as the Federal Bureau of Investigation (FBI), Drug Enforcement Administration (DEA), Bureau of Alcohol, Tobacco, Firearms and Explosives (ATF) and U.S. Secret Service
2.   Unlike local prosecutors, federal prosecutors are typically those who initiate a federal criminal investigation

F.   Tensions and conflicts sometimes exist between investigators and prosecutors if a case isn't prosecuted. Although officers can arrest based on probable cause, prosecutors are held to a much higher standard—proof *beyond a reasonable doubt*—in the courtroom
G.   Cases are not prosecuted if

1.   The complaint is invalid
2.   The prosecutor declines after reviewing the case
3.   The complainant refuses to prosecute
4.   The offender dies
5.   The offender is in prison or out of the country and cannot be returned
6.   No evidence or leads exist

H.   Administrative policy sometimes closes cases to further investigation
I.   In other cases, the report is valid but investigation reveals that witnesses have left the area or that no physical evidence remains at the crime scene
J.   Cases are *exceptionally cleared* when circumstances outside the investigation result in no charges being filed (e.g., the suspect dies)
K.   Motion hearings

1.   A motion is a request to the court for a decision on a specific legal issue

2. A motion can lead to a hearing, an appearance before the court to resolve the issue raised in the motion

3. If the defense files a *motion to suppress*, claiming that evidence was illegally obtained or a confession unconstitutionally extracted, and an evidentiary hearing is granted by the court, the possibility exists for the case to fold before ever going to trial, effectively resulting in nonprosecution

III. Preparing a Case for Prosecution

A. To prepare a case for court, review and evaluate all evidence, positive and negative, and the chain of custody; review all reports on the case, including transcripts of any depositions you have given; prepare witnesses; hold a pretrial conference with the prosecutor

B. Review and evaluate evidence

1. Concentrate on proving the elements of the crime and establishing the offender's identity

2. The pretrial *discovery process* requires the prosecution and defense to disclose to each other certain evidence they intend to use at trial, thus avoiding surprises

3. The *Brady rule* states that "the suppression by the prosecution of evidence favorable to the accused upon request violates due process where the evidence is material either to guilt or to punishment, irrespective of the good faith or bad faith of the prosecution"

4. Defense attorneys will try to *impeach* the testimony of prosecution witnesses; that is, they will try to discredit the testimony, to challenge the truth or accuracy of what a prosecution witness testified to under direct examination

5. Review and evaluate witnesses' statements for credibility

6. Assess the witness's relationship to the suspect and the victim

7. Establish the suspect's identity by eyewitness testimony, transfer evidence and supporting evidence such as motive, prior knowledge, opportunity and known modus operandi

8. Depositions: in many states, officers must provide a deposition before trial as part of the discovery

C. Review written reports of everything done during the investigation; also review the transcript of your own deposition

D. Prepare witnesses

1. Re-interview witnesses to refresh their memories

2. Describe trial procedures so they understand what will occur

3. Explain that they can testify only to facts from their own personal knowledge or from common knowledge, and emphasize that they must tell the truth

E. Pretrial conference: before testifying in court and after you have made the final case preparation, arrange for a pretrial conference with the prosecuting attorney

1. Organize the facts and evidence and prepare a summary of the investigation, including the focal points and main issues of the case, and an envelope containing copies of all reports and all other relevant documents
2. At the pretrial conference with the prosecutor, review all the evidence, discuss the strengths and weaknesses of the case and discuss the probable line of questioning by the prosecutor and the defense

F. Final preparations

1. Know what is expected and the rules of the court

   a. An officer will receive a *subpoena*, an order to appear before the court
   b. The *rule on witnesses* or *witness sequestration rule* dictates that witnesses usually are excluded from the courtroom during a trial to prevent one witness from hearing another witness's testimony
   c. A judge may have issued a *motion in limine*, a motion requesting the judge to issue a protective order against prejudicial questions or statements

2. Dress appropriately
3. Be on time

IV. The Trial

A. Trials occur within a construct called the *adversary system*, which establishes clearly defined roles for both the prosecution and the defense and sets the judge as the neutral party
B. The *judge*, or *magistrate*, presides over the trial; determines whether a witness is qualified and competent; addresses questions of law, including motions, objections and procedures; rules on the admissibility of evidence; keeps order; interprets the law for the jurors; and passes sentence if the defendant is found guilty
C. *Jurors* hear and evaluate the testimony of all witnesses. Called *fact finders*, jurors consider many factors other than the words spoken
D. *Legal counsel* presents the prosecution and defense evidence before the court and jury
E. *Defendants* may or may not take the witness stand
F. *Witnesses* present the facts as they know them. Police officers are witnesses for the prosecution

V.   Sequence of a Criminal Trial

    A.   A trial begins with a case being called from the court docket. If both the prosecution and the defense are ready, the case is presented before the court

    B.   The sequence in a criminal trial is as follows:

        1.   Jury selection
        2.   Opening statements by the prosecution and the defense
        3.   Presentation of the prosecution's case, cross-examination by the defense
        4.   Presentation of the defense's case, cross-examination by the prosecution
        5.   Rebuttal and surrebuttal testimony
        6.   Closing statements by the prosecution and the defense
        7.   Instructions to the jury
        8.   Jury deliberations to reach a verdict
        9.   Reading of the verdict
        10. Acquittal or passing of sentence

    C.   If the trial is before a judge without a jury, it is called a *bench trial*. In this case, the prosecution and the defense make their opening statements directly to the judge

    D.   *Direct examination* is the initial questioning of a witness or defendant by the lawyer who is using the person's testimony to further his or her case

    E.   *Cross-examination* is questioning by the opposing side to assess the validity of the testimony

    F.   After each side has presented its regular witnesses, both sides may present *rebuttal* and *surrebuttal* witnesses

        1.   The prosecution can call *rebuttal* witnesses to contradict the testimony (or evidence) presented by the defense
        2.   The defense, in turn, can call *surrebuttal* witnesses to contradict the testimony (or evidence) presented by the prosecution

VI.   While Waiting to Testify

    A.   Do not discuss the case while waiting in the hallway to testify; if a juror or another witness hears your statements, you may have created grounds for a mistrial

    B.   *De minimus communication*—a simple hello or giving of directions—is allowed

VII. Testifying under Direct Examination

    A.   The "win" for an investigator who testifies is to have established credibility

    B.   First impressions are critical

C.   Never walk in front of the judge or between the judge and the attorneys' tables; this area, called *the well*, is off-limits and is to be entered only if the judge so directs or permission is granted

D.   As you respond to questions, keep in mind the types of statements that are not admissible

E.   Inadmissible statements include:

   1.   Opinions and conclusions (unless the witness is qualified as an expert)
   2.   Hearsay
   3.   Privilege communication
   4.   Statements about character and reputation, including the defendant's criminal record

F.   Guidelines for effective testimony

   1.   Speak clearly, firmly and with expression
   2.   Answer questions directly; do *not* volunteer information
   3.   Pause briefly before answering
   4.   Refer to your notes if you do not recall exact details
   5.   Admit calmly when you do not know an answer
   6.   Admit any mistakes you make in testifying
   7.   Avoid police jargon, sarcasm and humor
   8.   Tell the complete truth as you know it

G.   Refer to your notes if you are uncertain of specific facts, but do not rely on them excessively

H.   Nonverbal factors

   1.   Do not underestimate the power of nonverbal factors as you testify
   2.   Communication is made up of several components:

      a.   *What* is said—the actual words spoken (accounts for 7% of the total message communicated)
      b.   *How* it is said—tone of voice, pitch, modulation and the like (38% of the message)
      c.   *Nonverbal factors*—body language, gestures, demeanor (55% of the message)

   3.   Important nonverbal elements include dress, eye contact, posture, gestures, mannerisms, rate of speech, tone of voice and facial expressions

I.   Strategies for excelling as a witness:

   1.   To excel as a witness, (1) set yourself up, (2) provoke the defense into giving you a chance to explain, (3) be unconditional and (4) do not stall
   2.   Get into the habit of thinking ahead to the trial while you are still out in the field. Ask yourself, "What if they ask me this in court?"

3. Be unconditional
4. Do not stall, and do not repeat the attorney's question

J. Expert testimony

1. In some instances, officers may qualify to testify as *expert witnesses*; in such cases, the restrictions on testimony are somewhat more relaxed
2. An *expert witness* is a person who has had special training, education or experience
3. To qualify as an expert witness, one must have as many of the following as possible:

   a. Present or prior employment in the specific field
   b. Active membership in a professional group in the field
   c. Research work in the field
   d. An educational degree directly related to the field
   e. Direct experience with the subject, if not employed in the field
   f. Papers, treatises or books published on the subject or teaching experience in it

VIII. Testifying under Cross-Examination

A. Post-trial interviews of jurors reveal body language or behaviors that can weaken a witness's credibility:

1. Using a defensive or evasive tone of voice
2. Appearing ill at ease or nervous
3. Avoiding eye contact
4. Crossing arms defensively across chest
5. Quibbling over common terms
6. Sitting stiffly
7. Looking to attorney for assistance during cross-examination
8. Cracking jokes inappropriately
9. Using lots of "ah's" or "uh's"

B. Jurors have noted that the following behaviors enhance credibility:

1. Displaying an even temperament on direct and cross
2. Not becoming angry or defensive when pressed
3. Appearing relaxed and at ease
4. Being likeable and polite
5. Maintaining eye contact with attorney and jury
6. Not being affected by interruptions or objections

C. During cross-examination, the defense attorney may

1. Be disarmingly friendly or intimidatingly rude
2. Attack your credibility and impartiality
3. Attack your investigative skill
4. Attempt to force contradictions or inconsistencies

  5. Ask leading questions or deliberately misquote you

  6. Ask for a simple answer to a complex question

  7. Use rapid-fire questioning

  8. Use the silent treatment

D. Maintain your dignity and impartiality and show concern for only the facts when being questioned by the defense attorney

E. If either attorney asks for any kind of *measurement* you did not personally make, including distance, time, height, weight, speed, age and the like, allow yourself some leeway. Either give an *approximation*—for example, "he was approximately 45 feet away"—or put your answer in brackets. *Brackets* provide a range—for example, "he was 40 to 50 feet away."

F. A key to testifying during cross-examination is to *never* volunteer any information

IX. Handling Objections

A. Three general types of objections common during trials are:

  1. Objections to the *form of the question*

  2. Objections to the *substance of the question*

  3. Objections to the *answer*

B. To avoid objections to your testimony, avoid conclusions and nonresponsive answers. Answer yes-or-no questions with "yes" or "no"

X. Concluding Your Testimony

A. Do not leave the stand until instructed to do so by counsel or the court

B. As you leave the stand, do not pay special attention to the prosecution, defense counsel, defendant or jury. Return immediately to your seat in the courtroom or leave the room if you have been sequestered

C. If you are told you may be needed for further testimony, remain available. If told you are no longer needed, leave the courtroom and resume your normal activities. To remain gives the impression that you have a special interest in the case

D. If you are in the courtroom at the time of the verdict, show neither approval nor disapproval at the outcome

E. If you have been a credible witness and told the truth, win or lose in court, you have done your job and should not take the outcome personally

XI. Advice on Testifying from a Seasoned, "Officer of the Year" Investigator

    A. Detective Richard Gautsch emphasizes three major areas to focus on when giving courtroom testimony: preparation, communication and credibility

    B. Preparation

        1. While testifying, an investigator should not use his or her report as a crutch or a script. It should be a safety net—seldom used. Constantly referring to a report gives the jury the impression that you do not know the case

        2. Officers should *study* their reports and the reports of fellow officers before testifying

    C. Communication

        1. Understand that words are a small part of communicating

        2. Expressions, demeanor, personality, appearance and more are what jurors use to form an opinion. If you remind them of the obstinate cop who wrote them a ticket for going two miles over the speed limit, they're going to sympathize with the defendant

    D. Credibility

        1. If jurors question your credibility, the case is in big trouble. If you are caught in a lie, an embellishment or an obvious omission, why should a juror believe anything you say?

        2. In the O. J. Simpson murder trial, a detective lied about whether he had ever used racial slurs. Even though it had nothing to do with the evidence he was presenting, once he lost his credibility, his testimony lost its value and, indeed, severely damaged the prosecution's case

    E. The lesson to be learned is never lie, exaggerate or embellish your testimony. It is more obvious to a jury than you may realize. Once you lose your credibility, it is nearly impossible to recover it. The truth can only strengthen a good case

XII. Summary

CRIMINAL INVESTIGATION: AN OVERVIEW

Test Bank

Chapter 1
Criminal Investigation: An Overview

Multiple Choice

1. The Latin term that means "to track or trace" and that relates most closely with contemporary police investigations is

    a. nolo contendere.
    b. voir dire.
    c. *vestigare.** (p. 8, Learning Objective: Describe what criminal investigation is.)
    d. certiorari.
    e. subpoena.

2. Which term describes a logical process in which a conclusion follows from specific facts?

    a. voir dire
    b. deductive reasoning* (p. 8, Learning Objective: Describe what criminal investigation is.)
    c. circumstantial evidence
    d. Locard's principle of exchange
    e. latent investigations

3. According to the text, most cases that are lost are lost during what part of the investigation?

    a. in the first hour* (p. 14, Learning Objective: Discuss what should be done initially at a crime scene.)
    b. before the 911 call is ever made
    c. in the forensic lab
    d. when witnesses recant testimony

4. Spontaneous statements uttered by a suspect at the time of a crime, concerning and closely related to actions involved in the crime, are referred to as what type of statements?

    a. *in flagrante delicto*
    b. exculpatory
    c. *res gestae** (p. 19, Learning Objective: Define the meaning and importance of *res gestae* statements.)
    d. uttering

5. In cases where officers were not able to complete the investigation for some reason, what may be required?

    a. redaction
    b. follow-up investigation* (p. 22, Learning Objective: Discuss who is responsible for solving crimes.)
    c. motion to dismiss
    d. waiver of a speedy trial

6. According to the text, when both the public and other professions within the justice system have unrealistic expectations of CSI abilities, law enforcement agencies are said to be suffering from what?

   a. Grissom effect
   b. TV syndrome
   c. CSI effect* (p. 22, Learning Objective: Describe how to determine whether a crime has been committed.)
   d. Peel disturbance

7. Crime mapping focuses on

   a. hot spots where crime occurs.* (p. 24, Learning Objective: Discuss who is responsible for solving crimes.)
   b. developing leads through the use of city maps and districts.
   c. the use of maps to direct officers to the scene.
   d. triangulating cell phone usage with criminal activity.

8. The act of sifting through the mountains of available information to find the data that pertains to an investigator's case is referred to as

   a. data dumping.
   b. motion to allow discovery from defense.
   c. data banking.
   d. data mining.* (p. 25, Learning Objective: Discuss who is responsible for solving crimes.)

9. Problem-oriented policing places a high value on new responses that are more

   a. task oriented.
   b. aggressive.
   c. preventive.* (p. 25, Learning Objective: Discuss who is responsible for solving crimes.)
   d. assertive.

10. Determining the optimal case assignment load, determining what factors are needed to solve crimes and reducing the number of crimes assigned for investigations that cannot be solved are all ways to increase

    a. investigative productivity.* (p. 26, Learning Objective: Discuss who is responsible for solving crimes.)
    b. an officer's workload.
    c. partnership with the community.
    d. data collection.

11.   The initial contact with law enforcement in a criminal investigation is usually made between a citizen and a

   a.   patrol officer.
   b.   civilian report taker.
   c.   dispatcher.* (p. 28, Learning Objective: Explain with whom investigators must relate.)
   d.   investigator.

12.   Whose staff can provide information and advice to investigators about legal issues, search and seizure, warrants, confessions and admissibility of evidence?

   a.   defense counsel
   b.   ACLU
   c.   prosecutor* (p. 28, Learning Objective: Explain with whom investigators must relate.)
   d.   federal task force

13.   Medical examiners and coroners' (ME/C) offices provide death investigation services locally and are responsible for what type of investigation of deaths?

   a.   autopsies
   b.   crime scene reconstruction
   c.   medicolegal
   d.   all of these choices* (p. 29, Learning Objective: Explain with whom investigators must relate.)

14.   Because definitions of crimes and their penalties vary considerably depending on where they occur, investigators must be familiar with

   a.   local ordinances, county ordinances and state statutes.* (p. 10, Learning Objective: Describe what criminal investigation is.)
   b.   zoning laws.
   c.   geographical boundaries of the local area.
   d.   all of these choices.

15.   A criminal's modus operandi is the details of

   a.   a criminal's multiple ordinance violations.
   b.   how, when and where a criminal usually operates.* (p. 10, Learning Objective: Describe what criminal investigation is.)
   c.   a multiple regression analysis to determine the suspect's operating methods.
   d.   a criminal's motive and opportunity.

16.   A logical process of investigation includes

   a.   delegating assigned tasks, deciding who completes the initial investigation and then turning the work over to the supervisor.
   b.   interrogating witnesses, taking numerous photos at the scene of the crime, interviewing the suspect and taking accurate notes of the process.

    c.   obtaining physical evidence legally, effectively interviewing witnesses, legally and effectively interrogating suspects, thoroughly developing leads and recording all details.* (p. 11, Learning Objective: Define the major goals of criminal investigation.)

    d.   developing, arresting and prosecuting a suspect.

17.   A fact is

    a.   an action, an event, a circumstance or an actual thing done.* (p. 13, Learning Objective: Describe what effective investigators do.)

    b.   a process of reasoning.

    c.   an action based on the known facts.

    d.   something that is known to all.

18.   An inference is

    a.   an assumption.

    b.   a process of reasoning by which a fact may be deduced.* (p. 13, Learning Objective: Describe what effective investigators do.)

    c.   an appropriate method of moving to the solution of the crime.

    d.   an expectation of guilt.

19.   What type of response time is necessary to increase the probability of arrest at the scene?

    a.   one minute or less* (p. 14, Learning Objective: Explain who usually arrives at a crime scene first.)

    b.   three to five minutes

    c.   five to ten minutes

    d.   any response within 15 minutes

20.   At a death scene, which would *not* be of immediate concern?

    a.   preserving the crime scene

    b.   identifying the body* (p. 18, Learning Objective: Describe what to do if a suspect is still at a crime scene or has recently fled the scene.)

    c.   identifying suspects

    d.   identifying witnesses

21.   Securing the crime scene is a major responsibility of the

    a.   dispatchers.

    b.   forensic specialists.

    c.   first officer(s) on the scene.* (p. 18, Learning Objective: Explain how the crime scene and evidence are protected and for how long.)

    d.   field supervisor.

22. A _____ approach to case investigation involves using specialists in various fields from within a particular jurisdiction.

    a. multijurisdictional
    b. multidisciplinary* (p. 31, Learning Objective: Explain with whom investigators must relate.)
    c. multipredictory
    d. multicriminalistic

23. Critical aspects of a successful investigation include thorough planning and preparation, efficient information management, a focus on effective communication and

    a. a competent medical examiner to analyze the physical evidence.
    b. advanced role definition and delineation of responsibilities.* (p. 31, Learning Objective: Explain with whom investigators must relate.)
    c. an understanding of the need for investigative productivity.
    d. a positive relationship with the prosecutor's office.

24. Which statement is *not* one of the components of CompStat?

    a. accurate and timely intelligence
    b. rapid deployment of resources
    c. effective tactics
    d. increase in arrests and convictions* (p. 24, Learning Objective: Discuss who is responsible for solving crimes.)
    e. relentless follow-up and assessment

25. Which process helps detectives use maps to understand the hunting patterns of serial criminals, to determine where these offenders might live and to identify offenders' next likely target?

    a. crime controls
    b. target hardening
    c. "bull's-eye" targeting
    d. crime mapping* (p. 24, Learning Objective: Discuss who is responsible for solving crimes.)

True/False

26. The best investigators follow their hunches, follow leads as they come in and attack cases with a random approach so as not to miss an important clue. (False, pp. 11–12, Learning Objective: Define the major goals of criminal investigation.)

27. A fact is an action, an event, a circumstance or an actual thing done. In contrast, an inference is a process of reasoning by which a fact may be deduced. (True, p. 13, Learning Objective: Explain the basic functions investigators perform.)

28. "Latent examination" refers to specialists trained in recording, identifying and interpreting the *minutiae* (minute details) of physical evidence, who usually work at crime scenes and in a crime lab. (False, p. 8, Learning Objective: Describe what criminal investigation is.)

29. The use of a siren to speed the response to the scene by patrol officers or investigators is sometimes of value, but the siren may cause the offender to flee the scene. (True, p. 16, Learning Objective: Discuss what should be done initially at a crime scene.)

30. The actions the first responders take at a crime scene have little to do with the value of the evidence for investigators and prosecutors. (False, p. 16, Learning Objective: Discuss what should be done initially at a crime scene.)

31. The media has a constitutional right to enter any crime scene to which the general public does not have access. (False, p. 20, Learning Objective: Describe how to determine whether a crime has been committed.)

32. A basic forensic theory which holds that objects that come in contact with each other always transfer material, however minute, to each other is referred to as Locard's principle of exchange. (True, p. 18, Learning Objective: Explain how the crime scene and evidence are protected and for how long.)

33. The specialty of a forensic specialist is the organized scientific collection and processing of evidence. (True, p. 21, Learning Objective: Describe how to determine whether a crime has been committed.)

34. Inquiries to the police from the defense counsel about a case should be referred to the prosecutor's office. (True, p. 29, Learning Objective: Explain with whom investigators must relate.)

35. Scientific evidence supports a belief that eyewitness identification is very credible, reliable and is responsible for solving many crimes. (False, p. 30, Learning Objective: Explain with whom investigators must relate.)

36. A crime scene must be protected until a suspect goes to trial. (False, p. 18, Learning Objective: Explain how the crime scene and evidence are protected and for how long.)

37. CompStat is a word that means computer statistics or comparison statistics. (True, p. 24, Learning Objective: Discuss who is responsible for solving crimes.)

38. Today the majority of law enforcement agencies use some degree of geographic information systems (GIS) or mapping technology to locate callers and to provide first responders with critical information before arriving on the scene. (True, p. 24, Learning Objective: Discuss who is responsible for solving crimes.)

39. Before any in-custody interrogation, an officer must read the *Miranda* warning to a suspect. (True, p. 17, Learning Objective: Describe what to do if a suspect is still at a crime scene or has recently fled the scene.)

40. In 1829 in England, Sir Henry Fielding gave birth to community policing when he stated, "The police are the public and the public are the police." (False, p. 28, Learning Objective: Explain with whom investigators must relate.)

41. Community policing is a philosophy that addresses public safety issues (such as crime, social disorder and fear of crime) by working through organizational strategies to support the systematic use of partnerships and problem-solving techniques. (True, p. 28, Learning Objective: Explain with whom investigators must relate.)

42. Community policing is a true philosophical shift rather than simply a program or set of programs. (True, p. 28, Learning Objective: Explain with whom investigators must relate.)

43. To demonstrate national unity in criminal statutes using the Model Penal Code, shoplifting is a felony in all states. (False, p. 10, Learning Objective: Describe what criminal investigation is.)

44. DNA was discovered in 1968 in England. (False, p. 9, Learning Objective: Explain the basic functions investigators perform.)

45. The Violent Criminal Apprehension Program (VICAP) mission is to facilitate cooperation, communication and coordination among federal law enforcement agencies only, and does not include local police agencies. (False, p. 31, Learning Objective: Explain with whom investigators must relate.)

Completion

46. Criminal investigation is a reconstructive process that uses _____ reasoning, which is a logical process in which a conclusion follows from specific facts. (deductive, p. 8, Learning Objective: Describe what criminal investigation is.)

47. The term MO means _____ _____. (modus operandi, p. 10, Learning Objective: Describe what criminal investigation is.)

48. One of the goals of criminal investigations is to present the best possible case to the _____. (prosecutor, p. 11, Learning Objective: Define the major goals of criminal investigation.)

49. Determining the _____ is more important than obtaining a conviction or closing a case. (truth, p. 11, Learning Objective: Define the major goals of criminal investigation.)

50. Successful investigations balance between _____ acquired by study and experience and the skills acquired by the artful application of learned techniques. (scientific knowledge, p. 11, Learning Objective: Explain the basic functions investigators perform.)

51. What was discovered in 1868 that changed scientific investigations forever? _____ (DNA, p. 9, Learning Objective: Explain the basic functions investigators perform.)

52. In what year was DNA first used in a criminal case in England to prove the innocence of a defendant? _____ (1986, p. 9, Learning Objective: Explain the basic functions investigators perform.)

53. The motto of the Pinkerton National Detective Agency was, "We never _____." (sleep, p. 7, Learning Objective: Describe what criminal investigation is.)

54. *Res gestae* statements are generally an exception to the _____ rule because they are usually very closely related to facts and are therefore admissible in court. (hearsay, p. 19, Learning Objective: Define the meaning and importance of *res gestae* statements.)

55. If no crime has been committed—for example, the matter is a _____ rather than a criminal situation—the victim should be told how to obtain assistance. (civil, p. 19, Learning Objective: Describe how to determine whether a crime has been committed.)

56. Investigators can use _____ tests to develop and lift fingerprints; discover flammable substances through vapor and fluid examination; detect drugs, explosive substances on hands or clothing, imprints of firearms on hands or bullet-hole residue; and conduct many other tests. (field, p. 19, Learning Objective: Describe how to determine whether a crime has been committed.)

Short Answer

57. What is the real purpose of a criminal investigation? (p. 10, Learning Objective: Define the major goals of criminal investigation.)

58. What are the major goals of a criminal investigation? (p. 11, Learning Objective: Define the major goals of criminal investigation.)

59. What are some characteristics of effective investigators? (pp. 12–14, Learning Objective: Describe which characteristics are important in investigators.)

60. After emergencies are dealt with, what are the first and most important functions of a first responder? (pp. 16–18, Learning Objective: Discuss what should be done initially at a crime scene.)

61. What type of statements are spontaneous statements made at the time of a crime, concerning and closely related to actions involved in the crime? They are often considered more truthful than later, planned responses. (p. 19, Learning Objective: Define the meaning and importance of *res gestae* statements.)

62. Protection against lawsuits includes what four elements? (p. 32, Learning Objective: Discuss how to avoid civil lawsuits.)

63. What legal statute states that anyone who acts under the authority of law and who violates another person's constitutional rights can be sued? (p. 32, Learning Objective: Discuss how to avoid civil lawsuits.)

64. Leaving out exculpatory evidence may lead to what sanctions? (p. 32, Learning Objective: Discuss how to avoid civil lawsuits.)

65. As a police investigator, what is one of the best ways to avoid lawsuits or to defend oneself if sued? (p. 32, Learning Objective: Discuss how to avoid civil lawsuits.)

66. What is the role of medical examiners and coroners? (p. 29, Learning Objective: Explain with whom investigators must relate.)

67. What's the difference between crime mapping and location intelligence? (p. 24, Learning Objective: Discuss who is responsible for solving crimes.)

68. Discuss the advantage of geographic profiling in a criminal investigation. Include a definition of the phrase "least effort" in your discussion. (pp. 24–25, Learning Objective: Discuss who is responsible for solving crimes.)

69. What are several ways to implement AVL/GPS technology in police work? In your answer, define AVL and GPS and describe their use. (p. 24, Learning Objective: Discuss who is responsible for solving crimes.)

70. What is the purpose of case screening? (p. 26, Learning Objective: Discuss who is responsible for solving crimes.)

71. Clarify the role and relationship investigators should have with the media and explain why this role is necessary. (p. 20, Learning Objective: Describe how to determine whether a crime has been committed.)

DOCUMENTING THE CRIME SCENE: NOTE TAKING, PHOTOGRAPHING AND SKETCHING

Test Bank

Chapter 2
Documenting the Crime Scene: Note Taking, Photographing and Sketching

Multiple Choice

1. Which are permanent written records of the facts of a case to be used in further investigation, in writing reports and in prosecuting the case?

   a. field notes
   b. tape recordings
   c. investigative notes* (p. 42, Learning Objective: Explain why notes are important in an investigation.)
   d. stenographer notes

2. Record all information that helps to answer the questions of

   a. Who? What? Which? When? How? and Why?
   b. Who? What? Where? When? How? and Why?* (p. 43, Learning Objective: Discuss what to record.)
   c. Which? When? Why? Where? and How many?
   d. Why? When? and Why or why not?

3. When taking notes, the investigator should

   a. ignore unimportant items.
   b. write only the important items.
   c. learn to select key facts and record them in abbreviated form.* (p. 44, Learning Objective: Discuss what to record.)
   d. never take notes but always memorize things verbatim and record them later.

4. One of the disadvantages of photographs is that

   a. they can be taken immediately and thus the crime scene processors have not prepared the scene.
   b. they are not selective.* (p. 47, Learning Objective: Compare and contrast advantages and disadvantages of crime scene photography and videography.)
   c. they are not admissible into court.
   d. they are only allowed in court if black and white.

5. When taking photographs/videotape, the investigator should

   a. take the primary points of concern or interest.
   b. take only those shots wanted by the prosecutor.
   c. examine the scene from all sides and take only the sides of the crime scene that show the best view.
   d. take sufficient photographs and/or videotape to reconstruct the entire scene.* (p. 50, Learning Objective: Determine what to photograph at a crime scene and in what sequence.)

6. Types of investigative photography include

   a. crime scene and mug shots.
   b. aerial, night and laboratory pictures.
   c. lineup photographs and those related to crime scenes.
   d. all of these choices.* (p. 51, Learning Objective: Compare and contrast the types of photography used in criminal investigations.)

7. Which of the following does a crime scene sketch accomplish?

   a. accurately portrays the physical facts
   b. relates to the sequence of events at the scene
   c. establishes the precise location and relationship of objects and evidence at the scene
   d. all of these choices* (p. 56, Learning Objective: Explain the various purposes of crime scene sketches.)

8. The basic purpose of field notes is to

   a. show the officer was at the scene.
   b. show the date and time of the incident.
   c. record all facts of the incident.* (p. 45, Learning Objective: Describe characteristics of effective notes.)
   d. all of these choices.

9. The amount of notes taken is determined by

   a. the conditions of each case.* (p. 43, Learning Objective: Discuss what to record.)
   b. whether the crime is a felony or not.
   c. department policy and procedure.
   d. calls for service.

10. Which plotting method establishes a straight line from one fixed point to another fixed point from which measurements are taken at right angles?

    a. baseline* (p. 60, Learning Objective: Differentiate between the different plotting methods used in sketches.)
    b. rectangular-coordinate
    c. triangulation
    d. cross-projection

11. The photographic technique in which a scene is photographed clockwise, with the first picture showing a specific object on one side of the photograph and the next picture showing the same object on the opposite side of the photograph, is called

    a. scoping.
    b. cross-projection photography.
    c. overlapping.* (p. 50, Learning Objective: Determine what to photograph at a crime scene and in what sequence.)
    d. triangulation.

12. The Bertillon identification system includes

   a.   a written description of a person.
   b.   a person's complete criminal record.
   c.   a photograph.
   d.   both a written description of a person and a photograph.* (p. 54, Learning Objective: Compare and contrast the types of photography used in criminal investigations.)

13. Which type of camera is more likely to result in convictions?

   a.   Polaroid
   b.   medium-format camera
   c.   point-and-shoot camera
   d.   video camera* (p. 48, Learning Objective: Decide on proper photographic equipment needed.)

14. Which of the following is *not* a disadvantage of photographs?

   a.   They do not show actual distances.
   b.   They are not selective.
   c.   They may be distorted.
   d.   Photographs are always admissible in court.* (p. 47, Learning Objective: Compare and contrast advantages and disadvantages of crime scene photography and videography.)

15. According to a national video forensics expert, what is the "new DNA for law enforcement"?

   a.   fingerprints
   b.   tire tracks
   c.   footprints
   d.   video analysis* (p. 52, Learning Objective: Compare and contrast advantages and disadvantages of crime scene photography and videography.)

16. The main problem with night photography is

   a.   lack of color.
   b.   shadows.
   c.   the cost of calling out a photographer.
   d.   proper illumination.* (p. 53, Learning Objective: Describe technical errors to avoid.)

17. Admissible photographs must be

   a.   noninflammatory.
   b.   material.
   c.   relevant.
   d.   all of these choices.* (p. 55, Learning Objective: Illustrate the basic rules to which evidence photographs must adhere.)

18. Photographs should be taken

    a. before officers leave the scene.
    b. only after the investigators complete a crime scene sketch.
    c. before tending to emergencies, to show the "true" scene as officers found it.
    d. before anything is disturbed.* (p. 51, Learning Objective: Describe technical errors to avoid.)

19. Sketch all serious crime and crash scenes

    a. after taking photographs.
    b. before anything is moved.
    c. both after taking photographs and before anything is moved.* (p. 57, Learning Objective: Identify what evidence to sketch.)
    d. neither after taking photographs nor before anything is moved.

20. Many agencies fail to do this with those tasked with videotaping a crime scene:

    a. provide enough videotape.
    b. provide adequate training.* (p. 47, Learning Objective: Compare and contrast advantages and disadvantages of crime scene photography and videography.)
    c. provide adequate supervision.
    d. provide enough portable power sources.

21. Photographs should be taken in the following order:

    a. specific objects, specific area, general area.
    b. specific area, general area, specific objects.
    c. general area, specific area, specific objects.* (p. 50, Learning Objective: Determine what to photograph at a crime scene and in what sequence.)
    d. micro to macro in all cases.

22. This type of photography may be best used for extensive, large-scale, outside areas:

    a. flash photography.
    b. aerial photography.* (pp. 52–53, Learning Objective: Compare and contrast the types of photography used in criminal investigations.)
    c. painting with light.
    d. walking flash.

23. Writing on the back of your photographs to identify them later is referred to as

    a. stacking.
    b. backing.* (p. 55, Learning Objective: Illustrate the basic rules to which evidence photographs must adhere.)
    c. cataloging.
    d. back-dating.

24. Showing the relationship between evidence on the walls and the floors of a room, by flattening out the walls on the sketch, allowing the viewer to look straight down into the sketch, is best done using which of the following methods?

    a.   compass-point
    b.   cross-projection* (p. 61, Learning Objective: Differentiate between the different plotting methods used in sketches.)
    c.   rectangular-coordination
    d.   doll-house

25. Which type of photography is often used to establish the identity of a subject, a location and in some cases criminal behavior?

    a.   surveillance* (pp. 51–52, Learning Objective: Compare and contrast the types of photography used in criminal investigations.)
    b.   infra-red
    c.   digital
    d.   mobile

26. Which process would enlarge the evidence to be viewed?

    a.   microphotography
    b.   macrophotography* (p. 54, Learning Objective: Compare and contrast the types of photography used in criminal investigations.)
    c.   paleontology
    d.   odontology

27. In which direction should the top of a sketch be oriented?

    a.   west
    b.   north* (p. 58, Learning Objective: Write the steps to take in making a rough sketch.)
    c.   south
    d.   east

28. Crime scene photographs are

    a.   substitutes for sketches.
    b.   substitutes for notes.
    c.   better than sketches.
    d.   none of these choices.* (p. 56, Learning Objective: Explain the various purposes of crime scene sketches.)

29. Providing proof that the image introduced into evidence is the same image taken at the crime scene is referred to as

    a.   redundancy.
    b.   image authentication.* (p. 56, Learning Objective: Illustrate the basic rules to which evidence photographs must adhere.)
    c.   concrete evidence.
    d.   pictometry.

30. A sketch drawn or personally witnessed by an investigator that accurately portrays a crime scene and that is allowed into evidence is referred to as what type of sketch?

    a. freehand
    b. exculpatory
    c. admissible* (p. 67, Learning Objective: Clarify when a sketch or a scale drawing is admissible in court.)
    d. courtroom

31. Which of the following statements about photographic resolution is *not* true?

    a. Resolution is commonly quantified by pixels.
    b. An image photographed with a high-resolution camera, if printed on a low-resolution printer, will not show fine detail clearly.
    c. A megapixel is roughly equivalent to a thousand dots.* (p. 50, Learning Objective: Describe technical errors to avoid.)
    d. A low-resolution image, if enlarged too much, will lose quality.

32. Record in notes the following items at the crime scene:

    a. services rendered.
    b. weather conditions.
    c. name, address and phone number of every person present.
    d. all of these choices.* (pp. 43–44, Learning Objective: Discuss what to record.)

33. Which type of photograph would best capture the immediate crime scene and the location of objects in the area or room?

    a. long-range shot
    b. medium-range shot* (p. 51, Learning Objective: Determine what to photograph at a crime scene and in what sequence.)
    c. close-range shot
    d. none of these choices

34. A major advance is the ability of computer software to stitch together digital photos of 180 degrees or more to create one 360-degree photo—a panoramic view of a crime scene that is interactive, allowing viewers, including jury members, to walk through it as though they were there. This type of 360-degree photographic view is called

    a. an aerial view.
    b. an exploded view.
    c. immersive imaging.* (p. 49, Learning Objective: Compare and contrast the types of photography used in criminal investigations.)
    d. walkthrough imaging.

35. What should be photographed first?

   a. the deceased
   b. weapons
   c. fragile evidence* (p. 50, Learning Objective: Determine what to photograph at a crime scene and in what sequence.)
   d. witnesses

36. According to the *Handbook of Forensic Services*, what should be used when photographing latent prints?

   a. flash and marker
   b. ruler and a pencil
   c. tripod and cable release* (p. 48, Learning Objective: Decide on proper photographic equipment needed.)
   d. macrolens and flashlight set at an oblique angle

37. These cameras are specially constructed to take pictures of fingerprints without distortion. They provide their own light through four bulbs, one in each corner. Removing a bulb from any corner provides slanted lighting to show fingerprint ridge detail. They are

   a. tripod cameras.
   b. fingerprint cameras.* (p. 48, Learning Objective: Decide on proper photographic equipment needed.)
   c. backlit cameras.
   d. blacklight cameras.

True/False

38. Digital photographs can create a virtual scene similar to Pictometry. (True, p. 53, Learning Objective: Compare and contrast the types of photography used in criminal investigations.)

39. Evidence not discernible to the naked eye can be detected by laser-beam photography. (True, p. 54, Learning Objective: Compare and contrast the types of photography used in criminal investigations.)

40. Notes are not admissible in court. (False, p. 46, Learning Objective: Explain why notes are important in an investigation.)

41. The purpose of a marker in a photograph is to show the location of the specific object being photographed. (False, p. 51, Learning Objective: Determine what to photograph at a crime scene and in what sequence.)

42. Microphotography is useful in criminal investigations because it renders bruises and injuries visible long after their actual occurrence. (False, p. 54, Learning Objective: Compare and contrast the types of photography used in criminal investigations.)

43. The first step in sketching a crime scene is to outline the area and the crime. (False, p. 57, Learning Objective: Write the steps to take in making a rough sketch.)

44. The basic purpose of crime scene photography is to record the entire crime scene permanently.* (True, p. 46, Learning Objective: Discuss purposes of crime scene photography.)

45. The basic purpose of note taking is to convict and punish offenders. (False, p. 45, Learning Objective: Describe characteristics of effective notes.)

46. A notebook is only a temporary report to record facts and has no real evidentiary value in itself. (False, p. 46, Learning Objective: Describe characteristics of effective notes.)

47. The advantages of videos include accurate representation of a crime scene and evidence, ability to show distance and sound capability to more fully document what is being seen. (True, p. 47, Learning Objective: Compare and contrast advantages and disadvantages of crime scene photography and videography.)

48. Photographs and videotapes reproduce the crime scene in detail primarily for presentation to the media. (False, p. 46, Learning Objective: Discuss purposes of crime scene photography.)

49. Digital cameras have not yet been approved for court use for crime scene photography. (False, pp. 47–48, Learning Objective: Decide on proper photographic equipment needed.)

50. To be admissible in court, photographs must be material, relevant, competent, accurate, free of distortion and noninflammatory. (True, p. 55, Learning Objective: Illustrate the basic rules to which evidence photographs must adhere.)

51. The first rough crime scene sketch is often an extremely important investigative aid. (True, p. 56, Learning Objective: Explain the various purposes of crime scene sketches.)

52. It is best to include every possible detail in a crime scene sketch. (False, p. 57, Learning Objective: Identify what evidence to sketch.)

53. Cameras may be stored wherever they are most readily available for use. (False, p. 49, Learning Objective: Decide on proper photographic equipment needed.)

54. Digital recorders are rapidly replacing notebooks in law enforcement note taking. (False, p. 43, Learning Objective: Discuss what to record.)

55. Note taking should never, under any circumstance, be delayed or postponed. (False, p. 42, Learning Objective: Demonstrate when to take notes.)

56. Checklists are a critical aspect of the law enforcement function, especially when it comes to crime scene photography. (True, p. 51, Learning Objective: Describe technical errors to avoid.)

57. If an item of evidence has inadvertently been moved before being photographed, put it back immediately and then resume taking photos. (False, p. 51, Learning Objective: Describe technical errors to avoid.)

58. Ultraviolet-light photography is used to document bite marks, neck strangulation marks and other impressions left from intentional injuries. (True, p. 54, Learning Objective: Compare and contrast the types of photography used in criminal investigations.)

59. The rough sketch must always be drawn to scale. (False, p. 57, Learning Objective: Write the steps to take in making a rough sketch.)

60. It is important to take crime scene photographs from eye level. (True, p. 51, Learning Objective: Describe technical errors to avoid.)

Completion

61. One of the ways a crime scene sketch can be used to assist an investigation is to _____ people. (interview, p. 56, Learning Objective: Explain the various purposes of crime scene sketches.)

62. _____ is commonly used in outdoor scenes but can also be used indoors. This process of locating evidence or other items uses straight-line measures from two fixed objects. (Triangulation, p. 60, Learning Objective: Differentiate between the different plotting methods used in sketches.)

63. A sketch that is drawn or personally witnessed by an investigator, that accurately portrays a crime scene and that is introduced as evidence is referred to as a(n) _____ sketch. (admissible, p. 67, Learning Objective: Clarify when a sketch or a scale drawing is admissible in court.)

64. Mug shots can be used in _____ lineups to help identify suspects. (photographic, p. 54, Learning Objective: Compare and contrast the types of photography used in criminal investigations.)

65. Writing your initials, the date the photo was taken, what the photo depicts and the direction of north on the back of a photograph is a procedure called _____. (backing, p. 55, Learning Objective: Illustrate the basic rules to which evidence photographs must adhere.)

66. The plotting method restricted to square or rectangular areas is the _____-coordinate method. (rectangular, p. 60, Learning Objective: Differentiate between the different plotting methods used in sketches.)

67. A crime scene sketch contains, among other things, the scale of the sketch, the direction of north and the name of the person making the sketch. This is referred to as the _____. (legend, p. 63, Learning Objective: Write the steps to take in making a rough sketch.)

68. The technique in which a scene is photographed clockwise, with the first picture showing an object on the right side of the photograph and the next picture showing the same object on the left side of the photograph, is called _____. (overlapping, p. 50, Learning Objective: Determine what to photograph at a crime scene and in what sequence.)

69. Take _____ shots first because they are the most subject to alteration by weather and security violations. (exterior, p. 50, Learning Objective: Determine what to photograph at a crime scene and in what sequence.)

70. To overcome defense challenges that a digital image was altered or otherwise tampered with, investigators must rigorously maintain the _____. (chain of custody, p. 55, Learning Objective: Illustrate the basic rules to which evidence photographs must adhere.)

71. Enhanced surveillance capability can be provided by using _____, thereby collecting critical intelligence without exposing officers. (robots, p. 52, Learning Objective: Decide on proper photographic equipment needed.)

Short Answer

72. When should the investigator start taking notes? (p. 42, Learning Objective: Demonstrate when to take notes.)

73. What type of items would one photograph in a laboratory? (pp. 53–54, Learning Objective: Compare and contrast the types of photography used in criminal investigations.)

74. What is immersive imaging? (p. 49, Learning Objective: Compare and contrast the types of photography used in criminal investigations.)

75. What kind of camera is useful for photographing trace evidence such as bloodstains and tool marks? (p. 48, Learning Objective: Decide on proper photographic equipment needed.)

76. What are trip cameras, and what are they used for? (p. 48, Learning Objective: Decide on proper photographic equipment needed.)

77. What typically determines where and how notes are to be filed? (p. 45, Learning Objective: Decide which notes to retain and where to file them.)

78. Imagine you are at the scene of a car accident involving two vehicles and a pedestrian. What evidence would you sketch? (p. 57, Learning Objective: Identify what evidence to sketch.)

79. When creating a scale drawing of a crime scene, what does an officer need to consider in order for the drawing to be admissible in court? (pp. 66–67, Learning Objective: Clarify when a sketch or a scale drawing is admissible in court.)

80. Briefly outline the six steps in making a sketch of a crime scene. (pp. 57–63, Learning Objective: Write the steps to take in making a rough sketch.)

81. Imagine you are at the scene of a homicide. The victim was murdered on the sidewalk in front of a public building on a busy street. Briefly record the photographs you need to take, and in what order they should be taken. (pp. 50–51, Learning Objective: Determine what to photograph at a crime scene and in what sequence.)

82. Explain what conditions a photograph needs to satisfy in order to be admitted as evidence in court. (pp. 55–56, Learning Objective: Illustrate the basic rules to which evidence photographs must adhere.)

83. How long does evidence, including photographic evidence, need to be kept? (p. 45, Learning Objective: Decide which notes to retain and where to file them.)

84. When would it be appropriate to use surveillance photography? (pp. 51–52, Learning Objective: Compare and contrast the types of photography used in criminal investigations.)

85. What are some of the advantages of videos? (p. 47, Learning Objective: Compare and contrast advantages and disadvantages of crime scene photography and videography.)

86. What are some of the disadvantages of videos? (p. 47, Learning Objective: Compare and contrast advantages and disadvantages of crime scene photography and videography.)

WRITING EFFECTIVE REPORTS

Test Bank

Chapter 3
Writing Effective Reports

Multiple Choice

1. The statement "the man could not walk a straight line" is an example of

    a. a fact.
    b. a conclusionary statement.* (p. 78, Learning Objective: Compare how to differentiate among facts, inferences and opinions.)
    c. an observation.
    d. any of these choices.

2. The term PC (probable cause) is needed in which report?

    a. crime report
    b. arrest report* (p. 80, Learning Objective: Summarize the common problems that occur in many police reports.)
    c. forensic report
    d. rough notes

3. Being concise means to

    a. leave out details.
    b. limit yourself to one paragraph.
    c. eliminate wordiness.* (p. 81, Learning Objective: Summarize the common problems that occur in many police reports.)
    d. be subjective.

4. Which of the following is *not* a benefit of a well-written report?

    a. It helps the criminal justice system operate more efficiently and effectively.
    b. It reduces liability for the department and officer.
    c. It reflects positively on the investigator who wrote it.
    d. It is geared subjectively to enhance prosecution.* (p. 89, Learning Objective: Explain why reports should be well written.)

5. Citizen Online Report Writing is appropriate for

    a. discovery crimes.* (p. 88, Learning Objective: Describe how reports are used.)
    b. involvement crimes.
    c. both discovery crimes and involvement crimes.
    d. neither discovery crimes nor involvement crimes.

6. Officers should *not* write reports in the

    a. past tense.
    b. passive voice.* (p. 84, Learning Objective: Summarize the common problems that occur in many police reports.)

    c.   active voice.

    d.   first person.

7.   Due process disclosure of what type of evidence must be determined and made by the prosecutor?

    a.   informal statements

    b.   informal attitudes

    c.   exculpatory information* (p. 80, Learning Objective: Describe characteristics of effective investigative reports.)

    d.   hearsay

8.   Which is *not* associated with some of the common problems with police reports?

    a.   confusing or unclear sentences

    b.   conclusions, assumptions and opinions in the report

    c.   missing or incomplete information

    d.   misspelled words

    e.   inability to type* (p. 74, Learning Objective: Summarize the common problems that occur in many police reports.)

9.   Investigative reports are read by many people and used for many purposes. Which of the following is *not* an example of how a report would typically be used?

    a.   Plan for future law enforcement services.

    b.   Compile statistics on crime in a given jurisdiction.

    c.   Provide information to insurance investigators.

    d.   Convey information to the victim or the victim's family.* (p. 74, Learning Objective: Describe how reports are used.)

10.   Once a report is written, the writer should

    a.   file it and forget it.

    b.   proofread it.* (p. 87, Learning Objective: Describe characteristics of effective investigative reports.)

    c.   immediately present it to the prosecution.

    d.   prepare for the appeal.

11.   The disposition of the case is stated in the _____ paragraph of a report narrative.

    a.   opening

    b.   final* (p. 75, Learning Objective: Explain whether form or content is more important.)

    c.   narrative

    d.   summary

12. In a police report, the majority of statements should be

    a. facts.* (p. 78, Learning Objective: Compare how to differentiate among facts, inferences and opinions.)
    b. inferences.
    c. opinions.
    d. conclusionary.

13. When organizing notes for a police report, officers should *not*

    a. use a table of contents.* (p. 75, Learning Objective: Explain whether form or content is more important.)
    b. place the notes in chronological order.
    c. use headings to guide the reader.
    d. prepare an outline.

14. Which of the following is true of writing completed in the active voice?

    a. The subject does not take any action.
    b. The subject of the sentence performs the actions.* (p. 84, Learning Objective: Describe characteristics of effective investigative reports.)
    c. The sentences are active in terms of the reader.
    d. Exact quotations are always used.

15. The most important step in report writing is to

    a. write with caution to avoid lawsuits.
    b. gather the facts.* (p. 78, Learning Objective: Compare how to differentiate among facts, inferences and opinions.)
    c. determine the motive.
    d. determine the modus operandi.

16. Which of the following statements is in the first person?

    a. "This officer made the arrest."
    b. "The arrest was made by this officer."
    c. "Previously this officer made this arrest."
    d. "I made the arrest."* (p. 84, Learning Objective: Describe characteristics of effective investigative reports.)

17. Words that have little emotional effect, for example, *cried*, are called

    a. emotive.
    b. psychological.
    c. denotative.* (p. 80, Learning Objective: Describe characteristics of effective investigative reports.)
    d. corroborating.

18. Words that have an emotional effect, such as *wept* or *blubbered*, are called

    a. denotative.
    b. connotative.* (p. 80, Learning Objective: Describe characteristics of effective investigative reports.)
    c. exculpatory.
    d. exclusionary.

19. Slanting, that is, including only one side of a story or only facts that tend to prove or support the officer's theory, can make a report

    a. objective.
    b. exclusionary.
    c. subjective.* (p. 80, Learning Objective: Describe characteristics of effective investigative reports.)
    d. exculpatory.

20. *Presynct*_DictaTrans field-based reporting system

    a. is paperless.
    b. combines voice and text in one application.
    c. requires minimal training.
    d. all of these choices.* (p. 87, Learning Objective: Explain whether form or content is more important.)

21. Approximately what percentage of an officer's time is spent writing reports?

    a. 10 percent
    b. 20 percent* (p. 72, Learning Objective: Explain why reports are important to an investigation.)
    c. 25 percent
    d. 5 percent

22. The words apparently or appeared can be used to

    a. justify expressing an opinion.
    b. make an inference stand out clearly as an inference.* (p. 78, Learning Objective: Compare how to differentiate among facts, inferences and opinions.)
    c. turn an inference into an objective statement.
    d. describe a fact.

23. Which of the following statements is most accurate?

    a. The car was traveling in excess of 90 mph.* (p. 79, Learning Objective: Compare how to differentiate among facts, inferences and opinions.)
    b. The suspect was taller than the bank guard.
    c. The witness refused to give a statement.
    d. The victim heard what happened.

24. One benefit of a well-written report is that it can

    a. reduce legal liability for the officer and the department.
    b. enhance an officer's career.
    c. make a positive impact on a prosecutor's case.
    d. all of these choices.* (p. 89, Learning Objective: Explain why reports should be well written.)

25. Which of the following statements is *not* true?

    a. Being brief is the same as being concise.* (p. 81, Learning Objective: Describe characteristics of effective investigative reports.)
    b. The way a report is written can have major consequences for the disposition of a case.
    c. Inferences can prove valuable in a report, provided they are based on sufficient evidence.
    d. Almost everything that a police officer does must be reduced to writing.

True/False

26. An effective report needs to be subjective for effective prosecution. (False, p. 80, Learning Objective: Describe characteristics of effective investigative reports.)

27. Officers should review their reports to make certain they are well organized. (True, p. 75, Learning Objective: Discuss who reads the reports.)

28. Reports are permanent written records of important facts in a case to be used in the future. (True, p. 72, Learning Objective: Explain why reports are important to an investigation.)

29. Reporters are never permitted to read police reports. (False, p. 74, Learning Objective: Discuss who reads the reports.)

30. Good report writing is a learned skill. (True, p. 75, Learning Objective: Explain whether form or content is more important.)

31. An inference is not really true or false; it is sound or unsound. (True, p. 78, Learning Objective: Compare how to differentiate among facts, inferences and opinions.)

32. Being objective means eliminating those facts from the report that may appear damaging to your case. (False, p. 80, Learning Objective: Describe characteristics of effective investigative reports.)

33. If an officer did not see who signed a check, the statement "the check was signed, John Doe" is more objective than "the check was signed by John Doe." (True, p. 80, Learning Objective: Compare how to differentiate among facts, inferences and opinions.)

34. An excellent report is more likely to cause the defendant to go to trial. (True, pp. 88–89, Learning Objective: Explain why reports should be well written.)

35. When writing a report, you should start a new paragraph when you change speakers, locations, time or ideas. (True, p. 84, Learning Objective: Explain whether form or content is more important.)

36. The statement "he saw what happened" is an objective statement based on fact. (False, p. 80, Learning Objective: Compare how to differentiate among facts, inferences and opinions.)

37. Recording or dictating reports is common in some departments. (True, p. 85, Learning Objective: Explain whether form or content is more important.)

38. The length of a report is the single most important factor in ensuring quality. (False, p. 81, Learning Objective: Describe characteristics of effective investigative reports.)

39. Officers should include all the facts in a report, even those that may appear to weaken the case against the charged individual. (True, p. 80, Learning Objective: Describe characteristics of effective investigative reports.)

40. An officer may use derogatory, biased terms referring to a person's race, ethnicity, religion or sexual preference in police reports. (False, p. 80, Learning Objective: Describe characteristics of effective investigative reports.)

41. Uniform Crime Reporting information is automatically aggregated in the CARE system. (True, p. 86, Learning Objective: Explain whether form or content is more important.)

42. One component of writing a report is to remember that many people will be reading the report and it is important to impress the audience with your writing skills. (False, p. 74, Learning Objective: Discuss who reads the reports.)

43. It doesn't matter whether a report is typed, written or printed—as long as others can read it easily. (True, p. 85, Learning Objective: Describe characteristics of effective investigative reports.)

44. The first person to evaluate your written report should be your supervisor. (False, p. 87, Learning Objective: Explain why reports should be well written.)

45. Officers should feel free to use police jargon in their notes, but should not use police jargon in their reports. (True, p. 74, Learning Objective: Summarize the common problems that occur in many police reports.)

Completion

46. A good report can make an excessive-force _____ less likely to be filed in the first place, and if it does go to court, less likely to be successful. (lawsuit, p. 85, Learning Objective: Explain why reports should be well written.)

47. Inferences are also referred to as _____ language. (conclusionary, (p. 78, Learning Objective: Compare how to differentiate among facts, inferences and opinions.)

48. When organizing notes for a report, list the facts of the investigation in _____ order. (chronological, p. 75, Learning Objective: Explain whether form or content is more important.)

49. An effective report uses the _____ tense, the _____ person and the _____ voice. (past, first, active, p. 78, Learning Objective: Describe characteristics of effective investigative reports.)

50. In the _____ voice, the subject of the sentence performs the actions. (active, p. 84, Learning Objective: Describe characteristics of effective investigative reports.)

51. Verbs in the _____ tense refer to events that have already occurred. (past, p. 84, Learning Objective: Describe characteristics of effective investigative reports.)

52. Once you have written your report, you should always take the following three steps: _____, _____ and _____ it. (evaluate, review, proofread, p. 87, Learning Objective: Describe characteristics of effective investigative reports.)

53. Being _____ means making every word count, without leaving out important facts. (concise, p. 81, Learning Objective: Describe characteristics of effective investigative reports.)

54. CARE stands for _____. (computer-assisted report entry, p. 86, Learning Objective: Explain whether form or content is more important.)

55. A way to increase clarity in reports is to include sketches and _____. (diagrams, p. 83, Learning Objective: Describe characteristics of effective investigative reports.)

Short Answer

56. Explain why it is necessary for officers to write clear reports. (pp. 89–90, Learning Objective: Explain why reports should be well written.)

57. List the characteristics of effective reports. (p. 78, Learning Objective: Describe characteristics of effective investigative reports.)

58. Describe how the report narrative should be structured and what to include in each part of the narrative. (p. 75, Learning Objective: Explain whether form or content is more important.)

59. List four benefits of citizen online reporting. (p. 88, Learning Objective: Describe how reports are used.)

60. Do you think form or content is more important in a police report? (p. 78, Learning Objective: Explain whether form or content is more important.)

61. Give a one-sentence example of an inference, and then rewrite the statement as a fact. (p. 78, Learning Objective: Compare how to differentiate among facts, inferences and opinions.)

62. What types of abbreviations should you avoid using in a report? (p. 83, Learning Objective: Describe characteristics of effective investigative reports.)

63. Briefly describe how citizen online reporting works. (p. 88, Learning Objective: Explain why reports should be well written.)

64. What is the difference between an officer's notes and a report? (p. 72, Learning Objective: Explain why reports are important to an investigation.)

65. How might a report be used to refresh a witness's memory? (p. 74, Learning Objective: Describe how reports are used.)

66. Give a one-sentence example of an opinion, and then rewrite the statement as a fact. (p. 78, Learning Objective: Compare how to differentiate among facts, inferences and opinions.)

67. How might a report be used to plan for future law enforcement services? (pp. 73–74, Learning Objective: Describe how reports are used.)

68. How would the writing of a report be different if a box-style format was used instead of the traditional narrative report? (p. 75, Learning Objective: Describe characteristics of effective investigative reports.)

69. Describe the difference between connotative and denotative language. (p. 80, Learning Objective: Compare how to differentiate among facts, inferences and opinions.)

70. Discuss the difference between inculpatory and exculpatory evidence and the role of the police report toward both. (p. 80, Learning Objective: Describe characteristics of effective investigative reports.)

SEARCHES

Test Bank

Chapter 4
Searches

Multiple Choice

1. In which 1984 case did the Supreme Court define a search as "a governmental infringement of a legitimate expectation of privacy?"

    a. *United States v. Ross*
    b. *United States v. Jacobsen** (p. 95, Learning Objective: Define what basic restriction is placed on all searches.)
    c. *Mapp v. Ohio*
    d. *Terry v. Ohio*

2. A lane search, or partitioning the area into lanes,

    a. can be adapted to any number of police personnel.* (pp. 108–109, Learning Objective: Outline what is included in organizing a crime scene search.)
    b. is intended to be used only with one officer.
    c. works well inside.
    d. must always be used with a traffic director.

3. Which of the following is *not* a goal of a search during an investigation?

    a. to establish that a crime was committed
    b. to establish when the crime was committed
    c. to identify who committed the crime
    d. to punish the offender* (p. 107, Learning Objective: Discuss what a successful crime scene search accomplishes.)

4. Which of the following do investigators *not* need to know in order to conduct an effective search?

    a. the legal requirements for searching
    b. the identity of the offender* (p. 96, Learning Objective: Outline what is required for an effective search.)
    c. the elements of the crime being investigated
    d. the items being searched for

5. The Fourth Amendment to the U.S. Constitution forbids what type of searches and seizures?

    a. illegal
    b. unsupervised
    c. unreasonable* (p. 96, Learning Objective: Identify which constitutional amendment restricts investigative searches.)
    d. undercover

6. In which of the following cases is a search *not* legal?

   a. The search is incidental to a lawful arrest.
   b. An officer stops a suspicious person and believes the person to be armed.
   c. An emergency exists.
   d. An officer conducts a search of a motorist for a driving infraction.* (p. 97, Learning Objective: Clarify what the preconditions and limitations of a legal search are.)

7. A way to determine if probable cause exists today is which test?

   a. plain-view doctrine
   b. totality-of-the-circumstances test* (p. 98, Learning Objective: Clarify what the preconditions and limitations of a legal search are.)
   c. voice stress test
   d. truth-in-evidence test

8. A judge may issue a search warrant if which of the following items are being sought by an officer?

   a. stolen or embezzled property* (p. 98, Learning Objective: Clarify what the preconditions and limitations of a legal search are.)
   b. property that is designed for noncriminal activity
   c. evidence that demonstrates a person is continuing criminal activity while on probation
   d. personal drug usage of medicinal marijuana

9. A search conducted with a warrant must be limited to

   a. only the specific room in the house.
   b. cars that are present on the property.
   c. only the specific area and items named in the warrant.* (p. 100, Learning Objective: Clarify what the preconditions and limitations of a legal search are.)
   d. only those items within the arm's-length rule.

10. Consent to search is valid only if given

   a. under duress.
   b. by a person who is not in control of the property.
   c. voluntarily.* (p. 100, Learning Objective: Clarify what the preconditions and limitations of a legal search are.)
   d. unknowingly.

11. *Terry v. Ohio* supported officers' right to

   a. question suspects with an attorney present.
   b. conduct a patdown or a frisk if they believe the person might be armed and dangerous.* (pp. 101–102, Learning Objective: Describe what precedents are established by the *Weeks, Mapp, Terry, Chimel, Carroll* and *Chambers* decisions.)
   c. conduct a full-body cavity search of an individual who is not in custody.
   d. search vehicles upon probable cause to do so.

12. Every lawful arrest is accompanied by a search of the arrested person. This is referred to as

   a. search of the person.
   b. search incident to arrest.* (pp. 102–103, Learning Objective: Describe what precedents are established by the *Weeks, Mapp, Terry, Chimel, Carroll* and *Chambers* decisions.)
   c. search upon complaint.
   d. search with consent.

13. The *Chimel* decision established that a search incidental to a lawful arrest must be made simultaneously with the arrest. A search incidental to arrest must be confined to

   a. the arrested person's body.* (p. 103, Learning Objective: Describe what precedents are established by the *Weeks, Mapp, Terry, Chimel, Carroll* and *Chambers* decisions.)
   b. the arrested person's body and car.
   c. the area within the suspect's immediate control.
   d. the general area.

14. Emergency circumstances (such as fire or officers hearing shots fired or screams) that allow officers to enter a home without a warrant are referred to as

   a. no-knock entries.
   b. high-risk entries.
   c. exigent circumstances.* (p. 103, Learning Objective: Discuss when a warrantless search is justified.)
   d. warrantless emergencies.

15. The *Carroll* decision established that with probable cause,

   a. automobiles may not be searched unless consent is given.
   b. houses may be searched if the person was arrested in the house.
   c. individuals associated with an arrested person may be searched.
   d. automobiles may be searched based on their obvious mobility.* (p. 104, Learning Objective: Describe what precedents are established by the *Weeks, Mapp, Terry, Chimel, Carroll* and *Chambers* decisions.)

16. *Mincey v. Arizona* established that

    a. officers may always search the premises when the search is associated with an arrest.
    b. while officers are on the premises pursuing their legitimate emergency activities, any evidence in plain view may be seized.* (p. 111, Learning Objective: Describe whether evidence left in plain view may be lawfully seized and whether it is admissible in court.)
    c. searching a location where there are illegal drugs is legal without a search warrant, owing to special federal antidrug legislation.
    d. officers may not seize evidence they find in plain view while pursuing emergency activities.

17. *Wyoming v. Houghton* (1999) held that an officer may search an automobile passenger's belongings simply because the officer suspects the driver has done something wrong. This ruling, which was intended to prevent drivers from claiming that illegal drugs or other contraband belongs to passengers rather than themselves, is referred to as the

    a. jump-seat exception.
    b. passenger patdown.
    c. passenger property exception.* (p. 102, Learning Objective: Discuss when a warrantless search is justified.)
    d. shotgun-seat exception.

18. The courts have ruled that when police take custody of a vehicle or other property, the police

    a. may not inventory the property without a court order.
    b. may not inventory the property without probable cause.
    c. may inventory the property.* (p. 104, Learning Objective: Describe what precedents are established by the *Weeks, Mapp, Terry, Chimel, Carroll* and *Chambers* decisions.)
    d. may search the property regardless of circumstances.

19. The most important limitation on searches is that they must be

    a. expedient in scope.
    b. narrow in scope.* (p. 96, Learning Objective: Define what basic restriction is placed on all searches.)
    c. broad in scope.
    d. prearranged by warrant.

20. Which rule said that courts would not accept evidence obtained by unreasonable search and seizure?

    a. silver-platter rule
    b. exclusionary rule* (p. 96, Learning Objective: Describe what the exclusionary rule is and how it affects investigators.)
    c. roots-of-the-tree rule
    d. rule of thumb

21. In *Nix v. Williams,* the Court said that if illegally obtained evidence (a statement, in this case, which led to a little girl's body) would, in all likelihood, eventually have been discovered legally (for example, by a large search party), it may be used. This is referred to as what exception to the exclusionary rule?

    a.   the inevitable-discovery doctrine* (p. 97, Learning Objective: Describe what the exclusionary rule is and how it affects investigators.)
    b.   the plain-view rule
    c.   the public safety rule
    d.   the eyes-on rule

22. Hopefully, a well-organized, thorough and proper organization of a crime scene search will result in

    a.   a meticulous search with no accidental destruction of evidence.* (p. 107, Learning Objective: Discuss what a successful crime scene search accomplishes.)
    b.   generating ideas about who might be a suspect.
    c.   ignoring some evidence that may have been found by accident.
    d.   identifying the motive.

23. In *United States v. Leon,* the court established that illegally obtained evidence may be admissible if the police were truly not aware they were violating a suspect's Fourth Amendment rights. In this case, the police were following up on a tip from an unreliable informant, which later invalidated the warrant. This exception is called the

    a.   sidewalk exception.
    b.   good-faith doctrine.* (p. 96, Learning Objective: Describe what the exclusionary rule is and how it affects investigators.)
    c.   public safety exception.
    d.   just-in-time exception.

24. Physical evidence is

    a.   blood-spattered.
    b.   on a person.
    c.   anything material and relevant. (p. 107, Learning Objective: Explain what physical evidence is.)
    d.   easily obtainable.

25. In *California v. Greenwood,* the Supreme Court ruled that

    a.   searches of homes are illegal.
    b.   searches of cars are legal if part of an inventory.
    c.   the curtilage rule applies to all evidence.
    d.   containers left on public property are open to search by police without a warrant.* (pp. 112–113, Learning Objective: Describe whether evidence left in plain view may be lawfully seized and whether it is admissible in court.)

True/False

26. The search of a vehicle does not require probable cause because vehicles are mobile. (False, p. 104, Learning Objective: Describe what precedents are established by the *Weeks, Mapp, Terry, Chimel, Carroll* and *Chambers* decisions.)

27. Dogs cannot be trained to search for explosives. (False, p. 116, Learning Objective: Outline how to use dogs in searches.)

28. Interior searches go from the general to the specific, usually in a circular pattern, covering all surfaces of a search area. (True, p. 110, Learning Objective: Define and compare interior and exterior search patterns.)

29. Plain-view evidence is admissible in court, no matter what the circumstances. (False, p. 111, Learning Objective: Describe whether evidence left in plain view may be lawfully seized and whether it is admissible in court.)

30. Officers may not seize contraband they discover during a legal search, but must ask consent. (False, p. 111, Learning Objective: Describe whether evidence left in plain view may be lawfully seized and whether it is admissible in court.)

31. Officers may use heat-sensing (thermal-scanning) devices without a warrant. (False, p. 112, Learning Objective: Describe whether evidence left in plain view may be lawfully seized and whether it is admissible in court.)

32. The common denominator of all search patterns is that they are designed to systematically locate any evidence at a crime scene or any other area where evidence might be found. (True, p. 108, Learning Objective: Define and compare interior and exterior search patterns.)

33. There are some instances in which evidence may not exist at the crime scene. (True, p. 107, Learning Objective: Outline what is included in organizing a crime scene search.)

34. In *Wyoming v. Houghton,* the court ruled that an officer may search the belongings of an automobile passenger simply because the officer suspects the driver has done something wrong. (True, p. 104, Learning Objective: Describe what precedents are established by the *Weeks, Mapp, Terry, Chimel, Carroll* and *Chambers* decisions.)

35. Under the consent once removed exception, officers can make a warrantless entry to arrest a suspect if consent to enter was given earlier to an undercover officer or informant. (True, p. 101, Learning Objective: Discuss when a warrantless search is justified.)

36. In *Georgia v. Randolph* (2006), the Supreme Court said, "If any party who is present and has authority to object to the search does object to the search, the police may not conduct the search on the authority of that party who gave consent." (True, p. 101, Learning Objective: Discuss when a warrantless search is justified.)

37. A search with consent must be voluntary. (True, p. 101, Learning Objective: Discuss when a warrantless search is justified.)

38. A search warrant can be issued to search for and seize property designed or intended for use in committing a crime. (True, p. 98, Learning Objective: Clarify what the preconditions and limitations of a legal search are.)

39. The consent to search must not be in response to an officer's claim of lawful authority or in response to a command or threat by an officer. (True, p. 101, Learning Objective: Discuss when a warrantless search is justified.)

40. Every lawful arrest is accompanied by a search of the arrested person to protect the arresting officers and others and to prevent destruction of evidence. (True, p. 102, Learning Objective: Describe what precedents are established by the *Weeks, Mapp, Terry, Chimel, Carroll* and *Chambers* decisions.)

41. During a stop of a moving vehicle, officers may search the vehicle and any closed containers in it without probable cause or consent. (False, p. 104, Learning Objective: Describe whether evidence left in plain view may be lawfully seized and whether it is admissible in court.)

42. One of the reasons that the courts allow an inventory of vehicles and property is to protect the owner's property. (True, p. 105, Learning Objective: Describe what precedents are established by the *Weeks, Mapp, Terry, Chimel, Carroll* and *Chambers* decisions.)

43. Property owners can consent to police entry or search even though a tenant or guest has lawful right of possession of the premises. (False, p. 101, Learning Objective: Discuss when a warrantless search is justified.)

44. *Illinois v. McArthur* (2001) ruled that officers may detain residents outside their homes until a search warrant can be obtained if necessary. (True, p. 102, Learning Objective: Describe what precedents are established by the *Weeks, Mapp, Terry, Chimel, Carroll* and *Chambers* decisions.)

45. The Fourth Amendment protects both people and places. (False, p. 96, Learning Objective: Identify which constitutional amendment restricts investigative searches.)

Completion

46. _____ searches are prohibited by the Fourth Amendment. (Unreasonable, p. 96, Learning Objective: Identify which constitutional amendment restricts investigative searches.)

47. When probable cause exists but there is no time to obtain a search warrant, the officer may conduct a search. This is an example of an emergency, or _____ circumstances. (exigent, p. 103, Learning Objective: Describe what precedents are established by the *Weeks, Mapp, Terry, Chimel, Carroll* and *Chambers* decisions.)

48. The *Carroll* decision established that automobiles may be searched without a warrant, largely based on the _____ of vehicles. (mobility, p. 104, Learning Objective: Describe what precedents are established by the *Weeks, Mapp, Terry, Chimel, Carroll* and *Chambers* decisions.)

49. The landmark decision in *Terry v. Ohio* established police officers' right to pat down or frisk a person they have stopped to question if they have reasonable suspicion that the person might be _____ and _____. (armed, dangerous, p. 102, Learning Objective: Describe what precedents are established by the *Weeks, Mapp, Terry, Chimel, Carroll* and *Chambers* decisions.)

50. In order to obtain a valid search warrant, officers must appear before a judge and establish probable cause to believe that the location contains evidence of a crime, and they must _____ describe that evidence. (specifically, p. 97, Learning Objective: Clarify what the preconditions and limitations of a legal search are.)

51. The Supreme Court has ruled that probable cause should be based on a totality-of-the-_____ test. (circumstances, p. 98, Learning Objective: Clarify what the preconditions and limitations of a legal search are.)

52. In a unanimous ruling in *United States v. Banks* (2003), the Supreme Court upheld the _____ entry into a suspected drug dealer's apartment 15 to 20 seconds after police knocked and announced themselves. (forced, p. 100, Learning Objective: Clarify what the preconditions and limitations of a legal search are.)

53. _____ _____ determines the extent of a search scene. (Department policy, p. 115, Learning Objective: Describe how to search a vehicle, a suspect and a dead body.)

54. A search conducted with a warrant must be limited to the specific area and specific items named in the warrant, in accordance with the _____ requirement. (particularity, p. 100, Learning Objective: Clarify what the preconditions and limitations of a legal search are.)

55. When asking for consent to search, it is good practice to get a(n) _____ answer before conducting a search, and even better practice to obtain a written consent to search. (affirmative, p. 101, Learning Objective: Discuss when a warrantless search is justified.)

Short Answer

56. Define *curtilage*. (p. 113, Learning Objective: Describe whether evidence left in plain view may be lawfully seized and whether it is admissible in court.)

57. Describe the "fruit-of-the-poisonous-tree" doctrine. (p. 96, Learning Objective: Describe what the exclusionary rule is and how it affects investigators.)

58. The courts have upheld the right of an officer to inventory a vehicle for what reasons? (p. 105, Learning Objective: Describe what precedents are established by the *Weeks, Mapp, Terry, Chimel, Carroll* and *Chambers* decisions.)

59. The search team leader is primarily responsible for which tasks? (p. 107, Learning Objective: Outline what is included in organizing a crime scene search.)

60. What is the plain-view doctrine? (pp. 111–112, Learning Objective: Describe whether evidence left in plain view may be lawfully seized and whether it is admissible in court.)

61. When is trash subject to search? (pp. 112–113, Learning Objective: Describe whether evidence left in plain view may be lawfully seized and whether it is admissible in court.)

62. What are the limits on a "dog-sniff" search for narcotics at a traffic stop? (p. 116, Learning Objective: Outline how to use dogs in searches.)

63. Describe limits on using thermal imaging in searches. (p. 112, Learning Objective: Describe whether evidence left in plain view may be lawfully seized and whether it is admissible in court.)

64. How would you proceed with the search of a dead body at a crime scene? What issues must be considered? (pp. 115–116, Learning Objective: Describe how to search a vehicle, a suspect and a dead body.)

65. Describe the "plain feel/touch" exception to the exclusionary rule. (pp. 111–112, Learning Objective: Describe whether evidence left in plain view may be lawfully seized and whether it is admissible in court.)

66. How would you organize a search for a murder weapon in an open field? (p. 107, Learning Objective: Define and compare interior and exterior search patterns.)

67. Describe a situation in which an officer might use an anticipatory warrant. (p. 100, Learning Objective: Discuss when a warrantless search is justified.)

68. Define an uncontaminated crime scene. (p. 107, Learning Objective: Define and compare interior and exterior search patterns.)

69. How would you organize a search for a murder weapon inside an apartment? (pp. 110–111, Learning Objective: Define and compare interior and exterior search patterns.)

70. Discuss whether dogs are subject to the same legal limitations on searches that officers are. (p. 116, Learning Objective: Outline how to use dogs in searches)

FORENSICS/ PHYSICAL EVIDENCE

Test Bank

Chapter 5
Forensics/Physical Evidence

Multiple Choice

1. Ultraviolet light is good for finding

    a. trace evidence such as semen or fibers.* (p. 130, Learning Objective: Identify the kind of evidence UV light can help discover.)
    b. bullet trajectories.
    c. paint or glass.
    d. tire tracks.

2. When evidence is collected, an officer should record in his or her notes the

    a. time the item was found and the disposition.
    b. time and date the item was found.
    c. time, date and location the item was found.
    d. time, date and location the item was found; the individual who found it; the case number; a description of the item; and who took it into custody.* (p. 131, Learning Objective: Explain what should be recorded in crime scene notes.)

3. Which term refers to the spiral pattern cut down the length of a firearm's barrel?

    a. rifling* (p. 162, Learning Objective: Explain how to mark and care for weapons used in crimes.)
    b. bore
    c. lands
    d. caliber markings

4. This type of fingerprint, which is not readily visible, consists of impressions of the ridges of the fingers, transferred to other surfaces by sweat on the ridges of the fingers or because the fingers carry residue of oil, blood, dirt or another substance. These prints are referred to as

    a. ten-print fingerprints.
    b. latent prints.* (p. 139, Learning Objective: Explain where fingerprints can be found and how they should be preserved.)
    c. ID-match prints.
    d. comparison prints.

5. Powders, Magnabrush techniques, laser technology, gelatin lifters and cyanoacrylate are all used to process what type of evidence?

    a. petechiae
    b. adipocre
    c. fingerprints* (pp. 141–143, Learning Objective: Explain where finger-prints can be found and how they should be preserved.)
    d. cadavers

6. AFIS stands for

   a. Automated Fingerprint Issuing Society.
   b. automatic fingerprint intake system.
   c. automatic fiber identification system.
   d. automated fingerprint identification system.* (p. 143, Learning Objective: Explain where fingerprints can be found and how they should be preserved.)

7. DNA testing is expensive and takes a lot of time. Because of this, laboratories require that

   a. samples be submitted for both the suspect and the victim.
   b. sufficient material be collected.
   c. the evidence be probative.
   d. all of these choices.* (p. 148, Learning Objective: Define DNA profiling.)

8. The number one mistake officers make in processing fingerprints with powders is

   a. over-processing fingerprints.* (p. 141, Learning Objective: Explain where fingerprints can be found and how they should be preserved.)
   b. misidentifying fingerprints.
   c. sneezing and destroying the print.
   d. selecting the wrong powder.

9. The types of prints taken of persons with reason to be at the crime scene location are referred to as _____ fingerprints.

   a. illusionary
   b. expectoratory
   c. elimination* (p. 143, Learning Objective: Explain where fingerprints can be found and how they should be preserved.)
   d. illuminating

10. Fingerprints can indicate

    a. age.
    b. race.
    c. gender.
    d. none of these choices.* (p. 145, Learning Objective: Describe what can and cannot be determined from fingerprints, DNA, bloodstains and hairs.)

11. In the examination of objects of physical evidence, class characteristics are important because they can

    a. place an item into a specific category.* (p. 139, Learning Objective: Identify the types of evidence most commonly found in criminal investigations and how to collect, identify and package each type.)
    b. distinguish one item from another.

c.   be used to trace the item to its manufacturer.
d.   define how the object was used by an individual.

12.   Integrity of evidence refers to the requirement that any item introduced in court must be in the same condition as when it was found at the crime scene. This is documented by the *chain of evidence,* also referred to as the

a.   missing link.
b.   chain of custody.* (p. 129, Learning Objective: Describe various methods of processing physical evidence.)
c.   chain of truth.
d.   all of these choices.

13.   The size and shape of chips and wear patterns in the blade of a screwdriver are _____ characteristics.

a.   individual* (p. 139, Learning Objective: Identify the types of evidence most commonly found in criminal investigations and how to collect, identify and package each type.)
b.   group
c.   class
d.   none of these choices

14.   DNA profiling can be done using

a.   blood only.
b.   fingerprints only.
c.   skin or hair cells only.
d.   cells from almost any part of the body.* (p. 147, Learning Objective: Define DNA profiling.)

15.   Hair analysis can reveal all but which of the following?

a.   which part of the body the hair came from
b.   the presence of drugs or poisons and consumer chemicals
c.   age and gender* (p. 158, Learning Objective: Explain how the identification of blood and hair can be useful.)
d.   blood-type group

16.   The most frequently located type of microscopic evidence is

a.   skin cells.
b.   hair.
c.   saliva droplets.
d.   fibers.* (p. 158, Learning Objective: Explain how the identification of blood and hair can be useful.)

17. A genetic fingerprint is obtained from a suspect's

    a. finger.
    b. DNA.* (p. 147, Learning Objective: Define DNA profiling.)
    c. hair.
    d. eye color.

18. When evidence is no longer needed, it is

    a. auctioned off.
    b. destroyed.
    c. returned to the owner.
    d. any of these may be appropriate.* (p. 138, Learning Objective: Describe methods of evidence disposal.)

19. A way of folding paper so that evidence does not fall out is referred as a

    a. drug hold.
    b. druggist fold.* (p. 132, Learning Objective: Describe various methods of packaging and transporting evidence to a department or a laboratory.)
    c. dime bag.
    d. doper bag.

20. Laboratory examination of _____ under a scanning electron microscope (SEM) is still considered a reliable analysis method, although enhancements in technology have been necessary.

    a. gunshot residue (GSR)* (p. 163, Learning Objective: Explain how to mark and care for weapons used in crimes.)
    b. DNA
    c. fingerprints
    d. retinal scans

21. What evidence can indicate whether a person is running, lost or carrying something heavy?

    a. fingerprints
    b. DNA
    c. footprints* (p. 159, Learning Objective: Describe where shoe and tire impressions can be found and how they should be preserved.)
    d. blood spatter

22. What type of evidence forms a substantive part of the case or has a legitimate and effective influence on the decision of the case?

    a. circumstantial
    b. material* (p. 125, Learning Objective: Describe various methods of processing physical evidence.)
    c. exculpatory
    d. *in flagrante delicto*

23. What type of evidence has been properly collected, identified, filed and continuously secured?

    a. relevant
    b. competent* (p. 125, Learning Objective: Describe various methods of processing physical evidence.)
    c. material
    d. exculpatory

24. This method is *not* recommended for developing latent fingerprints on unpainted wood, paper, cardboard or other absorbent surfaces.

    a. iodine fuming
    b. ninhydrin method
    c. powders* (p. 141, Learning Objective: Explain where fingerprints can be found and how they should be preserved.)
    d. thermal nitrate

25. Evidence disposal can occur

    a. continuously.
    b. annually.
    c. on a special date.
    d. all of these choices.* (True, p. 138, Learning Objective: Describe methods of evidence disposal.)

True/False

26. A mobile crime lab is a commercially customized van that provides compartments to hold equipment and countertops for processing evidence. (True, p. 128, Learning Objective: Describe various methods of processing physical evidence.)

27. Having equipment available for evidence processing is important, but having been trained in the use of the equipment is more important. (True, p. 128, Learning Objective: Describe various methods of processing physical evidence.)

28. During the search of a crime scene, it is generally easy to tell which items are evidence; the primary difficulty is in collecting the items. (False, p. 129, Learning Objective: Determine what qualifies as evidence.)

29. Probability serves no purpose in evidence; the lab must determine whether or not the evidence exactly matches the standard of comparison. (False, pp. 129–130, Learning Objective: Discuss common errors in collecting evidence.)

30. To simplify testimony in court, it is practical to have one officer collect the item of evidence and another take notes. (True, p. 131, Learning Objective: Identify evidence.)

31. Before, during and after its examination, evidence must be securely protected and properly stored. However, once it is ready for court, there are no issues regarding how it is stored. (False, p. 137, Learning Objective: Discuss methods of evidence storage.)

32. Automating evidence storage can prevent many problems. (True, p. 137, Learning Objective: Discuss methods of evidence storage.)

33. Evidence may be placed in any type of container, as long as it does not touch other evidence. (False, p. 132, Learning Objective: Describe various methods of packaging and transporting evidence to a department or a laboratory.)

34. It does not matter what color of fingerprint powder you use when dusting for prints. (False, p. 141, Learning Objective: Explain where fingerprints can be found and how they should be preserved.)

35. Deoxyribonucleic acid is used to compare sequences of nucleotides. (True, p. 147, Learning Objective: Define DNA profiling.)

36. Fingerprints are a type of evidence that requires a standard of comparison. (True, p. 130, Learning Objective: Discuss common errors in collecting evidence.)

37. Investigators should powder and lift every fingerprint they discover. (False, p. 141, Learning Objective: Explain where fingerprints can be found and how they should be preserved.)

38. Blood can be identified as animal or human. (True, p. 157, Learning Objective: Explain how the identification of blood and hair can be useful.)

39. Typewritten materials are untraceable and, therefore, impossible to link with a suspect. (False, p. 169, Learning Objective: Describe how to preserve such things as glass fragments, soil samples, safe insulation material, rope, tapes, liquids and documents.)

40. Locard's exchange principle basically states that a criminal always removes something from the crime scene or leaves behind incriminating evidence. (True, p. 123, Learning Objective: Describe various methods of processing physical evidence.)

41. Hairs are far more distinguishable than fibers. (False, p. 158, Learning Objective: Explain how the identification of blood and hair can be useful.)

42. Latent prints have been collected from human skin. (True, p. 140, Learning Objective: Explain where fingerprints can be found and how they should be preserved.)

43. DNA is extremely durable and generally unaffected by heat, sunlight, moisture, bacteria or mold. (False, p. 148, Learning Objective: Describe what can and cannot be determined from fingerprints, DNA, bloodstains and hairs.)

44. Investigators have used lip prints and lip impressions to solve cases. (True, p. 146, Learning Objective: Describe what can and cannot be determined from fingerprints, DNA, bloodstains and hairs.)

45. Evidence must be legally disposed of to prevent major storage problems. (True, p. 138, Learning Objective: Describe methods of evidence disposal.)

Completion

46. The type of evidence that links a suspect with a crime and is often found in fingerprints, footprints, bloodstains, hairs and fibers is called _____ evidence. (associative, p. 125, Learning Objective: Describe various methods of processing physical evidence.)

47. A tool _____ is an impression left by a tool on a surface. (mark, p. 160, Learning Objective: Illustrate how to preserve tools that might have been used in the crime, as well as the marks they made.)

48. The largest failure in gathering evidence is not the equipment available, but the lack of _____ in using it effectively. (training, p. 128, Learning Objective: Describe various methods of processing physical evidence.)

49. To determine what is evidence, first consider the apparent _____. (crime, p. 129, Learning Objective: Determine what qualifies as evidence.)

50. A _____ of comparison is an object, measure or model with which evidence is compared to determine whether both came from the same source. (standard, p. 130, Learning Objective: Discuss common errors in collecting evidence.)

51. When collecting evidence, take extreme care to prevent different pieces of evidence from touching each other, which can lead to _____ contamination. (cross, p. 131, Learning Objective: Discuss common errors in collecting evidence.)

52. The small lines on the palm side at the end of every human finger, which provide just enough roughness to help fingers retain objects, are known as _____ ridges. (friction, p. 139, Learning Objective: Explain where fingerprints can be found and how they should be preserved.)

53. Fingerprints are clear and _____ evidence of a person's identity. (positive, p. 145, Learning Objective: Describe what can and cannot be determined from fingerprints, DNA, bloodstains and hairs.)

54. For laboratories to process DNA evidence, the evidence must be _____ that is, tending to prove guilt or innocence. (probative, p. 148, Learning Objective: Define DNA profiling.)

55. In collecting hair samples, attempt to obtain 25 to 50 full hairs from the appropriate part of the suspect's body for _____ purposes. (comparison, p. 158, Learning Objective: Explain how the identification of blood and hair can be useful.)

Short Answer

56. Discuss the difference between individual and class characteristics. (p. 139, Learning Objective: Identify the types of evidence most commonly found in criminal investigations and how to collect, identify and package each type.)

57. Describe the basic types of equipment that a department would need to process a crime scene. (pp. 126–127, Learning Objective: Describe various methods of processing physical evidence.)

58. Once evidence is discovered, photographed and sketched, it is ready for collecting. How could you collect several different items in order to best avoid cross-contamination? (p. 131, Learning Objective: Discuss common errors in collecting evidence.)

59. How is it possible to collect scent from a crime scene? (p. 157, Learning Objective: Explain how the identification of blood and hair can be useful.)

60. Explain the difference between competent, material and relevant evidence. (p. 125, Learning Objective: Describe various methods of processing physical evidence.)

61. Describe the process of identifying and preserving the various types of fingerprints. (pp. 139–144, Learning Objective: Explain where fingerprints can be found and how they should be preserved.)

62. List and describe the evidence that would be most helpful in showing that a specific person was at a scene. (p. 129, Learning Objective: Identify evidence.)

63. How should an investigator avoid contaminating evidence? (p. 131, Learning Objective: Discuss common errors in collecting evidence.)

64. When would an investigator make use of an ultraviolet light? (p. 130, Learning Objective: Identify evidence.)

65. Why is the quality of a rolled fingerprint important? (p. 145, Learning Objective: Describe what can and cannot be determined from fingerprints, DNA, bloodstains and hairs.)

66. Why did the jury seem to disregard the DNA evidence in the O.J. Simpson case, and what suggestions do you have for avoiding such problems? (p. 148, Learning Objective: Define DNA profiling.)

67. Briefly describe the differences between latent, visible and plastic fingerprints. (pp. 139–140, Learning Objective: Explain where fingerprints can be found and how they should be preserved.)

68. Describe the type of evidence that might be found at the scene of a hit-and-run. How should this evidence be collected? (pp. 170–171, Learning Objective: Describe what evidence to collect in hit-and-run cases.)

69. Discuss how language analysis can contribute to an investigation. (p. 147, Learning Objective: Describe what can and cannot be determined from fingerprints, DNA, bloodstains and hairs.)

70. What can the examination of human skeletal remains contribute to an investigation? (p. 171, Learning Objective: Explain what can be determined from human skeletal remains.)

OBTAINING INFORMATION AND INTELLIGENCE

Test Bank

Chapter 6
Obtaining Information and Intelligence

Multiple Choice

1. In addition to physical evidence, three primary sources of information are available:

    a.   dispatchers, first responders and records clerks.
    b.   reports, records and databases; people who are not suspects in a crime but know something of the crime; and suspects in the crime.* (p. 180, Learning Objective: Describe the various sources of information that are available to investigators.)
    c.   reports, records and witnesses.
    d.   snitches, rats and informants.

2. The ultimate goal of interviewing and interrogating is to

    a.   identify the person who is to be arrested.
    b.   identify those responsible for a crime and eliminate the innocent from suspicion.* (p. 184, Learning Objective: Explain the goal of interviewing and interrogation.)
    c.   ensure proper punishment.
    d.   eliminate the innocent.

3. Two basic requirements for obtaining information are to

    a.   listen and observe.* (p. 186, Learning Objective: Outline what two requirements are needed to obtain information.)
    b.   listen and respond.
    c.   observe and analyze.
    d.   assess and evaluate.

4. Which of the following questions is most direct?

    a.   "Were you around the area of the corner of 5th and Main last night?"
    b.   "Where were you last night?"
    c.   "Did you assault George Smith at 5th and Main last night?"* (p. 186, Learning Objective: Clarify the difference between direct and indirect questions, and when to use each.)
    d.   "Why did you assault George?"

5. When conducting an interview, you should

    a.   interview all witnesses at once.
    b.   give first consideration to eyewitnesses.
    c.   give the *Miranda* warning first.
    d.   interview the victim or complainant first.* (p. 187, Learning Objective: Explain when and in what order individuals are interviewed.)

6. People may volunteer information if approached correctly. Consequently, the following technique is useful to demonstrate when conducting an interview.

   a. developing rapport* (pp. 188–189, Learning Objective: Discuss how to improve communication between the investigator, victims, witnesses or suspects.)
   b. developing an intimate relationship
   c. using bribery and gratuities
   d. using flattery and guile

7. The best place to interrogate a suspect is usually

   a. in the police vehicle.
   b. in the suspect's home.
   c. at the police department.* (p. 196, Learning Objective: Outline the two requirements of a place for conducting interrogations.)
   d. while the suspect is on the job.

8. Once a confession has been obtained, investigators should

   a. corroborate the confession using independent evidence.* (p. 201, Learning Objective: Clarify what significance a confession has in an investigation.)
   b. stop the investigation.
   c. let the confession prove the case.
   d. submit the case for prosecution based on the confession.

9. To improve communication,

   a. ask complex questions that will confuse the suspect and make him or her more likely to tell the truth.
   b. stand so that the suspect can see more of you.
   c. use a public setting.
   d. prepare your questions and tactics in advance.* (p. 184, Learning Objective: Discuss how to improve communication between the investigator, victims, witnesses or suspects.)

10. This type of interview technique calls for using a secluded, quiet place that is free of distractions. It is effective for obtaining information from victims and witnesses who are having difficulty remembering an event.

    a. reflective memory trips
    b. suppressed memory traps
    c. cognitive interview* (p. 190, Learning Objective: Describe techniques that are likely to assist recall as well as uncover lies.)
    d. subliminal inflection

11. If a public threat exists, questioning to reduce that threat may occur before the reading of the *Miranda* warning. Which case highlighted this issue?

   a. *New York v. Quarles** (pp. 194–195, Learning Objective: Explain what the *Miranda* warning is and when to give it.)
   b. *Mapp v. Ohio*
   c. *Lawson v. Kolender*
   d. *Arizona v. Mincey*

12. The fundamental distinction between the Fifth and Sixth Amendment right to counsel hinges on the issue of

   a. exigency.
   b. guilt.
   c. privacy.
   d. custody.* (p. 195, Learning Objective: Explain what the *Miranda* warning is and when to give it.)

13. When general, preliminary questioning occurs spontaneously on the street, it is called a

   a. field interview.* (p. 183, Learning Objective: Discuss what a sources-of-information file is and what it contains.)
   b. cite interview.
   c. site interrogation.
   d. field citation.

14. Which is not accepted by the courts as evidence?

   a. thermal imaging
   b. fingerprints
   c. DNA
   d. a polygraph* (p. 204, Learning Objective: Explain what a polygraph is and what its role in investigation and the acceptability of its results in court are.)

15. What may be used to help a victim or witness recall an incident?

   a. hypnosis* (p. 205, Learning Objective: Explain what a polygraph is and what its role in investigation and the acceptability of its results in court are.)
   b. electroshock therapy
   c. brain stimulation
   d. psychics

16. To be valid in court, a confession must always be

   a. written.
   b. voluntary.* (p. 200, Learning Objective: Describe what restrictions are placed on obtaining a confession.)
   c. an admission.
   d. witnessed by two or more people.

17. In *Miranda v. Arizona*, who won the ultimate appeal and why?

    a. Miranda, because he had been beaten to confess
    b. Miranda, because his rights had not been explained to him properly* (p. 191, Learning Objective: Explain what the *Miranda* warning is and when to give it.)
    c. Arizona, because the police had admonished Miranda properly
    d. Arizona, because Miranda voluntarily confessed

18. Under the *Bruton* rule, which resulted from *Bruton v. United States* (1968), a defendant's Sixth Amendment right to confront and cross-examine witnesses against him or her is violated if

    a. the defendant recants a confession.
    b. the defendant waives *Miranda* rights.
    c. a confessing defendant's statement is used against a nonconfessing defendant at their joint trial.* (pp. 201–202, Learning Objective: Clarify what significance a confession has in an investigation.)
    d. the witnesses recant.

19. Which of the following is *not* a recommended interrogation technique?

    a. minimizing the crime
    b. forcing responses
    c. inflating the ego
    d. none of these choices* (pp. 197–198, Learning Objective: Discuss what techniques to use in an interrogation.)

20. Information or data is not intelligence. Information needs which component to become intelligence?

    a. statistics
    b. computers
    c. analysis* (p. 207, Learning Objective: Identify the differences between information and intelligence.)
    d. data

21. Which of the following can be used to simultaneously monitor call activity on several lines?

    a. a pen register
    b. a dialed number recorder* (p. 181, Learning Objective: Discuss what a sources-of-information file is and what it contains.)
    c. an inventory tracking system
    d. caller ID

22. Which of the following statements about witnesses is false?

    a. Witnesses are often more confident in their knowledge of what happened than they are accurate.
    b. Witnesses rarely withhold information or provide it for ulterior motives, which is why officers can trust them as a source of information.* (p. 182, Learning Objective: Discuss what a sources-of-information file is and what it contains.)
    c. What witnesses think they see is a function of what they expected to see, what they wanted to see and what they actually saw.
    d. Many witnesses see only a part of the commission of a crime but testify as though they witnessed the entire event.

23. Which of the following is a characteristic of an effective interviewer/interrogator?

    a. optimistic
    b. confident
    c. sensitive
    d. all of these choices* (p. 184, Learning Objective: List the characteristics of an effective interviewer or interrogator.)

24. Which has been shown to be an effective interview technique to uncover lies?

    a. recording and videotaping the interview
    b. repetition* (p. 187, Learning Objective: Describe techniques that are likely to assist recall as well as uncover lies.)
    c. appealing to reason
    d. projecting the blame

25. Some research has found that the incidence of false confessions is

    a. directly related to the use of illegal, third-degree tactics.
    b. due to the incorrect use of the Miranda warning.
    c. lower when the suspect has no accomplices in the crime.
    d. higher than many believe and exacerbated by certain interrogation tactics.* (p. 201, Learning Objective: Describe what restrictions are placed on obtaining a confession.)

True/False

26. Audio and video recordings are being used more widely as evidence. (True, p. 187, Learning Objective: Describe techniques that are likely to assist recall as well as uncover lies.)

27. Once a suspect has confessed, the investigation should be ended and all of the facts presented to the prosecuting attorney. (False, p. 201, Learning Objective: Clarify what significance a confession has in an investigation.)

28. When at a crime scene, interview all witnesses together so that they can give an overall picture of the crime. (False, pp. 187–188, Learning Objective: Explain when and in what order individuals are interviewed.)

29. The *Miranda* warning advises suspects of their Fourth Amendment rights. (False, p. 191, Learning Objective: Explain when and in what order individuals are interviewed.)

30. When conducting an interrogation, officers should seek a place where the individual will likely feel the most stress. (False, p. 196, Learning Objective: Outline the two requirements of a place for conducting interrogations.)

31. Emotional barriers to communication include fear, anger, ingrained attitudes and prejudices, and the instinct for self-preservation. (True, p. 185, Learning Objective: Explain the emotional barriers to communication.)

32. Sympathy and empathy are the same. (False, pp. 188–189, Learning Objective: Discuss how to improve communication between the investigator, victims, witnesses or suspects.)

33. Since eyewitness testimony is not always reliable, it is generally regarded as irrelevant to investigating and prosecuting a case. (False, p. 182, Learning Objective: Discuss what a sources-of-information file is and what it contains.)

34. Information obtained through the use of truth serums is recognized by the courts as reliable and is admissible, provided a court order was obtained before the suspect received the serum. (False, p. 205, Learning Objective: Explain what a polygraph is and what its role in investigation and the acceptability of its results in court are.)

35. Interrogatory deception is a valuable tool for investigators. (True, p. 199, Learning Objective: Discuss what techniques to use in an interrogation.)

36. The Sixth Amendment right to counsel applies to anyone who is questioned by the police. (False, p. 195, Learning Objective: Explain what the *Miranda* warning is and when to give it.)

37. It is especially advantageous to officers to question someone suspected of involvement in a crime right after the crime has occurred. (True, p. 183, Learning Objective: Discuss what a sources-of-information file is and what it contains.)

38. During interrogation, it is permissible to tell a suspect that an accomplice has already confessed, when this is actually untrue. (True, p. 199, Learning Objective: Explain what third-degree tactics are and describe their place in interrogation.)

39. The ultimate goals of interviewing and interrogating are to identify those responsible for a crime and to eliminate the innocent from suspicion. (True, p. 184, Learning Objective: Explain the goal of interviewing and interrogation.)

40. The *Miranda* warning is not required during questioning by a private citizen who is not an agent of the government. (True, p. 192, Learning Objective: Explain what the *Miranda* warning is and when to give it.)

41. Polygraph results are admissible in court under some specific conditions. (False, p. 204, Learning Objective: Explain what a polygraph is and what its role in investigation and the acceptability of its results in court are.)

42. Hypnosis has been universally accepted by the courts. (False, p. 205, Learning Objective: Explain what a polygraph is and what its role in investigation and the acceptability of its results in court are.)

43. Truth serums are commonly used in criminal cases by the police (False, p. 205, Learning Objective: Explain what a polygraph is and what its role in investigation and the acceptability of its results in court are.)

44. Profilers are occasionally used by law enforcement. (True, p. 205, Learning Objective: Explain what a polygraph is and what its role in investigation and the acceptability of its results in court are.)

45. Officers may legally use deception during interviews. (True, p. 199, Learning Objective: Discuss what techniques to use in an interrogation.)

Completion

46. The _____ Amendment states that "[N]o person shall be compelled in any criminal case to be a witness against himself." (Fifth, p. 191, Learning Objective: Explain what the *Miranda* warning is and when to give it.)

47. A(n) _____ is anyone who can provide information about a case but who is not a complainant, witness, victim or suspect. (informant, p. 183, Learning Objective: Discuss what a sources-of-information file is and what it contains.)

48. _____ is the capacity to accurately perceive and respond to another person's thoughts and feelings. It is an active process rather than a passive experience. (Empathy, pp. 188–189, Learning Objective: Discuss how to improve communication between the investigator, victims, witnesses or suspects.)

49. The Miranda warning informs suspects of their _____ Amendment rights. (Fifth, p. 191, Learning Objective: Explain what the *Miranda* warning is and when to give it.)

50. The "question first" technique is also known as _____. (beachheading, p. 194, Learning Objective: Explain what the *Miranda* warning is and when to give it.)

51. Belittling a suspect is often effective, and is referred as _____ their ego. (deflating, p. 197, Learning Objective: Discuss what techniques to use in an interrogation.)

52. A(n) _____ question is to the point and limits the possibility of misinterpretation. (direct, p. 186, Learning Objective: Clarify the difference between direct and indirect questions, and when to use each.)

53. The _____ measures respiration and depth of breathing, changes in the skin's electrical resistance, and blood pressure and pulse. (polygraph, p. 203, Learning Objective: Explain what a polygraph is and what its role in investigation and the acceptability of its results in court are.)

54. The _____ interview method is especially effective for obtaining information from victims and witnesses who have difficulty remembering an event. (cognitive, p. 190, Learning Objective: Describe techniques that are likely to assist recall as well as uncover lies.)

55. A(n) _____ is the process of questioning those suspected of direct or indirect involvement in a crime. (interrogation, p. 184, Learning Objective: Explain the goal of interviewing and interrogation.)

Short Answer

56. What differences may arise in interviewing juveniles versus adults? (p. 202, Learning Objective: Discuss what to consider when questioning a juvenile.)

57. How should an investigator evaluate and corroborate information learned in interviews or interrogations? (p. 203, Learning Objective: Clarify what significance a confession has in an investigation.)

58. Describe a cognitive interview. (p. 190, Learning Objective: Describe techniques that are likely to assist recall as well as uncover lies.)

59. What are pen registers and how are they useful to investigators? (pp. 180–181, Learning Objective: Discuss what a sources-of-information file is and what it contains.)

60. Of what value is the FBI's National Crime Information Center (NCIC) to investigators? (p. 181, Learning Objective: Discuss what a sources-of-information file is and what it contains.)

61. Briefly discuss some of the approaches an officer can use in an interrogation. (pp. 197–198, Learning Objective: Discuss what techniques to use in an interrogation.)

62. What is a fusion center? (p. 208, Learning Objective: Identify the differences between information and intelligence.)

63. Outline the various scientific aids available to law enforcement for obtaining and evaluating information. (pp. 203–205, Learning Objective: Explain what a polygraph is and what its role in investigation and the acceptability of its results in court are.)

64. Under what conditions can a juvenile be used as an informant? (p. 202, Learning Objective: Discuss what to consider when questioning a juvenile.)

65. Describe the difference between an admission, a confession and an adoptive admission. (p. 200, Learning Objective: Describe what restrictions are placed on obtaining a confession.)

66. Discuss the legality of third-degree tactics in police interrogations. (p. 199, Learning Objective: Explain what third-degree tactics are and describe their place in interrogation.)

67. Describe the circumstances that must accompany a legally obtained confession. (p. 200, Learning Objective: Describe what restrictions are placed on obtaining a confession.)

68. Select one of the approaches to interrogation outlined in the text and describe how it might be used by an officer in dealing with a suspect. (pp. 197–198, Learning Objective: Discuss what techniques to use in an interrogation.)

69. How are foreign nationals to be treated when under detention or arrest, and why? (pp. 195–196, Learning Objective: Explain what the *Miranda* warning is and when to give it.)

70. Discuss the importance of rapport when interviewing a witness or interrogating a suspect. (p. 197, Learning Objective: Discuss how to improve communication between the investigator, victims, witnesses or suspects.)

IDENTIFYING AND ARRESTING SUSPECTS

Test Bank

Chapter 7
Identifying and Arresting Suspects

Multiple Choice

1. Surveillance, undercover assignments and raids are used only when

    a. the case is important.
    b. the case is a felony.
    c. normal methods of continuing the investigation fail to produce results.* (p. 224, Learning Objective: Describe when surveillance is used and what the objectives are.)
    d. terrorist activity or drug traffic are suspected.

2. The objective of surveillance is to

    a. obtain information that can be used to solve narcotics-related crimes.
    b. obtain information about people, their associates and their activities that may help solve a criminal case or protect a witness.* (p. 225, Learning Objective: Describe when surveillance is used and what the objectives are.)
    c. obtain information about anyone or anything.
    d. punish the offenders.

3. Which would *not* be one of the precautions for undercover agents?

    a. Write no notes that the subject can read.
    b. Carry police identification in case you need to make an arrest.
    c. Ensure that communication with headquarters is covert.
    d. Use drugs and alcohol to get in with the gang.* (p. 233, Learning Objective: Describe the objectives of undercover assignments and what precautions should be taken when going undercover.)

4. On a linear use-of-force continuum, where do "hard empty hand techniques" fall in relation to the use of a TASER or chemical agent?

    a. They fall to the left (i.e., they are more forceful).
    b. They fall to the right (i.e., they are less forceful).* (p. 242, Learning Objective: Clarify when and how much force is justified when making an arrest.)
    c. They are equivalent.
    d. They are not on the same use-of-force continuum.

5. When a person suddenly dies in police custody, it is often called

    a. excited delirium.* (p. 247, Learning Objective: Clarify when and how much force is justified when making an arrest.)
    b. use of deadly force.
    c. de facto arrest.
    d. nightcap provision.

6. *Field* or *show-up* identification is on-the-scene identification of a suspect by a victim or witness of a crime. The show-up must be

    a.   close in time to the incident.* (p. 215, Learning Objective: Define and compare the differences between field identifications and show-up identifications.)
    b.   close in location to the incident.
    c.   based on a warrant.
    d.   in conjunction with an attorney's consent.

7. Which method is *not* used to identify suspects?

    a.   field or show-up identification
    b.   mug shots
    c.   photographic identification or lineups
    d.   hearsay evidence* (p. 221, Learning Objective: Describe the four basic means of identifying a suspect.)

8. Which 2007 case established the use of "ramming" in pursuit as a use-of-force doctrine that the police use today?

    a.   *Mapp v. Ohio*
    b.   *Kim Wong Ark v. United States*
    c.   *Scott v. Harris** (p. 246, Learning Objective: Clarify when and how much force is justified when making an arrest.)
    d.   *United States v. Weeks*

9. Which of the following means is *not* used to develop suspects?

    a.   informants
    b.   physical evidence left at the crime scene
    c.   information in police files
    d.   none of these choices* (p. 216, Learning Objective: Describe how a suspect is developed.)

10. Which of the following are considered "nonlethal" weapons?

    a.   aerosols
    b.   ECDs
    c.   impact weapons
    d.   all of these choices* (pp. 243–245, Learning Objective: Clarify when and how much force is justified when making an arrest.)

11. Force necessary to overcome resistance offered during an arrest is referred to as

    a.   extraneous force.
    b.   reasonable force.* (p. 240, Learning Objective: Clarify when and how much force is justified when making an arrest.)
    c.   the Blue Hammer.
    d.   extralegal force.

12. Live lineups generally contain

    a. two to three individuals.
    b. four to five individuals.
    c. six to seven individuals.
    d. five to ten individuals.* (p. 222, Learning Objective: Explain how a proper lineup is created and how it is used.)

13. Psychological profiling

    a. is no longer used in police work.
    b. is used only in conjunction with a psychic.
    c. is 95 percent accurate in all cases.
    d. can help eliminate and develop suspects.* (p. 218, Learning Objective: Describe how a suspect is developed.)

14. In *United States v. Wade,* the Court said that a suspect must be informed of his or her right to have a lawyer present during what type of process?

    a. booking
    b. *Terry* stops
    c. invasive searches
    d. lineups* (p. 224, Learning Objective: Define the legal rights suspects have regarding participation in a lineup and relate which cases established these rights.)

15. What must be established before an arrest can be made?

    a. occurrence of a crime
    b. finding of a victim
    c. notification of suspect's lawyer
    d. probable cause* (p. 237, Learning Objective: Identify the probable cause that must exist for believing that a suspect has committed a crime.)

16. Wiretaps are legal when there is probable cause and they are

    a. ordered by the chief of police or sheriff.
    b. authorized by the district attorney.
    c. reviewed by a grand jury.
    d. authorized by a court.* (p. 230, Learning Objective: Explain when wiretapping is legal and identify the precedent case.)

17. A field identification is also called a

    a. hot stop.
    b. follow-up.
    c. shake-down.
    d. show-up.* (p. 215, Learning Objective: Define and compare the differences between field identifications and show-up identifications.)

18. Making a legal arrest, gaining information for warrants or even preventing crime can all be the result of

    a. criminal profiling.
    b. surveillance.* (p. 224, Learning Objective: Describe when surveillance is used and what the objectives are.)
    c. entrapment.
    d. pretextual traffic stops.

19. In *Whren v. United States* (1996), the Supreme Court affirmed that officers could stop vehicles to allay any suspicions even though they have no evidence of criminal behavior. This type of stop is referred to as a

    a. pretextual stop.* (p. 220, Learning Objective: Describe how a suspect is developed.)
    b. silver platter stop.
    c. *Terry* stop.
    d. racial profiling stop.

20. This 1985 court case eliminated the "fleeing-felon rule," banning law enforcement officers from shooting to kill a fleeing felon unless an imminent danger to life exists.

    a. *Argersinger v. Hamlin*
    b. *Brown v. Mississippi*
    c. *Terry v. Ohio*
    d. *Tennessee v. Garner** (p. 246, Learning Objective: Clarify when and how much force is justified when making an arrest.)

21. In the DEA smuggling case *United States v. Weaver* (1992), what did the Court rule?

    a. that race can be considered among other factors to use in developing suspects* (p. 220, Learning Objective: Describe how a suspect is developed.)
    b. that only agents of the same race as a suspect can work undercover to avoid racism charges
    c. that race can never be used as a factor in developing suspects
    d. that racial profiling is always illegal

22. The requirement of providing counsel to a suspect in a lineup that occurs after indictment or arraignment is known as the

    a. *Miranda* rule.
    b. Wade-Gilbert rule.* (p. 224, Learning Objective: Define the legal rights suspects have regarding participation in a lineup and relate which cases established these rights.)
    c. exclusionary rule.
    d. "fruits of the poisoned tree" rule.

23. In *United States v. Knotts* (1983), the Court ruled that installing and monitoring a bird dog tracking device in a public location

    a.   violates a suspect's rights.
    b.   is illegal.
    c.   does not violate a suspect's rights.* (p. 229, Learning Objective: Define the different types of surveillances.)
    d.   is inadmissible.

24. *Florida v. Riley* (1989) approved the warrantless aerial surveillance, noting that

    a.   there had to be at least 10,000 feet between the police airplane and the suspects.
    b.   there should be no reasonable expectation of privacy from the skies above.* (p. 229, Learning Objective: Define the different types of surveillances.)
    c.   this was a test case and was only approved once.
    d.   it must be in conjunction with a simultaneous ground-level surveillance.

25. In *Saucier v. Katz* (2001), the Supreme Court held that the guide for use of excessive force is that

    a.   the officer fears for his or her safety.
    b.   the force is objectively reasonable under Fourth Amendment excessive force analysis.* (p. 241, Learning Objective: Clarify when and how much force is justified when making an arrest.)
    c.   the suspect is armed.
    d.   the suspect presents a dangerous risk to the public.

True/False

26. A suspect does not have the right to a lawyer if a photographic lineup is used. (True, p. 221, Learning Objective: Define the legal rights suspects have regarding participation in a lineup and relate which cases established these rights.)

27. In *Schmerber v. California* (1966), the Court ruled that suspects may refuse to participate in a lineup, and such refusal may not be used against them in court. (False, p. 224, Learning Objective: Define the legal rights suspects have regarding participation in a lineup and relate which cases established these rights.)

28. Investigators should use at least five people of comparable race, height, weight, age and general appearance in police lineups. (True, p. 222, Learning Objective: Explain how a proper lineup is created and how it is used.)

29. The Supreme Court defined entrapment in *Sorrells v. United States* (1932) as essentially resting on whether or not the conception and planning of an

offense was by an officer, not a suspect. (True, p. 234, Learning Objective: Describe the objectives of undercover assignments and what precautions should be taken when going undercover.)

30. In *Katz v. United States,* the Supreme Court reversed the California decision, saying: "The Fourth Amendment protects people not places. . . ." (True, pp. 230–231, Learning Objective: Explain when wiretapping is legal and identify the precedent case.)

31. As far back as Title III of the Omnibus Crime Control and Safe Streets Act of 1968, the courts authorized court-ordered electronic surveillance of organized crime figures. (True, p. 231, Learning Objective: Explain when wiretapping is legal and identify the precedent case.)

32. The amount of time it takes to identify a suspect is directly correlated to the length of time it takes to solve a crime. (True, p. 214, Learning Objective: Define and compare the differences between field identifications and show-up identifications.)

33. Fixed surveillance is used when you know or suspect that a person is at or will come to a known location. (True, p. 227, Learning Objective: Define the different types of surveillances.)

34. Because race is part of a suspect's general description, racial profiling has been upheld by the courts as legal and constitutional. (False, p. 219, Learning Objective: Describe how a suspect is developed.)

35. Police officers are authorized to make an arrest for any criminal activity of which they are suspicious. (False, p. 236, Learning Objective: Define when a lawful arrest can be made.)

36. Electronic surveillance and wiretapping are considered forms of search and are therefore permitted only with probable cause and court order. (True, p. 230, Learning Objective: Explain when wiretapping is legal and identify the precedent case.)

37. TWS (through-the-wall surveillance) technology helps officers to determine if someone is in a room before putting themselves in harm's way and to save lives by using motion and images to differentiate between a hostage and a hostage taker. (True, p. 230, Learning Objective: Define the different types of surveillances.)

38. Pen registers and trap-and-trace devices are not considered forms of searches and do not need probable cause and a court order because subscribers waive their rights to privacy when using devices such as cell phones or telephones. (False, p. 230, Learning Objective: Explain when wiretapping is legal and identify the precedent case.)

39. *Gordon v. Warren Consolidated Board of Education* (1983) ruled that using undercover officers in high schools was unreasonable and therefore illegal. (False, p. 233, Learning Objective: Describe the objectives of undercover assignments and what precautions should be taken when going undercover.)

40. Officers working undercover should keep their real first name and date of birth. (True, p. 233, Learning Objective: Describe the objectives of undercover assignments and what precautions should be taken when going undercover.)

41. Some officers carry insurance to protect themselves against lawsuits. (True, p. 239, Learning Objective: Describe how officers leave themselves open to civil liability when making arrests.)

42. Investigators should keep in mind that eyewitness identification is highly fallible. (True, p. 216, Learning Objective: Relate how to assist witnesses in describing a suspect or a vehicle.)

43. Planning, organizing and executing a raid are somewhat similar to undertaking a small military attack on a specific target. (True, p. 234, Learning Objective: Discuss the precautions that should be taken when conducting a raid.)

44. Facts gathered after an arrest to justify probable cause are legally admissible as evidence of probable cause. (False, p. 237, Learning Objective: Identify the probable cause that must exist for believing that a suspect has committed a crime.)

45. Research has found that officers were significantly more likely to use higher levels of force with suspects encountered in disadvantaged neighborhoods. (True, p. 240, Learning Objective: Clarify when and how much force is justified when making an arrest.)

Completion

46. In moving surveillance, the surveillant may be referred to as a _____. (tail, p. 227, Learning Objective: Define the different types of surveillances.)

47. Police powers to arrest or search are restricted by the _____ Amendment. (Fourth, p. 236, Learning Objective: Define what constitutes an arrest.)

48. *Graham v. Connor* held that plaintiffs alleging excessive use of force need show only that the officer's actions were _____ under the standards of the Fourth Amendment. (unreasonable, p. 241, Learning Objective: Clarify when and how much force is justified when making an arrest.)

49. Identifying a weapon as less-lethal does not imply that it is _____ lethal. (never, p. 243, Learning Objective: Clarify when and how much force is justified when making an arrest.)

50. Stopping a vehicle when the officer's intent was not the real reason for the stop is called a _____ traffic stop. (pretextual, p. 220, Learning Objective: Describe how a suspect is developed.)

51. Suspects may _____ to participate in a lineup, but this decision can be used against them in court. (refuse, p. 224, Learning Objective: Define the legal rights suspects have regarding participation in a lineup and relate which cases established these rights.)

52. In _____ profiling, also known as criminal profiling, an attempt is made to identify an individual's mental, emotional and psychological characteristics. (psychological, p. 218, Learning Objective: Describe how a suspect is developed.)

53. Victims and witnesses should view _____ shots, as this may help identify a suspect believed to have a record. (mug, p. 217, Learning Objective: Clarify when mug shots are used.)

54. _____ identification is on-the-scene identification of a suspect by a victim or witness to a crime. (Field, p. 215, Learning Objective: Define and compare the differences between field identifications and show-up identifications.)

55. _____ profiling takes place when an officer focuses on an individual as a suspect based solely on that person's race. (Racial, p. 219, Learning Objective: Describe how a suspect is developed.)

Short Answer

56. Define *reasonable force.* (p. 240, Learning Objective: Clarify when and how much force is justified when making an arrest.)

57. Define *entrapment.* (p. 234, Learning Objective: Describe the objectives of undercover assignments and what precautions should be taken when going undercover.)

58. What precautions should be taken when conducting raids? (p. 235, Learning Objective: Discuss the precautions that should be taken when conducting a raid.)

59. At what point should an arrested individual be advised of his or her constitutional rights? (p. 238, Learning Objective: Define what constitutes an arrest.)

60. Describe the uses and value of psychological profiling. (p. 218, Learning Objective: Describe how a suspect is developed.)

61. Define the term *de facto arrest.* (p. 238, Learning Objective: Define what constitutes an arrest.)

62. Compile a list of some of the key items to ask about when helping a witness describe a suspect. (p. 216, Learning Objective: Relate how to assist witnesses in describing a suspect or a vehicle.)

63. Explain how geographic profiling can be used in criminal investigations. (pp. 218–219, Learning Objective: Describe how a suspect is developed.)

64. How does an officer determine whether photographic identification or lineup identification should be used to identify a suspect? (pp. 221–223, Learning Objective: Explain what photographic identification processes are and how to use them properly.)

65. Outline some of the suggestions discussed in the text for officers who are preparing to go undercover. (p. 223, Learning Objective: Describe the objectives of undercover assignments and what precautions should be taken when going undercover.)

66. How do the police establish the legal requirements for staging a raid? (p. 234, Learning Objective: Clarify how the police establish the legal requirements for staging a raid.)

67. After arresting a suspect, under what conditions are officers allowed to search the arrestee's home? (pp. 238–239, Learning Objective: Define what constitutes an arrest.)

68. Briefly outline some of the options available to an officer for controlling someone with non-lethal force. (pp. 243–245, Learning Objective: Clarify when and how much force is justified when making an arrest.)

69. If a suspect is at the scene of a crime, what methods can an officer use to identify the suspect at the scene? (pp. 214–215, Learning Objective: Define and compare the differences between field identifications and show-up identifications.)

70. Briefly outline some of the ways that surveillance can aid an investigation. (p. 225, Learning Objective: Describe when surveillance is used and what the objectives are.)

DEATH INVESTIGATIONS

Test Bank

Chapter 8
Death Investigations

Multiple Choice

1. Which of the following factors can assist in establishing time of death?

   a. victim's clothing
   b. presence of weapons
   c. rigor mortis* (p. 273, Learning Objective: Report the different factors that can aid in estimating time of death.)
   d. hair color

2. The type of "lust murderer" who is usually of above-average intelligence, methodical and cunning, and socially skilled, and who tricks victims into situations in which he can torture and then murder them, is called a(n),

   a. serial killer.
   b. organized offender.* (p. 290, Learning Objective: Explain why it is important to determine a motive in homicide investigations.)
   c. disorganized offender.
   d. mass murderer.

3. Which of the following statements is *not* true with regard to death investigations?

   a. Body temperature drops 2 to 3 degrees in the first hour after death.
   b. Rigor mortis appears first in the smaller muscles, such as those of the face.
   c. After about 36 hours, rigor mortis usually disappears in the same sequence as it appeared.
   d. Maximum lividity occurs within 15–20 hours after death.* (p. 275, Learning Objective: Report the different factors that can aid in estimating time of death.)

4. Premeditation would be a requirement in which case?

   a. first-degree murder* (p. 261, Learning Objective: Explain what degrees of murder are frequently specified.)
   b. second-degree murder
   c. excusable homicide
   d. justifiable homicide

5. Rigor mortis is at its maximum at about _____ hours after death.

   a. 6 to 8 hours
   b. 8 to 9 hours
   c. 12 to 24 hours* (p. 268–274), Learning Objective: Report the different factors that can aid in estimating time of death.)
   d. 36 to 48 hours

6. Deaths are classified by type as

    a. natural, accidental noncriminal, suicide, homicide (noncriminal and criminal.* (p. 260, Learning Objective: Outline the four categories of death.)
    b. natural, accidental, suicide, murder.
    c. accidental, suicide, murder, voluntary.
    d. either by accident or by the hands of another.

7. A dead body that sinks in water usually remains immersed for

    a. 5 to 7 days in warm water and 3 to 4 weeks in cold water.
    b. 8 to 10 days in warm water and 2 to 3 weeks in cold water.* (p. 277, Learning Objective: Explain the effect water has on a dead body.)
    c. 2 to 3 weeks in warm water and 5 to 6 weeks in cold water.
    d. none of these choices.

8. The first priority in a preliminary homicide investigation is to

    a. render aid to the victim.
    b. keep the media away from the area.
    c. identify the suspect.
    d. secure the safety of the scene.* (p. 269, Learning Objective: Identify the first priority in a homicide investigation.)

9. A common indicator of suicide using a knife is

    a. no weapon present.
    b. defensive wounds.
    c. wounds made through clothing.
    d. hesitation wounds.* (p. 282, Learning Objective: Describe the most frequent causes of unnatural death and how to determine whether a death is a suicide or a homicide.)

10. Most medical examinations of a deceased person are conducted primarily to

    a. prepare the body for burial.
    b. determine the deceased's identity.
    c. determine the time and cause of death.* (p. 279, Learning Objective: Outline the information provided by the medical examiner or coroner.)
    d. satisfy the state's legal requirement.

11. Noncriminal homicide includes

    a. justifiable homicide.* (p. 262, Learning Objective: Describe how excusable and justifiable homicide differ.)
    b. suicide.
    c. voluntary manslaughter.
    d. involuntary manslaughter.

12. A stiffening of portions of the body after death is referred to as

   a. desiccation.
   b. rigor mortis.* (p. 274, Learning Objective: Report the different factors that can aid in estimating time of death.)
   c. adipocere.
   d. livor mortis.

13. What may occur if a body is exposed to an extremely hot and dry climate?

   a. decomposition
   b. disarticulation
   c. mummification* (p. 276, Learning Objective: Report the different factors that can aid in estimating time of death.)
   d. skeletonization within 24 hours

14. Premeditation would be a requirement in which case?

   a. first-degree murder* (p. 263, Learning Objective: Explain what degrees of murder are frequently specified.)
   b. second-degree murder
   c. excusable homicide
   d. manslaughter

15. It can be assumed that a victim has died on land if

   a. the victim's eyes glisten when the body is brought out of the water.
   b. diatoms are found on the body.
   c. half of the victim's eye looks dry when the body is brought out of the water.* (p. 278, Learning Objective: Explain the effect water has on a dead body.)
   d. none of these choices.

16. If death is caused by carbon monoxide poisoning, lividity is

   a. white.
   b. dark blue or purple.
   c. absent.
   d. cherry red or strong pink.* (p. 275, Learning Objective: Report the different factors that can aid in estimating time of death.)

17. Which of the following is not an indication of suicide?

   a. defense wounds* (p. 282, Learning Objective: Describe the most frequent causes of unnatural death and how to determine whether a death is a suicide or a homicide.)
   b. hesitation wounds
   c. wounds under clothing
   d. weapon tightly clutched

18. Murder is classified as

    a. excusable homicide.
    b. nonfelonious homicide.
    c. criminal homicide.* (p. 261, Learning Objective: Define and classify homicide, murder and manslaughter.)
    d. justifiable homicide.

19. Most cases of hanging are

    a. homicides.
    b. accidents.
    c. suicides.* (p. 283, Learning Objective: Describe the most frequent causes of unnatural death and how to determine whether a death is a suicide or a homicide.)
    d. accidental homicides.

20. Shotgun wounds produce _____ than single bullets.

    a. smaller exit wounds
    b. smaller entry wounds
    c. both smaller exit and smaller entry wounds
    d. neither smaller exit nor smaller entry wounds* (p. 281, Learning Objective: Describe the most frequent causes of unnatural death and how to determine whether a death is a suicide or a homicide.)

21. The postmortem cooling process of the body is called

    a. adipocere.
    b. lividity.
    c. rigor mortis.
    d. algor mortis.* (p. 274, Learning Objective: Report the different factors that can aid in estimating time of death.)

22. A study of 800 homicide cases found that investigators are more likely to clear a homicide if

    a. there is at least one witness to the crime.
    b. they arrive at the scene within 30 minutes of being notified.* (p. 268, Learning Objective: Identify the first priority in a homicide investigation.)
    c. the incident is reported within 30 minutes to a 911 dispatcher.
    d. at least one detective assigned to the case attended the postmortem examination.

23. The criminal or noncriminal, felonious or nonfelonious taking of life by another human or by an agency, such as a government, is called

    a. murder.
    b. homicide.* (p. 261, Learning Objective: Define and classify homicide, murder and manslaughter.)
    c. manslaughter.
    d. crime against nature.

24. What type of murder usually includes the killing of three or more separate victims with a "cooling off" period between the killings?

    a.   mass murder
    b.   spree murder
    c.   serial murder* (pp. 289–290, Learning Objective: Explain why it is important to determine a motive in homicide investigations.)
    d.   disorganized killing

25. The study of poisons can determine the type of poison, the amount ingested, the approximate time ingested and the effect on the body. This field is referred to as

    a.   toxicology.* (p. 284, Learning Objective: Describe the most frequent causes of unnatural death and how to determine whether a death is a suicide or a homicide.)
    b.   odontology.
    c.   homeopathy.
    d.   entomology.

26. The poison known as the King of Poisons and the Poison of Kings is

    a.   arsenic.* (p. 284, Learning Objective: Describe the most frequent causes of unnatural death and how to determine whether a death is a suicide or a homicide.)
    b.   strychnine.
    c.   cyanide.
    d.   anthrax.

27. In assessing victim-offender relationships (VOR,), violence that is goal-directed predatory behavior used to exert control—such as a carjacker who shoots his victim before stealing the vehicle—is referred as what type of violence?

    a.   expressive violence
    b.   instrumental violence* (p. 286, Learning Objective: Describe the most frequent causes of unnatural death and how to determine whether a death is a suicide or a homicide.)
    c.   constructive violence
    d.   cognitive violence

28. Staging refers to

    a.   the positioning of the victim's body.
    b.   the manipulation of the scene around the victim's body.
    c.   both the positioning of the victim's body and the manipulation of the scene around the victim's body.* (p. 264, Learning Objective: Explain the special challenges presented by a homicide investigation.)
    d.   neither the positioning of the victim's body nor the manipulation of the scene around the victim's body.

True/False

29. Researchers have identified more than 100 compounds that are linked to decomposition in buried bodies. (False, p. 277), Learning Objective: Report the different factors that can aid in estimating time of death.)

30. Investigators are more likely to clear a homicide if they arrive within 30 minutes of being notified. (True, p. 268, Learning Objective: Identify the first priority in a homicide investigation.)

31. A lust murder is a sex-related homicide involving a sadistic, deviant assault. (True, pp. 289–290, Learning Objective: Explain why it is important to determine a motive in homicide investigations.)

32. The key element distinguishing manslaughter from murder is premeditation. (True, p. 263, Learning Objective: Explain the significance of premeditation.)

33. Examples of involuntary manslaughter include handling a firearm negligently; leaving poison where children may take it; and operating an automobile, boat or aircraft in a criminally negligent manner. (True, p. 261, Learning Objective: Define and classify homicide, murder and manslaughter.)

34. Two of the more difficult kinds of cases for a criminal investigator to handle are those related to missing persons and those involving unidentified human remains. (True, p. 272, Learning Objective: Explain how to identify an unknown homicide victim.)

35. In *Flippo v. West Virginia* the Supreme Court determined that there is a general "murder scene exception" to the search warrant requirements of the Fourth Amendment. (False, p. 268, Learning Objective: Explain the special challenges presented by a homicide investigation.)

36. More Americans die by suicide than homicide. (True, p. 266, Learning Objective: Explain the special challenges presented by a homicide investigation.)

37. A person who is addicted to or uses crack cocaine regularly may have what is called a "crack thumb." (True, p. 266, Learning Objective: Outline what information and evidence can be obtained from a victim.)

38. First-degree murder requires premeditation and the intent to cause death. (True, p. 261, Learning Objective: Explain what degrees of murder are frequently specified.)

39. More officers lose their lives to suicide than homicide. (True, p. 267, Learning Objective: Explain the special challenges presented by a homicide investigation.)

40. Profiles of serial killers show they are usually sane; they know right from wrong but simply do not care. (True, pp. 289, Learning Objective: Explain why it is important to determine a motive in homicide investigations.)

41. Equivocal death investigations are those inquiries that are open to interpretation as to the cause of death. (True, p. 264, Learning Objective: Explain the special challenges presented by a homicide investigation.)

42. Lack of a note generally precludes the possibility of suicide. (False, p. 267, Learning Objective: Explain the special challenges presented by a homicide investigation.)

43. In general, decomposition is increased by lower temperatures and decreased by higher temperatures. (False, p. 276, Learning Objective: Report the different factors that can aid in estimating time of death.)

44. The cornea clouds more rapidly if the eyes remain closed after death. (False, p. 276, Learning Objective: Explain what physical evidence is usually found in homicides.)

45. All murders are homicides. (True, p. 261, Learning Objective: Define and classify homicide, murder and manslaughter.)

46. It is not common procedure to exhume a body for medical examination. (True, p. 279, Learning Objective: Outline the information provided by the medical examiner or coroner.)

47. Insects can offer valuable clues as to the time a body was left or buried. (True, p. 276), Learning Objective: Report the different factors that can aid in estimating time of death.)

48. Unlike workplace violence, school violence usually occurs without warning. (False, p. 288, Learning Objective: Outline the similarities that exist between school and workplace mass murders.)

49. Unfortunately, the U.S. Justice Department does not have a national program to help law enforcement agencies, medical examiners and others identify missing persons who have been murdered or have died of other causes. (False, p. 272, Learning Objective: Explain how to identify an unknown homicide victim.)

Completion

50. Criminal _____ involves creating a situation that results in an unreasonable risk of death or great bodily harm. (negligence, p. 264, Learning Objective: Define and classify homicide, murder and manslaughter.)

51. _____ is the killing of one person by another. (Homicide, p. 261, Learning Objective: Define and classify homicide, murder and manslaughter.)

52. A key difference between first- and second-degree murder is the element of _____. (premeditation, p. 263, Learning Objective: Explain the significance of premeditation.)

53. A forensic _____ can examine various types of insects to assist in estimating the time of death. (entomologist, p. 276, Learning Objective: Report the different factors that can aid in estimating time of death.)

54. In _____ asphyxiation, sexual gratification is sought by placing a rope around the neck and causing just enough restriction to result in semi-consciousness. (autoerotic, p. 284, Learning Objective: Describe the most frequent causes of unnatural death and how to determine whether a death is a suicide or a homicide.)

55. Ted Bundy, John Wayne Gacy and Andrew Cunanan were well-known _____ murderers. (serial, p. 289, Learning Objective: Explain why it is important to determine a motive in homicide investigations.)

56. Killing an individual as part of a legally ordered execution is considered _____ homicide. (justifiable, p. 262, Learning Objective: Describe how excusable and justifiable homicide differ.)

57. "Heat of passion" is the alternative to premeditation and assumes an act was committed when the suspect suddenly became extremely emotional. It is commonly referred to as _____ rather than murder. (manslaughter, p. 261, Learning Objective: Explain the significance of premeditation.)

58. Violence that stems from hurt feelings, anger or rage is called _____ violence. (expressive, p. 286, Learning Objective: Describe the most frequent causes of unnatural death and how to determine whether a death is a suicide or a homicide.)

59. Postmortem lividity, also referred to as _____, is a dark blue or purple discoloration that can be seen on a dead body. (livor mortis, p. 275, Learning Objective: Report the different factors that can aid in estimating time of death.)

60. After 9/11, _____ analysis is the preferred method of identification of human remains from mass disasters. (DNA, p. 272, Learning Objective: Explain how to identify an unknown homicide victim.)

Short Answer

61. How can police departments address homicide proactively? (p. 294, Learning Objective: Describe how the conventional wisdom about homicide has changed in some departments.)

62. What are some examples of an equivocal death situation? (pp. 264–266, Learning Objective: Explain the special challenges presented by a homicide investigation.)

63. Compare the different indicators in gunshot wounds in an apparent suicide versus a homicide. (p. 281, Learning Objective: Describe the most frequent causes of unnatural death and how to determine whether a death is a suicide or a homicide.)

64. Describe autoerotic asphyxiation. (p. 284, Learning Objective: Describe the most frequent causes of unnatural death and how to determine whether a death is a suicide or a homicide.)

65. Describe the postmortem interval and its effect on an investigation. (p. 273, Learning Objective: Report the different factors that can aid in estimating time of death.)

66. Describe some of the signs of death that officers can use to determine if a victim is dead when they arrive at the scene. (p. 269, Learning Objective: Describe how to establish that death has occurred.)

67. Compare the key difference between murder and involuntary manslaughter or criminal negligence. What are two key elements that are missing from the latter two items? (p. 261, Learning Objective: Define and classify homicide, murder and manslaughter.)

68. Why do you think the police have such a high suicide rate within their profession? (pp. 267–268, Learning Objective: Explain the special challenges presented by a homicide investigation.)

69. Discuss the importance of the case of *Flippo v. West Virginia* (1999), and how it relates to searches at homicide scenes. (p. 268, Learning Objective: Identify the first priority in a homicide investigation.)

70. What similarities exist regarding the killer in both school and workplace mass murders? (p. 288, Learning Objective: Outline the similarities that exist between school and workplace mass murders.)

71. What are some factors that can help in determining time of death? (p. 273, Learning Objective: Report the different factors that can aid in estimating time of death.)

72. What were the lessons learned by the Miami-Dade homicide unit in their investigation of the "Moonberry Pond Murder"? (p. 294, Learning Objective: Describe how the conventional wisdom about homicide has changed in some departments.)

73. How is investigating a murder committed by a serial killer different from investigating any other type of homicide? (p. 289, Learning Objective: Explain why it is important to determine a motive in homicide investigations.)

74. Describe the difference between expressive violence and instrumental violence. (p. 286, Learning Objective: Describe the most frequent causes of unnatural death and how to determine whether a death is a suicide or a homicide.)

75. Discuss the difference between defense wounds and hesitation wounds. (pp. 281–282, Learning Objective: Describe the most frequent causes of unnatural death and how to determine whether a death is a suicide or a homicide.)

ASSAULT, DOMESTIC VIOLENCE, STALKING AND ELDER ABUSE

Test Bank

Chapter 9
Assault, Domestic Violence, Stalking and Elder Abuse

Multiple Choice

1. One-third of the women killed in the United States are murdered by their husbands or boyfriends, and as many as 90 percent of women are stalked before the murder. This is a clear example of

    a. mass murder.
    b. target hardening.
    c. femicide.* (p. 314, Learning Objective: Explain what constitutes stalking.)
    d. fratricide.

2. Physical evidence that indicates the severity of an assault may include all but which of the following?

    a. broken dishes
    b. overturned furniture
    c. bruises and lacerations
    d. the mental state of the offender* (p. 305, Learning Objective: Describe what evidence is likely to be at the scene of an assault.)

3. An unlawful attack by one person on another in order to inflict severe bodily injury and which often involves use of a dangerous weapon and is a felony is called

    a. aggravated assault.* (p. 303, Learning Objective: Compare how simple assault differs from aggravated assault.)
    b. mayhem.
    c. attempted murder.
    d. assault with a deadly weapon.

4. The cycle of violence involves

    a. tension-building, the battering episode and the honeymoon.* (p. 306, Learning Objective: Define what constitutes domestic violence.)
    b. intimacy, arguments and making up.
    c. premarital sex, alcohol and the honeymoon period.
    d. threats, battering and compliance.

5. An example of an indicator crime is

    a. a hit-and-run offense.
    b. harassing phone calls.
    c. a prior offense involving the same victim and suspect.
    d. all of these choices.* (p. 309, Learning Objective: Define what constitutes domestic violence.)

6. Aggravated assault requires

   a. a threat made to the victim.
   b. attempted bodily injury to the victim.
   c. severe bodily injury to the victim.* (p. 303, Learning Objective: Compare how simple assault differs from aggravated assault.)
   d. a weapon.

7. An act toward the commission of a crime that is more complete than a threat or gesture is referred to as what type of act?

   a. overt act* (p. 303, Learning Objective: Articulate the elements of simple assault, aggravated (felonious) assault and attempted assault.)
   b. subversive act
   c. covert act
   d. preliminary act

8. Intentionally causing another person to fear immediate bodily harm or death or intentionally inflicting or attempting to inflict bodily harm on the person is called what?

   a. mayhem
   b. simple assault* (p. 303, Learning Objective: Compare how simple assault differs from aggravated assault.)
   c. aggravated assault
   d. assault with a deadly weapon

9. Of the three elements included in the crime of aggravated assault, investigators must prove

   a. two of the three.
   b. all three.
   c. only one.* (p. 303, Learning Objective: Articulate the elements of simple assault, aggravated (felonious) assault and attempted assault.)
   d. all three, plus intent.

10. Healed injuries not visible to the naked eye may be revealed through

    a. microphotography.
    b. limited or restricted wavelength photography.
    c. specific, refined wavelength photography.
    d. reflective ultraviolet photography.* (p. 305, Learning Objective: Describe what evidence is likely to be at the scene of an assault.)

11. Which of the following is *not* true about "battered-woman syndrome"?

    a. It is based on the concept of duress.
    b. It results from the cycle of violence.
    c. It may be used as a court defense for women who murder their abusers.
    d. It is a myth.* (p. 308, Learning Objective: Define what constitutes domestic violence.)

12. Over time, the three-stage cycle of abuse (or violence) typically

    a. increases in frequency.
    b. increases in severity.
    c. increases in both severity and frequency.* (p. 306, Learning Objective: Define what constitutes domestic violence.)
    d. decreases in both severity and frequency.

13. The majority of stalking cases are categorized as _____ stalking.

    a. acquaintance
    b. stranger
    c. cyber
    d. intimate or former intimate* (p. 314, Learning Objective: Explain what constitutes stalking.)

14. Elder abuse is

    a. almost always reported.
    b. reported about half the time.
    c. severely underreported.* (p. 317, Learning Objective: Describe what constitutes elder abuse, and how prevalent elder abuse is.)
    d. always a social service concern, not a law enforcement issue.

15. The term *in loco parentis* refers to the fact that

    a. one form of domestic violence is when parents abuse their children.
    b. some abusers were victims of abuse at the hands of their own parents.
    c. teachers are allowed to use force to maintain discipline.* (p. 302, Learning Objective: Explain when force is legal.)
    d. none of these choices.

16. The dynamics of same-sex domestic violence are similar to those of opposite-sex domestic violence in many respects. Which of the following statements is *not* true?

    a. The cause is cyclical, escalates over time and maintains a commonality in characteristics of batterers.
    b. When the law enforcement response to domestic violence incidents involving heterosexual and same-sex couples is compared, it is noted that the couples receive similar treatment.
    c. Same-sex victims rarely are afforded the same protection as heterosexuals.
    d. Same-sex victims are always afforded the same protection as heterosexuals.* (p. 308, Learning Objective: Define what constitutes domestic violence.)

17. Historically, officers are more likely to be assaulted while responding to what type of calls?

    a. robbery
    b. domestic violence* (p. 304, Learning Objective: Define what constitutes domestic violence.)
    c. elder abuse
    d. homicide

18. Studies have shown that the ties between _____ and violence are unmistakable and that this type of behavior is a predictor of abusive or violent behavior.

    a. property crimes
    b. abuse or cruelty to animals* (p. 309, Learning Objective: Define what constitutes domestic violence.)
    c. internecine rivalry
    d. fraud and embezzlement

19. Which of the following has proved to be effective in a coordinated approach and seems best suited to dealing with the continuous cycle of domestic violence?

    a. long sentences
    b. specialized units within police departments and prosecutors' offices* (p. 311, Learning Objective: Define what constitutes domestic violence.)
    c. large fines and jail terms
    d. mandatory GPS tracking

20. Batterer intervention programs (BIPs) have found that batterer rehabilitation is significantly affected by what the offender actually has to lose, for example, home ownership, employment and marriage. These variables are referred to as the offender's

    a. stake in conformity.* (p. 312, Learning Objective: Define what constitutes domestic violence.)
    b. natural selection.
    c. family code model.
    d. cycle of recovery.

21. Which of the following is *not* a type of stalker?

    a. intimate or former intimate partner
    b. stranger
    c. simple obsessional and love obsessional
    d. autoerotic* (p. 314, Learning Objective: Explain what constitutes stalking.)

22. By the year 2000, how many domestic violence cases resulted in arrests?

    a. 10 percent
    b. 50 percent* (p. 306, Learning Objective: Define what constitutes domestic violence.)
    c. 15 percent
    d. 60 percent

23. Which of the following is *not* a form of elder abuse?

    a. abandonment
    b. self-neglect
    c. verbal threats
    d. failure to resuscitate* (p. 317, Learning Objective: Describe what constitutes elder abuse, and how prevalent elder abuse is.)

24. The type of weapon used most frequently in domestic violence cases is

    a. a firearm.
    b. furniture.
    c. a blunt object.* (p. 307, Learning Objective: Define what constitutes domestic violence.)
    d. a knife or sharp object.

25. Current or former spouses, opposite-sex cohabiting partners, same-sex cohabiting partners and even dating relationships may all be described using which of the following terms.

    a. intimate partners* (p. 307, Learning Objective: Define what constitutes domestic violence.)
    b. cycle of intimacy
    c. offender-partner cycle
    d. life partner cycle

True/False

26. Although the majority of abuse victims are women, women may also perpetrate domestic violence. (True, p. 308, Learning Objective: Define what constitutes domestic violence.)

27. An assault committed in self-defense is legal and justifiable. (True, p. 302, Learning Objective: Explain when force is legal.)

28. Research has shown that law enforcement agencies are placing a higher priority on responding to domestic violence calls. (True, p. 312, Learning Objective: Define what constitutes domestic violence.)

29. Officers should not disregard the victim as a potential attacker in a domestic violence case. (True, p. 308, Learning Objective: Define what constitutes domestic violence.)

30. Establishing that an act was an attempted assault requires proof of intent along with ability to commit the crime. (False, p. 303, Learning Objective: Articulate the elements of simple assault, aggravated (felonious) assault and attempted assault.)

31. The term *elder abuse* applies to the physical and emotional abuse, financial exploitation and general neglect of the elderly. (True, p. 317, Learning Objective: Describe what constitutes elder abuse, and how prevalent elder abuse is.)

32. Some states now require an offender who violates a domestic order of protection to wear a global positioning system (GPS) monitoring device. (True, p. 313, Learning Objective: Define what constitutes domestic violence.)

33. In some instances, teachers and bus drivers are allowed to use reasonable physical force. (True, p. 302, Learning Objective: Explain when force is legal.)

34. Women constitute the offenders in nearly one eighth of all family violence incidents. (True, p. 308, Learning Objective: Define what constitutes domestic violence.)

35. The first antistalking laws were passed in Massachusetts in 2005. (False, p. 315, Learning Objective: Explain what constitutes stalking.)

36. A restraining order issued in one county may not be valid in the next county. (False, p. 313, Learning Objective: Define what constitutes domestic violence.)

37. Self-neglect is a form of elder abuse in many states. (True, p. 317, Learning Objective: Describe what constitutes elder abuse, and how prevalent elder abuse is.)

38. Research has found that children who witness abuse or are abused themselves are more likely to abuse a spouse or child when they become adults. (True, p. 306, Learning Objective: Define what constitutes domestic violence.)

39. Some stalking laws are more prohibitive and require that specific threats, or credible threats, must be made to the victim. (True, p. 315, Learning Objective: Explain what constitutes stalking.)

40. In some states, the police themselves can issue an emergency protective order in domestic violence cases. (True, p. 313, Learning Objective: Define what constitutes domestic violence.)

41. Computer technology is used to harass approximately 50 percent of all stalking victims. (False, p. 314–315, Learning Objective: Explain what constitutes stalking.)

42. Research supports a connection between animal cruelty as a child and domestic violence as an adult. (True, p. 309, Learning Objective: Define what constitutes domestic violence.)

43. Full faith and credit is a provision of the Violence Against Women Act of 1994. (True, p. 313, Learning Objective: Define what constitutes domestic violence.)

44. The use of restraining orders for stalkers has not proven to be very effective. (True, p. 308) Learning Objective: Explain what constitutes stalking.)

45. More women than men are victims of stalking. (True, p. 314, Learning Objective: Explain what constitutes stalking.)

Completion

46. When responding to cases of domestic violence, officers should wait for _____ prior to entering the scene. (backup, p. 309, Learning Objective: Define what constitutes domestic violence.)

47. Cruelty toward _____ is often a predictor of abuse or violent behavior. (animals, p. 309, Learning Objective: Define what constitutes domestic violence.)

48. The _____ of assault include the intent to cause injury, the severity of the injury inflicted and whether a dangerous weapon was used. (elements, p. 303, Learning Objective: Articulate the elements of simple assault, aggravated (felonious) assault and attempted assault.)

49. When investigating assault, the investigator should _____ the victim's information with physical evidence. (corroborate, p. 305, Learning Objective: Compare how to prove the elements of both simple and aggravated assault.)

50. Love _____ stalkers have no prior relationship with their victim but become fixated on that person, often a celebrity, believing they belong together. (obsessional, p. 314, Learning Objective: Explain what constitutes stalking.)

51. The initial phase of the three-phase cycle of violence is referred to as the _____ phase. (tension-building, p. 306, Learning Objective: Define what constitutes domestic violence.)

52. Simple assault must involve the commission of a(n) _____ act towards carrying out the intention. (overt, p. 303, Learning Objective: Compare how simple assault differs from aggravated assault.)

53. For an act to be considered an assault, _____ to do bodily harm to another must be proved. (intent, p. 302, Learning Objective: Define what constitutes assault.)

54. In general, any _____ that would lead an officer to make an arrest in any other situation also applies to domestic situations. (evidence, p. 310, Learning Objective: Define what constitutes domestic violence.)

55. _____ violence is a pattern of behavior involving physical, sexual, economic and emotional abuse, alone or in combination, by an intimate partner, often to establish and maintain power and control over the other partner. (Domestic, p. 306, Learning Objective: Define what constitutes domestic violence.)

Short Answer

56. What are some of the indicators of financial abuse of the elderly? (pp. 318–319, Learning Objective: Describe what constitutes elder abuse, and how prevalent elder abuse is.)

57. Describe cyberstalking and how it has grown exponentially in the last few years. (p. 314–315, Learning Objective: Explain what constitutes stalking.)

58. What are first actions that an officer should take upon arriving at the scene of an assault? (p. 305, Learning Objective: Describe what evidence is likely to be at the scene of an assault.)

59. Compare and contrast the use of mandatory arrest policies for domestic abuse with alternatives to arrest policies. What have studies found in comparing the two issues? (p. 311, Learning Objective: Define what constitutes domestic violence.)

60. What makes stalking such a unique crime? (p. 315, Learning Objective: Explain what constitutes stalking.)

61. Describe how GPS technology is being used to enforce restraining orders. (p. 313, Learning Objective: Define what constitutes domestic violence.)

62. List five signs of physical abuse of the elderly and five questions law enforcement officers might ask to determine whether a person is the victim of such abuse. (p. 318, Learning Objective: Describe what constitutes elder abuse, and how prevalent elder abuse is.)

63. Describe the differences between simple and aggravated assault. (p. 302, Learning Objective: Compare how simple assault differs from aggravated assault.)

64. Describe some of the special challenges in investigating assaults. (p. 304–305, Learning Objective: Describe what special challenges are posed by an assault investigation.)

65. Where did the term "rule of thumb" originate and what effect did it have on early domestic violence cases? (p. 306, Learning Objective: Define what constitutes domestic violence.)

66. Discuss the impact of a poor response or no-response policy to domestic violence cases. What happened in the Tracy Thurman case that highlighted the need for mandated responses? (p. 313–314, Learning Objective: Define what constitutes domestic violence.)

67. Describe the special challenges posed by elder abuse or dependent adult investigations. (p. 317–318, Learning Objective: Describe what constitutes elder abuse, and how prevalent elder abuse is.)

68. Define domestic violence. (p. 312, Learning Objective: Define what constitutes domestic violence.)

69. Describe the relation between the terms *battery* and *assault.* (p. 302 Learning Objective: Define what constitutes assault.)

70. How would you recognize abuse indicators, known as forensic markers, on an elderly abuse victim who is a resident in a long-term care facility? (pp. 319–320, Learning Objective: Describe what constitutes elder abuse, and how prevalent elder abuse is.)

SEX OFFENSES

Test Bank

Chapter 10
Sex Offenses

Multiple Choice

1. A particularly difficult type of sexual assault is date rape, sometimes called

    a. acquaintance rape.* (p. 335, Learning Objective: Explain what evidence to seek in date rape cases.)
    b. social rape.
    c. fraternal rape.
    d. sexual battery.

2. The key distinction between human trafficking and smuggling lies in

    a. the international implications.
    b. the need for labor.
    c. the individual's freedom of choice.* (p. 330, Learning Objective: Identify the key distinction between human trafficking and human smuggling.)
    d. government collusion.

3. Acknowledging the severe and dangerous nature of drug-assisted sexual assaults, the Drug-Induced Rape Prevention and Punishment Act, signed in 1996, allows courts to impose prison sentences up to _____ on anyone who distributes an illicit drug to someone intending to commit sexual assault.

    a. 5 years
    b. 10 years
    c. 20 years* (p. 335, Learning Objective: Explain what evidence to seek in date rape cases.)
    d. life

4. The largest number of people illegally trafficked into the United States are from

    a. Mexico and Central America.
    b. eastern Europe and Russia.
    c. east Asia and the Pacific.* (pp. 328–329, Learning Objective: Identify the key distinction between human trafficking and human smuggling.)
    d. South America.

5. When arriving at the scene of a rape case, officers should look for

    a. evidence of a struggle.
    b. stained or torn clothing.
    c. semen and bloodstains.
    d. all of these choices.* (p. 334, Learning Objective: Describe what type of evidence is often obtained in sex offense investigations.)

6. The element of sexual assault most difficult to prove in court is

    a. the act of sexual intercourse.
    b. that the act was committed with a person other than a spouse.
    c. that the act was committed without the consent of the victim.
    d. that the act was committed against the victim's will and by force.*
    (p. 333, Learning Objective: Identify the elements of sexual assault.)

7. In what type of interview do you carefully question the victim about the rapist's behavior, analyze the behavior to ascertain the motivation underlying the assault and then compile a profile of the individual likely to have committed the crime?

    a. sexual predator profile
    b. victim's behavioral interview
    c. latent sexuality probe
    d. behavior-oriented interview* (p. 340, Learning Objective: Define blind reporting and its advantages.)

8. A common "date rape" drug is

    a. aspirin.
    b. morphine.
    c. Rohypnol.* (p. 335, Learning Objective: Explain what evidence to seek in date rape cases.)
    d. mescaline.

9. The pleasure of complete domination over another person is what drives the

    a. masochist.
    b. exhibitionist.
    c. sadist.* (p. 331, Learning Objective: Describe how sex offenses are classified.)
    d. voyeur.

10. Statutory rape is

    a. sexual intercourse under threat of force.
    b. the rape of a spouse.
    c. any sex act that violates a state statute, regardless of mutual consent.
    d. sexual intercourse with a minor.* (p. 331 Learning Objective: Define the elements of rape and how it is classified.)

11. In a sexual assault case, it is best that the interviewer of the victim

    a. always be a male officer.
    b. always be a female officer.
    c. be an officer who is the same gender as the victim.
    d. be a police officer with the proper training and attitude.* (pp. 338–339, Learning Objective: Define blind reporting and its advantages.)

12. Rapists are often divided into two categories: _____ rapists and _____ rapists.

    a. anger, pleasure
    b. anger, power* (pp. 341–342, Learning Objective: Define blind reporting and its advantages.)
    c. pain, pleasure
    d. aggravated, simple

13. The main side effect of Rohypnol is

    a. nausea.
    b. amnesia.* (p. 335, Learning Objective: Explain what evidence to seek in date rape cases.)
    c. drowsiness.
    d. aggression.

14. Sexual penetration refers to an intrusion into a victim's

    a. anal opening.
    b. genital opening.
    c. mouth.
    d. any of these choices.* (p. 331, Learning Objective: Describe how sex offenses are classified.)

15. Certain offenders are likely to be obsessed with keeping trophies and recordings of their assaults, and therefore any search warrant applications in such cases should include photographs, records, scripts, letters, diaries, audiotapes, videotapes and newspaper reports of the crime. These offenders are called

    a. serial killers.
    b. sexual sadists.* (p. 341, Learning Objective: Define blind reporting and its advantages.)
    c. mass murderers.
    d. lone wolf killers.

16. The success of blind reporting hinges on

    a. whether trust can be established between the victim and the investigator.* (p. 338, Learning Objective: Define blind reporting and its advantages.)
    b. whether the victim is willing to prosecute.
    c. the investigator's willingness to accept a blind report.
    d. whether the victim is willing to commit immediately to an investigation.

17. What method has been used with sexual offenders in 16 states amid widespread controversy?

    a.　medical castration
    b.　chemical castration
    c.　civil commitment* (p. 344, Learning Objective: Explain whether recent laws have reduced or increased the penalties for sexual assault and why.)
    d.　the death penalty

18. The Supreme Court has clarified its limitation on civil commitments, saying that there must be

    a.　proof of physical or chemical castration.
    b.　proof of an offender's serious difficulty in controlling his behavior.* (p. 344, Learning Objective: Explain whether recent laws have reduced or increased the penalties for sexual assault and why.)
    c.　a statement under oath that the offender promises not to reoffend.
    d.　concurrent registration for life of any sex offender.

19. Which law finally required states to release any relevant information about registered sex offenders necessary to maintain and protect public safety, and allows disclosure of information collected under a state registration program for any purpose permitted under the laws of the state?

    a.　Jacob's Law
    b.　Megan's Law* (pp. 344–345) Learning Objective: Define which three federal statutes form the basis for sex offender registries.)
    c.　Jon Benet Ramsey Law
    d.　Little Lindbergh Law

20. In April 1998, what did the Supreme Court decide in regard to constitutional challenges that claimed that the Sexual Offender Registration and Notification Act's notification requirements represented an unconstitutional added punishment?

    a.　They agreed and overturned them.
    b.　They rejected the argument and retained the laws.* (p. 346, Learning Objective: Define which three federal statutes form the basis for sex offender registries.)
    c.　They decided to compromise and only register those offenders who voluntarily agreed to be listed as a term of their parole.
    d.　They disagreed and resentenced all sex offenders to a "life" parole.

21. What type of reporting allows sexual assault victims to retain their anonymity and confidentiality while sharing critical information with law enforcement, and also permits victims to gather legal information from law enforcement without having to commit immediately to an investigation?

    a.　third-party reporting
    b.　ex parte reporting

    c.   blind reporting* (p. 338, Learning Objective: Define blind reporting and its advantages.)

    d.   self-reporting

22.   A "date rape" drug that can be found in an odorless, colorless liquid form or as a pill or white powder and that has psychological effects including confusion, depression, anxiety, sleeplessness, drug craving and paranoia is called MDMA or

    a.   marijuana.

    b.   heroin.

    c.   Ecstasy.* (p. 335, Learning Objective: Explain what evidence to seek in date rape cases.)

    d.   mescaline.

23.   A "date rape" drug that is found in a white powder form and that can cause hallucinations, lost sense of time and identity, distorted perceptions of sight and sound, feeling out of control, impaired motor function, breathing problems, convulsions, vomiting, out-of-body experiences, memory problems, a dream-like feeling, numbness and loss of coordination is

    a.   Ecstasy.

    b.   peyote.

    c.   alpha-omega.

    d.   ketamine.* (p. 335, Learning Objective: Explain what evidence to seek in date rape cases.)

24.   Which of the following is *not* a sex offense?

    a.   incest

    b.   bigamy

    c.   child molestation, sodomy and rape

    d.   pornography* (p. 330, Learning Objective: Describe how sex offenses are classified.)

25.   Incest is sexual intercourse with a(n)

    a.   brother, sister or parent.* (p. 331, Learning Objective: Describe how sex offenses are classified.)

    b.   first cousin.

    c.   blood relative.

    d.   animal.

True/False

26.   Sexual assaults are among the easiest cases to investigate because victims usually know their attackers. (False, p. 333, Learning Objective: Outline the special challenges that exist in investigating sex offenses.)

27. Sexual penetration does not occur until semen is produced in the victim's body. (False, p. 331, Learning Objective: Describe how sex offenses are classified.)

28. When investigating the scene of a sexual assault, it is best to set up a command center at the victim's home to ensure that she feels safe. (False, p. 334 Learning Objective: Outline the special challenges that exist in investigating sex offenses.)

29. The only difference between single and serial murderers of prostitutes is the number of victims they have killed. (False, p. 327) Learning Objective: Identify the key distinction between human trafficking and human smuggling.)

30. Recent research has shown that most victims of human trafficking were used for commercial sex acts. (True, p. 327, Learning Objective: Identify the key distinction between human trafficking and human smuggling.)

31. As a safety feature, newly produced Rohypnol pills turn blue when added to liquids, but older pills, which are still available, have no color. (True, p. 335, Learning Objective: Explain what evidence to seek in date rape cases.)

32. Emergency medical personnel can contribute valuable information to the investigation of a sexual assault because they are frequently the earliest responders to the scene of the crime. (True, p. 334, Learning Objective: Describe what type of evidence is often obtained in sex offense investigations.)

33. Making obscene phone calls is a crime. (True, p.326, Learning Objective: Identify the key distinction between human trafficking and human smuggling.)

34. Today, all states have enacted laws requiring sex offenders to register within their states to help law enforcement agencies manage offenders released from secure confinement. (True, p. 345, Learning Objective: Define which three federal statutes form the basis for sex offender registries.)

35. GPS technology is now being used to protect victims of sexual assault by providing information as to the victim's whereabouts in the event that the attacker attempts another assault. (False, p. 346 Learning Objective: Define which three federal statutes form the basis for sex offender registries.)

36. A victim who consents to a sexual act but who has an emotional disturbance, mental illness or retardation, or who is attacked while on drugs or unconscious, is still considered giving "true consent" which negates a criminal act. (False, p. 333, Learning Objective: Identify the elements of sexual assault.)

37. Rohypnol is one of the newest drugs to be used in date rape crimes and its effects are still not fully understood by scientists. (False, p. 336, Learning Objective: Explain what evidence to seek in date rape cases.)

38. In most sex offenses, victims know their attackers. (True, p. 326, Learning Objective: Identify the elements of sexual assault.)

39. Police should not accept blind reporting because it limits their investigation of the crime. (False, p. 338, Learning Objective: Define blind reporting and its advantages.)

40. Because of right-to-privacy issues, the Supreme Court has rejected legislation by states that adopted policies of flagging driver's-license and vehicle registration files of registered sex offenders as a means of keeping law enforcement authorities informed of address changes, vehicle information and personal data. (False, p. 346, Learning Objective: Define which three federal statutes form the basis for sex offender registries.)

41. The civil commitment of sex offenders has been ruled unconstitutional. (False, p. 344, Learning Objective: Explain whether recent laws have reduced or increased the penalties for sexual assault and why.)

42. Preassaultive behavior of rapists may include having fantasies about successful sexual relationships and the planning of an attack. (True, pp. 342–343, Learning Objective: Define blind reporting and its advantages.)

43. Digital penetration is a form of sexual penetration. (True, p. 331, Learning Objective: Describe how sex offenses are classified.)

44. Police should allow professional medical personnel to obtain the personal details of a sexual attack. (False, pp. 338–339, Learning Objective: Outline the special challenges that exist in investigating sex offenses.)

Completion

45. The characteristic of excessive force may identify a rapist as a _____. (sadist, pp. 341–342, Learning Objective: Describe how sex offenses are classified.)

46. Additional evidence in date rape cases may include the presence of _____ in the victim's system. (alcohol and/or drugs, p. 335, Learning Objective: Explain what evidence to seek in date rape cases.)

47. Rapists are classified as _____ rapists and _____ rapists. (power, anger, p. 341, Learning Objective: Define blind reporting and its advantages.)

48. The police may use _____ to trace obscene phone calls if given a signed affidavit from the victim stating the facts related to the calls. (traps, p. 326, Learning Objective: Identify the key distinction between human trafficking and human smuggling.)

49. _____ exposure is the act of revealing one's genitals to another person to such an extent as to shock the other's sense of decency. (Indecent, p. 331, Learning Objective: Describe how sex offenses are classified.)

50. _____ abuse involves fettering, binding or otherwise physically restraining, whipping or torturing for sexual gratification. (Sadomasochistic, p. 331, Learning Objective: Describe how sex offenses are classified.)

51. Rape is often classified as either forcible or _____. (statutory, p. 331, Learning Objective: Define the elements of rape and how it is classified.)

52. _____ reporting allows victims to gather information from law enforcement without having to commit to an investigation. (Blind, p. 338, Learning Objective: Define blind reporting and its advantages.)

53. Sex _____ means the recruitment, harboring, transportation, provision or obtaining of a person for the purpose of a commercial sex act in which a commercial sex act is induced by force, fraud or coercion. (trafficking, p. 327, Learning Objective: Identify the key distinction between human trafficking and human smuggling.)

54. The three most common date rape drugs are Rohypnol, GHB and _____. (ketamine, p. 335, Learning Objective: Explain what evidence to seek in date rape cases.)

Short Answer

55. Describe the role of medical personnel in the process of investigating a sexual assault. (pp. 336–338 Learning Objective: Outline the special challenges that exist in investigating sex offenses.)

56. What type of information should officers attempt to gain when interviewing the victim of a date rape? (p. 338–340, Learning Objective: Explain what evidence to seek in date rape cases.)

57. What special considerations should be made in dealing with the victim of a sexual assault? (pp. 333–334, Learning Objective: Describe what type of evidence is often obtained in sex offense investigations.)

58. Discuss the issue of human trafficking and how it differs from smuggling. (p. 328–330, Learning Objective: Identify the key distinction between human trafficking and human smuggling.)

59. What important steps should responding officers carry out when they first arrive at the scene of a sexual assault? (p. 334, Learning Objective: Outline the special challenges that exist in investigating sex offenses.)

60. What are some of the concerns that victims of sexual assault have in facing a jury? (p. 343, Learning Objective: Clarify what is generally required to obtain a conviction in sexual assault cases.)

61. Explain the procedure called blind reporting. Why is it used, and how effective or ineffective has it been? What are the benefits and drawbacks of this procedure? (p. 338, Learning Objective: Define blind reporting and its advantages.)

62. What type of information should officers attempt to gain when interviewing the victim of a sexual offense? (pp. 338–340, Learning Objective: Explain what modus operandi factors are important in investigating a sexual assault.)

63. Explain the concept of civil commitment of sex offenders following sentences served. What is the rationale behind such legislation? Have the courts generally upheld such measures? (p. 344, Learning Objective: Explain whether recent laws have reduced or increased the penalties for sexual assault and why.)

64. Describe the elements that are necessary to obtain a conviction in a sexual assault case. (p. 343, Learning Objective: Clarify what is generally required to obtain a conviction in sexual assault cases.)

65. What are the arguments for and against sex offender registries and notification laws? (pp. 344–346, Learning Objective: Define which three federal statutes form the basis for sex offender registries.)

66. Discuss the difference between sex crimes that involve aggression toward a victim and victimless acts between consenting adults. (p. 330, Learning Objective: Describe how sex offenses are classified.)

67. How does fantasy play a part in the decision of what to list in the search warrant when searching the home of a suspected rapist or sexual assault suspect? (p. 341, Learning Objective: Describe what type of evidence is often obtained in sex offense investigations.)

68. In addition to the police, which agencies play a role in the investigation of a sexual assault, and how are they involved? (p. 343, Learning Objective: Identify agencies that can assist in a sexual assault investigation.)

69. How have laws regarding sexual assault crimes changed over the past 25 years? (pp. 343–344 Learning Objective: Explain whether recent laws have reduced or increased the penalties for sexual assault and why; Learning Objective: Define which three federal statutes form the basis for sex offender registries.)

70. Discuss how investigators can trace obscene telephone calls and texts, and what barriers exist in identifying some callers? (p. 326, Learning Objective: Identify the key distinction between human trafficking and human smuggling.)

CRIMES AGAINST CHILDREN

Test Bank

Chapter 11
Crimes against Children

Multiple Choice

1. Physical indicators of child neglect may include

    a. sleep disorders.
    b. begging and stealing food.
    c. being wary of adults.
    d. frequent hunger and poor hygiene.* (p. 364, Learning Objective: Identify what things can indicate child neglect or abuse.)

2. What agency is responsible for investigating crimes involving the U.S. mail, including child pornography and child sexual abuse offenses? It is the lead agency in the federal government's efforts to eliminate the production and distribution of such material.

    a. the FBI's CyberCrime Unit
    b. the U.S. Postal Inspection Service* (p. 375, Learning Objective: Describe the three law enforcement approaches that are models to combat child sexual exploitation.)
    c. the Secret Service
    d. Homeland Security

3. Which three law enforcement approaches have emerged as models to combat child sexual exploitation?

    a. protecting children online, developing a reporting mechanism for child sexual exploitation and imposing tougher penalties for sex crimes against children
    b. special task forces, strike forces and law enforcement networks* (p. 374, Learning Objective: Describe the three law enforcement approaches that are models to combat child sexual exploitation.)
    c. stiffer penalties for offenders, special task forces and increased budgets for programs that investigate crimes against children
    d. none of these choices

4. The most common habitual child sex abuser is the

    a. mesomorph.
    b. hebephile.
    c. pedophile.* (pp. 369–370, Learning Objective: Explain what types of evidence are important in child neglect or abuse cases.)
    d. pederast.

5. Which of the following is a risk factor contributing to increased chance of child maltreatment?

    a.   special needs that increase caregiver burden
    b.   all of these choices.* (p. 356, Learning Objective: Discuss the effects of child abuse.)
    c.   social isolation
    d.   community violence

6. Sex offenders, particularly those who abuse young children, are referred to as

    a.   vultures.
    b.   chicken hawks.* (p. 369, Learning Objective: Explain how a pedophile might typically react to being discovered.)
    c.   buzzards.
    d.   robins.

7. To assist in preventing sex crimes against children, parents should

    a.   avoid exposing children to sexual information, as it may cause them to get into trouble.
    b.   encourage children to think of sex as frightening, so that they will be more likely to protect themselves against sexual abuse.
    c.   educate their children about sex and sexual abuse that might occur.* (p. 381, Learning Objective: Discuss how crimes against children can be prevented.)
    d.   insist that sex education be banned from the schools.

8. Failure to provide adequate food, clothing, shelter, love, attention or proper supervision can be construed as child

    a.   neglect.* (p. 353, Learning Objective: Identify the four common types of maltreatment.)
    b.   pedophilia.
    c.   trolling.
    d.   incest.

9. When children talk about a sexual assault, they

    a.   often exaggerate the details.
    b.   generally relate the truth.* (p. 359, Learning Objective: Determine whether children are generally truthful when talking about abuse.)
    c.   often lie for revenge.
    d.   will never lie.

10. Using children in pornography is best defined as an example of

    a.   neglect.
    b.   exploitation.* (p. 371, Learning Objective: Describe the types of sex rings that exist in the United States related to child abuse and sexual exploitation.)

    c.   abandonment.

    d.   kidnapping.

11.   When interviewing children, interrogators should avoid asking the question, _____ because it tends to sound accusatory.

    a.   "What?"

    b.   "Where?"

    c.   "Why?"* (p. 361, Learning Objective: Discuss which factors to consider in interviewing child victims.)

    d.   "When?"

12.   The Child Protection Act prohibits

    a.   child kidnapping.

    b.   child pornography.* (p. 371, Learning Objective: Describe what the Child Protection Act involves.)

    c.   child neglect and abandonment.

    d.   all of these choices.

13.   The most frequent type of child abduction is committed by

    a.   someone who intends to kidnap the child.

    b.   one of the child's parents.* (p. 377, Learning Objective: Identify the most common type of child abduction.)

    c.   someone who is not related to the child.

    d.   a complete stranger.

14.   A syndicated sex ring is

    a.   a well-structured organization that recruits children, produces pornography and delivers sexual services.* (p. 370, Learning Objective: Describe the types of sex rings that exist in the United States related to child abuse and sexual exploitation.)

    b.   an environment in which pedophiles can exchange experiences and trade or sell explicit photographs of children.

    c.   organized primarily by the age of the children who are targeted by pedophiles.

    d.   all of these choices.

15.   Babysitters should

    a.   never believe children when they talk about abuse in their home.

    b.   avoid taking care of children when a questionable relative is staying in the house.

    c.   always request and check references of families that they don't know.

    d.   be selected carefully by parents.* (p. 381, Learning Objective: Discuss how crimes against children can be prevented.)

16. It is believed that for every report of abuse the police and child protective services receive, how many cases are unreported?

   a. 25
   b. 10* (p. 352, Learning Objective: Describe the crimes that are frequently committed against children.)
   c. 5
   d. 50

17. Which of the following should be a red flag to investigators working possible child fatality cases?

   a. signs of malnourishment
   b. records from 911 call centers
   c. an unreasonable delay in seeking medical attention, because the injuries may have been caused by abuse
   d. all of these choices* (p. 368, Learning Objective: Identify what things can indicate child neglect or abuse.)

18. Most reports of child abuse are made by

   a. third parties.* (p. 359, Learning Objective: Describe who usually reports crimes against children.)
   b. the victim.
   c. the family.
   d. the offender.

19. The National Center for Missing and Exploited Children (NCMEC) has a congressionally mandated program that is a reporting mechanism for child sexual exploitation. What is it called?

   a. Kid's Law
   b. CyberTipline* (p. 374, Learning Objective: Describe what the Child Protection Act involves.)
   c. To Catch a Crook
   d. CyberCops

20. Constantly belittling a child is a form of

   a. emotional abuse.* (p. 353, Learning Objective: Identify the four common types of maltreatment.)
   b. physical abuse.
   c. sexual abuse.
   d. none of these choices.

21. When interviewing children in a sexual abuse investigation, which of the following is *not* a consideration?

   a. the child's attention span
   b. the child's reputation for being truthful* (p. 359, Learning Objective: Discuss which factors to consider in interviewing child victims.)

c. the child's age
d. the child's ability to describe what happened

22. Behavioral indicators of child sexual abuse include

a. withdrawal.
b. bizarre sexual behavior.
c. an unwillingness to change clothes in front of others.
d. all of these choices.* (p. 364, Learning Objective: Identify what things can indicate child neglect or abuse.)

23. The acronym CART stands for

a. Community Alert and Respond Tactics.
b. Child Abuse Rescue Team.
c. Child Abuse and Runaway Tracking.
d. Child Abduction Response Team.* (p. 379, Learning Objective: Define the AMBER Alert program.)

24. Which of the following is *not* a critical step in interviewing children in a sexual abuse case?

a. talking in terms of good touch, bad touch
b. asking the child to promise to testify in court* (p. 362, Learning Objective: Discuss which factors to consider in interviewing child victims.)
c. building rapport with the child
d. discussing anatomical identification

25. MSBP stands for

a. Multiple Sexual Biological Perversions.
b. Misoped Sadist Biological Pedophile.
c. Multiphase Sexual Bipolar Physical.
d. Munchausen Syndrome by Proxy.* (p. 365, Learning Objective: Identify what things can indicate child neglect or abuse.)

True/False

26. Girls are much more likely than boys to be victimized by sexual abuse. (False, p. 354, Learning Objective: Explain the most common form of child maltreatment and how serious it is.)

27. Sexual abuse victims are significantly more likely to be arrested for violence as adults. (False, p. 356, Learning Objective: Discuss the effects of child abuse.)

28. Child abuse and neglect affect a significant proportion of children's lives, and children who have been abused are more aggressive and have higher levels of impaired social functioning than their counterparts. (True, p. 356, Learning Objective: Discuss the effects of child abuse.)

29. Not all states have enacted child abuse and neglect laws. (False, p. 357, Learning Objective: Describe the three components typically included in child abuse/neglect laws.)

30. An offender's computer is a good source of information when arresting an individual for child pornography. (True, p. 372, Learning Objective: Describe what the Child Protection Act involves.)

31. Pictures of children's injuries should be taken quickly because children heal faster than adults. (True, p. 363, Learning Objective: Explain what types of evidence are important in child neglect or abuse cases.)

32. Venereal disease or other sexually transmitted diseases are an indicator of possible child sexual abuse. (True, p. 364, Learning Objective: Identify what things can indicate child neglect or abuse.)

33. In cases of sexual assault, the child's description of the acts or experiences will probably not be normal for their age. (True, p. 361, Learning Objective: Determine whether children are generally truthful when talking about abuse.)

34. Investigators should never make use of the "cognitive interview technique" with children. (False, p. 361, Learning Objective: Discuss which factors to consider in interviewing child victims.)

35. In the vast majority of child abuse cases, children tell the truth to the best of their ability. (True, p. 350) Learning Objective: Determine whether children are generally truthful when talking about abuse.)

36. Childhood abuse or neglect has not been linked with a history of delinquency. (False, p. 364, Learning Objective: Discuss the effects of child abuse.)

37. Once an abducted child is taken to a foreign country, there is no way to get that child back. (False, p. 378, Learning Objective: Identify the most common type of child abduction.)

38. A child's history of physical abuse predisposes the child to violence in later years. (True, p. 356, Learning Objective: Discuss the effects of child abuse.)

39. Most pedophiles use force to gain control over their victims. (False, p. 369, Learning Objective: Explain how a pedophile might typically react to being discovered.)

40. The AMBER Alert plan was enacted in response to the sexual assault of a young girl in Minnesota in 1989. (False, pp. 378–379, Learning Objective: Define the AMBER Alert program.)

41. The use of anatomical dolls in the interview process is widely recognized as an important factor in apprehending pedophiles. (False, p. 361, Learning Objective: Discuss which factors to consider in interviewing child victims.)

42. Child pornography is a highly organized, multimillion-dollar industry. (True, p. 371, Learning Objective: Describe what the Child Protection Act involves.)

43. SIDS is often a factor in cases of child neglect. (False, p. 366, Learning Objective: Explain what types of evidence are important in child neglect or abuse cases.)

44. The Unborn Victims of Violence Act, or Laci and Conner's Law, allows separate punishment for the harming of a child in utero. (True, p. 354, Learning Objective: Explain the most common form of child maltreatment and how serious it is.)

45. Children who are afflicted with osteogenesis imperfecta (OI) may display some of the telltale symptoms of child abuse. (True, p. 366, Learning Objective: Explain what types of evidence are important in child neglect or abuse cases.)

Completion

46. Commercial _____ of children involves the use of children with monetary or other material gain as a direct or indirect goal. (exploitation, p. 371, Learning Objective: Describe what the Child Protection Act involves.)

47. _____ Alert is an early-warning network that law enforcement can use to quickly convey key information to the general public via television and radio soon after a child has been abducted. (AMBER, pp. 378–379, Learning Objective: Define the AMBER Alert program.)

48. In a _____ sex ring, pedophiles keep their activities and photographs totally secret. (solo, p. 370, Learning Objective: Describe the types of sex rings that exist in the United States related to child abuse and sexual exploitation.)

49. Some groups that use rituals or ceremonial acts to draw their members into a certain belief system, also known as _____, occasionally include child sexual abuse in their rituals. (cults, p. 370, Learning Objective: Describe the types of sex rings that exist in the United States related to child abuse and sexual exploitation.)

50. Child abuse has been identified as the biggest single cause of _____ of young children. (death, p. 355, Learning Objective: Identify the biggest single cause of death of young children.)

51. Constantly belittling a child is a form of _____ abuse. (emotional, p. 353, Learning Objective: Identify the four common types of maltreatment.)

52. _____ are the most likely suspects in physical abuse. (Parents, p. 365, Learning Objective: Identify what things can indicate child neglect or abuse.)

53. Emotional damage from child abuse may include impaired self-concept as well as increased levels of aggression, anxiety and tendency toward _____. (self-destructiveness, p. 355, Learning Objective: Discuss the effects of child abuse.)

54. Children who are reported missing by their parents are often _____. (runaways, p. 376, Learning Objective: Discuss the challenges presented by a missing child report.)

55. A misoped is someone who _____ children. (hates, p. 369, Learning Objective: Explain how a pedophile might typically react to being discovered.)

Short Answer

56. Describe a "transition sex ring" and how someone might get involved. (p. 370, Learning Objective: Describe the types of sex rings that exist in the United States related to child abuse and sexual exploitation.)

57. What conditions would have to be present to consider moving a child from the home into protective custody without a hearing? (p. 358, Learning Objective: Clarify when a child should be taken into protective custody.)

58. How does a pedophile normally react when discovered? (p. 371, Learning Objective: Explain how a pedophile might typically react to being discovered.)

59. Discuss the rationale for mandated reporters, and describe who is given the role of mandated reporter. (pp. 359–360, Learning Objective: Describe who usually reports crimes against children.)

60. Discuss the differences between a misoped, hebephile and pedophile. (p. 369, Learning Objective: Explain how a pedophile might typically react to being discovered.)

61. List and discuss the various indicators of child neglect. (p. 364, Learning Objective: Identify what things can indicate child neglect or abuse.)

62. What criteria should officers consider to determine whether a runaway child is endangered? (p. 378, Learning Objective: Discuss the challenges presented by a missing child report.)

63. Discuss why child abuse has not historically been considered a crime. (pp. 351–352, Learning Objective: Describe the crimes that are frequently committed against children.)

64. Describe the four common types of maltreatment, and give an example for each. (p. 353, Learning Objective: Identify the four common types of maltreatment.)

65. When investigating child fatalities, which individuals should officers consider as potential witnesses? (p. 367, Learning Objective: Explain the challenges involved in investigating crimes against children.)

66. Describe some recent accomplishments of the Innocent Images National Initiative (IINI). (p. 375, Learning Objective: Describe the three law enforcement approaches that are models to combat child sexual exploitation.)

67. What are some of the reasons that children run away from their families? (p. 376, Learning Objective: Discuss the challenges presented by a missing child report.)

68. Discuss the three components that are included in child abuse/neglect laws. (p. 356, Learning Objective: Describe the three components typically included in child abuse/neglect laws.)

69. What kinds of questions are pertinent for officers considering criminal charges against a parent who has abducted his or her child? (p. 378, Learning Objective: Identify the most common type of child abduction.)

70. Describe the rules and procedures that the courts have changed in order to resolve some of the problems associated with children providing testimony in court. (p. 380, Learning Objective: Discuss how crimes against children can be prevented.)

ROBBERY

Test Bank

Chapter 12
Robbery

Multiple Choice

1. Generally, the three elements of robbery are

   a. the wrongful taking of another person's property, through the use of force, against the person's will.
   b. theft with a gun, by a person, against another person.
   c. the wrongful taking of personal property, from a person or in the person's presence, against the person's will by force or threat of force.* (p. 395, Learning Objective: Identify the elements of the crime of robbery.)
   d. the intentional theft, of personal property, from another against their will.

2. False robbery reports may be identified by

   a. unusual delay in reporting the offense.
   b. lack of correspondence with the physical evidence.
   c. improbable events.
   d. all of these choices.* (p. 401, Learning Objective: Identify what physical evidence can link a suspect with a robbery.)

3. Robberies committed by a lone robber tend to

   a. be crimes of opportunity.* (p. 389 Learning Objective: Define robbery.)
   b. involve younger victims.
   c. include firearms.
   d. involve injuring the victim.

4. The main elements of robbery include

   a. using weapons.
   b. force or fear.* (p. 395, Learning Objective: Identify the elements of the crime of robbery.)
   c. physical harm to the victim.
   d. any loss over $200.

5. Bank robberies are investigated by

   a. local police.
   b. state officers.
   c. the FBI.
   d. the FBI, in joint investigation with local police and sheriff's departments.* (p. 393, Learning Objective: List the types of robbery in which the FBI and state officials become involved.)

6. Which of the following is a true statement?

   a. Amateur, solitary offenders tend to rob banks at the end of the day.
   b. Professionals prefer to operate when there are fewer customers, such as at opening time.* (p. 393, Learning Objective: List the types of robbery in which the FBI and state officials become involved.)
   c. Gangs of robbers always rob at midday.
   d. Note passers only enter the bank at closing.

7. Which of the following categories are used to define robbery?

   a. residential, commercial, street and personal
   b. residential, commercial, street and vehicle driver* (p. 390, Learning Objective: Classify robberies.)
   c. personal, commercial, street and vehicle
   d. street, home and business

8. Physical evidence at the scene of a robbery might include which of the following?

   a. fingerprints
   b. shoe prints
   c. restraining devices
   d. all of these choices* (p. 400, Learning Objective: Identify what physical evidence can link a suspect with a robbery.)

9. Deterrents to convenience store robberies include

   a. keeping outdoor pay phones in good working condition.
   b. dimming the lights inside and outside of the store.
   c. elevating the cash-register area.* (p. 390, Learning Objective: Classify robberies.)
   d. all of these choices.

10. Residential robberies are also referred to as

    a. home-invading robberies.* (p. 390, Learning Objective: Classify robberies.)
    b. stop and robs.
    c. neighborhood mugging.
    d. smash and grabs.

11. Which of the following correctly lists priorities at a hostage situation?

    a. save lives, recover property and gain evidence for an arrest
    b. preserve life, apprehend the hostage taker and recover or protect property* (p. 396, Learning Objective: Describe the factors to consider in responding to a robbery-in-progress call.)
    c. preserve life, apprehend the hostage taker and protect witnesses
    d. kill the hostage taker and rescue the victim

12. An indicator of a false robbery report is

    a.   an exceptionally detailed description of the offender.
    b.   an exceptionally vague description of the offender.
    c.   a lack of cooperation.
    d.   all of these choices.* (p. 401, Learning Objective: Identify what physical evidence can link a suspect with a robbery.)

13. Most residential robberies occur

    a.   in the early morning.
    b.   around noon.
    c.   in the early evening.* (p. 390, Learning Objective: Classify robberies.)
    d.   around midnight.

14. The most frequent victims of robbery are

    a.   older people.*
    b.   middle-aged people.
    c.   youths.
    d.   both middle-aged and older people. (p. 389, Learning Objective: Define robbery.)

15. In most robberies, the robber

    a.   makes an oral demand.* (p. 389, Learning Objective: Define robbery.)
    b.   makes a written demand.
    c.   uses gestures.
    d.   uses a firearm.

16. The first priority in hostage situations is to

    a.   recover or protect property.
    b.   apprehend the hostage taker.
    c.   preserve life.* (p. 396, Learning Objective: Describe the factors to consider in responding to a robbery-in-progress call.)
    d.   none of these choices.

17. To prosecute for the crime of robbery, officers must

    a.   prove at least one element of the crime.
    b.   prove at least two elements of the crime.
    c.   prove all elements of the crime.* (p. 398, Learning Objective: Explain how to prove each element of robbery.)
    d.   have recovered the stolen property for use as evidence.

18. A robbery occurring at a loan company would be classified as a _____ robbery.

    a. residential
    b. street
    c. commercial* (p. 390, Learning Objective: Classify robberies.)
    d. vehicle-driver

19. A recent innovation in robbery investigations is

    a. automatic alarms activated by the presence of a weapon.
    b. retina pattern recognition.
    c. facial recognition systems.* (p. 393, Learning Objective: List the types of robbery in which the FBI and state officials become involved.)
    d. stun guns.

20. Which one of the following items is *not* negotiable in dealing with a hostage taker?

    a. food
    b. media access
    c. transportation (p. 397, Learning Objective: List the types of robbery in which the FBI and state officials become involved.)
    d. reduced penalties

21 Which one of the following is *not* characteristic of robberies?

    a. They are committed by strangers rather than by acquaintances.
    b. The offender lives within a few miles (five or ten) of the robbery.* (p. 389, Learning Objective: Define robbery.)
    c. Youths committing them tend to operate in groups and to use strong-arm tactics more frequently than do adults.
    d. Middle-aged and older people tend to be the victims.

22. Today, officers have the advantage of using Global Information Software (GIS) to

    a. map all incidents of robberies.* (p. 401, Learning Objective: Identify what physical evidence can link a suspect with a robbery.)
    b. identify all robbers.
    c. track all known vehicles.
    d. map potential victims.

23. This psychological effect may occur when hostages report that they have no ill feelings toward the hostage takers and, further, that they feared the police more than they feared their captors.

    a. Seattle syndrome
    b. bait-and-switch

    c.   Stockholm syndrome* (p. 397, Learning Objective: Describe the factors to consider in responding to a robbery-in-progress call.)

    d.   butterfly effect

24.   Why would clothing and disguises discarded by the robber upon leaving the scene be valuable evidence if discovered?

    a.   They may have identifying marks on them.

    b.   The robber may have left his/her ID in them.

    c.   The victim may recognize the owner.

    d.   They may provide DNA evidence.* (p. 400, Learning Objective: Identify what physical evidence can link a suspect with a robbery.)

25.   This system may be of great assistance in identifying a stolen vehicle that might be serving as a getaway car, even as robbers speed away at 100 mph.

    a.   facial recognition systems

    b.   automatic license plate recognition (ALPR)* (p. 396 Learning Objective: List the types of robbery in which the FBI and state officials become involved.)

    c.   GPS locaters

    d.   spike strips

True/False

26.   Amateur bank robbers usually demand that dye packs be left out of any money bags that are handed over by the teller. (False, p. 394, Learning Objective: List the types of robbery in which the FBI and state officials become involved.)

27.   In a robbery situation, use of force must be directly aimed against the victim or it will not hold up in the courts of law. (False, p. 399, Learning Objective: Explain how to prove each element of robbery.)

28.   Officers should rush hostage takers in order to catch them off-guard. (False, p. 397, Learning Objective: Describe the factors to consider in responding to a robbery-in-progress call.)

29.   Carjacking is a category of robbery that involves taking a motor vehicle by force or threat of force. (True, pp. 391–392, Learning Objective: Define carjacking.)

30.   In hostage situations, bait money is often used to lure bank robbers out of the building. (False, p. 394, Learning Objective: List the types of robbery in which the FBI and state officials become involved.)

31.   Convenience stores that have already been robbed are less likely to be robbed again. (False, p. 390, Learning Objective: Classify robberies.)

32. Finding an MO that matches a previous robbery is a strong indicator that the same robber committed the crime. (False, p. 400, Learning Objective: Describe the modus operandi information to obtain in a robbery case.)

33. Bank robberies are committed by amateurs as well as by habitual criminals because of the large sums of money involved. (True, p. 393, Learning Objective: List the types of robbery in which the FBI and state officials become involved.)

34. Robbers may use various types of disguises to keep from being identified, including ski masks, paper sacks and other types of clothing. (True, p. 400, Learning Objective: Identify what descriptive information is needed to identify suspects and vehicles.)

35. Commercial robberies are usually better planned than street robberies. (True, p. 390, Learning Objective: Classify robberies.)

36. Robbery victims are the least likely of all victims of violent crime to face an armed offender. (False, p. 400, Learning Objective: Identify what descriptive information is needed to identify suspects and vehicles.)

37. Most robberies do not result in personal injury. (True, p. 389, Learning Objective: Define robbery.)

38. Lack of cooperation in the investigation of a robbery is almost absolute proof that the robbery was staged. (False, p. 401, Learning Objective: Identify what physical evidence can link a suspect with a robbery.)

39. Most street robberies involve large sums of money. (False, p. 390, Learning Objective: Classify robberies.)

40. Because robbery is inherently serial, mapping it has proven successful. (True, p. 401, Learning Objective: Identify what physical evidence can link a suspect with a robbery.)

41. As an essential element of robbery, the robber must have no legal right to the property. (True, p. 395, Learning Objective: Identify the elements of the crime of robbery.)

42. The Stockholm syndrome refers to a situation in which hostages attack the hostage takers because they know they are about to be killed. (False, p. 397, Learning Objective: Describe the factors to consider in responding to a robbery-in-progress call.)

43. "In the presence of a person" means that the victim does not need to actually see the robber take the property. (True, p. 395, Learning Objective: Identify the elements of the crime of robbery.)

44. Most robbers carry a weapon or other threatening item or indicate to the victim that they are armed. (True, p. 389, Learning Objective: Define robbery.)

45. The speed of robbery, its potential for violence and the usual lack of evidence at the scene do not really pose special challenges for investigators. (False, p. 398, Learning Objective: Explain the special challenges that are posed by a robbery investigation.)

Completion

46. Robbery is the _____ taking of another's property through force or intimidation. (felonious, p. 389, Learning Objective: Define robbery.)

47. The first priority in a hostage situation is to preserve _____. (life, p. 396, Learning Objective: Describe the factors to consider in responding to a robbery-in-progress call.)

48. _____ robbery is both a federal and a state offense. (Bank, p. 393, Learning Objective: Classify robberies.)

49. The phenomenon in which hostages begin to identify with and sympathize with their captors is known as the _____ syndrome. (Stockholm, p. 397, Learning Objective: Describe the factors to consider in responding to a robbery-in-progress call.)

50. Most robbers are visibly armed with a weapon or dangerous device and make a(n) _____ demand of the victim. (oral, p. 389, Learning Objective: Define robbery.)

51. Many commercial robberies are committed by individuals with criminal records; therefore, their _____ should be compared with those of past robberies. (modus operandi [or MO], p. 400, Learning Objective: Describe the modus operandi information to obtain in a robbery case.)

52. About 8 percent of convenience stores account for more than _____ percent of all convenience store robberies. (50, p. 390, Learning Objective: Classify robberies.)

53. When responding to a robbery in progress, it is often best to arrive quietly to prevent the taking of _____. (hostages, p. 395, Learning Objective: Describe the factors to consider in responding to a robbery-in-progress call.)

54. _____ _____ know that many Asian families distrust banks and keep large amounts of cash and jewelry in their homes. (Home invaders, p. 390, Learning Objective: Define home invaders.)

55. A robbery occurring at a loan company is classified as a _____ robbery. (commercial, p. 390, Learning Objective: Classify robberies.)

Short Answer

56. Explain some of the special challenges that are posed by a robbery investigation. (p. 389, Learning Objective: Explain the special challenges that are posed by a robbery investigation.)

57. What are some of the advantages to the passage of time with regard to hostage scenarios? (p. 397, Learning Objective: Describe the factors to consider in responding to a robbery-in-progress call.)

58. Describe some of the main distinguishing characteristics between professional and amateur bank robbers. (pp. 393–394, Learning Objective: List the types of robbery in which the FBI and state officials become involved.)

59. What are the first steps that an officer should take when responding to a robbery-in-progress call? (pp. 395–396, Learning Objective: Describe the factors to consider in responding to a robbery-in-progress call.)

60. U.S. Code Title 18, Section 2113, defines the elements of the federal crime of bank robbery. Why is there joint jurisdiction with local police or sheriffs and the FBI in investigations of this crime? (p. 393, Learning Objective: List the types of robbery in which the FBI and state officials become involved.)

61. How is the concept of modus operandi applied in robbery investigations? List some modus operandi information that is important in such investigations. (p. 400, Learning Objective: Describe the modus operandi information to obtain in a robbery case.)

62. What are some of the strategies that have been developed in order to deter bank robberies? (pp. 393–394, Learning Objective: List the types of robbery in which the FBI and state officials become involved.)

63. Why is the technology of automatic license plate recognition (ALPR) so important in the investigation of robbery cases? (p. 396, Learning Objective: Explain the special challenges that are posed by a robbery investigation.)

64. Describe some of the components that would contribute to an ideal negotiation scenario with a hostage taker. (pp. 396–398, Learning Objective: List the types of robbery in which the FBI and state officials become involved.)

65. What indicators might an investigator look for to determine whether a robbery is being falsely reported? (p. 401, Learning Objective: Identify what physical evidence can link a suspect with a robbery.)

66. What conflicts between tactics may occur when deciding whether to use a direct assault by SWAT officers or a crisis negotiation team (CNT)? (pp. 396–397 Learning Objective: Describe the factors to consider in responding to a robbery-in-progress call.)

67. Define the elements of a takeover robbery, and explain why this type of robbery is so costly. (p. 393, Learning Objective: List the types of robbery in which the FBI and state officials become involved.)

68. Provide five to six examples of physical evidence that might be found at a robbery scene. (pp. 400–401, Learning Objective: Identify what physical evidence can link a suspect with a robbery.)

69. What issues should officers consider when dealing with the victims or witnesses of a robbery? (p. 398, Learning Objective: Explain the special challenges that are posed by a robbery investigation.)

70. What are the three main elements for the crime of robbery? For each element, provide examples of one or two questions that investigators should ask when interviewing the victim. (pp. 398–399, Learning Objective: Explain how to prove each element of robbery.)

BURGLARY

Test Bank

Chapter 13
Burglary

Multiple Choice

1. Most burglars are convicted on circumstantial evidence. For this reason,

   a. any physical evidence at the burglary scene is of the utmost importance.* (p. 418–419, Learning Objective: Describe what physical evidence is often found at a burglary scene.)
   b. officers should collect only the most critical evidence.
   c. officers should determine if fingerprints are available before working to process the crime scene.
   d. none of these choices.

2. A go-between who receives stolen goods for resale is called a

   a. broker.
   b. dealer.
   c. fence.* (p. 422, Learning Objective: Define the elements of the offense of receiving stolen goods.)
   d. pawn broker.

3. Most burglary laws increase the severity of the crime of burglary if the burglar possesses

   a. burglary tools.
   b. explosives or a weapon.* (p. 413, Learning Objective: Explain what determines the severity of a burglary.)
   c. gloves.
   d. police radio scanners.

4. The national burglary clearance rate is

   a. less than 13 percent.* (p. 415, Learning Objective: Identify the basic difference between burglary and robbery.)
   b. over 30 percent.
   c. nearly 66 percent.
   d. usually around 82 percent.

5. Which of the following is suggested as a strategy to prevent burglaries?

   a. Know where the nearest police department is located.
   b. Program all telephones in the building to speed-dial 911.
   c. Provide clearly visible addresses on stores and homes.* (pp. 422–423, Learning Objective: Describe what measures may be taken to prevent burglary.)
   d. All of these choices.

6. Burglary elements include the unlawful entry of a structure to commit

   a.   any crime.
   b.   a felony or theft.* (pp. 412–413, Learning Objective: Identify three elements that are present in laws defining burglary.)
   c.   a felony only.
   d.   a crime against property.

7. False alarms for burglary account for up to what percentage of all alarm calls?

   a.   50 percent
   b.   75 percent
   c.   90 percent
   d.   96 percent* (p. 415, Learning Objective: Explain how to proceed to a burglary scene and what to do on arrival.)

8. Most burglaries occur in

   a.   occupied homes.
   b.   occupied businesses.
   c.   unoccupied homes and businesses.* (p. 410, Learning Objective: Identify the basic difference between burglary and robbery.)
   d.   unoccupied businesses.

9. Which is *not* a common way of entering a safe?

   a.   punching
   b.   peeling
   c.   pounding* (p. 418, Learning Objective: Explain how safes are broken into.)
   d.   pulling

10. Breaking and entering is a form of which type of evidence?

   a.   presumptive* (p. 413, Learning Objective: Describe what additional elements can be included in burglary.)
   b.   circumstantial
   c.   physical
   d.   inadmissible

11. Modus operandi (MO) can be used in burglary cases to

   a.   identify individual burglary suspects.
   b.   determine, to some degree, that the same person is committing a series of burglaries.* (p. 420, Learning Objective: Identify what modus operandi factors are important in burglary.)
   c.   make arrests of suspects.
   d.   none of these choices.

12. Which of the following legitimate businesses should investigators partner with to search for stolen goods?

    a.   pawnshops
    b.   secondhand stores
    c.   flea markets
    d.   all of these choices* (p. 421, Learning Objective: Explain where to search for stolen property.)

13. A primary element of the crime of possession of burglary tools is

    a.   none of these choices.
    b.   both of these choices.
    c.   possession of any tool that could be used to commit burglary.
    d.   an intent to use a tool or permit its use to commit burglary.* (p. 414, Learning Objective: Identify the elements of the crime of possession of burglary tools.)

14. The main difference between burglary and robbery is that

    a.   robbery is committed in the daytime.
    b.   robbery is a crime against property.
    c.   burglary is a crime against property.* (p. 410, Learning Objective: Identify the basic difference between burglary and robbery.)
    d.   burglary is a crime against a person.

15. In some states, which of the following can be considered as structures in a commercial burglary?

    a.   cell phone towers
    b.   railroad cars* (p. 412, Learning Objective: Explain the two basic classifications of burglary.)
    c.   oil rigs
    d.   water towers

16. Which acronym refers to an aggressive form of verified response policy?

    a.   ECV* (p. 415, Learning Objective: Explain how to proceed to a burglary scene and what to do on arrival.)
    b.   NCIC
    c.   RxPATROL
    d.   CPTED

17. The most common method of entrance in burglary is

    a.   jimmying a door.* (p. 417, Learning Objective: Describe the most frequent means of entry to commit burglary.)
    b.   breaking a side or rear window.
    c.   entering through the roof.
    d.   tunneling in under walls.

18. Important evidence in a burglary is

    a. safe insulation.
    b. tool marks.
    c. paint chips.
    d. any of these choices.* (p. 419, Learning Objective: Describe what physical evidence is often found at a burglary scene.)

19. The term *target hardening* refers to

    a. accepting that fact that burglaries happen in all parts of the world.
    b. altering physical characteristics of a property to make it less vulnerable.* (p. 423, Learning Objective: Describe what measures may be taken to prevent burglary.)
    c. taking out additional insurance to cover losses in the event of a burglary.
    d. none of these choices.

20. Burglars seek to

    a. confront their victims directly and immediately.
    b. hide and then confront their victims after a period of time.
    c. avoid contact with victims.* (p. 410, Learning Objective: Identify the basic difference between burglary and robbery.)
    d. either confront their victims directly and immediately or hide and then confront their victims after a period of time, depending on the burglar.

21. Most amateur burglars are between the ages of

    a. 8 and 12.
    b. 15 and 25.* (p. 414, Learning Objective: Identify the elements of the crime of possession of burglary tools.)
    c. 13 and 19.
    d. There are no "amateur" burglars.

22. Intent to commit the crime is

    a. never an element of burglary.
    b. occasionally an element of burglary, depending on state laws.
    c. always an element of burglary.* (p. 412, Learning Objective: Identify three elements that are present in laws defining burglary.)
    d. an irrelevant, often peripheral element of burglary.

23. Which of the following is *not* an element of burglary under the routine activity theory?

    a. the presence of likely or motivated offenders
    b. poor economic conditions* (p. 411, Learning Objective: Identify three elements that are present in laws defining burglary.)
    c. the presence of suitable targets
    d. an absence of guardians to prevent the crime

24. Most burglars are convicted on _____ evidence.

    a. ex parte
    b. direct
    c. dissociate
    d. circumstantial* (p. 418, Learning Objective: Describe what physical evidence is often found at a burglary scene.)

25. CPTED is a procedure that relates to

    a. verified response policy
    b. punching a safe
    c. target hardening* (p. 423, Learning Objective: Describe what measures may be taken to prevent burglary.)
    d. hit-and-run burglary

True/False

26. Police do not need to obtain a search warrant before inspecting pawnshop records. (True, p. 421, Learning Objective: Explain where to search for stolen property.)

27. Research shows that premises that have previously been burglarized are likely to be burglarized again. (True, p. 422, Learning Objective: Describe what measures may be taken to prevent burglary.)

28. The fact that a buyer paid a very low price in comparison to an item's actual value can be used as evidence that the buyer knew the item was stolen or illegally obtained. (True, p. 422, Learning Objective: Define the elements of the offense of receiving stolen goods.)

29. DNA is not important in burglary investigations. (False, pp. 419–420, Learning Objective: Describe what physical evidence is often found at a burglary scene.)

30. Entering a safe using a sledge and chisels or other instrument to chop a hole in the bottom of a safe is called chopping. (True, p. 418, Learning Objective: Explain how safes are broken into.)

31. Professional residential burglars tend to operate solo, since this lessens the risk of getting caught. (False, p. 411, Learning Objective: Explain the two basic classifications of burglary.)

32. "Jimmying" is the most common method of entry to commit burglary. (True, p. 417, Learning Objective: Describe the most frequent means of entry to commit burglary.)

33. A *hit-and-run* burglary is the same as a *smash-and-grab* burglary. (True, p. 417, Learning Objective: Describe the most frequent means of entry to commit burglary.)

34. Many people, such as mechanics and carpenters, possess tools that might be used in a burglary, but use them for legitimate means. (True, p. 406) Learning Objective: Identify the elements of the crime of possession of burglary tools.)

35. A burglary is only classified as residential if the structure or dwelling entered is inhabited at the time of the burglary. (False, p. 414, Learning Objective: Explain the two basic classifications of burglary.)

36. In terms of classifying burglary, some state laws consider vehicles, trailers and railroad cars as commercial structures. (True, p. 412, Learning Objective: Explain the two basic classifications of burglary.)

37. An attempt to unlawfully enter a structure to commit a theft, even if unsuccessful, still counts as a burglary. (True, p. 410, Learning Objective: Define burglary.)

38. Residential burglaries are often committed by one or more juveniles or young adults who live in the same community. (True, p. 411, Learning Objective: Explain the two basic classifications of burglary.)

39. Most retail burglaries occur at night or on weekends. (True, p. 412, Learning Objective: Explain the two basic classifications of burglary.)

40. Some burglars steal just for the excitement of committing the crime and evading detection. (True, p. 414, Learning Objective: Identify the elements of the crime of possession of burglary tools.)

41. Burglars prefer corner homes that allow them to see people approaching from a variety of directions. (True, p. 416, Learning Objective: Explain how to proceed to a burglary scene and what to do on arrival.)

42. If other crimes are committed along with a burglary, the additional crimes are legally considered separate and must be proven separately. (True, p. 413, Learning Objective: Explain what determines the severity of a burglary.)

43. Profiling and mapping have no useful applications in burglary investigations. (False, p. 420, Learning Objective: Identify what modus operandi factors are important in burglary.)

44. The charge of receiving stolen goods can be used when possession of stolen items can be demonstrated but insufficient evidence exists to prove actual theft. (True, p. 422, Learning Objective: Define the elements of the offense of receiving stolen goods.)

45. A "slam puller" is a tool commonly used to pull a safe. (False, p. 414, Learning Objective: Identify the elements of the crime of possession of burglary tools.)

Completion

46. A _____ burglary is one that occurs in buildings, structures or attachments that are used as or are suitable for dwellings. (residential, p. 410, Learning Objective: Explain the two basic classifications of burglary.)

47. Breaking and entering is strong _____ evidence that a crime is intended, meaning that it provides a reasonable basis for belief that the crime was intended. (presumptive, p. 413, Learning Objective: Describe what additional elements can be included in burglary.)

48. The method that is opposite of pulling a safe is _____ a safe. (punching, p. 418, Learning Objective: Explain how safes are broken into.)

49. Burglary of a church would be considered a _____ burglary. (commercial, p. 412, Learning Objective: Explain the two basic classifications of burglary.)

50. Burglars can use a code _____ to duplicate the electronic signal emitted from an automatic garage door opener. (grabber, p. 417, Learning Objective: Describe the most frequent means of entry to commit burglary.)

51. The type of burglary in which a window is broken and items taken from the other side is known as a _____-and-grab burglary. (smash, p. 417, Learning Objective: Identify three elements that are present in laws defining burglary.)

52. A pattern of burglaries appearing in a cluster are one element of a(n) _____ that may indicate that the same burglar is responsible for the crimes. (modus operandi, p. 420, Learning Objective: Identify what modus operandi factors are important in burglary.)

53. The _____ of property stolen does not determine the severity of a burglary. (value, p. 413, Learning Objective: Explain what determines the severity of a burglary.)

54. The word *burglar* comes from the German words _____ (meaning "house") and _____ (meaning "thief"). (*burg, laron*, p. 409, Learning Objective: Define burglary.)

55. Many cities have established _____ operations to catch individuals who purchase stolen goods for resale. (sting, p. 422, Learning Objective: Define the elements of the offense of receiving stolen goods.)

Short Answer

56. Why is the collection of DNA at burglary scenes an increasing priority for law enforcement? (pp. 419–420, Learning Objective: Describe what physical evidence is often found at a burglary scene.)

57. Outline the elements of the crime of burglary. (p. 412, Learning Objective: Explain the two basic classifications of burglary.)

58. What are some measures to enhance security in order to prevent burglary? (p. 423, Learning Objective: Describe what measures may be taken to prevent burglary.)

59. What are the elements of the offense of receiving stolen goods? (p. 422, Learning Objective: Define the elements of the offense of receiving stolen goods.)

60. Define what it means to "enter a structure" in relation to burglary. (p. 412, Learning Objective: Identify three elements that are present in laws defining burglary.)

61. Describe what is involved in crime prevention through environmental design (CPTED). (p. 423, Learning Objective: Describe what measures may be taken to prevent burglary.)

62. Explain how burglary differs from robbery. (p. 410, Learning Objective: Identify the basic difference between burglary and robbery.)

63. Why is it important to record and describe the modus operandi of a burglary? (p. 420, Learning Objective: Identify what modus operandi factors are important in burglary.)

64. What do officers mean when they refer to a burglary as a "combination" safe job? (p. 416 Learning Objective: Explain how to proceed to a burglary scene and what to do on arrival.)

65. How does Enhanced Call Verification work? Why might some departments choose to adopt this program? (p. 415, Learning Objective: Explain how to proceed to a burglary scene and what to do on arrival.)

66. Choose two methods of entering a safe and describe the process and tools involved. (p. 418, Learning Objective: Explain how safes are broken into.)

67. Which areas of the crime scene should investigators process in a residential burglary? Provide examples. (p. 416, Learning Objective: Explain how to proceed to a burglary scene and what to do on arrival.)

68. What are the benefits of modern safes that are designed without spindles? (p. 418, Learning Objective: Explain how safes are broken into.)

69. What should officers do when they are responding to a burglary call? (pp. 414–415, Learning Objective: Explain how to proceed to a burglary scene and what to do on arrival.)

70. Describe the types of evidence found at a burglary involving a safe. (p. 419, Learning Objective: Describe what physical evidence is often found at a burglary scene.)

LARCENY/THEFT, FRAUD AND WHITE-COLLAR CRIME

Test Bank

Chapter 14
Larceny/Theft, Fraud and White-Collar Crime

Multiple Choice

1. The cost of insurance scams totals over _____ dollars a year.

   a. 100 million
   b. 25 billion
   c. 40 billion* (p. 443, Learning Objective: Discuss the common means of committing fraud.)
   d. 2 trillion

2. Thieves who go around neighborhoods targeting mailboxes with their flags up, searching for envelopes containing checks and other forms of payment, are referred to as

   a. taggers.
   b. flaggers.* (p. 433, Learning Objective: Define the common types of larceny.)
   c. flagellators.
   d. grabbers.

3. The greatest percentage of loss in the retail industry is due to

   a. bookkeeping or administrative errors.
   b. internal theft.* (p. 433, Learning Objective: Define the common types of larceny.)
   c. shoplifting.
   d. vendor fraud.

4. Most bicycle thefts are committed by

   a. juveniles.* (p. 432, Learning Objective: Define the common types of larceny.)
   b. professional bicycle theft rings.
   c. adult amateurs.
   d. solo professionals.

5. The primary motive for all types of larceny is usually

   a. spite.
   b. revenge.
   c. monetary gain.* (p. 429, Learning Objective: Differentiate larceny from burglary and robbery.)
   d. the excitement of stealing.

6. Theft may include all but which of the following?

    a. petty theft
    b. crimes against the person* (p. 429, Learning Objective: Differentiate larceny from burglary and robbery.)
    c. grand theft
    d. larceny

7. The telephone fraud that occurs when rates are increased without notification is

    a. cramming.
    b. fluffing.* (p. 444, Learning Objective: Discuss the common means of committing fraud.)
    c. gouging.
    d. slamming.

8. Altering the price on a garment in a store is considered

    a. embezzlement.
    b. fraud.
    c. larceny.* (p. 434, Learning Objective: Define the common types of larceny.)
    d. a gray-collar crime.

9. To prosecute for shoplifting, it is important to prove that the suspect

    a. left the store with the merchandise.
    b. knew the value of the merchandise.
    c. intended to steal the merchandise.* (p. 435, Learning Objective: Discuss whether a shoplifter must leave the premises before being apprehended.)
    d. left the store with the merchandise, knew the value of the merchandise, and intended to steal the merchandise.

10. Jewelry is most often stolen by

    a. juvenile amateurs.
    b. adult amateurs.
    c. professionals.* (p. 436, Learning Objective: Explain when the FBI would become involved in a larceny/theft investigation.)
    d. gang members.

11. In larceny/theft, what determines whether the offense is grand or petty?

    a. the amount* (p. 429, Learning Objective: Compare the two major categories of larceny and describe how to determine them.)
    b. a judge
    c. a jury
    d. the physical evidence

12. A term that refers to the unexplained or unauthorized loss of inventory, merchandise, cash or any other asset from a retail establishment due to employee theft, shoplifting, organized retail crime, administrative errors and vendor fraud is

    a. stop loss.
    b. shrinkage.* (p. 433, Learning Objective: Define the common types of larceny.)
    c. frommage.
    d. dark figure of inventory.

13. The telephone scam in which consumers are billed for unauthorized or misleading charges is

    a. cramming.* (p. 444, Learning Objective: Discuss the common means of committing fraud.)
    b. fluffing.
    c. gouging.
    d. slamming.

14. The number one consumer fraud complaint to the Federal Trade Commission in 2006 was

    a. insurance fraud.
    b. telemarketing fraud.
    c. identify theft.* (p. 448, Learning Objective: Describe what form of larceny/theft headed the FTC's top 10 consumer fraud complaints in 2006.)
    d. copyright violation.

15. Which of the following is *not* an element in check fraud?

    a. forgery
    b. issuing worthless checks
    c. issuing insufficient-fund checks
    d. using an access device* (p. 445, Learning Objective: Clarify the common types of check fraud.)

16. Larceny differs from robbery in that larceny

    a. is a misdemeanor.
    b. involves no force or threat of force.* (p. 429, Learning Objective: Differentiate larceny from burglary and robbery.)
    c. involves illegally entering a structure.
    d. has a monetary limit.

17. The title of the agency that deals with art theft is called NSAF, an acronym that stands for

    a. National Security Art File.
    b. National Safety Art File.
    c. National Scientific Art File.
    d. National Stolen Art File.* (p. 437, Learning Objective: Explain when the FBI would become involved in a larceny/theft investigation.)

18. The telephone scam in which companies charge undisclosed fees for calls made from pay phones or hotel rooms is

    a. cramming.
    b. fluffing.
    c. gouging.* (p. 444, Learning Objective: Discuss the common means of committing fraud.)
    d. slamming.

19. This refers to groups, gangs and sometimes individuals who are engaged in illegally obtaining merchandise through both theft and fraud as part of a commercial enterprise.

    a. organized retail crime (ORC)* (pp. 435–436, Learning Objective: Define the common types of larceny.)
    b. "shop till you drop" groups
    c. commercial robbery program (CRP)
    d. theft and robbery gangs (TRG)

20. Which of the following statements is true?

    a. Kiting is form of embezzlement.* (pp. 453–454, Learning Objective: Define white-collar crime and explain what offenses are often included in this crime category.)
    b. *Leakage* and *shrinkage* are interchangeable terms.
    c. Poachers who harvest cactus plants illegally are called burls.
    d. Looping is a method used in credit-card scams.

21. The third and final step of the money laundering cycle is

    a. integration.* (p. 453, Learning Objective: Define white-collar crime and explain what offenses are often included in this crime category.)
    b. placement.
    c. structuring.
    d. layering.

22. Victims of telemarketing fraud are most commonly

    a. middle-class.
    b. recently married.
    c. elderly.* (p. 434, Learning Objective: Discuss the common means of committing fraud.)
    d. immigrants.

23. Confidence people are known to take money from others using which of these schemes?

    a. phony home repairs* (p. 442, Learning Objective: Discuss the common means of committing fraud.)
    b. poaching
    c. property flipping
    d. all of these choices

24. Which section of the FBI is responsible for investigating Ponzi schemes?

    a.   JAG
    b.   DNR
    c.   NFCF
    d.   FCS* (p. 428, Learning Objective: Differentiate larceny from burglary and robbery.)

25. Which of the following statements regarding jurisdictional issues is *not* true?

    a.   The monetary value of the loss plays a role in determining who is assigned the case.
    b.   The monetary threshold for jewelry theft is $5,000.
    c.   The monetary threshold for art theft is $25,000.* (p. 456, Learning Objective: Explain how the monetary loss value of certain thefts, frauds or other economic crimes influences which agency has jurisdiction over a criminal investigation.)
    d.   Some crimes have no monetary threshold that must be exceeded before the federal government gains jurisdiction.

True/False

26. Shoplifting is the most frequently occurring type of larceny. (False, p. 431, Learning Objective: Differentiate larceny from burglary and robbery.)

27. To the experienced livestock person, brands are a readable language, read from left to right, top to bottom and outside to inside. (True, p. 438, Learning Objective: Define the common types of larceny.)

28. Changing the UPC bar code on merchandise so it rings up differently at checkout is commonly called bait and switch. (False, p. 435, Learning Objective: Define the common types of larceny.)

29. The term *numismatic theft* refers specifically to the theft of valuable ancient coins. (False, p. 437, Learning Objective: Define the common types of larceny.)

30. The theft of timber is no longer a problem because of strict environmental regulations and security measures taken by logging companies. (False, p. 438, Learning Objective: Define the common types of larceny.)

31. Boosting is the same thing as shoplifting. (True, p. 433, Learning Objective: Define the common types of larceny.)

32. Jamming, the unauthorized switch of a long-distance carrier, represents the fastest-growing category of complaint to the FCC. (False, p. 444, Learning Objective: Define what fraud is and how it differs from larceny/theft.)

33. Shrinkage refers to the explained loss of inventory, merchandise, cash or any other asset from a retail establishment. (False, p. 433, Learning Objective: Define the common types of larceny.)

34. In confidence games, the mark refers to the victim. (True, p. 441, Learning Objective: Define what fraud is and how it differs from larceny/theft.)

35. Theft of art objects is considered a major international criminal activity. (True, p. 437, Learning Objective: Explain when the FBI would become involved in a larceny/theft investigation.)

36. The most common type of insurance fraud is the creation of bogus insurance schemes in which con artists collect premiums for policies that do not exist. (False, p. 443, Learning Objective: Discuss the common means of committing fraud.)

37. Simply walking out of the store without paying for an item in one's possession is not shoplifting. (True, p. 435, Learning Objective: Discuss whether a shoplifter must leave the premises before being apprehended.)

38. Bicycle thefts are difficult to investigate because thieves can ride the bikes into areas that patrol cars cannot go. (False, p. 432, Learning Objective: Define the common types of larceny.)

39. Farmers create a market for stolen pesticides and herbicides by purchasing them at reduced rates. (True, p. 439, Learning Objective: Define the common types of larceny.)

40. Common equity skimming schemes involve use of shell companies, corporate identity theft and use of bankruptcy/foreclosure to dupe homeowners and investors. (True, p. 442, Learning Objective: Discuss the common means of committing fraud.)

41. The FBI has jurisdiction in jewel thefts in which the jewels are moved intrastate. (False, p. 437, Learning Objective: Explain when the FBI would become involved in a larceny/theft investigation.)

42. Altering the price of an item is considered shoplifting. (True, p. 434, Learning Objective: Define the common types of larceny.)

43. Purse snatching, pocket picking, theft from coin machines, shoplifting, bicycle theft, theft from motor vehicles, theft from buildings, theft of motor vehicle accessories and jewelry theft are all types of larceny/theft. (True, p. 431, Learning Objective: Define the common types of larceny.)

44. Embezzlement is the fraudulent appropriation of property by a person to whom it has been entrusted. (True, p. 453, Learning Objective: Define white-collar crime and explain what offenses are often included in this crime category.)

45. Shoplifting accounts for more store losses than employee theft. (False, p. 433, Learning Objective: Discuss whether a shoplifter must leave the premises before being apprehended.)

Completion

46. Cattle are ear marked and _____ marked, commonly with a knife, according to branding protocol. (wattle, p. 438, Learning Objective: Define the common types of larceny.)

47. The phrase "goods or property" refers to all forms of _____ property, real or personal. (tangible, p. 429, Learning Objective: Describe the elements of larceny/theft.)

48. The _____ -release limit is the maximum dollar amount that may be paid with a charge or credit card without getting authorization from the central office. (floor, p. 447, Learning Objective: Discuss the common means of committing fraud.)

49. Structuring, or _____, is a method of avoiding federal reporting requirements by breaking large amounts of cash into increments of less than $10,000. (smurfing, p. 453, Learning Objective: Define white-collar crime and explain what offenses are often included in this crime category.)

50. Prosecution tactics in which civil and criminal sanctions are pursued at the same time are known as _____ proceedings. (parallel, p. 456, Learning Objective: Define white-collar crime and explain what offenses are often included in this crime category.)

51. _____ is a term used to describe the activity of individuals who pretend to be what they are not. (Fraud, p. 441, Learning Objective: Discuss the common means of committing fraud.)

52. The _____ value at the time of the theft is generally used to determine value of property stolen. (market, p. 429, Learning Objective: Compare the two major categories of larceny and describe how to determine them.)

53. _____ is one of the basic elements of check fraud. (Forgery, p. 446, Learning Objective: Clarify the common types of check fraud.)

54. When any credit card transaction must be checked, regardless of the amount of the purchase, the policy is called _____. (zero floor release, p. 447 Learning Objective: Discuss the common means of committing fraud.)

55. Shoplifting, also known as _____, involves taking items from retail stores without paying for them. (boosting, p. 433, Learning Objective: Discuss whether a shoplifter must leave the premises before being apprehended.)

Short Answer

56. Describe the three steps of the money laundering cycle. (p. 453, Learning Objective: Define white-collar crime and explain what offenses are often included in this crime category.)

57. What are the main problems in investigating environmental crimes? (p. 455, Learning Objective: Describe the main problems in prosecuting environmental crime.)

58. Explain the difference between short-con games and long-con games, and give examples of each. (p. 441, Learning Objective: Discuss the common means of committing fraud.)

59. What are the elements of the crime of larceny by debit or credit card? (p. 447, Learning Objective: Explain what the elements of the crime of larceny by debit or credit card are.)

60. Why would the FBI become involved in larceny/theft, fraud, white-collar and environmental crime cases? (p. 428, Learning Objective: Differentiate larceny from burglary and robbery.)

61. Describe the law concerning found property. (p. 430, Learning Objective: Describe what legally must be done with found property.)

62. How does the text define identify theft? (pp. 447–448, Learning Objective: Describe what form of larceny/theft headed the FTC's top 10 consumer fraud complaints in 2006.)

63. What legislation made identify theft a federal crime, and why? (p. 448, Learning Objective: Describe what form of larceny/theft headed the FTC's top 10 consumer fraud complaints in 2006.)

64. Outline five forms of white-collar or economic crime. (p. 451, Learning Objective: Define white-collar crime and explain what offenses are often included in this crime category.)

65. Explain how larceny differs from burglary and robbery. What elements, if any, do these crimes have in common? (pp. 429–430, Learning Objective: Differentiate larceny from burglary and robbery.)

66. Compare the two major categories of larceny and theft and describe how to determine them, giving an example for each category. (p. 430, Learning Objective: Compare the two major categories of larceny and describe how to determine them.)

67. Outline the FBI's two-pronged approach to investigating money laundering. (p. 453, Learning Objective: Discuss the FBI's two-pronged approach to investigating money laundering.)

68. Define fraud. How does it differ from theft? (p. 441, Learning Objective: Define what fraud is and how it differs from larceny/theft.)

69. Outline the three main criteria for an object to be eligible for entry into the NSAF. (p. 437, Learning Objective: Explain when the FBI would become involved in a larceny/theft investigation.)

70. Describe some of the investigative challenges of cargo thefts and "leakage." (pp. 439–440, Learning Objective: Define the common types of larceny.)

MOTOR VEHICLE THEFT

Test Bank

Chapter 15
Motor Vehicle Theft

Multiple Choice

1. With this type of system, the engine recognizes only the preprogrammed key(s) assigned to the car.

   a. immobilizer system* (p. 476, Learning Objective: Discuss how to help prevent motor vehicle theft.)
   b. panic alarm
   c. stop-and-go system
   d. GPS system

2. Which of the following agencies cooperates with the police in motor vehicle theft?

   a. FTA
   b. NICB* (p. 471, Learning Objective: Identify what two agencies can help investigate motor vehicle theft.)
   c. GMC
   d. none of these choices

3. Which of the following is a type of physical evidence that officers should search for in a vehicle theft case?

   a. latent prints
   b. accident damage
   c. evidence that rake and pick guns were used
   d. all of these choices* (p. 470, Learning Objective: Discuss why false reports of auto theft are sometimes made.)

4. In order to rule out the possibility of a false report of vehicle theft, officers should check to see if

   a. the vehicle was reclaimed by a loan company.
   b. the vehicle was reported stolen because someone wanted to provide an alibi for crashing the car or being late to an appointment.
   c. the vehicle was accidentally misplaced in a parking lot.
   d. all of these choices.* (p. 470, Learning Objective: Discuss why false reports of auto theft are sometimes made.)

5. A crime in which a stolen vehicle assumes the identity of a legally owned, or nonstolen, vehicle of a similar make and model is called

   a. counterfeiting.
   b. vehicle cloning.* (p. 470, Learning Objective: Discuss why false reports of auto theft are sometimes made.)
   c. strip and ship.
   d. invisible theft.

6. What does NCIC stand for?

    a. National Criminal Information Commission
    b. National Cooperative Information Commission
    c. National Crime Information Center* (p. 471, Learning Objective: Identify what two agencies can help investigate motor vehicle theft.)
    d. National Car and Identity Center

7. When the police use a car to try to trap a car theft suspect by placing it in a high crime area, the vehicle is called a _____ car.

    a. hot
    b. decoy
    c. bait* (p. 474, Learning Objective: Describe how to improve effectiveness in recognizing stolen vehicles.)
    d. gotcha

8. A juvenile or young person who takes a car for some "thrills or excitement" may be guilty of

    a. carjacking.
    b. joyriding.* (p. 466, Learning Objective: Identify the six major categories of motor vehicle theft.)
    c. aggravated car theft.
    d. petite theft.

9. Which of the following is *not* recommended as a way to improve an officer's ability to recognize stolen vehicles?

    a. Keep a "hot sheet" in the car.
    b. Learn the common characteristics of stolen vehicles.
    c. Frequently drive through the poorest neighborhoods.* (pp. 471–472, Learning Objective: Describe how to improve effectiveness in recognizing stolen vehicles.)
    d. Take time to check suspicious persons and vehicles.

10. The VIN of an automobile is

    a. always the same as the EN number.
    b. the registration number.
    c. chosen by the owner as a personal identifying feature.
    d. an unduplicated number assigned to a motor vehicle by the manufacturer.* (p. 465, Learning Objective: Explain what a VIN is and why it is important.)

11. For purposes of theft, the definition of a motor vehicle includes which of the following?

    a. homemade motor vehicles, such as kit cars* (p. 468, Learning Objective: Discuss the elements of the crime of unauthorized use of a motor vehicle.)
    b. hang-gliders
    c. sailboats
    d. remote-controlled vehicles

12. A possible indication of a stolen vehicle might include which of the following?

    a. a single plate on a car that requires two plates
    b. dirty plates on a clean car
    c. a sloppily applied dealer's sticker
    d. all of these choices* (p. 472, Learning Objective: Describe how to improve effectiveness in recognizing stolen vehicles.)

13. Someone who needs an alibi or a cover-up for an accident or even for misplacing the car may

    a. call the police and confess.
    b. steal a car.
    c. deface their own car.
    d. file a false police report.* (p. 469, Learning Objective: Discuss why false reports of auto theft are sometimes made.)

14. If an officer stops a vehicle, what might suggest that the car is stolen?

    a. hesitation in answering the officer's questions
    b. all of these choices* (p. 472, Learning Objective: Describe how to improve effectiveness in recognizing stolen vehicles.)
    c. over-politeness
    d. nervousness

15. The profit on stripped auto parts and accessories is

    a. extremely low.
    b. fairly low.
    c. moderate.
    d. extremely high.* (p. 467, Learning Objective: Identify the six major categories of motor vehicle theft.)

16. A business that takes stolen cars apart to sell the parts for a profit is known as a

    a. strip-and-peel shop.
    b. chop shop.* (p. 467, Learning Objective: Identify the six major categories of motor vehicle theft.)
    c. midnight auto supply.
    d. shake and bake.

17. The NICB Web site suggests a four-layered approach to combat auto theft: common sense, visible and audible warning devices, immobilizing devices and what?

    a. slide-lock devices
    b. tinted windows
    c. tracing devices* (p. 476, Learning Objective: Discuss how to help prevent motor vehicle theft.)
    d. self-deflating tires

18. The most important means of identifying an automobile is its

    a.   title and registration.
    b.   license plates.
    c.   VIN.* (p. 465, Learning Objective: Explain what a VIN is and why it is important.)
    d.   make and model.

19. Transporting a stolen vehicle across state lines is a violation of what act?

    a.   Harrison Act
    b.   Wickersham Act
    c.   Mann Act
    d.   Dyer Act* (p. 469, Learning Objective: Explain how the Dyer Act assists in motor vehicle theft investigations.)

20. What is the name of the program instituted in New York City that gives the police permission to stop any vehicle being driven between 1 A.M. and 5 A.M. if the vehicle has a sticker indicating that the owner of the vehicle participates in this program?

    a.   HEAT
    b.   CAT* (pp. 473–474, Learning Objective: Describe how to improve effectiveness in recognizing stolen vehicles.)
    c.   ATTF
    d.   NVIP

21. The elements of motor vehicle theft are

    a.   intentionally taking or driving a motor vehicle without the consent of the owner or the owner's authorized agent.* (p. 468, Learning Objective: Discuss the elements of the crime of unauthorized use of a motor vehicle.)
    b.   taking a motor vehicle from the owner with the intent to sell or remove the vehicle.
    c.   taking an automobile with the intent to sell the automobile.
    d.   joyriding for pleasure or for criminal activity.

22. Legitimate ownership of a motor vehicle exists when the vehicle is any but which of the following?

    a.   owned by a private person or company
    b.   being sold by an authorized dealership
    c.   in the factory being manufactured
    d.   being loaned to another* (p. 468, Learning Objective: Discuss the elements of the crime of unauthorized use of a motor vehicle.)

23. Motor vehicle thefts are often associated with

    a. organized crime rings.
    b. joyriding, transportation, commission of another crime, stripping vehicles for parts and accessories or reselling vehicles for profit.* (pp. 465–468, Learning Objective: Identify the six major categories of motor vehicle theft.)
    c. cars, trucks, construction equipment and even recreational equipment.
    d. carjacking, robbery, getaway cars and car bombings.

24. The state with the most auto thefts is currently

    a. New York.
    b. New Jersey.
    c. Texas.
    d. California.* (p. 464, Learning Objective: Explain what a VIN is and why it is important.)

25. Most stolen vehicles are recovered within how many hours?

    a. 2
    b. 10
    c. 24
    d. 48* (p. 472, Learning Objective: Describe how to improve effectiveness in recognizing stolen vehicles.)

True/False

26. Installing brighter lights in areas where cars are parked has been successfully used to combat auto theft. (True, p. 473, Learning Objective: Discuss how to help prevent motor vehicle theft.)

27. K-9 vehicles are much more likely to be stolen than other police vehicles. (False, p. 475, Learning Objective: Discuss how to help prevent motor vehicle theft.)

28. Construction equipment is rarely stolen. (False, p. 476, Learning Objective: Discuss how to help prevent motor vehicle theft.)

29. Snowmobiles do not generally have specific identification numbers. (False, p. 478, Learning Objective: Discuss how to help prevent motor vehicle theft.)

30. One method of improving an officer's ability to find stolen motor vehicles is by developing a checking system to rapidly determine whether a suspicious vehicle is stolen. (True, p. 471, Learning Objective: Describe how to improve effectiveness in recognizing stolen vehicles.)

31. One characteristic of a stolen vehicle is that it has only one license plate when two are required. (True, p. 472, Learning Objective: Describe how to improve effectiveness in recognizing stolen vehicles.)

32. Most motor vehicle thefts are local problems involving locally stolen and recovered vehicles. (True, p. 472, Learning Objective: Describe how to improve effectiveness in recognizing stolen vehicles.)

33. The Dyer Act made vehicle theft a federal crime. (False, p. 469, Learning Objective: Explain how the Dyer Act assists in motor vehicle theft investigations.)

34. The secure-idle system is a means of preventing the theft of construction vehicles. (False, p. 475, Learning Objective: Discuss how to help prevent motor vehicle theft.)

35. The VIN for each vehicle contains information on the assembly plant where the vehicle was made. (True, p. 465, Learning Objective: Explain what a VIN is and why it is important.)

36. A motor vehicle includes any self-propelled devices for moving people or property or for pulling implements, whether operated on land, in the water or in the air. (True, p. 468, Learning Objective: Explain what types of vehicles are considered "motor vehicles.")

37. A stolen vehicle driven by a criminal is more likely to be involved in a motor vehicle crash. (True, p. 466, Learning Objective: Identify the six major categories of motor vehicle theft.)

38. There is a specific meaning, other than as an identifier for a specific vehicle, for each of the digits in a VIN. (True, p. 465, Learning Objective: Explain what a VIN is and why it is important.)

39. A large market exists for stolen airbags. (True, p. 467, Learning Objective: Identify the six major categories of motor vehicle theft.)

40. The Honda Accord is currently the most stolen auto in the United States. (True, p. 464, Learning Objective: Explain what a VIN is and why it is important.)

41. A vehicle stolen for joyriding is generally kept longer than one stolen for transportation. (False, p. 466, Learning Objective: Identify the six major categories of motor vehicle theft.)

42. The NICB serves as a clearinghouse for information on stolen cars. (True, p. 471, Learning Objective: Explain what a VIN is and why it is important.)

43. Vehicle insurance fraud is a major economic crime that affects every premium payer through increased insurance rates. (True, p. 470, Learning Objective: Define embezzlement of a motor vehicle.)

44. Trucks and trailers are generally stolen by professional thieves. (True, p. 476, Learning Objective: Discuss how to help prevent motor vehicle theft.)

45. High-end luxury cars are the usual targets of cloning. Escalades, Lexus RX 300s, Z4s and BMW 5 Series are among the models most widely reported as cloned by local detectives (True, p. 470, Learning Objective: Define embezzlement of a motor vehicle.)

Completion

46. Setting up a _____ operation is one method of combating motor vehicle theft. (sting, p. 473, Learning Objective: Describe how to improve effectiveness in recognizing stolen vehicles.)

47. VIN stands for _____. (vehicle identification number, p. 465, Learning Objective: Explain what a VIN is and why it is important.)

48. NICB stands for National _____ Crime Bureau. (Insurance, p. 471, Learning Objective: Explain what a VIN is and why it is important.)

49. A(n) _____ shop may help vehicle owners dispose of a car for insurance fraud purposes. (chop, p. 467, Learning Objective: Identify the six major categories of motor vehicle theft.)

50. If someone answers an ad in the newspaper for a particular car for sale, takes the car for a test drive and never returns it, it is considered a case of motor vehicle _____. (embezzlement, pp. 467–468, Learning Objective: Define embezzlement of a motor vehicle.)

51. No two VINs are _____. (identical, p. 465, Learning Objective: Explain what a VIN is and why it is important.)

52. A(n) _____ is generally a youth who takes a motor vehicle for only temporary use. (joyrider, p. 466, Learning Objective: Identify the six major categories of motor vehicle theft.)

53. The National Motor Vehicle Theft Act is also known as the _____ Act. (Dyer, p. 469, Learning Objective: Explain how the Dyer Act assists in motor vehicle theft investigations.)

54. Some _____ cars are equipped with telematic technology, which enables the transfer of information between the car and a remote computer. (bait, p. 474, Learning Objective: Describe how to improve effectiveness in recognizing stolen vehicles.)

55. The Dyer Act was amended in 1945 to include _____. (aircraft, p. 469, Learning Objective: Explain how the Dyer Act assists in motor vehicle theft investigations.)

Short Answer

56. Explain how vehicle cloning is carried out, who the typical perpetrators are and how this crime may be linked to other crimes. (pp. 470–471) Learning Objective: Define embezzlement of a motor vehicle.)

57. What are the six major categories of motor vehicle theft? (p. 465, Learning Objective: Identify the six major categories of motor vehicle theft.)

58. How does PlateScan work? (p. 474, Learning Objective: Describe how to improve effectiveness in recognizing stolen vehicles.)

59. Why would someone file a false vehicle theft report? (p. 469, Learning Objective: Discuss why false reports of auto theft are sometimes made.)

60. What is the purpose of the Dyer Act? (p. 469, Learning Objective: Explain how the Dyer Act assists in motor vehicle theft investigations.)

61. What are some of the red flags that might indicate theft of construction and agricultural vehicles? Give an example from each of the following categories outlined by the National Equipment Register (NER): transport; use and location; equipment and markings; and price. (p. 477, Learning Objective: Discuss how to help prevent motor vehicle theft.)

62. Describe the elements of the crime of interstate transportation of a motor vehicle. (p. 469, Learning Objective: Discuss why false reports of auto theft are sometimes made.)

63. Discuss the vulnerability of police cars to theft. What are some of the primary concerns, and what technological innovations have been employed to prevent the theft of patrol cars? (p. 475, Learning Objective: Describe how to improve effectiveness in recognizing stolen vehicles.)

64. What two agencies can help investigate motor vehicle theft, and what does each agency offer in terms of assistance? (p. 471, Learning Objective: Identify what two agencies can help investigate motor vehicle theft.)

65. What are some of the characteristics of the driver of a stolen vehicle? (p. 472, Learning Objective: Describe how to improve effectiveness in recognizing stolen vehicles.)

66. Why are trucks, trailers, construction vehicles and construction equipment stolen? What are some of the most commonly stolen pieces of equipment in these categories? (pp. 476–477, Learning Objective: Discuss how to help prevent motor vehicle theft.)

67. List and explain the steps you would take and the questions you would ask when questioning the driver of a vehicle you suspect is stolen. (p. 472, Learning Objective: Describe how to improve effectiveness in recognizing stolen vehicles.)

68. How is the routine activity approach applied to motor vehicle theft? (p. 474, Learning Objective: Describe how to improve effectiveness in recognizing stolen vehicles.)

69. What types of information can you learn from a VIN, and how would this information verify that the VIN on the car belongs on the car you are examining? (p. 465, Learning Objective: Explain what a VIN is and why it is important.)

70. What kinds of strategies have police departments developed to combat auto theft? (p. 473, Learning Objective: Describe how to improve effectiveness in recognizing stolen vehicles.)

ARSON, BOMBS AND EXPLOSIVES

Test Bank

Chapter 16
Arson, Bombs and Explosives

Multiple Choice

1. Alligatoring is

    a. the checking of charred wood.* (p. 492, Learning Objective: Describe common burn indicators.)
    b. the formation of irregular cracks in glass due to heat.
    c. the charring of just the surface of wood.
    d. a sure sign of arson.

2. The majority of automobile fires are

    a. accidental.
    b. arson.* (pp. 496–497, Learning Objective: Make a checklist of what to look for when investigating suspected arson of a vehicle.)
    c. natural.
    d. of undetermined cause.

3. Arson is a

    a. Part One Index crime.* (p. 483, Learning Objective: Describe how fires are classified.)
    b. Part Two Index crime.
    c. Part Three Index crime.
    d. misdemeanor.

4. The fire triangle consists of which of the following three elements?

    a. oxygen, fire and heat
    b. fuel, heat and warmth
    c. wood, warmth and fire
    d. air, fuel and heat* (p. 491, Learning Objective: Explain what the fire triangle is and why it is important in arson investigations.)

5. Private insurance investigators

    a. interfere with law enforcement and fire investigations and should be kept away.
    b. are supportive but not helpful.
    c. can assist fire and police efforts in investigating fire losses.* (p. 489, Learning Objective: Explain who is responsible for detecting and investigating arson.)
    d. can offer bounties on arsonists.

6. Blue smoke results from the burning of which of the following?

   a.   alcohol* (p. 493, Learning Objective: Explain how fires normally burn.)
   b.   vegetable compounds
   c.   sulfur or nitric acid
   d.   none of these choices

7. Fires are classified as all but which of the following?

   a.   natural or accidental
   b.   criminal or accidental
   c.   suspicious or of unknown origin
   d.   natural and technological* (p. 484, Learning Objective: Describe how fires are classified.)

8. Crazing is

   a.   the checking of charred wood.
   b.   the formation of irregular cracks in glass due to heat.* (p. 492, Learning Objective: Describe common burn indicators.)
   c.   how deeply the wood is burned.
   d.   burnt glass.

9. If a bomb is found, the most important rule in handling the suspect package is to

   a.   get the package submerged in water as quickly as possible.
   b.   wear bomb-proof gloves when removing the package from the scene.
   c.   not touch the package.* (p. 499, Learning Objective: Identify what to pay special attention to when investigating explosions and bombings.)
   d.   have at least three officers surround the package and cover it gently with a bomb-resistant tarp.

10. The purpose of the law enforcement officer in an arson investigation is to

   a.   support the fire officer with the investigation.
   b.   provide protection for the fire officer.
   c.   assist with the criminal investigation.
   d.   work cooperatively with the fire officer to handle the criminal part of the investigation.* (pp. 487–489, Learning Objective: Explain who is responsible for detecting and investigating arson.)

11. What resource has become increasingly useful in bomb detection and in searches for evidence following explosions and has been in constant demand since 9/11?

   a.   field deployable electronic sensors
   b.   K-9s* (p. 499, Learning Objective: Identify what to pay special attention to when investigating explosions and bombings.)
   c.   electronic "sniffers"
   d.   robots

12. Which of the following statements is *not* true?

    a. More than one point of origin indicates arson.
    b. Fires normally burn outward.* (p. 493, Learning Objective: Describe how to determine a fire's point of origin. and DYK: Explain how fires normally burn.)
    c. The point of origin is established by finding the area with the deepest char.
    d. Fires are drawn toward ventilation and follow fuel paths.

13. Yellow or brownish smoke results from the burning of which of the following?

    a.   alcohol
    b.   petroleum
    c.   sulfur, nitric acid or hydrochloric acid* (p. 493, Learning Objective: Explain how fires normally burn.)
    d.   drugs

14. Which of the following is *not* one of the five classes of explosive incidents in the United States?

    a.   terrorist or extreme activity
    b.   emotionally disturbed persons
    c.   revenge and/or protest* (p. 497, Learning Objective: Identify what to pay special attention to when investigating explosions and bombings.)
    d.   recovered military ordnance or commercial explosives

15. A disrupter is

    a.   another term used to describe an arsonist.
    b.   someone who accidentally disturbs the scene of an arson fire.
    c.   a device that uses gunpowder to fire a jet of water into an explosive with the intent of making it safe.* (p. 500, Learning Objective: Identify what to pay special attention to when investigating explosions and bombings.)
    d.   a common type of igniter used to start fires.

16. Which of the following agencies or groups is *not* among the common partners in an arson investigation?

    a.   the news media
    b.   ATF
    c.   AIT* (p. 489, Learning Objective: Explain who is responsible for detecting and investigating arson.)
    d.   insurance companies

17. Female arsonists usually burn

    a.   the property of strangers.
    b.   the property of someone known to them.
    c.   their own property.* (p. 486, Learning Objective: Detail what degrees of arson the Model Arson Law establishes.)
    d.   another female's property.

18. Preparing to burn a building without actually doing so is _____ arson.

    a. aggravated
    b. second-degree
    c. simple
    d. attempted* (p. 486, Learning Objective: Define aggravated and simple arson.)

19. Which is *not* one of the fire department's basic roles?

    a. fire investigation
    b. arson detection
    c. arson investigation* (p. 488, Learning Objective: Explain who is responsible for detecting and investigating arson.)
    d. determining the cause of a fire

20. Which of the following is *not* part of the initial procedure that officers should take when responding to a bomb threat?

    a. Ensure that a search for secondary explosive devices has been conducted.
    b. Establish procedures to document personnel entering and exiting the scene.
    c. Ensure that the scene has been secured.
    d. Ensure that a search warrant has been procured in order to execute a full search of the premises.* (p. 500, Learning Objective: Identify what to pay special attention to when investigating explosions and bombings.)

21. A sniffer is

    a. another term used when referring to a canine in a K-9 unit.
    b. a detection device that takes a sample of air and identifies the approximate quantities of explosive material in the sample.* (p. 500, Learning Objective: Identify what to pay special attention to when investigating explosions and bombings.)
    c. a detection device that takes a sample of air and identifies the quality of the smoke and what type of igniter was used to set the fire.
    d. none of these choices.

22. If a person dies in a fire set by an arsonist, the death is

    a. involuntary manslaughter.
    b. voluntary manslaughter.
    c. second-degree murder.
    d. first-degree murder.* (p. 486, Learning Objective: Define aggravated and simple arson.)

23. Pipe bombs, nail bombs and other bombs disguised to escape detection are referred to as

   a. local explosive devices (LEDs).
   b. disguised explosive devices (DEDs)
   c. improvised explosive devices (IEDs).* (p. 497, Learning Objective: Identify what to pay special attention to when investigating explosions and bombings.)
   d. dangerous explosive devices (DEDs).

24. A homemade explosive that Richard Reid, the "shoe bomber," carried aboard American Airlines Flight 63 from Paris to Miami in 2001 was made from

   a. dynamite.
   b. TATP or triacetone triperoxide.* (p. 498, Learning Objective: Identify what to pay special attention to when investigating explosions and bombings.)
   c. C-4 military explosive.
   d. 2-methyloctane.

25. Catalytic combustion detectors are

   a. the most common type of flammable vapor detector used by arson investigators.* (p. 491, Learning Objective: Identify what to pay special attention to when investigating explosions and bombings.)
   b. recently developed instruments for detecting the presence of an explosive bomb.
   c. a remote-controlled instrument for approaching and analyzing unknown explosive devices.
   d. none of these choices.

True/False

26. Arson fires usually show the same burn patterns as regular fires. (False, p. 493, Learning Objective: Explain how fires normally burn.)

27. Strikers start fires because of an irresistible urge or passion for fire. (False, p. 487, Learning Objective: Detail what degrees of arson the Model Arson Law establishes.)

28. Knowing the fire's point of origin is of little importance to an arson investigator. (False, pp. 492–493, Learning Objective: Describe how to determine a fire's point of origin.)

29. Evidence of accelerants is a primary form of physical evidence at an arson scene. (True, p. 491, Learning Objective: Discuss what accelerants are and which are most commonly used in arson.)

30. It is difficult to determine whether the victim is a suspect in arson cases. (True, p. 490, Learning Objective: Describe what special challenges exist in investigating arson.)

31. ATF is responsible for alcohol, tobacco, firearms and explosive investigations. (True, p. 489, Learning Objective: Explain who is responsible for detecting and investigating arson.)

32. Among children, fireplay involves malice and the intent to harm. (False, p. 486, Learning Objective: Detail what degrees of arson the Model Arson Law establishes.)

33. Female arsonists usually burn their own property rather than that of others. (True, p. 486, Learning Objective: Detail what degrees of arson the Model Arson Law establishes.)

34. Arson investigations are usually joint investigations involving both law enforcement and fire officers. (True, pp. 487–488, Learning Objective: Explain who is responsible for detecting and investigating arson.)

35. Fire marshals have extralegal powers to summon witnesses, subpoena records and take statements under oath that police officers do not have. (True, p. 488, Learning Objective: Explain who is responsible for detecting and investigating arson.)

36. A rapid, intensely hot fire results in small, flat alligatoring. (False, p. 492, Learning Objective: Describe common burn indicators.)

37. Arson is a combination of crimes against persons and property. (True, p. 483, Learning Objective: Describe how fires are classified.)

38. Juveniles have a higher rate of involvement in arson crimes than any other Index crime. (True, p. 486, Learning Objective: Detail what degrees of arson the Model Arson Law establishes.)

39. Large, rolling blisters indicate a slow, weak heat. (False, p. 492, Learning Objective: Describe common burn indicators.)

40. Arson has the highest clearance rate by arrest of all Index crimes. (False, p. 490, Learning Objective: Explain who is responsible for detecting and investigating arson.)

41. Matches, candles, lighters or chemical devices can all be used as accelerants. (False, p. 491, Learning Objective: Identify the common igniters that are used in arson.)

42. Black smoke results from the burning of petroleum. (True, p. 493, Learning Objective: Explain how fires normally burn.)

43. The most commonly used flammable liquid accelerant is gasoline. (True, p. 491, Learning Objective: Discuss what accelerants are and which are most commonly used in arson.)

44. The basic difference between aggravated and simple arson is that aggravated arson involves malicious intent. (False, pp. 485–486, Learning Objective: Define aggravated and simple arson.)

45. A fire caused by faulty wiring is classified as a natural fire. (False, p. 494, Learning Objective: Describe how fires are classified.)

Completion

46. White smoke results from the burning of _____. (vegetable matter, p. 493, Learning Objective: Explain how fires normally burn.)

47. A fire in which there is no evidence to indicate whether the fire was natural, accidental or incendiary is classified as a fire of _____ _____. (undetermined origin, p. 491, Learning Objective: Describe how fires are classified.)

48. The most common and accurate types of flammable vapor detectors used by arson investigators are _____ combustion detectors. (catalytic, p. 491, Learning Objective: Discuss what accelerants are and which are most commonly used in arson.)

49. The breaking off of surface pieces of concrete or brick due to intense heat is referred to as _____. (spalling, p. 492, Learning Objective: Describe common burn indicators.)

50. In arson cases, _____ is the prime element in the corpus delicti. (burning, p. 485, Learning Objective: Describe what factors indicate the likelihood of arson.)

51. Burn _____ are visible evidence of the effects of heating or partial burning. (indicators, p. 492, Learning Objective: Describe common burn indicators.)

52. Brown stains around a spall indicate use of a(n) _____. (accelerant, p. 492, Learning Objective: Describe common burn indicators.)

53. The boundary between charred and uncharred material is called a line of _____. (demarcation, p. 492, Learning Objective: Describe common burn indicators.)

54. A(n) _____ warrant is issued when it is necessary for a government agent to search a property to determine a fire's cause and origin. (administrative, pp. 495–496, Learning Objective: Discuss when administrative and criminal warrants are issued.)

55. _____ cocktails are one kind of explosive. (Molotov, p. 486, Learning Objective: Define aggravated and simple arson.)

Short Answer

56. Describe the two-part warrant process that is required by the U.S. Supreme Court for investigating fires involving crime. (pp. 495–496, Learning Objective: Explain when a warrant is needed for investigating a fire scene and identify the precedent case.)

57. Outline the elements of the crime of arson. (p. 485, Learning Objective: Identify the elements of arson.)

58. Why would an investigator use a K-9 in an arson investigation? (p. 494, Learning Objective: Describe what factors indicate the likelihood of arson.)

59. Why would an arson investigator interview a firefighter as part of the arson investigation? (p. 495, Learning Objective: Explain who is responsible for detecting and investigating arson.)

60. Summarize the Model Arson Law. (p. 486, Learning Objective: Detail what degrees of arson the Model Arson Law establishes.)

61. What is a striker? (p. 487, Learning Objective: Detail what degrees of arson the Model Arson Law establishes.)

62. When responding to a fire scene, what should an officer observe, note and record? (p. 490, Learning Objective: Describe what special challenges exist in investigating arson.)

63. Describe three special challenges to arson investigation. (p. 490, Learning Objective: Describe what special challenges exist in investigating arson.)

64. Explain the concept of the fire triangle. (p. 491, Learning Objective: Explain what the fire triangle is and why it is important in arson investigations.)

65. List the common motives for arson and explain how they help investigators locate suspects. (p. 487, Learning Objective: Detail what degrees of arson the Model Arson Law establishes.)

66. When investigating a case of arson, how does an officer uncover the burning pattern? (p. 493, Learning Objective: Explain how fires normally burn.)

67. Describe the difference between accelerants and igniters, and give three examples of each. (p. 491, Learning Objective: Discuss what accelerants are and which are most commonly used in arson and Learning Objective: Identify the common igniters that are used in arson.)

68. How should an officer investigate a vehicle fire? (pp. 496–497, Learning Objective: Make a checklist of what to look for when investigating suspected arson of a vehicle.)

69. Describe some of the recent technological innovations in bomb detection. (pp. 499–501, Learning Objective: Identify what to pay special attention to when investigating explosions and bombings.)

70. Why is it important to photograph and videotape an arson fire? (p. 494, Learning Objective: Describe what factors indicate the likelihood of arson.)

71. Describe how to find the point of origin in a fire and what it can reveal to the investigator. (pp. 492–493, Learning Objective: Describe how to determine a fire's point of origin.)

COMPUTER CRIME

Test Bank

Chapter 17
Computer Crime

Multiple Choice

1. What type of material should *not* be used when packaging electronic evidence?

    a. waxed paper
    b. cardboard
    c. plastic materials* (p. 532, Learning Objective: Explain how electronic evidence should be stored.)
    d. paper bags

2. A zombie is a

    a. certain type of computer virus.
    b. computer that has been rendered immobile by a virus.
    c. computer used by hackers to copy other computer programs.
    d. computer that has been taken over by another computer.* (p. 515, Learning Objective: Identify the two key characteristics of computer crime.)

3. A secretly attached program that monitors a computer system and waits for an error to occur so that the weakness may be exploited is called a

    a. shadow bomb.
    b. logic bomb.* (p. 514, Learning Objective: Identify the two key characteristics of computer crime.)
    c. super-program.
    d. turtle.

4. A virus attack may replace or destroy data on the computer's hard drive and

    a. identify bank accounts and financial records.
    b. leave a "back door" open for later entry.* (p. 517, Learning Objective: Identify the two key characteristics of computer crime.)
    c. obtain one's access codes.
    d. defraud the end user.

5. Port scanning is

    a. looking for access into a computer.* (p. 514, Learning Objective: Identify the two key characteristics of computer crime.)
    b. scanning for a portable computer that is using a wireless system.
    c. removing data.
    d. linking access codes.

6. Which of the following is *not* one of the three general categories of cyber-criminals?

    a.   crackers
    b.   vandals
    c.   criminals
    d.   IT professionals* (p. 535, Learning Objective: Explain how computer crime can be categorized.)

7. Which of the following statements about reshipper schemes is correct?

    a.   These schemes typically involve employees of the U.S. Postal Service, UPS, FedEx or other such businesses.
    b.   The masterminds of reshipper schemes often initiate contact with their victims in chat rooms.* (pp. 518–519, Learning Objective: Explain how computer crime can be categorized.)
    c.   Scam artists who organize these schemes are frequently charged with sabotage.
    d.   These schemes typically involve intercepting a computer being shipped, installing spyware and resending the computer to its final destination.

8. The USA PATRIOT Act, signed by President George W. Bush in 2001, grants

    a.   roving authority to the FBI and other law enforcement agents to serve orders on communications carriers.* (p. 537, Learning Objective: Describe what motivates different types of cybercriminals.)
    b.   total authority to the FBI for wiretapping the communication lines of any U.S. citizen.
    c.   total authority to the FBI to arrest any noncitizen who is under suspicion of using communication lines to plan a terrorist attack.
    d.   all of these choices.

9. NW3C stands for

    a.   North West Computer Crime Center.
    b.   National White Collar Crime Center.* (p. 511, Learning Objective: Identify the two key characteristics of computer crime.)
    c.   New West Crime Center Corporation.
    d.   none of these choices.

10. Which of the following statements is true?

    a.   A static IP address does not fluctuate and is thus more secure
    b.   A dynamic IP address fluctuates and is thus more secure.* (p. 515, Learning Objective: Identify the two key characteristics of computer crime.)
    c.   An ISP is a unique number, analogous to a phone number.
    d.   An IP address is directly linked to the location of the building where the computer can be found.

11. Theft of intellectual property

    a.   involves the theft of ideas, not property.

    b.   is hacking into a computer and stealing individual programs, not ideas.

    c.   involves the pirating of proprietary information and copyrighted material.* (p. 519, Learning Objective: Explain how computer crime can be categorized.)

    d.   only applies to written material.

12. Which of the following statements is *not* true?

    a.   A virus attack could lead to the hacking of evidence logs and hijacking of department reports.

    b.   Security of the police department's computers is basically a nonissue, because most police departments have highly trained computer specialists on staff.* (p. 537, Learning Objective: Describe what motivates different types of cybercriminals.)

    c.   Systems that control computer-aided dispatch, records management applications and offender databases should be a top priority for security.

    d.   Any computer in the department that is attached to a phone line is accessible by unauthorized people outside the department.

13. Computer evidence is

    a.   next to impossible to destroy.

    b.   destroyed only by fire or intense heat.

    c.   easy to destroy.* (p. 522, Learning Objective: Describe what forms electronic evidence and other computer crime evidence may take.)

    d.   preserved by magnetic fields.

14. Computer disks should be stored away from

    a.   strong light.

    b.   magnetic fields.

    c.   dust.

    d.   all of these choices.* (p. 533, Learning Objective: Explain how electronic evidence should be stored.)

15. Skimming is defined as

    a.   monitoring data traveling along a data network.

    b.   scavenging through a business's garbage looking for useful information.

    c.   exploiting the telephone system's vulnerabilities to acquire free access and usage in a dial-up Internet provider system.

    d.   a method in which a device is placed in a card reader to record sensitive information.* (p. 514, Learning Objective: Identify the two key characteristics of computer crime.)

16. Electronic evidence and other computer crime evidence may take the form of

    a.   printers and scanners.
    b.   VCRs and GPS devices.
    c.   telephones and fax machines.
    d.   all of these choices.* (pp. 526–527, Learning Objective: Describe what forms electronic evidence and other computer crime evidence may take.)

17. Intentionally destroying computer information, programs or hardware using a logic bomb is classified as

    a.   embezzlement.
    b.   espionage.
    c.   extortion.
    d.   sabotage.* (p. 514, Learning Objective: Identify the two key characteristics of computer crime.)

18. Which of the following specialists are frequently consulted in the team approach to investigating computer crime?

    a.   the victim who owns the equipment
    b.   database processing technicians
    c.   auditors
    d.   all of these choices* (p. 538, Learning Objective: Explain what approach is often required in investigating computer crime.)

19. What is the name for the process, often considered synonymous with phishing, that involves acquiring unauthorized access to a computer or network through a message using an IP address which appears to be from a trusted host, in an attempt to commit identity theft?

    a.   snarking
    b.   spoofing* (p. 519, Learning Objective: Explain how computer crime can be categorized.)
    c.   sniping
    d.   shadowing

20. Common protocol for processing a crime scene involving electronic evidence includes which of the following?

    a.   Photographing and diagramming the placement of all computer terminals.
    b.   Holding the IT staff in quarantine until reinforcements arrive.
    c.   Obtaining a search warrant.* (p. 523, Learning Objective: Describe the common protocol for processing a crime scene involving electronic evidence.)
    d.   Unplugging all computers, telephones and printers.

21. The biggest difference between traditional evidence and computer evidence is the latter's

    a.   electronic nature.
    b.   lack of availability.
    c.   storage on discs.
    d.   fragility.* (p. 522, Learning Objective: Describe the special challenges that are presented by computer-related crimes.)

22. Cybercrime is

    a.   a local problem.
    b.   a transnational problem.* (p. 511, Learning Objective: Identify the two key characteristics of computer crime.)
    c.   strictly a federal problem.
    d.   a minor problem when compared to the losses to the public caused by street crime.

23. Most computer crimes are

    a.   not reported.* (p. 520, Learning Objective: Describe the special challenges that are presented by computer-related crimes.)
    b.   reported in excessive amounts to local authorities.
    c.   reported frequently.
    d.   reported to the federal government.

24. A malicious program hidden inside an apparently harmless, legitimate program, intended to carry out unauthorized or illegal functions, is called a

    a.   salami slice.
    b.   logic bomb.
    c.   super-zapper.
    d.   Trojan horse.* (p. 514, Learning Objective: Identify the two key characteristics of computer crime.)

25. IC3 stands for

    a.   Internet Computer Three.
    b.   International Computer Classification Corporation.
    c.   Internet Crime Complaint Center.* (p. 511, Learning Objective: Identify the two key characteristics of computer crime.)
    d.   none of these choices.

True/False

26. An attempt to get victims to disclose personal, sensitive information such as passwords and bank account numbers is referred to as phishing. (True, p. 518, Learning Objective: Explain how computer crime can be categorized.)

27. Adware is a covert way to advertise on Web sites without having to pay a fee. (False, p. 514, Learning Objective: Identify the two key characteristics of computer crime.)

28. When removing a computer from a site, the first thing the investigator should do, for safety, is to turn the machine off and unplug the computer from the wall. (False, p. 529, Learning Objective: Identify different precautions you should take when handling PC media.)

29. Electronic evidence is fragile. (True, p. 522, Learning Objective: Describe the special challenges that are presented by computer-related crimes.)

30. Keystroke logging is a specific maneuver that initiates a "denial of service" attack. (False, p. 514, Learning Objective: Identify the two key characteristics of computer crime.)

31. The suffixes ".com," ".gov," and ".int" are common examples of an ISP. (False, p. 516, Learning Objective: Identify the two key characteristics of computer crime.)

32. The Privacy Protection Act establishes that investigators are allowed to seize drafts of newsletters or Web pages if there is reason to believe that the seizure is necessary in order to prevent death or serious bodily injury. (True, p. 534, Learning Objective: Discuss whether "deleted" data are really deleted.)

33. The terms *Internet* and *Web* are basically interchangeable. (False, p. 515, Learning Objective: Identify the two key characteristics of computer crime.)

34. Virus attacks rank as the most common crime against a computer. (True, p. 512, Learning Objective: Identify the two key characteristics of computer crime.)

35. Investigators do not need to be concerned that digital evidence may also contain physical evidence such as DNA, fingerprints or serology. (False, p. 527, Learning Objective: Describe what forms electronic evidence and other computer crime evidence may take.)

36. Most computer crimes are committed by insiders. (False, p. 535, Learning Objective: Explain whether most cybercrimes against businesses are committed by insiders or outsiders.)

37. Very few states have enacted computer crime statutes. (False, p. 537, Learning Objective: Explain what approach is often required in investigating computer crime.)

38. Unlike computer hard drives, the electronic memory devices within cell phones can be completely erased, leaving no possibility of retrieving deleted items. (False, p. 532, Learning Objective: Discuss whether "deleted" data are really deleted.)

39. Most computer crimes are not prosecuted. (True, p. 510, Learning Objective: Identify the two key characteristics of computer crime.)

40. Perverted Justice is an Internet-based organization that is committed to assisting victims of cybercrime. (False, p. 539, Learning Objective: Explain what approach is often required in investigating computer crime.)

41. A search warrant is not needed to search a computer connected to the Internet, because there is no expectation of privacy. (False, p. 526, Learning Objective: Discuss how an investigator with a search warrant should execute it in a computer crime investigation.)

42. Cybercriminals are solitary by nature and do not operate in groups. (False, p. 535, Learning Objective: Define how cybercriminals may be categorized.)

43. Cyberterrorism is a premeditated, politically motivated attack against information, computer systems, computer programs and data that results in violence against noncombatant targets. (True, p. 520, Learning Objective: Explain how computer crime can be categorized.)

44. Spyware is most commonly used to infiltrate national security systems, with the ultimate goal of disarming national defense systems. (False, p. 514, Learning Objective: Identify the two key characteristics of computer crime.)

45. Worms are more powerful and destructive than viruses. (True, p. 518, Learning Objective: Explain how computer crime can be categorized.)

Completion

46. The FBI defines computer crime as "that which involves the addition, deletion, change or theft of _____ from a computer." (information, p. 513, Learning Objective: Explain how computer crime can be categorized.)

47. Child pornography, fraud and gambling are examples of crimes in which the computer is used as a(n) _____. (tool, p. 517, Learning Objective: Explain how computer crime can be categorized.)

48. A computer program such as Internet Explorer that accesses and displays data from the Internet or other networks is called a(n) _____. (browser, p. 514, Learning Objective: Explain how computer crime can be categorized.)

49. Data _____ is the residual physical representation of data that have been erased. (remanence, p. 534, Learning Objective: Discuss whether "deleted" data are really deleted.)

50. _____ involves the hijacking of a domain name in order to redirect online traffic toward a bogus Web site. (Pharming, p. 519, Learning Objective: Explain how computer crime can be categorized.)

51. When UCE, also known as _____, is distributed on a massive scale with malicious or contentious content or with intent to defraud, it becomes criminal. (spam, p. 519, Learning Objective: Explain how computer crime can be categorized.)

52. Because successful criminal prosecution of intellectual property theft requires reliable investigative resources, the Cyber Division and the Intellectual Property Rights Division were created by the _____ to investigate intellectual property theft and fraud. (FBI, p. 519, Learning Objective: Explain how computer crime can be categorized.)

53. Most e-crimes are handled _____ without involving legal action or law enforcement. (internally, p. 520, Learning Objective: Describe the special challenges that are presented by computer-related crimes.)

54. _____ is any procedure used in cryptography to convert plain text into cipher-text to prevent anyone but the intended recipient from reading the data. (Encryption, p. 526, Learning Objective: Explain the basic tenet for first responders at a computer crime scene.)

55. Computer crimes can also include hidden messages or images, which may appear as an innocent cover message or picture. The Greek word for "hidden writing" refers to this process as _____. (steganography, p. 526, Learning Objective: Explain the basic tenet for first responders at a computer crime scene.)

Short Answer

56. Outline some examples of the type of computer crime evidence that may be found in an investigation. (p. 529, Learning Objective: Describe what forms electronic evidence and other computer crime evidence may take.)

57. Describe the three general categories of cybercriminals and their respective motivations. (p. 535, Learning Objective: Define how cybercriminals may be categorized.)

58. How can computer crimes be prevented? Who is primarily responsible for putting new policies into place? (pp. 540–541, Learning Objective: Discuss how computer crimes can be prevented.)

59. Discuss some of the difficulties in reporting, investigating and prosecuting Internet crimes that are transnational in scope. (pp. 522–523; Learning Objective: Describe the special challenges that are presented by computer-related crimes.)

60. Outline the NetSmartz program, including its mission and how it has been implemented. (p. 539, Learning Objective: Discuss how computer crimes can be prevented.)

61. Discuss some of the challenges of investigating a business environment versus a stand-alone computer. (p. 527, Learning Objective: Describe what forms electronic evidence and other computer crime evidence may take.)

62. List and briefly describe the various resources (agencies or organizations) available to help law enforcement investigate computer crimes. (p. 539, Learning Objective: Explain what approach is often required in investigating computer crime.)

63. What are the elements of common protocol for processing a crime scene involving electronic evidence? (pp. 523–524, Learning Objective: Describe the common protocol for processing a crime scene involving electronic evidence.)

64. What are some of the guidelines investigators must adhere to when dealing with physical evidence in a computer crime case? (pp. 527–530, Learning Objective: Identify different precautions you should take when handling PC media.)

65. What are some of the essential questions that investigators should ask when interviewing employees and staff at a business or organization that has been the victim of computer crime? (pp. 524-525, Learning Objective: Explain the basic tenet for first responders at a computer crime scene.)

66. How could the Privacy Protection Act (PPA) impact a computer crime investigation? What issues should be considered? (p. 534, Learning Objective: Explain whether most cybercrimes against businesses are committed by insiders or outsiders.)

67. Describe the basic elements of a "reshipper scheme." (pp. 518–519, Learning Objective: Explain how computer crime can be categorized.)

68. Explain why a business or organization might be reluctant to report a computer crime. (p. 520, Learning Objective: Describe the special challenges that are presented by computer-related crimes.)

69. Define the "ON/OFF rule" and explain why it is imperative in any cybercrime investigation. (p. 524, Learning Objective: Explain the basic tenet for first responders at a computer crime scene.)

70. What did the Supreme Court decide in the case of *Ashcroft v. Free Speech Coalition* (2002) where the issue involved the use of "virtual" child pornography? (pp. 522–523, Learning Objective: Describe the special challenges that are presented by computer-related crimes.)

A DUAL THREAT: DRUG-RELATED CRIME AND ORGANIZED CRIME

Test Bank

Chapter 18
A Dual Threat: Drug-Related Crime and Organized Crime

Multiple Choice

1. Using restrictive restraint devices and procedures, such as handcuffing subjects behind their back and placing them facedown, can lead to

   a. complaints of abuse.
   b. back injuries.
   c. positional asphyxia.* (p. 564, Learning Objective: Explain what the major legal evidence in prosecuting drug use and possession is.)
   d. loss of evidence.

2. Examples of physical evidence of possession or use of controlled substances include

   a. the drugs and the apparatus associated with their abuse.
   b. the suspect's appearance and behavior.
   c. blood and urine tests.
   d. all of these choices.* (p. 562, Learning Objective: Explain what the major legal evidence in prosecuting drug use and possession is.)

3. In a drug investigation, officers can avoid charges of entrapment by

   a. having a third party buy the drugs.
   b. making two or more buys.* (pp. 566–567, Learning Objective: Discuss what precautions to take in undercover drug buys and how to avoid a charge of entrapment.)
   c. making an immediate arrest that is witnessed.
   d. using marked buy money.

4. Drugs can be classified as

   a. depressants, stimulants, narcotics, hallucinogens, cannabis or inhalants.* (p. 551, Learning Objective: Explain how drugs are commonly classified.)
   b. street drugs, prescription drugs and designer drugs.
   c. uppers, downers and everything in between.
   d. depressants, stimulants and hallucinogens.

5. Which of the following is *not* a distinctive characteristic of organized crime?

   a. high-profit and continued-profit crimes
   b. definite organization and control
   c. strong ideological foundation* (p. 575, Learning Objective: Explain the distinctive characteristics of organized crime and its major activities.)
   d. protection through corruption

6. If an officer observes what appears to be a drug buy,

    a. the officer can make warrantless arrest if there is probable cause.* (p. 565, Learning Objective: Explain when an on-sight arrest can be made for a drug buy.)
    b. the officer needs to gather physical evidence from the scene before making an arrest.
    c. the officer must set up a buy in order to prove that a transfer of drugs has taken place.
    d. the officer should call for reinforcements immediately.

7. Drug addiction is

    a. a sudden disease.
    b. a progressive disease.* (p. 561, Learning Objective: Explain what the major legal evidence in prosecuting drug use and possession is.)
    c. fairly easy to cure once addicts admit they need help.
    d. not considered a disease.

8. Organized crime is *not* involved in which of the following victimless crimes?

    a. loan-sharking
    b. sports bribery
    c. employment of illegal aliens
    d. none of these choices* (p. 576, Learning Objective: Outline what crimes organized crime is typically involved in.)

9. Rohypnol is a

    a. narcotic.
    b. depressant.* (pp. 556–557, Learning Objective: Describe what drugs are most commonly observed on the street, in the possession of users and seized in drug raids, and what the most frequent drug arrest is.)
    c. hallucinogen.
    d. stimulant.

10. Barbiturates are classified as

    a. narcotics.
    b. depressants.* (p. 551, Learning Objective: Explain how drugs are commonly classified.)
    c. hallucinogens.
    d. stimulants.

11. Which of the following crime networks has been called the fastest-growing criminal organization in the United States?

    a. the Triads
    b. the LCN

c.   Eurasian Organized Crime (EOC)* (p. 579, Learning Objective: Outline what crimes organized crime is typically involved in.)

d.   the Mexican Mafia

12.   The primary emphasis of the Federal Drug Enforcement Administration is to

a.   stop the flow of drugs.* (p. 572, Learning Objective: Clarify what agency provides unified leadership in combating illegal drug activities and what its primary emphasis is.)

b.   apprehend users.

c.   rehabilitate addicts.

d.   educate the public regarding the dangers of drug abuse.

13.   What act did the federal government pass in 1914 that made the sale or use of certain drugs illegal?

a.   the Sullivan Act

b.   the Mann Act

c.   the Harrison Narcotics Act* (p. 548, Learning Objective: Discuss what act made it illegal to sell or use certain narcotics and dangerous drugs.)

d.   the Little Lindbergh Law

14.   Designer drugs are

a.   created by adding something to an existing drug.

b.   created by omitting something from an existing drug.

c.   high-profit drugs for dealers.

d.   all of these choices.* (p. 558. Learning Objective: Describe what drugs are most commonly observed on the street, in the possession of users and seized in drug raids, and what the most frequent drug arrest is.)

15.   Crack

a.   is substantially more expensive than cocaine.

b.   has 10 times less impact than cocaine.

c.   has 10 times more impact than cocaine.* (p. 552, Learning Objective: Describe what drugs are most commonly observed on the street, in the possession of users and seized in drug raids, and what the most frequent drug arrest is.)

d.   is less addictive than cocaine.

16.   Which of the following provides revenue to law enforcement for antidrug efforts?

a.   fines

b.   asset forfeiture* (pp. 572–573, Learning Objective: Clarify what agency provides unified leadership in combating illegal drug activities and what its primary emphasis is.)

c.   prosecution

d.   incarceration

17. The major legal evidence in prosecuting drug sale cases is

    a. identification of a known user.
    b. identification of a known seller.
    c. the actual transfer of the drug from the seller to the buyer.* (p. 564, Learning Objective: Describe what the major legal evidence in prosecuting drug sale and distribution is.)
    d. actual possession of the drug.

18. The RICO Act of 1970 is one of the major federal acts that

    a. make it permissible to use circumstantial rather than direct evidence to enforce conspiracy violations.* (p. 576, Learning Objective: Identify what organized crime activities are specifically made crimes by law.)
    b. aim to stop the flow of drugs.
    c. make it easier for prosecutors to charge and convict those apprehended in the sale of illegal drugs.
    d. make the use of pen registers legal in the investigation of criminal networks.

19. Surveillance is used in narcotics investigations to

    a. protect the money put up to make the buy.
    b. provide credibility for the buy.
    c. provide information to establish probable cause for an arrest.
    d. all of these choices.* (pp. 565–566, Learning Objective: Explain when an on-sight arrest can be made for a drug buy.)

20. With reference to drugs, OTC stands for

    a. Office of Trading Control.
    b. Official Technological Commission.
    c. Operation Traffic Control.
    d. over-the-counter.* (p. 558, Learning Objective: Describe what drugs are most commonly observed on the street, in the possession of users and seized in drug raids, and what the most frequent drug arrest is.)

21. Designer drugs, which are illicit drugs that are offshoots of the legal drugs from which they are created, may cause the muscles to stiffen and give the appearance of someone suffering from Parkinson's disease. These illicit drugs are referred to as what type of drugs?

    a. analogs* (p. 558, Learning Objective: Describe what drugs are most commonly observed on the street, in the possession of users and seized in drug raids, and what the most frequent drug arrest is.)
    b. parasites
    c. lemurs
    d. bonding agents

22. Drugs found on a person during a legally conducted search

    a. may be seized.* (p. 561, Learning Objective: Explain what the major legal evidence in prosecuting drug use and possession is.)
    b. may not be seized under the exclusionary rule.
    c. may not be seized under the plain feel exception.
    d. may not be seized under the "fruit-of-the-poisonous-tree" doctrine.

23. Which of the following is *not* one of the four groups that make up the Mafia?

    a. the Neopolitan Camorra
    b. the Sacra Corona Unita
    c. the Fratelli Gambino* (p. 577, Learning Objective: Outline what crimes organized crime is typically involved in.)
    d. the 'Ndrangheta Mafia

24. Club drugs, prescription narcotics and ultra-pure forms of DXM, an ingredient found in OTC cough medication,

    a. can all be purchased online and shipped directly to the user's home—transactions that are extremely difficult for law enforcement to detect.* (p. 568, Learning Objective: Discuss what precautions to take in undercover drug buys and how to avoid a charge of entrapment.)
    b. are not available online because of stricter regulations.
    c. may be restricted for online purchase by requiring ID and are relatively easy for law enforcement to detect.
    d. can no longer be shipped to a person's residence, only to medical facilities.

25. The U.S. Congress has defined a drug addict as

    a. any person who habitually uses any habit-forming narcotic drug so as to endanger the public morals, health, safety or welfare.
    b. any person who is or has been so far addicted to the use of habit-forming narcotic drugs as to have lost the power of self-control with reference to the addiction.
    c. any person who both habitually uses any habit-forming narcotic drug so as to endanger the public morals, health, safety or welfare, and is or has been so far addicted to the use of habit-forming narcotic drugs as to have lost the power of self-control with reference to the addiction.* (p. 561, Learning Objective: Explain what the major legal evidence in prosecuting drug use and possession is.)
    d. none of these choices.

True/False

26. Ecstasy is a commonly used name for MDMA. (True, p. 556, Learning Objective: Describe what drugs are most commonly observed on the street, in the possession of users and seized in drug raids, and what the most frequent drug arrest is.)

27. The vast majority of hard-narcotics users once used marijuana. (True, p. 555, Learning Objective: Describe what drugs are most commonly observed on the street, in the possession of users and seized in drug raids, and what the most frequent drug arrest is.)

28. Methamphetamine is a synthetic stimulant that looks like cocaine but is made from toxic chemicals and easily obtained over-the-counter products. (True, p. 555, Learning Objective: Describe what drugs are most commonly observed on the street, in the possession of users and seized in drug raids, and what the most frequent drug arrest is.)

29. Prison gangs are not connected to organized crime or drug manufacture or sale. (False, p. 579, Learning Objective: Outline what crimes organized crime is typically involved in.)

30. Capital flight is interchangeable with money laundering, and both are illegal. (False, p. 579, Learning Objective: Explain how drugs are commonly classified.)

31. Many visitors to a residence or place of business, particularly at odd hours, who stay for a limited amount of time may be an indication of drug sales. (True, p. 565, Learning Objective: Explain when an on-sight arrest can be made for a drug buy.)

32. A sting is a reverse buy. (True, p. 567, Learning Objective: Discuss what precautions to take in undercover drug buys and how to avoid a charge of entrapment.)

33. "Head shops" sell products that help the end user ingest drugs. (True, p. 567, Learning Objective: Discuss what precautions to take in undercover drug buys and how to avoid a charge of entrapment.)

34. Water lines or electrical cords running to a basement or outbuilding are a possible indication of indoor marijuana growing. (True, p. 571, Learning Objective: Explain what hazards exist in raiding a clandestine drug laboratory.)

35. LSD is derived from lysergic acid, from a fungus that grows on rye and other grains. (True, p. 557, Learning Objective: Describe what drugs are most commonly observed on the street, in the possession of users and seized in drug raids, and what the most frequent drug arrest is.)

36. The most dangerous drugs are Schedule I drugs. (True, p. 550, Learning Objective: Describe when it is illegal to use or sell narcotics or dangerous drugs.)

37. A pupilometer allows police to check if someone is under the influence of alcohol or drugs by measuring the pupils in their eyes as subject to light. (True, p. 561, Learning Objective: Explain what the major legal evidence in prosecuting drug use and possession is.)

38. The production of LSD involves ingredients such as strong acids and bases, flammable solvents and very explosive and poisonous chemicals. (False, p. 568, Learning Objective: Describe what drugs are most commonly observed on the street, in the possession of users and seized in drug raids, and what the most frequent drug arrest is.)

39. Mescaline and peyote are stimulants. (False, p. 551, Learning Objective: Explain how drugs are commonly classified.)

40. Autonomous robotics can enhance officers' safety in investigating a suspected meth lab and can be an important force multiplier. (True, p. 570, Learning Objective: Explain what hazards exist in raiding a clandestine drug laboratory.)

41. Local patrol officers can provide very limited information concerning organized crime. (False, p. 580, Learning Objective: Describe the investigator's primary role in dealing with the problem of organized crime.)

42. Because of their experience with drugs, drug users are not likely to sell drugs themselves. (False, p. 564, Learning Objective: Describe what the major legal evidence in prosecuting drug sale and distribution is.)

43. A victimless crime is an illegal activity in which all involved are willing participants. (True, pp. 576–577, Learning Objective: Outline what crimes organized crime is typically involved in.)

44. Crack is a derivative of heroin. (False, p. 552, Learning Objective: Describe what drugs are most commonly observed on the street, in the possession of users and seized in drug raids, and what the most frequent drug arrest is.)

45. A flashroll is something used by a mule to smuggle drugs. (False, p. 567, Learning Objective: Discuss what precautions to take in undercover drug buys and how to avoid a charge of entrapment.)

Completion

46. Rohypnol is one of the _____ drugs. (club, p. 556, Learning Objective: Describe what drugs are most commonly observed on the street, in the possession of users and seized in drug raids, and what the most frequent drug arrest is.)

47. _____ is the most widely available and most commonly used illicit drug in the United States. (Marijuana, pp. 554–555, Learning Objective: Describe what drugs are most commonly observed on the street, in the possession of users and seized in drug raids, and what the most frequent drug arrest is.)

48. _____ is produced by mixing cocaine with baking soda and water. (Crack, p. 552, Learning Objective: Describe what drugs are most commonly observed on the street, in the possession of users and seized in drug raids, and what the most frequent drug arrest is.)

49. People under the influence of illicit stimulants such as cocaine may exhibit extremely agitated and incoherent behavior, a condition known as excited _____. (delirium, pp. 562–564, Learning Objective: Explain what the major legal evidence in prosecuting drug use and possession is.)

50. _____, also known as "roofie," is 10 times more potent than Valium. (Rohypnol, pp. 556–557, Learning Objective: Describe what drugs are most commonly observed on the street, in the possession of users and seized in drug raids, and what the most frequent drug arrest is.)

51. A major indication of indoor marijuana growing operations is excessive use of _____. (electricity, p. 571, Learning Objective: Explain what hazards exist in raiding a clandestine drug laboratory.)

52. Concealing drugs in any opening of a human or animal is called _____. (body packing, p. 562, Learning Objective: Explain what the major legal evidence in prosecuting drug use and possession is.)

53. It is illegal to possess or use narcotics or other dangerous drugs without a _____. (prescription, p. 550, Learning Objective: Describe when it is illegal to use or sell narcotics or dangerous drugs.)

54. Crank is a street name for _____. (methamphetamine, p. 555, Learning Objective: Describe what drugs are most commonly observed on the street, in the possession of users and seized in drug raids, and what the most frequent drug arrest is.)

55. It is illegal to sell or distribute narcotics or other dangerous drugs without a _____. (license, p. 550, Learning Objective: Describe when it is illegal to use or sell narcotics or dangerous drugs.)

Short Answer

56. Describe how SkySeer drones have been used in the war against drugs. (p. 572, Learning Objective: Clarify what agency provides unified leadership in combating illegal drug activities and what its primary emphasis is.)

57. Summarize the crimes that organized crime is typically involved in. (p. 576, Learning Objective: Outline what crimes organized crime is typically involved in.)

58. Outline the role of the federal Drug Enforcement Administration (DEA) in attacking illegal drug activities. (p. 572, Clarify what agency provides unified leadership in combating illegal drug activities and what its primary emphasis is.)

59. What is the controversy over the government's involvement in policing victimless crimes? (pp. 576–577, Learning Objective: Outline what crimes organized crime is typically involved in.)

60. Describe the connection between bookmaking and loan-sharking, explaining why organized crime groups are perfectly poised to engage in both of these enterprises. (p. 577, Learning Objective: Outline what crimes organized crime is typically involved in.)

61. What are some of the precautions that officers should take in undercover drug buys? (pp. 566–567, Learning Objective: Discuss what precautions to take in undercover drug buys and how to avoid a charge of entrapment.)

62. Describe the various types of physical evidence of possession or use of controlled substances, giving examples of each type. (p. 562, Learning Objective: Explain what the major legal evidence in prosecuting drug use and possession is.)

63. Describe the conditions that must be met in order for an officer to make an on-sight arrest for a drug buy. (p. 565, Learning Objective: Explain when an on-sight arrest can be made for a drug buy.)

64. What are some safety concerns investigators should have when entering a clandestine drug lab? (pp. 568–570, Learning Objective: Explain what hazards exist in raiding a clandestine drug laboratory.)

65. Which is more effective: intervention of partnerships with third parties, or law-enforcement-only approaches? Why? (pp. 573–574, Learning Objective: Clarify what agency provides unified leadership in combating illegal drug activities and what its primary emphasis is.)

66. What are some indicators of a clandestine meth lab that an investigator could detect from the outside of a building? (p. 568, Learning Objective: Explain what hazards exist in raiding a clandestine drug laboratory.)

67. How are club drugs and designer drugs similar? How are they different? (pp. 556–558, Learning Objective: Describe what drugs are most commonly observed on the street, in the possession of users and seized in drug raids, and what the most frequent drug arrest is.)

68. What is the purpose of asset forfeitures? How does it help law enforcement? (p. 572) Learning Objective: Clarify what agency provides unified leadership in combating illegal drug activities and what its primary emphasis is.)

69. Choose one of the organized crime groups detailed in the text and describe some of its elements, including the origin of the group, the typical crimes the group engages in and what special challenges the organization creates for investigators. (pp. 577–580, Learning Objective: Outline what crimes organized crime is typically involved in.)

70. What role has the federal government played since 2010 to help law enforcement and communities fight drug abuse? (p. 574, Learning Objective: Describe what the key to reducing drug abuse is.)

CRIMINAL ACTIVITIES OF GANGS AND OTHER DANGEROUS GROUPS

Test Bank

Chapter 19
Criminal Activities of Gangs and Other Dangerous Groups

Multiple Choice

1. Which of the following is a characteristic of a street gang, as opposed to a drug gang?

   a. small structure
   b. loose leadership* (p. 592, Learning Objective: Outline how to classify gangs.)
   c. controlled competition
   d. narrow age range

2. Which of the following may be an important indicator of satanic or cult activity?

   a. the *Book of Shadows*
   b. booby traps
   c. painted rocks
   d. all of these choices* (p. 617, Learning Objective: Explain what may be involved in ritualistic crime.)

3. What percentage of known offenders involved in hate crimes are White?

   a. 62 percent* (p. 609, Learning Objective: Articulate the primary motivation for bias or hate crimes, and identify who is most frequently targeted in such crimes.)
   b. 45 percent
   c. 93 percent
   d. 11 percent

4. A flash mob is an example of

   a. gang behavior that is atypical because it involves a large portion of the gang at the same time.
   b. swarming.
   c. illegal gang activity.
   d. all of these choices.* (p. 599, Learning Objective: Describe the types of crimes gangs typically engage in.)

5. A special problem in investigating illegal activities of gangs is the multitude of suspects and the

   a. fact that most are juveniles.
   b. unreliability or fear of witnesses.* (p. 603, Learning Objective: Discuss what special challenges are involved in investigating illegal activities of gangs.)

c.   fact that courts have not upheld gang statutes.

d.   fact that gangs are interracial.

6.   The three-pronged approach to address the gang problem uses a balance of which three strategies?

a.   intervention, motivation and suppression

b.   prevention, intervention and suppression* (p. 605, Learning Objective: Describe what strategies have been used to combat a gang problem.)

c.   intervention, transition and motivation

d.   penetration, suppression and prevention

7.   Which of the following is *not* an important type of record to keep in dealing with any gang problem?

a.   gang vehicle file

b.   gang member pointer file

c.   gang member illegal activities file

d.   gang member drug preferences file* (p. 603, Learning Objective: Explain what kinds of records to keep on gangs.)

8.   Which of the following is one of the models used to explain the relationship between gangs and crime?

a.   enhancement model* (p. 599, Learning Objective: Describe the types of crimes gangs typically engage in.)

b.   aggravation model

c.   criminal model

d.   professional model

9.   A gang's graffiti can provide all of the following pieces of information about the gang except one. Which one does it *not* reveal?

a.   territory

b.   members

c.   leadership

d.   arrest records* (pp. 603–604, Learning Objective: Discuss what special challenges are involved in investigating illegal activities of gangs.)

10.   Which of the following is *not* a sign that a youth may be in a gang?

a.   admits to "hanging out" with kids in gangs

b.   uses unusual hand signals to communicate with friends

c.   has been in trouble with police

d.   wears baggy jeans with underwear showing* (p. 602, Learning Objective: Describe how to identify gang members.)

11. OMGs have become a major distributor of _____ in the United States.

    a.   crack
    b.   heroin
    c.   marijuana
    d.   methamphetamine* (p. 598, Learning Objective: Outline how to classify gangs.)

12. Investigators dealing with youths they suspect may be engaging in cult-related activities should inquire into which of the following?

    a.   the music the youths listened to
    b.   whether the youths dabbled in astrology
    c.   whether the youths played with Ouija boards or tarot cards
    d.   all of these choices* (p. 617, Learning Objective: Identify indicators of ritualistic crimes.)

13. One hypothesis to explain the relationship between gangs and crime is the facilitation model, which posits that

    a.   gang membership promotes drug involvement, which in turn facilitates violence.* (p. 599, Learning Objective: Describe the types of crimes gangs typically engage in.)
    b.   gangs attract members who are already delinquent or criminally involved, and their antisocial behaviors facilitate their acceptance into the gang.
    c.   gangs attract those who are already delinquent or criminally involved, and membership further facilitates their preexisting antisocial behavior.
    d.   none of these choices.

14. What are the two most common defenses cited for gang members in court?

    a.   self-defense and following the orders of gang leadership
    b.   self-defense and being under the influence of alcohol/drugs* (p. 607, Learning Objective: Explain two defense strategies that are commonly used by gang members' lawyers in court.)
    c.   being under the influence of alcohol/drugs and racial discrimination on the part of the police
    d.   following the orders of gang leadership and racial discrimination on the part of the police

15. The majority of hate crimes are based on

    a.   social class.
    b.   religion.
    c.   race.* (p. 608, Learning Objective: Articulate the primary motivation for bias or hate crimes, and identify who is most frequently targeted in such crimes.)
    d.   sexual orientation.

16. The Crips are associated with

    a.   green and yellow shirts.
    b.   blue or purple bandannas.* (p. 602, Learning Objective: Describe how to identify gang members.)
    c.   red or green colors.
    d.   black and gold scarves or rags.

17. Which of the following is *not* a common purpose of graffiti as used by gangs?

    a.   marking a gang's turf
    b.   disrespecting a rival gang or gang member
    c.   sending a message
    d.   informing the general public that they exist* (p. 604, Learning Objective: Outline how to classify gangs.)

18. Which of the following would *not* be one of the signs of a ritualistic homicide?

    a.   missing body parts such as heart, genitals, left hand, tongue, index finger
    b.   urine or human or animal feces smeared on body or found in body cavities
    c.   wax drippings, oils, incense or ritual powders on the body
    d.   missing clothing* (p. 618, Learning Objective: Identify indicators of ritualistic crimes.)

19. Which group may be associated with mutilated animals, grave robbery and desecration of churches and human remains?

    a.   motorcycle gangs
    b.   stoner gangs* (pp. 614–615, Learning Objective: Describe what a ritualistic crime is.)
    c.   MS-13
    d.   Aryan Brotherhood

20. What was the decision in the U.S. Supreme Court's 2003 case, *Virginia v. Black*?

    a.   It upheld all hate crime legislation.
    b.   It upheld a Virginia law banning cross burning, saying the statute did not violate the First Amendment.
    c.   It struck down a Virginia law banning cross burning, saying the statute violated the First Amendment.* (p. 613, Learning Objective: Articulate the primary motivation for bias or hate crimes, and identify who is most frequently targeted in such crimes.)
    d.   It ruled that any hate crime legislation would always be too "broad," and thus unconstitutional.

21. One of the latest technological innovations to aid in the fight against gangs is

    a. TAGRS.* (p. 604, Learning Objective: Describe what strategies have been used to combat a gang problem.)
    b. Facebook.
    c. the LA-FI database.
    d. NRM.

22. Which of the following is *not* one of the common reasons that people join gangs?

    a. the neighborhood they live in
    b. the amount of money they have* (pp. 591–592, Learning Objective: Analyze whether the gang problem is increasing or decreasing.)
    c. the fact that family and friends are also involved in gangs
    d. parent-child relationship problems

23. Which of the following statements is true?

    a. Members of the military possess specialized skills that pose a unique threat to law enforcement personnel.
    b. Service members, as well as dependents and relatives, have been identified as gang members.
    c. Gangs have been identified on international military installations.
    d. All of these choices.* (p. 594, Learning Objective: Outline how to classify gangs.)

24. The Southern Poverty Law Center is a

    a. watchdog organization for bias and hate crimes.* (p. 608, Learning Objective: Articulate the primary motivation for bias or hate crimes, and identify who is most frequently targeted in such crimes.)
    b. law group that lobbies for hate crime legislation.
    c. law group that lobbies to protect freedom of speech even for those who may be considered to have committed hate crimes.
    d. an antipolice advocate.

25. Which of the following is *not* an example of a cult discussed in the text?

    a. Hare Krishna
    b. NRM
    c. Branch Davidians
    d. 666* (p. 613, Learning Objective: Discuss what a cult is, and explain a better way to refer to cults)

True/False

26. Hybrid gangs, a new generation of gangs, are singularly focused on making money from drugs, robberies and prostitution. (True, p. 593, Learning Objective: Outline how to classify gangs.)

27. Individuals involved in the occult are typically imaginative overachievers who possess high self-esteem. (False, p. 615, Learning Objective: Describe what a ritualistic crime is.)

28. Research indicates that as a gang's organization increases, so does its level of criminal involvement. (True, p. 594, Learning Objective: Describe the types of crimes gangs typically engage in.)

29. The defense of "diminished capacity" is one of the most common defense strategies used by gang members. (True, p. 607, Learning Objective: Explain two defense strategies that are commonly used by gang members' lawyers in court.)

30. The homeless are often overlooked as frequent victims of hate crime. (True, p. 609, Learning Objective: Articulate the primary motivation for bias or hate crimes, and identify who is most frequently targeted in such crimes.)

31. Occult groups have four levels of activity: dabbling, serious involvement, criminal involvement and ascension to leadership. (False, p. 614, Learning Objective: Describe what a ritualistic crime is.)

32. High-ranking gang members are often able to exert their influence on the street from within prison. (True, p. 593, Learning Objective: Outline how to classify gangs.)

33. The first step in dealing with a gang problem is to keep a record of all graffiti tags in the defined area. (False, p. 600, Learning Objective: Identify the first step in dealing with a gang problem.)

34. Charles Manson and David Berkowitz, both serial murderers, have been shown to have had links to Satanism. (True, pp. 619–620, Learning Objective: Identify indicators of ritualistic crimes.)

35. Black men in interracial relationships are one of the groups at highest risk for hate crime. (False, p. 608, Learning Objective: Articulate the primary motivation for bias or hate crimes, and identify who is most frequently targeted in such crimes.)

36. The threat of federal prison has been shown to be an important deterrent of gang violence and is recognized as a valuable strategy for law enforcement to use in the war against gangs. (True, pp. 606–607, Learning Objective: Describe what strategies have been used to combat a gang problem.)

37. Occult murders are usually sacrificial shootings, with gunshot wounds distributed in the form of a cross. (False, p. 618, Learning Objective: Identify indicators of ritualistic crimes.)

38. When dealing with gang members, it is important for officers to communicate that they do not respect the individual or the gang. (False, p. 604, Learning Objective: Discuss what special challenges are involved in investigating illegal activities of gangs.)

39. Research has found minimal public support for harsher penalties for offenders who commit hate crimes than for offenders who commit identical crimes with no biased motivation. (True, p. 613, Learning Objective: Articulate the primary motivation for bias or hate crimes, and identify who is most frequently targeted in such crimes.)

40. Gang members often refuse to use pleas of diminished capacity and self-defense because this runs counter to the value placed on masculinity and strength in most gangs. (False, p. 607, Learning Objective: Explain two defense strategies that are commonly used by gang members' lawyers in court.)

41. Hate crime is a relatively new development in the United States. (False, p. 608, Learning Objective: Articulate the primary motivation for bias or hate crimes, and identify who is most frequently targeted in such crimes.)

42. Magick can be described as a prescribed form of religious or mystical ceremony. (False, p. 614, Learning Objective: Discuss what a cult is, and explain a better way to refer to cults)

43. Most cases of ritualistic homicide are dismissed in court because most juries disbelieve outlandish charges of Satanism and human sacrifice. (True, p. 618, Learning Objective: Identify indicators of ritualistic crimes.)

44. It is believed that partnering with the community, parents and schools will provide a more effective response to the issue of gangs. (True, p. 606, Learning Objective: Describe what strategies have been used to combat a gang problem.)

45. The number of gangs in large cities ranges from 1,500 to 2,000. (False, p. 591, Learning Objective: Analyze whether the gang problem is increasing or decreasing.)

Completion

46. In a cult, the color _____ may stand for energy, sexuality or physical life. (red, p. 614, Learning Objective: Discuss what a cult is, and explain a better way to refer to cults)

47. A(n) _____ _____ involves behaviors that, although motivated by bias, are not criminal acts. (hate incident, p. 610, Learning Objective: Articulate the primary motivation for bias or hate crimes, and identify who is most frequently targeted in such crimes.)

48. A(n) _____ is a verbal spell. (incantation, p. 614, Learning Objective: Discuss what a cult is, and explain a better way to refer to cults)

49. A(n) _____ crime is a crime committed with or during a ceremony. (ritualistic, p. 614, Learning Objective: Describe what a ritualistic crime is.)

50. A new breed of increasingly violent street gangs appearing through the country is _____ gangs, whose members are generally young and particularly profit driven. (hybrid, p. 593, Learning Objective: Outline how to classify gangs.)

51. The best sources of information on gang activities are _____ members, who are more likely to be cooperative with the police than hard-core members. (peripheral, p. 594, Learning Objective: Outline how to classify gangs.)

52. _____ graffiti is usually highly artistic and very detailed. (Hispanic, p. 595, Learning Objective: Outline how to classify gangs.)

53. A _____ file is one way that investigators can keep track of gang members' street names and legal names. (moniker, p. 603, Learning Objective: Explain what kinds of records to keep on gangs.)

54. Gangs are now sending members across the country and into the nation's heartland to take advantage of new territory, diminished _____ from other gangs and law enforcement agencies with less experience in dealing with gang activity. (competition, p. 591, Learning Objective: Analyze whether the gang problem is increasing or decreasing.)

55. A _____ of Satanism often incorporates religious articles stolen from churches. (Black Mass, p. 614, Learning Objective: Describe what a ritualistic crime is.)

Short Answer

56. Indicate whether gang activity is increasing or decreasing, and describe why this is difficult to determine. (p. 591, Learning Objective: Analyze whether the gang problem is increasing or decreasing.)

57. Outline the ways that gangs are currently classified. (pp. 592–593, Learning Objective: Outline how to classify gangs.)

58. Discuss the various strategies currently in use by communities that are working to suppress gang activity and violence. (pp. 605–606, Learning Objective: Describe what strategies have been used to combat a gang problem.)

59. Describe the difference between a hate crime and a hate incident. (pp. 608–610, Learning Objective: Articulate the primary motivation for bias or hate crimes, and identify who is most frequently targeted in such crimes.)

60. List the types of ritualistic crimes that investigators should be aware of. (p. 614, Learning Objective: Describe what a ritualistic crime is.)

61. Describe the two defense strategies that are commonly used by gang members. What specifically should investigators document to aid the prosecution, and why? (p. 607, Learning Objective: Explain two defense strategies that are commonly used by gang members' lawyers in court.)

62. Describe three possible signs that a homicide is ritualistic. (p. 618, Learning Objective: Identify indicators of ritualistic crimes.)

63. List and briefly discuss the kinds of records investigators should keep on gangs and gang members. (pp. 602–603, Learning Objective: Explain what kinds of records to keep on gangs.)

64. Outline what a cult is and what factors to be aware of when investigating cult activities. (pp. 613–617, Learning Objective: Discuss what a cult is, and explain a better way to refer to cults)

65. Describe bias and hate crimes and what motivates the offenders. (pp. 608–609, Learning Objective: Articulate the primary motivation for bias or hate crimes, and identify who is most frequently targeted in such crimes.)

66. Give some examples of variables that affect whether agencies report hate crimes. (pp. 610–612, Learning Objective: Articulate the primary motivation for bias or hate crimes, and identify who is most frequently targeted in such crimes.)

67. How can officers identify gang members? What are some of the indicators? (pp. 601–602, Learning Objective: Describe how to identify gang members.)

68. What are some of the special challenges involved in investigating illegal activities of gangs? (pp. 603, Learning Objective: Discuss what special challenges are involved in investigating illegal activities of gangs.)

69. What are some of the legislative challenges to hate or bias crimes? (pp. 613, Learning Objective: Articulate the primary motivation for bias or hate crimes, and identify who is most frequently targeted in such crimes.)

70. What are the special challenges involved in investigating ritualistic crimes? (p. 619, Learning Objective: Describe special challenges involved in investigating ritualistic crimes.)

TERRORISM AND HOMELAND SECURITY

Test Bank

Chapter 20
Terrorism and Homeland Security

Multiple Choice

1. The primary destruction resulting from a dirty bomb is usually a result of

   a. radiation.
   b. panic.* (p. 636, Learning Objective: Describe the various methods terrorists may use.)
   c. nerve damage.
   d. widespread fire.

2. NIMS stands for

   a. National Information Management System.
   b. National Identification Management System.
   c. National Incident Management System.* (p. 645, Learning Objective: Describe what the Law Enforcement Officers Safety Act authorizes.)
   d. National Intelligence Monitoring System.

3. The group HAMAS is

   a. literally the Party of God, a militia group or a political party that first emerged as a faction in Lebanon following the Israeli invasion in 1982.
   b. a militant Palestinian Islamic movement in the West Bank and Gaza Strip.* (p. 629, Learning Objective: Outline what groups are commonly identified as Islamic terrorist organizations.)
   c. a broad-based Islamic militant organization founded by Osama bin Laden in the late 1980s.
   d. a group formed in the refugee camps in the West Bank of Israel.

4. Weapons of mass destruction (WMDs) can contain

   a. biological elements.
   b. all of these choices.* (pp. 635–636, Learning Objective: Describe the various methods terrorists may use.)
   c. chemical agents.
   d. nuclear agents.

5. The Al-Aqsa Martyrs Brigades are

   a. literally the Party of God, a militia group and a political party that first emerged as a faction in Lebanon following the Israeli invasion in 1982.
   b. a militant Palestinian Islamic movement in the West Bank and Gaza Strip.
   c. a broad-based Islamic militant organization founded by Osama bin Laden in the late 1980s.
   d. a group formed in the refugee camps in the West Bank of Israel.* (p. 629, Learning Objective: Outline what groups are commonly identified as Islamic terrorist organizations.)

6. Certain experts believe that because of the difficulty in obtaining materials, the least likely type of terrorism to occur is

   a. domestic terrorism.
   b. bioterrorism.* (p. 635, Learning Objective: Describe the various methods terrorists may use.)
   c. nuclear terrorism.
   d. street terrorism.

7. Which of the following is *not* one of the ways in which the USA PATRIOT Act significantly improved the nation's counterterrorism efforts?

   a. allowing investigators to use the tools available to investigate organized crime and drug trafficking
   b. facilitating information sharing and cooperation among government agencies so they can better "connect the dots"
   c. updating the law to reflect new technologies and new threats, as well as increase the penalties for those who commit or support terrorist crimes
   d. allowing for political assassinations with presidential approval* (p. 639, Learning Objective: Describe how the USA PATRIOT Act enhances counterterrorism efforts by the United States.)

8. "Terrorism that initiates, or threatens to initiate, the exploitation or attack on information systems" is the FBI's definition of which type of terrorism?

   a. bioterrorism
   b. cyberterrorism* (pp. 636–637, Learning Objective: Describe the various methods terrorists may use.)
   c. international terrorism
   d. nuclear terrorism

9. What did members of Aum Shinrikyu, a new-age cult, release into the Tokyo subway system, killing 12 and sending 5,000 to the hospital?

   a. anthrax
   b. sarin gas* (pp. 635–636, Learning Objective: Describe the various methods terrorists may use.)
   c. hydrochloric acid
   d. cyanide gas

10. Which of the following is *not* a type of chemical weapon?

   a. blood agents
   b. immune agents* (p. 636, Learning Objective: Describe the various methods terrorists may use.)
   c. blistering agents
   d. nerve agents

11. A sleeper cell is

    a. a group of terrorists who are in training in Afghanistan.
    b. a group of terrorists who blend into a community until called to action.* (p. 642, Learning Objective: Explain the three-tiered model of al-Qaeda terrorist attacks.)
    c. a group of individuals who only plan terrorist activities.
    d. a group of terrorist recruits who are awaiting weapons and explosives.

12. What does ALF stand for?

    a. Al-Qaeda Liberation Front
    b. Animal Liberation Front* (pp. 632–633, Learning Objective: Discuss what domestic terrorist groups exist in the United States.)
    c. Anti-Liberation Front
    d. Anarchists Liberation Front

13. Which of the following crimes is *not* normally associated with funding terrorism?

    a. contract killing* (p. 637, Learning Objective: Describe the various methods terrorists may use.)
    b. money laundering
    c. extortion and protection rackets
    d. document forging

14. The "contagion effect" refers to

    a. the way terror spreads after a terrorist act.
    b. the use of infectious disease as a weapon by terrorists.
    c. the fact that the coverage of terrorism inspires more terrorism.* (p. 645, Learning Objective: Describe what the Law Enforcement Officers Safety Act authorizes.)
    d. the spread of biological or chemical weapons of mass destruction.

15. The FBI categorizes terrorism in the United States as either

    a. domestic or international.* (p. 628, Learning Objective: Explain how the FBI classifies terrorist acts.)
    b. local or national.
    c. local or international.
    d. domestic or foreign.

16. Which was a case of domestic terrorism?

    a. first World Trade Center bombing in 1993
    b. bombing of the Marine Barracks in Lebanon in 1982
    c. bombing of the Alfred P. Murrah Federal Building in Oklahoma City in 1985* (p. 628, Learning Objective: Explain how the FBI classifies terrorist acts.)
    d. 9/11 attacks

17. The Earth Liberation Front (ELF) is an example of what type of organization?

     a.   cyberterrorist
     b.   bioterrorist
     c.   ecoterrorist* (p. 633, Learning Objective: Discuss what domestic terror-
          ist groups exist in the United States.)
     d.   cryptoterrorist

18. A common tactic that enables a weaker state or nonstate entity, such as a
     terrorist group, to achieve an advantage over a stronger adversary is known
     as what?

     a.   asymmetric warfare* (p. 628, Learning Objective: Explain how the FBI
          classifies terrorist acts.)
     b.   apathetic contagion
     c.   antiparallel deconfliction
     d.   antithetical engagement

19. The term *intifada* means

     a.   holy war.
     b.   uprising.* (p. 629, Learning Objective: Outline what groups are
          commonly identified as Islamic terrorist organizations.)
     c.   martyr.
     d.   secret army.

20. At the federal level, what is the name of the lead agency for responding to
     acts of domestic terrorism?

     a.   OSHA
     b.   INS
     c.   Homeland Security/FEMA* (p. 638, Learning Objective: Identify the two
          lead agencies in combating terrorism.)
     d.   FBI

21. The number one priority in any terrorist-preparedness plan should be

     a.   securing adequate firepower.
     b.   implementation of profiling standards.
     c.   communication between local, state and federal law enforcement
          agencies.* (p. 644, Learning Objective: Identify a key to successfully
          combating terrorism.)
     d.   ready deployment of CDC personnel.

22. Which of the following is *not* one of the four common types of chemical
     weapons?

     a.   nerve agents
     b.   blood agents

   c.   choking agents
   d.   "knockout" agents* (p. 636, Learning Objective: Describe the various methods terrorists may use.)

23. The Army of God is

   a.   a group out of the Middle East operating in the United States.
   b.   a pro-life, antiabortion group in the United States.* (p. 632, Learning Objective: Discuss what domestic terrorist groups exist in the United States.)
   c.   a group in Lebanon that has threatened the United States.
   d.   white supremacists who seek to split the United States by racial divides.

24. The method most likely to be used by terrorists is

   a.   nuclear weapons.
   b.   toxic chemicals.
   c.   explosives.* (p. 634, Learning Objective: Describe the various methods terrorists may use.)
   d.   armed attack.

25. Which toxin is both a biological and a chemical weapon, is more than 1,000 times as poisonous as cyanide and, in its purest form, can kill an adult in an amount no bigger than a grain of table salt?

   a.   strychnine
   b.   anthrax
   c.   ricin* (p. 636, Learning Objective: Describe the various methods terrorists may use.)
   d.   mad cow disease

True/False

26. Guidelines used to avoid conflict between different law enforcement agencies are called de-escalation protocols. (False, p. 644, Learning Objective: Identify a key to successfully combating terrorism.)

27. Community policing and Homeland Security are similar in that both are proactive. (True, pp. 647–648, Learning Objective: Discuss the balances that must be maintained in investigating terrorism.)

28. Hydrochloric acid is a chemical agent that requires perfect conditions and a poor emergency response to cause heavy casualties; however, if it is properly released in a well-populated area, it has the potential to cause tens of thousands of casualties. (False, p. 636, Learning Objective: Describe the various methods terrorists may use.)

29. In the past, the sharing of information among agencies responsible for preventing and responding to terrorism has been relatively simple and straightforward. (False, p. 639, Learning Objective: Describe how the USA PATRIOT Act enhances counterterrorism efforts by the United States.)

30. Terrorist groups commonly collaborate with organized criminal groups to deal drugs, arms and, in some instances, people. (True, p. 637, Learning Objective: Describe the various methods terrorists may use.)

31. Terrorists may use arson as a way of attacking a target. (True, p. 634, Learning Objective: Describe the various methods terrorists may use.)

32. Technological terrorism includes attacks on technology, as well as the use of technology. (True, p. 636, Learning Objective: Describe the various methods terrorists may use.)

33. As of 2011, there are three levels of threat in the DHS security advisory system: low, elevated and imminent threat. (False, p. 639, Learning Objective: Describe how the USA PATRIOT Act enhances counterterrorism efforts by the United States.)

34. Terrorist activities are heavily supported by drug money. (True, p. 637, Learning Objective: Describe the various methods terrorists may use.)

35. WMDs do not include biological agents such as anthrax, botulism and smallpox, which are classified separately. (False, p. 635, Learning Objective: Describe the various methods terrorists may use.)

36. Terrorist targets are typically symbolic. (True, p. 641, Learning Objective: Identify the first line of defense against terrorism in the United States.)

37. Terrorism is a relatively new form of human conflict that has emerged only in the modern age. (False, p. 627, Learning Objective: Describe what most definitions of terrorism have in common.)

38. It is a federal crime to commit an act of terrorism against a mass transit system. (True, p. 639, Learning Objective: Explain what federal office was established as a result of 9/11.)

39. In the war against terrorism, it is important that all law enforcement keep as close an eye on domestic terrorists as they do on the international variety. (True, p. 631, Learning Objective: Discuss what domestic terrorist groups exist in the United States.)

40. Federal officials are the most important resource for combating terrorism. (False, pp. 640–641, Learning Objective: Identify the first line of defense against terrorism in the United States.)

41. It is of vital importance that all patrol officers remain distrustful of Arab Americans until they are able to ascertain their citizenship. (False, p. 646, Learning Objective: Identify two major concerns related to the war on terrorism.)

42. Hometown Security and Homeland Security basically mean the same thing. (True, p. 640, Learning Objective: Identify the first line of defense against terrorism in the United States.)

43. In general, law enforcement experiences from the war on drugs are not applicable to the war on terrorism. (False, p. 639, Learning Objective: Describe how the USA PATRIOT Act enhances counterterrorism efforts by the United States.)

44. Civil liberties are not a major concern in the war on terrorism. (False, p. 646, Learning Objective: Identify two major concerns related to the war on terrorism.)

45. Americans should remain alert to indicators of biological warfare especially in areas of high population, because the aftereffects of such attacks, also referred to as the "contagion effect," can be lethal. (False, p. 645, Learning Objective: Describe what the Law Enforcement Officers Safety Act authorizes.)

Completion

46. The informal banking system based on trust and bartering in the Middle East is called _____. (*hawala*, p. 637, Learning Objective: Describe the various methods terrorists may use.)

47. The _____, a new development in the war against terrorism, is an effective and efficient mechanism to exchange information and intelligence. (fusion center, p. 640, Learning Objective: Describe how the USA PATRIOT Act enhances counterterrorism efforts by the United States.)

48. The first spontaneous Palestinian revolt in Gaza and the West Bank was called the _____. (*intifada*, p. 629, Learning Objective: Explain how the FBI classifies terrorist acts.)

49. _____ extremists believe in a pro-Marx stance that the rich must be brought down and the poor elevated. (Left-wing, p. 632, Learning Objective: Discuss what domestic terrorist groups exist in the United States.)

50. Most terrorist acts result from _____ with a religious, political or social system or policy and frustration resulting from an inability to change it through acceptable, nonviolent means. (dissatisfaction, p. 627, Learning Objective: Describe what motivates most terrorist attacks.)

51. The members of _____ groups are typically heavily armed and often frustrated and socially unable to cope with change. (militia, p. 632, Learning Objective: Discuss what domestic terrorist groups exist in the United States.)

52. Many terrorist operations are financed by _____ groups and wealthy Arabs sympathetic to the group's cause. (charitable, p. 637, Learning Objective: Describe the various methods terrorists may use.)

53. The most feared type of attack by Americans is _____. (nuclear, p. 636, Learning Objective: Describe the various methods terrorists may use.)

54. The Party of God, or _____, is a militia group and political party that first emerged in Lebanon following the Israeli invasion of that country in 1982. (Hezbollah, p. 629, Learning Objective: Outline what groups are commonly identified as Islamic terrorist organizations.)

55. Radiation presence and amount can be detected using a handheld _____. (dosimeter, p. 636, Learning Objective: Describe the various methods terrorists may use.)

Short Answer

56. What are the two main concerns related to the war on terrorism? Explain each one briefly. (p. 646, Learning Objective: Identify two major concerns related to the war on terrorism.)

57. Describe what motivates most terrorist attacks. Briefly discuss motivations for both international and domestic terrorism. (pp. 627–628, Learning Objective: Describe what motivates most terrorist attacks.)

58. What are the two lead agencies that work to combat terrorism? How do their roles differ? (pp. 638–639, Learning Objective: Identify the two lead agencies in combating terrorism.)

59. Outline the different categories of methods that terrorists use in an attack. Give an example of each type of attack. (pp. 633–637, Learning Objective: Describe the various methods terrorists may use.)

60. How does the patrol officer in the field participate in the prevention of terrorism? (pp. 640–641, Learning Objective: Identify the first line of defense against terrorism in the United States.)

61. What new technologies are being used to increase border security and contribute to homeland security? (pp. 644–645, Learning Objective: Describe what the Law Enforcement Officers Safety Act authorizes.)

62. Outline the main elements of the USA PATRIOT Act. (p. 639, Learning Objective: Describe how the USA PATRIOT Act enhances counterterrorism efforts by the United States.)

63. How is white-collar crime linked to terrorism? (p. 641, Learning Objective: Identify the first line of defense against terrorism in the United States.)

64. Describe how the intelligence cycle works, and how it is affected by the operational style of law enforcement. (pp. 643–644, Learning Objective: Explain the three-tiered model of al-Qaeda terrorist attacks.)

65. Discuss whether community policing can be effective in the post-9/11 era, in terms of guarding against further terrorist attacks. (pp. 647–648, Learning Objective: Discuss the balances that must be maintained in investigating terrorism.)

66. Discuss the changes to the threat advisory program that were enacted in 2011 and describe the main difference in the new program. (p. 639, Learning Objective: Describe how the USA PATRIOT Act enhances counterterrorism efforts by the United States.)

67. How can local law enforcement officers serve the counterterrorism effort in the first two stages of al-Qaeda terrorist attacks? (pp. 641–642, Learning Objective: Identify the first line of defense against terrorism in the United States.)

68. Describe the five goals that have been outlined as priorities for the DHS. (p. 639, Learning Objective: Explain what federal office was established as a result of 9/11.)

69. Briefly outline the three-tiered model of al-Qaeda terrorist attacks. (p. 642, Learning Objective: Explain the three-tiered model of al-Qaeda terrorist attacks.)

70. Why do some criticize homeland security as "the monster that ate criminal justice"? (pp. 626–627, Learning Objective: Describe what most definitions of terrorism have in common.)

PREPARING FOR AND PRESENTING CASES IN COURT

Test Bank

Chapter 21
Preparing for and Presenting Cases in Court

Multiple Choice

1. What type of evidence tends to show innocence of the accused and must be disclosed?

    a. expectoratory
    b. exculpatory* (p. 654, Learning Objective: Describe how to review a case.)
    c. excruciating
    d. excoriating

2. Direct examination of witnesses is done by

    a. prosecution counsel only.
    b. defense counsel only.
    c. both prosecution and defense counsel.* (p. 662, Learning Objective: Describe the usual sequence in a criminal trial.)
    d. the judge.

3. Which of the following takes place last in a criminal trial?

    a. opening statements
    b. instructions to the jury* (p. 662, Learning Objective: Describe the usual sequence in a criminal trial.)
    c. jury selection
    d. presentation of the defense's case

4. Roles are clearly defined for both the prosecution and the defense because we have what type of legal system?

    a. adversarial* (p. 660, Learning Objective: Explain what occurs during the pretrial conference.)
    b. contentious
    c. federalist
    d. accusatory

5. Which of the following are parts of communication?

    a. words
    b. expressions, appearance
    c. demeanor, personality
    d. all of these choices* (p. 670, Learning Objective: Describe the key to testifying during cross-examination.)

6. Once a report is written, the writer should

    a.   staple the pages together if it is more than one page, and file it.
    b.   evaluate it.* (p. 658, Learning Objective: Describe how to review a case.)
    c.   immediately show it to the prosecutor for approval.
    d.   give a copy to both the prosecution and defense.

7. The most important rule for eradicating fear of testifying in court is to always

    a.   assist with the conviction of the suspect.
    b.   inform the prosecutor of your plans during testimony.
    c.   understand what the problems are with the case.
    d.   tell the truth.* (p. 654, Learning Objective: Identify the most important rule to eradicate fear of testifying in court.)

8. Which of the following is inadmissible for an officer to make in court?

    a.   statements including obscenity or vulgarity
    b.   statements about the defendant's behavior at the time of arrest
    c.   statements about the defendant's criminal record* (p. 663, Learning Objective: Explain what kinds of statements are inadmissible in court.)
    d.   none of these choices

9. At the pretrial conference with the prosecutor, investigators should do all but which one of the following?

    a.   review all evidence
    b.   discuss strengths and weaknesses of the case
    c.   discuss the probable line of questioning by prosecutor and defense
    d.   ask the defendant if he or she "did it"* (p. 659, Learning Objective: Explain what occurs during the pretrial conference.)

10. When officers are finished testifying, they should

    a.   leave the stand.
    b.   leave the stand when dismissed.* (p. 670, Learning Objective: Explain how to avoid objections to your testimony.)
    c.   conclude with a statement.
    d.   thank the jury.

11. When testifying, it is recommended that officers either give an approximation or use brackets in their statements, which is another way of

    a.   providing a range.* (p. 668, Learning Objective: Describe what defense attorney tactics to anticipate.)
    b.   using a defensive tone.
    c.   employing hand gestures.
    d.   quoting directly from the report.

12. Which of the following is *not* contained in a final report?

    a. statements, admissions and confessions
    b. photographs and sketches
    c. summary of negative evidence
    d. the officer's recommendation to the jury* (p. 654, Learning Objective: Outline what to include in the final report.)

13. Which of the following terms refers to witnesses called by the prosecution?

    a. subpoena
    b. the rule on witnesses
    c. surrebuttal
    d. rebuttal* (p. 662, Learning Objective: Describe the usual sequence in a criminal trial.)

14. The Brady rule grew out of a landmark Supreme Court case that relates to the

    a. well of evidence.
    b. discovery process.* (p. 657, Learning Objective: Describe how to review a case.)
    c. rule on witnesses.
    d. cross-examination.

15. If a case is exceptionally cleared, this means that

    a. no charges are being filed because the prosecutor did not share evidence with the defender.
    b. the testimony of the officer was exceptional.
    c. no charges are being filed because of something that happened outside the investigation.* (p. 656, Learning Objective: Explain why some cases are not prosecuted.)
    d. the motion in limine was not upheld.

16. Inadmissible statements include all but which of the following forms of evidence?

    a. opinions of witnesses
    b. privileged communication
    c. hearsay
    d. direct evidence* (p. 663, Learning Objective: Explain what kinds of statements are inadmissible in court.)

17. In order to be prosecuted, a case requires that the prosecutor is able to present

    a. a confession.
    b. proof beyond a reasonable doubt.* (p. 656, Learning Objective: Discuss how to prepare a case for court.)
    c. proof of probable cause.
    d. motive, means and opportunity.

18. The purpose of the pretrial conference is to

    a. review the case to determine strengths and weaknesses.* (p. 659, Learning Objective: Explain what occurs during the pretrial conference.)
    b. predetermine answers to possible questions.
    c. get acquainted with the prosecuting attorney.
    d. try for a plea bargain.

19. Defendants in a case must

    a. take the witness stand and testify.
    b. answer questions if they elect to take the witness stand.* (pp. 660–661, Learning Objective: Explain what occurs during the pretrial conference.)
    c. be represented by counsel.
    d. remain silent.

20. Redirect examination follows

    a. direct examination.
    b. re-cross-examination.
    c. cross-examination.* (p. 662, Learning Objective: Describe the usual sequence in a criminal trial.)
    d. surrebuttal.

21. When officers testify, it is advisable for them to admit

    a. mistakes in prior testimony.
    b. when they do not understand a question.
    c. when they do not know an answer.
    d. all of these choices.* (p. 663, Learning Objective: Describe how to testify most effectively.)

22. Which of the following statements is true?

    a. Defense attorneys will try to impeach the testimony of prosecution witnesses.* (p. 657, Learning Objective: Describe how to review a case.)
    b. An officer who mishandles his or her testimony in court can be impeached from the investigation.
    c. Any witness moving through the well can automatically be impeached by the judge.
    d. A witness in court will be impeached if he or she does not look directly at the jury when testifying.

23. Officers who are waiting to testify may speak to jurors or other witnesses as long as the communication is _____, such as a simple hello or the giving of directions.

    a. de minimus* (p. 662, Learning Objective: Describe the usual sequence in a criminal trial.)
    b. exculpatory

c. veneer
d. de facto

24. Officers who testify in court should

a. dress appropriately and be on time.
b. admit when they have made a mistake in testifying.
c. admit when they don't know the answer to the question.
d. all of these choices.* (p. 663, Learning Objective: Describe how to testify most effectively.)

25. The prosecutor is described by the text as the

a. arbitrator.
b. gatekeeper of the court system.* (p. 655, Learning Objective: Describe the relative importance of the prosecutor in the court system.)
c. mediator.
d. trier of facts.

True/False

26. The law is interpreted for the jurors by the bailiff. (False, p. 660, Learning Objective: Explain what occurs during the pretrial conference.)

27. A trial before a judge without a jury is referred to as a bench trial. (True, pp. 661–662, Learning Objective: Describe the usual sequence in a criminal trial.)

28. Statements about the defendant's criminal record and reputation as a law-breaker are admissible before a jury. (False, p. 663, Learning Objective: Explain what kinds of statements are inadmissible in court.)

29. Officers testifying during cross-examination should volunteer information whenever they have the opportunity to contribute. (False, p. 669, Learning Objective: Describe how to testify most effectively.)

30. It is fine to discuss the case with other witnesses scheduled for the trial, unless the judge has ordered that this not occur. (False, p. 662, Learning Objective: Describe the usual sequence in a criminal trial.)

31. In a criminal trial, the prosecution presents its case first. (True, p. 662, Learning Objective: Describe the usual sequence in a criminal trial.)

32. A motion that requests the judge to issue a protective order against prejudicial questions or statements is called a motion to suppress. (False, p. 660, Learning Objective: Explain what occurs during the pretrial conference.)

33. Most criminal cases are resolved without a trial. (True, p. 656, Learning Objective: Explain why some cases are not prosecuted.)

34. If the defense claims that your testimony does not agree with that of other officers, you should amend your testimony to eliminate possible jury perceptions of a disorganized and ineffective police department. (False, p. 668, Learning Objective: Describe what defense attorney tactics to anticipate.)

35. Phrases such as "I believe" or "to the best of my recollection" may leave a negative impression on the jury. (True, p. 663, Learning Objective: Explain when to use notes while testifying.)

36. The prosecutor may choose not to prosecute if the complainant refuses to prosecute. (True, p. 656, Learning Objective: Explain why some cases are not prosecuted.)

37. It is acceptable for law enforcement officers to offer opinions and conclusions when testifying. (False, p. 663, Learning Objective: Explain what kinds of statements are inadmissible in court.)

38. While testifying, an investigator should always refer to his or her report as a script to ensure consistency. (False, p. 663, Learning Objective: Explain when to use notes while testifying.)

39. Videotaped testimony is never allowed, so trials must be postponed until all witnesses are able to appear in court. (False, p. 658, Learning Objective: Describe how to review a case.)

40. The "win" for an investigator who testifies is to have established credibility. (True, p. 662, Learning Objective: Clarify what the "win" is for an investigator who testifies in court.)

41. Nonverbal factors can be important when a person testifies in court. (True, p. 664, Learning Objective: Describe what nonverbal elements can influence courtroom testimony positively and negatively.)

42. Investigators should include a summary of all negative or exculpatory evidence developed during the investigation in a report to the prosecuting attorney. (True, p. 654, Learning Objective: Outline what to include in the final report.)

43. Officers and investigators should review all reports on the case prior to going to trial, but only if they did not write the reports. (False, p. 658, Learning Objective: Describe how to review a case.)

44. An expert witness is a person who has special training, education or experience in an area. (True, p. 665, Learning Objective: Discuss strategies that can make testifying in court more effective.)

45. Law enforcement officers find it important to embellish testimony in many cases. (False, p. 670, Learning Objective: Explain how to avoid objections to your testimony.)

Completion

46. The _____ Amendment protects defendants against self-incrimination. (Fifth, p. 660, Learning Objective: Explain what occurs during the pretrial conference.)

47. Police officers are generally witnesses for the _____. (prosecution, p. 661, Learning Objective: Explain what occurs during the pretrial conference.)

48. To avoid objections to an officer's testimony, he or she should avoid _____ and nonresponsive answers. (conclusions, pp. 669–670, Learning Objective: Explain how to avoid objections to your testimony.)

49. _____ examination is the initial questioning of a witness or defendant by the lawyer who is using the person's testimony to further his or her case. (Direct, p. 662, Learning Objective: Describe the usual sequence in a criminal trial.)

50. The main goal for an officer who testifies is to establish _____ . (credibility, p. 662, Learning Objective: Clarify what the "win" is for an investigator who testifies in court.)

51. _____ communication, such as saying hello or giving directions, is permissible while waiting to testify. (De minimus, p. 662, Learning Objective: Describe the usual sequence in a criminal trial.)

52. _____ witnesses are used by the defense to contradict the testimony or evidence presented by the prosecution. (Surrebuttal, p. 662, Learning Objective: Describe the usual sequence in a criminal trial.)

53. The witness _____ rule is designed to prevent witnesses from hearing each other's statements during testimony. (sequestration, p. 660, Learning Objective: Explain what occurs during the pretrial conference.)

54. Gestures, eye movement and facial expressions are all forms of _____. (nonverbal communication, p. 664, Learning Objective: Describe what nonverbal elements can influence courtroom testimony positively and negatively.)

55. The _____ process requires that the prosecution and the defense disclose to each other certain evidence they intend to use at trial. (discovery, p. 657, Learning Objective: Describe how to review a case.)

Short Answer

56. Briefly outline the seven elements of the final report prepared by an investigating officer. (p. 654, Learning Objective: Outline what to include in the final report.)

57. Discuss the Brady rule and how it relates to evidence in a criminal trial. (p. 657, Learning Objective: Describe how to review a case.)

58. What mitigating circumstances might explain a case that is ultimately not prosecuted? (p. 656, Learning Objective: Explain why some cases are not prosecuted.)

59. What should an officer plan to discuss with the prosecutor at a pretrial conference? (p. 659, Learning Objective: Explain what occurs during the pretrial conference.)

60. Discuss the impact of *Daubert v. Merrell-Dow Pharmaceuticals, Inc.,* for expert witness testimony. (p. 665, Learning Objective: Discuss strategies that can make testifying in court more effective.)

61. What are the four strategies suggested in the text for excelling as a witness? (pp. 664–665, Learning Objective: Discuss strategies that can make testifying in court more effective.)

62. Describe nonverbal factors connected with testimony. (p. 664, Learning Objective: Describe what nonverbal elements can influence courtroom testimony positively and negatively.)

63. Briefly outline the usual sequence of events in a criminal trial. (p. 661, Learning Objective: Describe the usual sequence in a criminal trial.)

64. What are some of the tactics a defense attorney might use to cross-examine a prosecution witness? (p. 667, Learning Objective: Describe what defense attorney tactics to anticipate.)

65. The text details eight guidelines for effective testimony in court, the first of which is to "speak clearly, firmly and with expression." List the other seven guidelines for effective testimony. (p. 663, Learning Objective: Describe how to testify most effectively.)

66. When being cross-examined, how can an officer enhance his or her credibility in the eyes of the jury? Briefly outline some behaviors to avoid as well as some behaviors to display. (pp. 665–667, Learning Objective: Describe the key to testifying during cross-examination.)

67. When should an investigator refer to his or her notes? (p. 663, Learning Objective: Explain when to use notes while testifying.)

68. Detective Richard Gautsch emphasizes three major areas to focus on when giving courtroom testimony. What are these three areas, and which do you think would be most challenging for you? (p. 670, Learning Objective: Explain how to avoid objections to your testimony.)

69. List and explain or describe the types or kinds of statements that are inadmissible in court. (p. 663, Learning Objective: Explain what kinds of statements are inadmissible in court.)

70. How can an officer avoid objections to his or her testimony in court? (pp. 669–670, Learning Objective: Explain how to avoid objections to your testimony.)

SORTING INFORMATION AND ASSIGNING PRIORITIES

Challenge Exercise

Have students read through the following detailed information, taken from an actual case. Once they have reviewed it, ask them to give detailed responses in writing to the Challenge Questions below that explain as fully as possible the steps they would take to investigate and resolve this case.

Serial Shootings

The county of San Juan has had a busy day. During the past twelve hours, three people have been shot. One is dead and two are in the hospital in critical condition. The suspect has not been identified, and investigators have not been able to determine any known connection between the three victims.

One of the surviving victims, John Richards, age 37, told the investigators that he was just driving along North Canyon Road, in an unincorporated part of the county, at approximately 1:30 p.m. when an individual waved him down. When Richards got out of his car, the suspect shot him twice, once in the leg and once in the arm. The only reason Richards escaped was that another car drove up and the suspect ran away, to the west of where Richards had been shot. The driver of the other car did see the other man running away, but did not get a clear glimpse of him. He recalls that the individual had on jeans and some type of jacket, he thinks. He did not see the suspect driving a car of any type. However, Richards was able to describe the suspect as a white male in his late 20s or early 30s, around 6 feet tall and slender. The suspect was wearing jeans, a T-shirt, and no jacket, even though the temperature was about 35 degrees at the time and a mixture of snow and rain was falling from the sky. Richards did mention that he had seen a fairly new Ford pickup, probably white and purple, parked on the side of the road, but he did not know if this was connected to the suspect.

The deceased victim, George Johnston, of Denver, Colorado, age 29, had mentioned something about a truck when officers first arrived, called to the area at approximately 2:00 p.m. He then passed out and did not regain consciousness. Johnston was found on Middle Canyon Road by a semitruck driver who was passing through and radioed police on his CB at about 1:50 p.m. The third -victim, Jeremy Steen, was unconscious when officers arrived and has not regained consciousness since he was taken to the hospital. Steen was found by a motorist on Smith Road, which connects to North Canyon Road and is a dead end residential road. The motorist, who was on her way to her house on Smith Road, called 911 on her cell phone at approximately 3:15 p.m. However, based on his body temperature and the amount of blood loss, ambulance attendants estimated that Steen was probably shot somewhat earlier, at some time between 1:30 p.m. and 2:30 p.m. The motorist who found Steen mentioned that she saw a white, possibly Ford pick-up truck turn off Smith Road onto North Canyon Road a few seconds before she made the left turn from North Canyon Road onto Smith Road, towards her home. However, the vehicle was some distance away from her, much too far for her to distinguish either its driver or a license plate.

One individual, who lives in the area of the first known shooting, stopped the -officers and mentioned that he had heard two shots, that he then looked out of the window of his house and he did see a larger blue pick-up of an unknown brand and year driving down the road toward the city of Rounder. He said that he saw what seemed to be a man driving and that he had on what seemed to be a baseball cap, turned backward. He has no idea if this vehicle was connected to the incident, but it seemed to be leaving from a stopped position and was gaining speed as it drove away.

The news media has learned of the three shootings and several television stations and print reporters are in the area of the three shootings. One television station went live and reported the purple and white pick-up and the description of the suspect as a "person of interest". Dispatch and the television station have received several telephone calls. Two of the calls seem to offer a lead. One of them was from a man who said his roommate had left earlier that day with a gun and was very angry about something. The second was a call in which a woman's voice stated, "I know who did this" before hanging up the line. Dispatch is working to trace this second call, which was made from a cell phone, but has had technical issues in tracing the exact number from which it was made. The fact that these issues are arising may be coincidence, but they may also indicate that the call is a prank, and that whoever made it was savvy enough about technology to ensure that it could not be traced. It is frustrating that attention and resources have to be spent on a potential joke at such a difficult time. However, at this point the police cannot afford not to follow up on any potential lead. Meanwhile, the media director for one of the local television stations has demanded full information on the case, saying that if he does not get it, he will go public with what he has from listening to the police scanner.

In the past forty-five minutes, dispatch has received three telephone calls of possible shots fired. One report is from the city of Rounder, the largest city in the county. The two other reports are from along South Jim Creek, a mountainous area south of the city. If a line is drawn on a map from the site of the original shootings on North Canyon Road and Upper North Canyon Road, through the city of Rounder, to the region where shots were reported near South Jim Creek, the shooter (assuming the same person is responsible for all these incidents) seems to be moving in a consistent direction, heading south. South Jim Creek, an isolated and somewhat poor rural community, is one of a handful of such settlements in the south part of the county. A slender strip of unincor-porated land, including a state park that is mostly deserted at this time of year, is all that stands between these southernmost settlements and the border with neighboring Yucaipa county.

There is one additional report of a car speeding through the city of Rounder and not stopping for a stale red light. The complaint was from the wife of an off-duty city of Rounder police officer, who was driving through an intersection where she had right-of-way (a green light) when she saw a car approaching suddenly from her left. By accelerating out of the intersection, she managed to avoid being hit. She described the car involved in the near miss as a green, later-model sedan, possibly a Chevrolet, but was not able to get the license number, since she was focused first on getting out of the way and then on calming her children, who were in the back seat.

One piece of information that you have is that the city of Broadview, about ten miles away, but on the edge of the mountains and south of South Jim Creek, reported two incidents of shots fired from a moving vehicle last week. The city of Broadview has not caught the individual(s), but they do have a description of a car as well as a truck. The truck is described as being dark in color, with a license plate starting with the letter M or N; the car is a larger, newer model, possibly blue, with unknown plates. The witnesses are uncertain of the information and no additional information is known.

Since the incident may involve the city of Rounder, the Rounder Police Department is now involved and the Chief of Patrol has asked to meet to confer with the officer in charge for the sheriff's department. The state patrol has learned of the incidents and has offered its services as well as additional manpower to the sheriff's department.

Most recently dispatch has received a call from the city of Longtown, in the northern part of Yucaipa county, reporting that they have received calls of shots fired along a strip mall on the north end of the city. There is no known connection to the shooting in your county, but the Longtown Police Department has some information, from a witness, about a Ford truck, darker in color and with a license plate starting with the letter M, in the area when the shots were fired. The city of Longtown shift commander has called to notify you that he is sending two investigators with all of the information that they have on this incident to the sheriff's department. They will arrive in a few minutes, and you must be prepared to talk to them as well as receive their information.

You have a very serious, still-developing case on your hands. The case will probably take massive amounts of resources due to the multiple crime scenes and the involvement of many victims, many departments and a murder. In short, you are overwhelmed with information, and don't know how it all fits together.

Challenge Questions

1. What are your priorities in terms of the investigation?
2. What resources will be needed?
3. What would you suggest for the use of the multiple agencies that are offering assistance?
4. Who should be in charge of the investigation? Who has jurisdiction in this case, and in what areas?
5. How will you organize the information that you have available?
6. What leads will you give priority to?
7. What would the role of the District Attorney be at this point in the investigation?
8. What is the role of victim services in this case?
9. How will you protect the people who may be in the shooter's path without draining resources you need for the investigation? How will you warn people without creating a panic?
10. How will you deal with the gathering media storm?